Assessing Object Relations Phenomena

edited by

Morton Kissen

Assessing Object Relations Phenomena

edited by

Morton Kissen

INTERNATIONAL UNIVERSITIES PRESS, INC.

MADISON CONNECTICUT

Library of Congress Cataloging-in-Publication Data

Assessing object relations phenomena.

Bibliography: p.
Includes index.
1. Object relations (Psychoanalysis) 2. Mental illness—Diagnosis. 3. Rorschach test. 4. Psychological tests. 5. Psychotherapy. I. Kissen, Morton.
RC455.4.023A86 1986 616.89'17 86-10513
ISBN 0-8236-0445-4

Manufactured in the United States of America

In memory of my
father, Louis Kissen

CONTENTS

Contributors ix
Introduction 3

I: THE RORSCHACH

1. Rorschach Thought Organization and Transference Enactment in the Patient-Examiner Relationship
George I. Athey, Jr. 19

2. Self-Experience and Reality Testing: Synthesis of an Object Relations and an Ego Psychological Model on the Rorschach
Alan Sugarman 51

3. An Object Relations Understanding of Borderline Phenomena on the Rorschach
Alan Sugarman 77

4. Preconditions for Internalization: Introjective, Projective, and Boundary Phenomena in the Rorschach
Michael K. Harty 89

5. An Object Representation Approach to Rorschach Assessment
Howard D. Lerner 127

6. An Object Relations View of the Borderline Defenses: A Rorschach Analysis
Steven H. Cooper and David Arnow 143

II: OTHER TESTS

7. Object Relations Aspects of Human Figure Drawings
Morton Kissen 175

8. Combined Use of Human Figure Drawings and the Early Memories Test in Assessing Object Relations Phenomena
Morton Kissen 193

9. An Object Relational Theory of Affect Maturity: Applications to the Thematic Apperception Test
Anne E. Thompson 207

10. Bionian Interpretation of the Wechsler Scales: Paranoid-Schizoid Operations
Richard M. Billow 225

III: THE TESTING PROCESS

11. Therapeutic Exploration of Object Relations Patterns Observable During the Testing Process
Morton Kissen 271

12. Treatment Implications of Object Relationships As They Unfold During the Diagnostic Interaction
Fred Shectman and Michael K. Harty 279

IV: PSYCHOSOCIAL STATES

13. Assessing Children's Mental Construction of the Object
Bonnie Batter Slade 307

14. Meshing Character Structures in Marriage Partners
Morton Kissen 323

15. Experiential and Structural Aspects of the (C) Rorschach Response in Patients with Narcissistic Character Pathology
Paul M. Lerner 333

16. Self- and Object Representation in Borderline Disorders
Henry M. Bachrach and Frederic J. Levine 349

Name Index 375
Subject Index 379

CONTRIBUTORS

David Arnow. Ph.D.
Clinical Fellow in Psychology, Department of Psychiatry, Massachusetts General Hospital and Bunker Hill Health Center, Harvard Medical School.

George I. Athey, Jr., Ph.D.
Staff Psychologist at the C. F. Menninger Memorial Hospital, Supervisor of Neuropsychological Testing in the Department of Education of the Menninger Foundation, Topeka, Kansas.

Henry M. Bachrach. Ph.D.
Director of Psychological Training, Saint Vincent's Hospital, New York City.

Richard M. Billow. Ph.D.
Associate Professor, Doctoral and Postdoctoral Programs, Institute of Advanced Psychological Studies, Adelphi University.

Steven H. Cooper. Ph.D.
Instructor of Psychiatry (Psychology), Massachusetts Mental Health Center and The Cambridge Hospital, Harvard Medical School.

Michael K. Harty. Ph.D.
Director of Psychological Services, The Crittenton Center, and private practice, Kansas City, Missouri.

Morton Kissen. Ph.D.
Associate Professor, Assistant Director, Postdoctoral Psychotherapy Program, Institute of Advanced Psychological Studies, Adelphi University. Editor, *From Group Dynamics to Group Psychoanalysis.*

Howard D. Lerner. Ph.D.
Assistant Professor, Department of Psychiatry, University of Michigan Medical School. Coeditor, *Borderline Phenomena and the Rorschach Test.*

Paul M. Lerner. ED.D.
Department of Psychiatry, Faculty of Medicine, University of Toronto. Chief Psychologist, Department of Psychiatry, Mount Sinai Hospital, Toronto, Ontario. Editor, *A Handbook of Rorschach Scales.* Coeditor, *Borderline Phenomena and the Rorschach Test.*

Frederic J. Levine. Ph.D.
Associate Professor and Coordinator of Clinical Psychology Internship Training in the Department of Mental Health Science at the Hahnemann Medical College and Hospital, Philadelphia, Pennsylvania.

Fred Shectman. Ph.D.
Director, Adult Outpatient Diagnostic and Consultation Service, Menninger Foundation, Topeka, Kansas.

Bonnie Batter Slade. Ph.D.
Clinical Psychologist, Private Practice, Palm Bay, Florida.

Alan Sugarman, Ph.D.
Associate Professor, California School of Professional Psychology, San Diego, California. Clinical Associate in Adult and Child Psychoanalysis, San Diego Psychoanalytic Institute. Assistant Clinical Professor of Psychiatry, University of California, San Diego. Coeditor, *Borderline Phenomena and the Rorschach Test.*

Anne E. Thompson. Ph.D.
Assistant Professor, Program in Counseling and Consulting Psychology, Harvard University, Graduate School of Education.

Assessing Object Relations Phenomena

INTRODUCTION

MORTON KISSEN

Interest in object relations theory and its implications for the psychotherapy process has in recent years become widespread. The earlier contributions of Jacobson (1964), Klein (1946) and the British analysts (Fairbairn, 1952; Winnicott, 1965; Balint, 1968; Guntrip, 1968) have been aptly summarized in the recent systematic contributions of Kernberg (1975, 1976, 1980), which have perhaps done most to popularize the object relations approach to understanding and treating the difficult, more severely disturbed patient. Although this approach has most often been associated with therapeutic models for work with characterologically impaired and borderline patients (Balint, 1968; Giovacchini, 1972, 1975, 1976; Kernberg 1976), it has also been productively applied in work with less disturbed neurotic patients. Indeed, Kernberg (1970) has used object relations constructs to establish a clinically useful diagnostic continuum ranging from high-level and fairly well integrated neurotic personalities at one end to lower-level borderline personality organizations at the other.

In outlining this continuum, Kernberg makes it quite clear that he does not believe in separating issues of diagnostic assessment from those of therapeutic process. The two are integrally related to one another and are equally important. An accurate assessment of object relations phenomena allows both for a more trenchant and articulate operational definition of certain key object relations constructs and for their rigorous therapeutic application. To this twofold end, the present volume will focus on various major issues involved in such an assessment.

Since a number of summaries of the antecedents of modern object relations theory have already appeared (Sutherland, 1963; Tuttman, Kaye, and Zimmerman, 1981), no attempt will be made in this introduction to offer a systematic presentation of the history of the object relations approach. Instead, a number of issues intrinsic to object relations theory will be outlined. First, the core *phenomenological* focus implicit in all object relations approaches will be illuminated. Next, the important connections between the *dynamic* principles of Freudian theory, the *structural* principles of ego psychological theory, and the *process* principles of object relations theory will be presented. The relationship of the latter two approaches to the more content-oriented principles of the earlier model will be explored. Next, a developmental schema will be presented for the clinically discernible object relations stages of psychosocial maturation. Throughout, emphasis will be placed on operational definition of three object relations constructs—*self-representation, object representation*, and *ego identity state*—having particular relevance for both diagnostic assessment and therapeutic process. Finally, an overview of the present volume will suggest the varied ways in which the chapters to follow are clinically linked with these key constructs.

The Phenomenological Focus Implicit in the Object Relations Model

Kernberg's masterful efforts to relate object relations constructs to the borderline defense mechanisms of *splitting, projective identification, idealization*, and *self-depreciation*, though intended to elucidate the various clinical aspects of the borderline patient, have given us a terminology that, while very popular, remains nonetheless at some remove from actual clinical experience. Many clinicians have been deterred by such highly abstract concepts as splitting and have wondered how such theoretically dense constructs can be clinically applied. Pruyser (1975), in particular, has questioned the clinical and phenomenological relevance of this very complex metapsychological idea. After all, when we use such terms as *split-off part-objects* to describe our sense of the structural and psychodynamic issues involved in our work with borderline patients, what is it that we are actually saying about our experience with them? On examination, it turns out that we are trying to illuminate some of the more *narcissistic* features of their interpersonal relationships with others. The lack in these patients of any warm, vibrant, and continuous emotional contact is the experiential process (having a quite *functional* significance) that we are attempting to capture in the term *part-object relationship*. Similarly, when we describe a patient's interaction with authority figures in terms of self-representations and object representations, are we actually clarifying matters or making them more dense and complex than they need be? Kernberg

(1966) has given us the conceptual grid for such a seemingly metatheoretical description of psychodynamic events via his elucidation of various interpersonal relationships as essentially involving self-representations, object representations, and their associated affect states. Thus, a particular individual might react to the therapist in an overly timid and compliant fashion. For Kernberg, this would involve the self-representation of an intimidated individual confronting a harsh, critical object representation. The experience is associated with affects of fearfulness. Essentially, these object relational terms are being used to capture the inner phenomenological state of the patient in an emotionally meaningful fashion. Occasionally, due to the excessive abstractness of these formulations, they fail to do this effectively.

Mayman (1967) and a number of other psychologists (Athey, 1974; Allen, 1977; Sugarman, 1977; Lerner, 1980) have begun to focus more attention on the usefulness of object relations concepts in diagnostic assessment of a broad variety of patients. Mayman in particular has begun to explore the phenomenological utility of object relations constructs when applied to a number of projective tests (i.e. the Rorschach and Early Memories tests). In a recent paper (Mayman, 1976), he noted the essentially experience-distant character of most earlier metapsychological formulations of psychological test responses (i.e. impulse-defense configurations, structural and broadly characterological statements, psychodynamic inferences of a more speculative nature, etc.). He points out that much in our earlier conceptualizations has stemmed from the structural theories of the ego psychologists. These theories, particularly as elaborated in the work of Rapaport (1960), have a highly abstract and metapsychological character. Mayman feels that these conceptions have taken us further and further away from our own experience and that of our patients. We need somehow to approach our subject so as to capture the feelingful immediacy of phenomenal experience. For Mayman, the modern object relations approach offers precisely the conceptual tool needed.

Object Relations Theory as a Phenomenological Foundation for the Earlier Freudian and Ego Psychological Approaches

Many of our clinical conceptualizations, with regard to both diagnostic assessment and psychotherapy, have until recently involved a complex melding of the basic principles of Freudian psychodynamic theory with the more structural emphasis of the ego psychological model. Freud initially tended to view the patient as struggling with inner conflicts and anxieties, many of which appeared to link up with sexual and aggressive drive inhibition. The push-pull, hydraulic discharge model implicit in Freud's earliest psychodynamic theories had a definite tension-reduction character. Most symptoms were seen as stemming from inefficient and largely self-destructive struggles against inner drives and impulses. The neurotic and his symptoms seemed aptly reflected in this need-reduction model of psychic motivation.

Most psychological assessments and therapeutic endeavors influenced by this early psychodynamic model tended to emphasize the conflicts and struggles underlying various neurotic symptoms. Thus a given patient's oedipal conflicts would be scrupulously (and occasionally quite speculatively) analyzed and interpreted. In a similar fashion, a given individual's oral or anal reactions or inhibitions might be explored. Such an approach seemed linked to a rather intellectual, analytic, and basically mechanistic conceptual model of both diagnostic assessment and treatment. Speculative intellectual interpretations were the mainstay of this approach, which involved a definite risk of *wild analysis*.

Partially in response to the excessive psychodynamic speculations of this early Freudian model, a *structural* theory was evolved from Freud's later constructs (1923) of id, ego, and superego. The writings of Hartmann (1939), Schafer (1954), and Rapaport (1960) all began to focus on the more structural aspects of Freud's psychoanalytic approach. Psychological assessments tended to consist of an analysis of impulse-defense configurations rather than of more speculative dynamic formulations. Therapeutic recommendations were formulated in terms of ego development, self-esteem, and the enhancement of competence striving (White, 1960). The ego psychoanalytic model of treatment (Blanck and Blanck, 1974), stressing ego psychological diagnosis, maturational expectations, and ego-supportive interventions, has evolved from the structural aspects of Freudian theory. The ego psychoanalytic approach has been melded with object relations concepts and applied to the treatment of character disorders and other difficult patients by Kernberg (1975) and Giovacchini (1976). The notion of ego development along a continuum from primary process to secondary process thinking and defensive and adaptive functioning is basic to the work of both men.

The object relations model is a central feature of the contributions of both Kernberg and Giovacchini. The object relations approach of the latter stems from the earlier conceptions of Winnicott (1965) and consists of a treatment model in which the therapist is viewed as a *transitional object* who can be internalized by the patient as an identification substitute for the deficient and inadequate preoedipal mother of the patient. In Giovacchini's theory of the therapeutic process with characterologically impaired patients, the therapist provides an *analytic introject* for the patient as a substitute for the constricting introjects that have been internalized during the symbiotic phase of the patient's ego development. The parent (probably the mother) was not able to provide *good enough* nurturance during the preoedipal, largely nonverbal phase of the patient's development. The therapist's task, consequently, is to provide a transitional object relationship via a relatively consistent, well-bounded, and anxiety-free interpretive environment. The analytic setting, according to Giovacchini, naturally provides the patient the identificatory experience so sorely needed.

Kernberg's object relations approach stems at least in part from his development of a continuum for the diagnostic assessment of character pathology (1970). He notes that at higher diagnostic levels neurotic defense mechanisms such as regression, projection, displacement, and reaction-formation predominate. At lower levels, the borderline defenses of splitting, projective identification, idealization, and self-depreciation are predominant. Kernberg recommends a classical analytic approach consisting of a stringent reliance on interpretations within a context of technical neutrality and few parameters for patients at the higher levels. For patients at the lower end of the diagnostic continuum, he recommends an *expressive* psychotherapy with ego-supportive parameters. The extremely aggressivized behavioral and ideational reactions of the borderline patient frequently require firm structuring and prohibitions (and occasionally hospitalization), above and beyond the interpretive focus on borderline defensive maneuvers that is so basic to Kernberg's treatment model. The object relations aspects of Kernberg's diagnostic and therapeutic models necessitate a study of the self- and object representations and the associated affect states implicit in the borderline patient's heavy reliance on splitting and projective identification.

The phenomenally evident self-representational states of the characterologically impaired and borderline patient are basic to the object relations approaches of both Giovacchini and Kernberg and also to the earlier object relations models of the therapeutic process developed by Winnicott (1965) and Balint (1968). In a recent paper (1981) I developed the centrality of the projective identification mechanism for a variety of object relations approaches to the treatment of difficult patients. The therapist's task in most of these models is to empathically contain the patient's projected self-representational states and does not involve, to any great extent, interpretive procedures. Essentially, the therapist must provide a *containing* experience of a preinterpretive and largely nonverbal nature for these difficult patients.

The modern object relations model of the therapeutic process builds, then, upon the earlier Freudian psychodynamic and the subsequent ego psychoanalytic treatment models. It adds a phenomenological grounding to these earlier, largely metapsychological models. This grounding is provided by a focus on ego identity states, self-experience (self-representations), and perceptions with regard to significant others (object representations). Despite the seeming metapsychological complexity of some of Giovacchini's and Kernberg's therapeutic formulations, they nevertheless essentially involve a focus on self psychology. These conceptions must therefore be viewed as largely phenomenological in nature. Sutherland (1963) has very clearly articulated some of the phenomenological lacks in the traditional psychoanalytic metapsychological models: "Most psychoanalysts have found the models put forward so far to have only limited relevance to their practice: and for those with more theoretical interests, the awareness of this gap between theory and practice has confirmed their lack of enthusiasm for them" (p. 110).

Mayman (1976) has begun to approach the same functional issue in the sphere of diagnostic assessment. He notes the lack of practical clinical relevance in the traditional Freudian and ego psychological models and suggests that the modern object relations approach has the *process* aspects that can be seen as a corrective to the experience-distant aspects of the earlier models. He stresses, too, the significant phenomenological potential implicit in object relations theory and notes that this model provides a systematic conceptual grid for capturing clinically relevant process aspects of self-experience.

Object Relations Viewed from the Perspective of Psychosocial Phases of Maturation and Development

Object relations theory has particular relevance for current notions regarding psychosexual and psychosocial development. Indeed, when viewed from a developmental perspective, the object relations model has very powerful and practical implications for both diagnostic assessment and psychological treatment of various pathological conditions. The implications are particularly powerful for the diagnosis and treatment of so-called difficult, characterologically impaired patients, in whom the *narcissistic* aspects of psychopathology predominate. Thus, a diagnostic assessment from an object relations perspective often discerns in such patients the existence of certain developmental lags and deficiencies which need to be corrected. The proper therapy for such deficiencies must provide object relational experiences that allow for a more benign and progressive form of maturational growth.

Winnicott's notion (1965) of the *transitional object* has, as noted above, been integrated into the model developed by Giovacchini (1976) for treating patients suffering from character disorders. Giovacchini assumes that the various ego, self-esteem, and identity disturbances so often seen in the character disorders stem essentially from traumatic environmental experiences and lack of "good enough" parenting in the early developmental histories of these patients. The therapeutic task thus becomes the creation of an analytic setting that can ultimately be internalized by the patient (in the form of a functional analytic introject) as a corrective to earlier, more ego-disruptive, and constricting introjects. Thus, according to Giovacchini, the analyst provides the patient a growth-inducing maturational experience by providing the transitional object that was earlier unavailable.

The psychotherapy process with character disorders, then, is focused largely on the developmental phases *preceding* the so-called period of identity and object constancy occurring at approximately three years of age. The developmental framework of object relations theory has been most closely studied and applied to the preoedipal and hence preneurotic patient.

There is an implicit series of stages and processes in the development of early object relations which underlies both diagnosis and therapy when they are viewed from an object relations theoretical perspective. Freud's developmental model, which ended at the postoedipal period of latency (approximately, from the age of eight to preadolescence) involved a psychosexual ladder and was descriptively applied to character pathology by Abraham (1927), who noted the existence of oral, anal, and phallic character types. Wilhelm Reich (1949) later developed an elaborate technical model for therapeutic work with the various character armors and resistances so often seen in these patients.

The more ego psychologically oriented work of Erikson (1959) culminated in his articulation of a *psychosocial* ladder paralleling Freud's earlier description of character development from a psychoeconomic perspective. Erikson viewed the oral phase as involving psychosocial issues around the evolution of a sense of basic trust, and the anal phase as involving issues of personal autonomy and a sense of control over the outer environment. He extended his view of the developmental stages through adulthood and middle age, in which the evolution of a solid sense of ego identity, generativity, and integrity provides the primary developmental themes.

The developmental model most intimately related to object relations theory, however, has tended to focus on the earliest two phases of Freud's psychosexual ladder, which basically precede the stage in which a solid sense of object constancy and nonnarcissistic relatedness has evolved. Most character disorders fail to attain the stage of maturational development at which empathic relatedness to a whole object becomes possible. Much of the focus in the diagnosis and treatment of character disorders has thus been on the narcissistic aspects of interpersonal functioning. Kohut (1971) has developed an elaborate conceptualization and treatment model focusing on the *echo transference* needs of these patients. Kernberg (1975) has developed an even more elaborate diagnostic formulation of the character disorders, focusing upon the borderline personality organization and associated primitive defense mechanisms. His treatment model, in contrast to Kohut's emphasis on the *mirroring* needs of the narcissistic patient in the transference, stresses the severely regressed patient's need for an *expressive* therapeutic intervention in which defense confrontations, ego-supportive parameters and direct prohibitions of narcissistic acting-out behavior are selectively employed.

Kernberg, as we have seen, emphasizes the need for a solid interpretive focus on the pathological defensive maneuvers of borderline patients, particularly their reliance on splitting and ego dissociation. His focus on splitting derives from his earlier object relations conceptualizations (1966) with regard to the developmental shifts in the process of early ego identity establishment. He notes that the most basic units of ego identity organization involve primitive entities consisting of a fairly simple self-representation, an equally simple object representation, and an associated affect state. At the earliest stages of development there is a narcissistic quality to these self-organizational units, and the object representations are essentially of a part-object nature. There is also a fairly great degree of dissociation between self-object representational units organized around positive affects and those organized around negative affects. Kernberg's conception of splitting highlights the significance of these dissociated self-organizational units for both the diagnosis and the treatment of severe characterological disorders. His treatment model contains an implicit ego-developmental model in which the various maturational phases of object relations development involve, in varying degrees, an unconscious striving toward the building up of stable self-object organizational units and the establishment of enduring object-libidinal cathexes within the ego identity system.

Much of the therapeutic focus with severely regressed or narcissistically damaged patients is thus directed to that developmental period so cogently described by Mahler (1952) as the *symbiotic* stage. Virtually all theorists have noted the *rapprochement* crisis as the critical developmental fixation point for both character disorders and borderline states. This phase of ego maturation and object relational development follows the earliest phases of development, in which *autistic* issues predominate. Most forms of psychotic pathology are viewed as linked to this much more primitive phase of development.

Kwawer (1979) has viewed the boundary disturbances in the Rorschach inkblot responses of borderline patients along a continuum of interpersonal differentiation. The most primitive forms of response consist largely of the essentially autistic object relational mode of *narcissistic mirroring*. The next, slightly more sophisticated phase involves intense aspirations toward *symbiotic merger* and self-object representational fusion. The next level reflects somewhat weak but nevertheless discernible strivings toward *separation and division*, while the final phase consists of the beginnings of a primitive ego identity organization centering about *metamorphosis and transformation*. Kwawer thus offers us an interesting developmental grid for depicting the struggles of the self toward ego identity articulation and a more empathic form of relatedness to early objects. His maturational grid dovetails nicely with Horner's recent formulation (1979) of the stages of development of early object relations and their associated pathologies.

Horner traces the process of object relations development from the earliest phase following birth, that of primary and secondary infantile autism, in which there is no capacity for attachment to an object, through the stage of normal symbiosis (4–5 months) and then through a primitive separation-individuation striving period culminating in the rapprochement crisis and, finally, the emergence of ego identity and object constancy at approximately the third year. There is a rather speculative character to Horner's linkage of particular pathological conditions to specific developmental fixation points (i.e. the psychopathic personality is seen as consisting of an object relational fixation at the period of secondary autism, and the schizoid character as fixated to the postsymbiotic but prerapprochement period of separation-individuation). It is unlikely that we have at present sufficient clinical data to make such linkages between nosological forms of character pathology and specific stages of early object relational development. Nevertheless, Horner's maturational stages provide us still another systematic conceptual grid for depicting early object relations development. This conceptualization of the earliest maturational phases from an object relations perspective goes well beyond Freud's psychosexual and Erikson's psychosocial interpretations.

Three Object Relations Constructs Relevant to the Plan of the Present Volume

A basic object relations model can be derived from a melding of the more complex concepts of the object relations theorists with the framework for action-oriented and more phenomenological inference developed by Mayman (1963) and Schafer (1976, 1978). This model requires only three operationally definable clinical concepts and can be easily applied both to the psychotherapy process and to a broad variety of psychological test data.

The three object relations terms to be operationally defined and exemplified through projective test responses in this volume are those of *self-representation, object representation,* and *ego state*. A number of authors (Mayman 1963, 1967, 1976; Jacobson, 1964; Kernberg, 1966; and Horner, 1979) have offered definitions of these clinically relevant constructs. The following definitions are simple enough to be operationalized in both psychological testing and therapeutic experience and are underlying assumptions of the clinical and conceptual thinking throughout the present volume.

Self-representation. The various physiognomic modes by which the individual symbolizes an experiential image of himself and its associated affects. The individual may utilize verbal or nonverbal means for expressing these internalized units of self-perception. Although these self-perceptions may be experienced at a relatively conscious, preconscious, or even unconscious level, they are most likely to be consciously available.

Object representation. The various physiognomic modes by which the individual symbolizes an experiential image of a significant other and its associated affects. These units of object perception may be expressively captured either verbally or nonverbally. They too may be experienced at a relatively conscious, preconscious, or unconscious level, but are most likely to be consciously available.

Ego state. More complex and relatively differentiated units of self- and object representation and their associated affects. The composite of these experiential states defines essential aspects of an individual's self-organization. When viewed using a *structural* mode of observation and inference, they define the individual's central sense of identity. From a more *adaptive* vantage point, these experiential entities define the individual's characterological style. At a very personal and experiential level these ego states may be felt as undesirable and foreign to the individual's core sense of identity and more idealized strivings, but on the other hand they may be felt as intimately essential aspects of the self-concept. Foreign-seeming and experientially unpleasant ego states may be operationally defined as *introjects*. More intimately comfortable ego states can be operationally defined as *identifications*.

A number of projective tests offer an opportunity for operational demonstrations of these three object relations constructs. In the present volume, the Rorschach inkblots, the Thematic Apperception Test, the human figure drawing test, the intelligence test, and the Early Memories Test provide ideal instruments for assessing these object relations phenomena. The assumption underlying the volume is that an adequate phenomenological assessment of these phenomena can lead to a more solid and comprehensive understanding of the therapeutic process viewed from an object relations perspective.

Overview and Scope of the Volume

The phenomenological focus of the present volume will allow for an application of basic operationalizable principles of object relations theory to both diagnostic assessment and psychotherapy. The assessment process will first be studied from the vantage point of the Rorschach inkblot test. The first section of the present volume contains a number of chapters that clarify the object relational features of this widely used projective instrument. The study of self- and object representational processes reflected in inkblot responses, particularly those obtained from patients manifesting severe characterological disorders and borderline conditions, will be the primary focus of the first section (chapters 1–6).

The next section of the volume (chapters 7–10) will consider self- and object representational processes from the perspective of projective and non-projective instruments that have particularly noteworthy object relational characteristics. The human figure drawing, Early Memories, and Thematic Apperception tests are the projective instruments included. The figure drawing test will be viewed as an instrument particularly suitable for the clarification of self-representational units. The Early Memories and Thematic Apperception tests, on the other hand, are seen as instruments particularly suitable for the study of object representational units and more complex ego identity states. The object relations features of the Wechsler Intelligence Scales will also be outlined in this second section.

The third section (chapters 11–12) will explore object relations in the testing process and their implications for an object relations approach to psychotherapy.

The fourth and final section (chapters 13–16) will focus on an exploration of the self- and object representational processes underlying certain important psychosocial states. The interaction of married couples will be studied from an object relations perspective, with particular emphasis on their meshing characterological structures. Experiential and structural aspects of children and patients with narcissistic character pathology or borderline personality organization will also be explored.

In short, then, the present volume systematically studies the object relational patterns manifested in test responses, assuming their relevance to an object relations model of the psychotherapy process.

It will not be possible to make further theoretical and clinical advances in our understanding of the various ego defects and characterological disturbances without a solidly systematic study of object relations phenomena from the perspective of an ego psychologically grounded developmental continuum. We now have the beginnings of such a developmental continuum and can specify, at least somewhat tentatively, the developmental level of the self- and object representations in various pathological states. The present volume is a contribution to this process of systematization of object relations theory and its application to both assessment and psychotherapy.

References

Abraham, K. (1927), *Selected Papers on Psycho-Analysis*. London: Hogarth Press.

Allen, J. (1977), Ego states and object relations. *Bull. Menn. Clin.*, 41:522–539.

Athey, G. (1974), Schizophrenic thought organization, object relations and the Rorschach test. *Bull. Menn. Clin.*, 38:406–429.

Balint, M. (1968), *The Basic Fault: Therapeutic Aspects of Regression*. London: Tavistock.

Blanck, G., & Blanck, R. (1974), *Ego Psychology: Theory and Practice*. New York: Columbia University Press.

Erikson, E. (1959), Growth and crises of the healthy personality. In: Identity and the Life Cycle. *Psychological Issues,* Monogr. 1. New York: International Universities Press, 1959, pp. 50–100.

Fairbairn, W. (1952), *An Object-Relations Theory of the Personality*. New York: Basic Books.

Freud, S. (1923), The ego and the id. *Standard Edition*, 19:13–66. London: Hogarth Press, 1961.

Giovacchini, P. (1976), *Psychoanalysis of Character Disorders*. New York: Aronson.

——— Ed. (1972), *Tactics and Techniques in Psychoanalytic Therapy*. New York: Science House.

——— ed. (1975), *Tactics and Techniques in Psychoanalytic Therapy. Vol. II: Countertransference*. New York: Aronson.

Guntrip, H. (1968), *Schizoid Phenomena, Object Relations and the Self*. New York: Basic Books.

Hartmann, H. (1939), *Ego Psychology and the Problems of Adaptation*. New York: International Universities Press, 1958.

Horner, A. (1979), *Object Relations and the Developing Ego in Therapy*. New York: Aronson.

Jacobson, E. (1964), *The Self and the Object World*. New York: International Universities Press.

Kernberg, O. (1966), Structural derivatives of object relationship. *Internat. J. Psycho-Anal.*, 47:236–253.

——— (1970), A psychoanalytic classification of character pathology. *J. Amer. Psychoanal. Assn.*, 18:800–822.

——— (1975), *Borderline Conditions and Pathological Narcissism*. New York: Aronson.

——— (1976), *Object Relations Theory and Clinical Psychoanalysis*. New York: Aronson.

——— (1980), *Internal World and External Reality*. New York: Aronson.

Kissen, M. (1981), Therapeutic use of self- and object representations in the treatment of character disorders. Unpublished manuscript.

Klein, M. (1946). Notes on some schizoid mechanisms. In: *Development in Psycho-Analysis*, ed. M. Klein, P. Heimann, S. Isaacs, & J. Riviere. London: Hogarth Press, 1952, pp. 292–320.

Kohut, H. (1971), *The Analysis of the Self*. New York: International Universities Press.

Kwawer, J. (1979), Borderline phenomena, interpersonal relations and the Rorschach test. *Bull. Menn. Clin.*, 43:515–524.

Lerner, P., & Lerner, H. (1980), Rorschach assessment of primitive defenses in borderline personality structure. In: *Borderline Phenomena and the Rorschach Test*, ed. J. Kwawer, H. Lerner, P. Lerner, & A. Sugarman. New York: International Universities Press, pp. 257–274.

Mahler, M. (1952), On childhood psychosis and schizophrenia: Autistic and symbiotic infantile psychoses. *The Psychoanalytic Study of the Child*, 7:286–305. New York: International Universities Press.

Mayman, M. (1963), Psychoanalytic study of the self-organization with psychological tests. In: *Recent Advances in the Study of Behavior Change: Proceedings of the Academic Assembly on Clinical Psychology*, ed. B. Wigdor. Montreal: McGill University Press, pp. 97–117.

——— (1967), Object representations and object relationships in Rorschach responses. *Internat. J. Psycho-Anal.*, 31:17–24.

——— (1976), Psychoanalytic theory in retrospect and prospect. *Bull. Menn. Clin.*, 40:199–210.

Pruyser, P. (1975), What splits in "splitting"? A scrutiny of the concept of splitting in psychoanalysis and psychiatry. *Bull. Menn. Clin.*, 39:1–46.

Rapaport, D. (1960), The Structure of Psychoanalytic Theory: A Systematizing Attempt. *Psychological Issues,* Monogr. 6. New York: International Universities Press.

Reich, W. (1949), *Character Analysis*. New York: Noonday.

Schafer, R. (1954), *Psychoanalytic Interpretation in Rorschach Testing*. New York: International Universities Press.

——— (1976), *A New Language for Psychoanalysis*. New Haven: Yale University Press.

——— (1978), *Language and Insight*. New Haven: Yale University Press.

Sugarman, A. (1977), Object relations theory: A reconciliation of phenomenology and ego psychology. *Bull. Menn. Clin.*, 41:113–130.

Sutherland, J. (1963), Object-relations theory and the conceptual model of psychoanalysis. *Brit. J. Med. Psychol.*, 36:109–121.

Tuttman, S., Kaye, C., & Zimmerman, M., eds. (1981), *Object and Self: A Developmental Approach*. New York: International Universities Press.

White, R. (1960), Competence and the psychosexual stages of development. In: *Nebraska Symposium on Motivation*, ed. M. Jones. Lincoln: University of Nebraska Press, pp. 97–141.

Winnicott, D. (1965), *The Maturational Processes and the Facilitating Environment*. New York: International Universities Press.

Part I
The Rorschach

Chapter 1

RORSCHACH THOUGHT ORGANIZATION AND TRANSFERENCE ENACTMENT IN THE PATIENT-EXAMINER RELATIONSHIP

GEORGE I. ATHEY, JR.

When the meaning of Rorschach test functioning is considered from a psychoanalytic ego psychological point of view, several basic issues arise. These include the relationship between object relations and thought organization on the Rorschach, as well as essential functions in the Rorschach response process pertinent to thought organization, object relations, and the patient-examiner relationship.

The clinical utility of this approach can be seen through an examination of a series of cases differing in Rorschach thought organization but sharing a set of events in the patient-examiner relationship that I have termed *transference enactment*. Specifically, these patients evidence reactions to the initial introduction of the Rorschach task and subsequent noteworthy feelings toward the examiner. Such events are clarified by examiner inquiry and may be understood in terms of transference of psychodynamic conflict. Close examination of these transference events demonstrates how the patient's manner of experiencing and handling the transference feelings is regulated by the structure of his or her thought organization.

Thus, these events provide one sort of confirmation of the predictive validity of thought organization for the type of relationship structures which may emerge in transference phenomena, and suggest the importance of pursuing the subtleties of the patient-examiner relationship in Rorschach inquiry.

Object Relations and Thought Organization

Various models of the relationship between object relations and thought organization have arisen from consideration of patients (specifically, psychotic and borderline patients) who exhibit noteworthy shifts in the formal organization of their thinking on the Rorschach. With reference to schizophrenic functioning, Blatt and his colleagues (Blatt and Ritzler, 1974; Blatt and Wild, 1976) have offered a boundary deficit model. In addition, Kernberg (1975) has provided a developmental model of object relations which spans the entire spectrum of psychopathology and which has implications for any effort to employ a Rorschach metapsychology of human functioning. Kernberg's concepts will be reviewed in a cursory manner; the reader desiring more comprehensive treatment is referred to Smith (1980).

The Boundary Deficit Hypothesis

Blatt and his colleagues were among the first to offer a rationale for the relationship between object relations and thought organization on the Rorschach. They postulated a superordinate concept of "boundary deficit" whereby different intensities of "thought disorder" along a continuum of Rorschach scores (for example, fabulized combination, confabulation, contamination) were viewed as reflecting different intensities of "loss of boundary" between separate ideas. Such loss of conceptual boundaries was seen as a process that runs parallel, within the domain of thinking, to the progressive loss of boundary between self and other which may occur in regressive representation or experience of relationships. Their ideas find most direct application in the evaluation of schizophrenic patients, in whom symbiotic relationship concerns abound and for whom fusion experiences may occur in the clinical relationship.

Blatt's formulations point to parallels which may exist between thought organization and object relations for groups of patients, but cannot account for differences which may emerge in individual patients' thinking and object representation, explicate the meaning of different types or degrees of boundary loss, or offer any explanation of how boundaries become "lost." By contrast, an earlier paper of my own (Athey, 1974) offered clinical illustrations of the substantive difference in the clinical functioning and treatment response of two patients who manifested distinctly different types of disordered thinking (confabulation and contamination), though sharing the same primitive relationship concerns regarding loss of identity and of boundary between self and other. In only one (the "contaminator") did fusion actually occur in the immediate experience of the treatment relationship.

The point of view adopted by that paper and the present one follows the model of psychoanalytic diagnosis offered by Shevrin and Shectman (1973), according to which formal processes of representation (thought organization) and the content of concerns about personal relationships thus organized (object relations), while different sides of the same coin, need not always exist at the same level of regression or fixation.

Kernberg's Object Relations Paradigms

The basic object relations paradigms offered by Kernberg (1975) provide structural models of key "relationship states" associated with psychotic, borderline, and neurotic (or nonborderline character pathology) modes of adjustment. These paradigms allow for some independence between object relations content and its level of structural representation. For example, while borderline patients retain a strong interest in symbiotic relationships, they have progressed to a point of conflicted separation-individuation (by contrast with psychotic patients, whose current experience is dominated by symbiosis or fusion), but cannot proceed sufficiently beyond this experience to firmly establish integrated experiences of self and other.

Kernberg has spoken to the unique contributions psychological testing can make to diagnosis of borderline personality in particular, viewing selective emergence of primary process thinking on less structured psychological tests—a finding that has been confirmed empirically by Singer (1977)—as one of the *structural* indications of borderline personality, alongside his object relations paradigms of differentiation and reintegration. Unfortunately, these two structural indications have not been genuinely integrated. Rather, the notion of levels of thought organization appears to have been bootlegged into Kernberg's views by way of the aforementioned paradigms of object relations states. One is left with a sequence of paradigms which do not form a smooth continuum, but rather a series of discontinuous states separated by "quantum leaps"[1] of intrapsychic development. No provision is made for systematic progression or regression to bridge these various states.[2]

In brief, Kernberg's structural paradigms of object relations states may be seen as representing, in the abstract, nodal points of confluence between lingering early concerns about relationships (content, represented in some patients as a character style) and specific levels of reality attunement in the formal representation of these concerns (structural aspects of the paradigms). Such confluence might be expected as the eventual focal point in transference-

[1] I am indebted to Dr. Irwin C. Rosen for this metaphor, which he used in a discussion following Dr. Kernberg's presentation of his initial formulations at an open scientific meeting of the Topeka Psychoanalytic Association, 1972.

[2] This type of discontinuous series is remarkably similar to the pseudounitary dimension of thought disorder involving fabulized combination, confabulation, and contamination.

and-regression-fostering clinical relationships, in which the current experience of certain concerns may result in a rekindling of the very type of object representation which was concurrent with those original concerns in the past. However, it is precisely through assessment of Rorschach thought organization that one may assess the extent to which the patient is or is not likely to represent object relations concerns at a particular regressive level.

Modes of Approach to Rorschach Thought Organization

In drawing a distinction between thought organization and object relations, I am equating thought organization with the level of integration of those psychological functions mentioned by Shevrin and Shectman as having object relations characteristics. Application of the notion of thought organization to varying levels of regressed experience requires a shift from a unitary conception of primary process thinking as ''thought disorder.'' A description of distinctive levels of thought organization may provide for a less unitary view. This model is an extension and refinement of one offered earlier (Athey, 1974). Three major efforts provide the historical context for the model I am proposing now in greater detail: (1) Rapaport (Rapaport, Gill, and Schafer, 1945), (2) Holt (Holt and Havel, 1960; Holt, 1963), and (3) Johnston and Holzman (1976).

Rapaport

In their primary work on the application of psychological tests to clinical diagnosis, Rapaport and his colleagues discussed primary process thinking on the Rorschach under the rubric of ''deviant verbalizations,'' and analyzed such responses in terms of an overall dimension of altered (pathological increase or loss of) ''distance'' from the reality task. They offered three major categories of responses reflecting such qualitative alterations in distance from reality—fabulized combinations, confabulations, and contaminations. Fabulized combinations were seen as involving the assertion of an unrealistic relationship between two percepts that is considered realistic purely by virtue of the contiguity of the blot areas involved. Confabulations were seen as instances involving determination of the response by associative processes to the exclusion of reality cues in the blot. Contamination was seen as involving a single percept representing two different things simultaneously.

Holt

The first major extension of Rapaport's work was accomplished by Holt. Holt's multitude of score types was not neatly arranged into hierarchical groupings, nor were the various scores consistently related to the two basic primary process mechanisms (condensation and displacement) which Holt had underscored in originating his scoring system (see Urist, 1980). Rather, each score was considered as posing a particular degree of "defense demand," which might then be met more or less successfully by the patient's defensive or control efforts within the response.

If one groups Holt's scores of formal deviations of thinking in terms of the defense demand assigned them in his manual, some similarities may be sensed among scores at each level, but scores within levels may represent qualitatively different types of thought process. The untoward effect of this state of affairs is to consider primary process as a unitary dimension differing only in severity of challenge to a person's defenses or in degree of distance from conventional social discourse.

Johnston and Holzman

The most recent system of scoring primary process thinking, the Thought Disorder Index, builds upon Holt's earlier work and includes considerations originally put forth by Wiener (1966) concerning implications of object representation for formal thought organization. In this system, four distinct levels of primary process thinking have been delineated, representing qualitative differences in "pathology of verbal responses." These levels are presented as reflections of "reality contact and the ability to maintain an appropriate cognitive focus" (p. 1). While for the most part the groupings of scores within levels of pathology suggest common organizing principles within levels, the authors do not fully spell out these implications.

The first level is a major addition to the three classical scores of Rapaport, though borrowing from Rapaport's notion of "peculiar" responses, and is defined in the greatest detail—"moderate idiosyncrasies which are probably only rarely noticed in ordinary conversation, although an accumulation of them might result in a lack of clarity. . . . there is some slight intrusion of an idiosyncratic set, or . . . some difficulty in maintaining a clear unambiguous focus" (p. 5). "They suggest [that the patient] may have some trouble dealing appropriately with some tasks, or that he responds idiosyncratically but not bizarrely. . . . such a person may be 'on the fringe,' but he is still in tune with his surroundings" (p. 22).

The other levels are not conceptualized in similar detail. Thus, accumulation of scores at the second level is described as conveying "loss of moorings, shaky reality contact" (p. 22). The third level is not explicitly defined and the fourth is viewed as reflecting the fact that "reality contact appears to have completely broken down" (p. 33). The second level contains certain fabulized combinations, the third confabulation, and the fourth contamination.

Emphasis is placed on a unitary conception of degree of pathology, represented as distance from conventional social reality. This view is similar to that of Holt, who offered parallels to his defense-demand ratings in terms of the degree of impact such verbalizations might have in the context of a social gathering.

A Binary Multimodal Approach to Rorschach Thought Organization

I would like to offer an alternative model which remains close to the traditional ordering of severity of primary process thinking scores, but which defines these groupings in ways which provide some guiding perspective on the general common meaning of various scores within groups, and simultaneously affords some understanding of the different modes of representation reflected by different levels. In so doing, it is necessary to integrate an understanding of these scores with an understanding of the Rorschach response process and to postulate the healthy forms of thought organization from which the various pathological modes represent deviations. Thus the model is an attempt to delineate a continuum of thinking from secondary to primary process modes, which Urist (1980) has encouraged, while retaining the useful distinctions between qualitative modes of organization within this continuum.

Rapaport has eloquently described certain aspects of the Rorschach response process—specifically, the ''cogwheeling of the progress of perceptual organization with the associative process'' which occurs in the subjective emergence of a Rorschach response (Rapaport, Gill, and Schafer, 1945, p. 276). Various primary process qualities of responses may be viewed as deriving from preparatory aspects of cogwheeling—aspects which would ordinarily remain unconscious—reaching conscious awareness.[3] Such an event reflects a disturbance in the normal articulation and integration of subjective experience with objective reality.

Normal Perceptual-Experiential Enrichment

The integration of subjective experience and reality is viewed as contained (in a normal, growth-fostering manner) within a reality-oriented mode by the reciprocal influence of two processes: (1) restraint of the subjective associative process by the perceptual-representational[4] realities of the blot,

[3] This process was made more explicit by Rapaport in relation to the Word Association Test.

[4] For brevity, hereafter termed simply ''perceptual'' when emphasis is placed on external stimulus givens, or ''representational'' when emphasis is placed on internal objective priorities finding nascent perceptual anchoring in a blot area.

and (2) enrichment and guidance of the perceptual differentiation-integrative reorganization process of percept formation by the associative process. The notion of excessive "distance" or "closeness" seems to be Rapaport's way of indicating an imbalance in these two processes—closeness referring to excessive perceptual reality adherence and distance referring to excessive associative elaboration and reconstruction. Unfortunately, Rapaport has also used the phrase "loss of distance" on the Rorschach to refer to the patient's excessive involvement with a percept. This suggests a different meaning of the word "distance," such as in the capacity to maintain a balanced perspective on one's associative processes in relation to objective reality (that is, self-observation), which is lost when inappropriate involvement with a percept occurs. It would be better to maintain a more consistent and univocal terminology: loss of distance (from the percept) should perhaps be thought of as excessive distance from the blot reality or excessive involvement with the associative process.[5]

The normal means of maintaining appropriate distance from or closeness to reality and simultaneously conveying unique subjective experience include (1) fabulation—the attribution of ideational or affective specificity to a percept in a way which can fit the reality of the blot and the essential identity of the percept, and (2) combination (and in particular, construction) responses[6] —viewing differentiated parts of the blot as in relation to each other in an accurate and appropriate fashion. These processes reflect, respectively, the enriching and reorganizing influences of the associative process on percept formation, and might be labeled generically in relation to Rapaport's response process as reflecting "successful associative embellishment" and "successful perceptual organization."

Use of fabulation and combination as two basic anchoring frames of reference within healthy thought organization finds some support in a recent empirical study (Athey, Fleischer, and Coyne, 1980), in which a factor of Productive Thought Organization was defined substantially by these two

[5] Concerning the Word Association Test, Rapaport has presented parallel notions regarding closeness to and distance from the verbal stimulus. The difference on the Rorschach is that the perceptual nature of the blot area is in part selected by a process of differentiation and integration which proceeds concomitantly with association. While the stimulus word is provided for the patient on the Word Association Test, the blot stimulus undergoes an insidious shift from an agent of external reality to a liaison between external and internal reality.

[6] W+ reflects unusual success in perceptual differentiation and reintegration which may or may not involve seeing two different percept areas in combination. Construction responses involve this sort of reintegration, but do not necessarily require the whole blot. Becker (1956) has used the concept of construction responses in distinguishing among different levels of maturity of W responses in his genetic level scoring system, depending upon whether the W must first be "broken" by the patient before integrating the various parts.

scores. This view is consistent as well with another study (Blatt, Brenneis, Schimek, and Glick, 1976), which used patients who gave only combination responses as the normal-range comparison group for other groups giving fabulized combinations, confabulations, and contaminations.

Urist (1980), in a review of psychoanalytic theory pertinent to primary process thinking, has underscored the importance of the basic mechanisms of condensation and displacement for delineating a continuum of primary and secondary process thinking. He has also pointed out the difficulty in relating structural concepts to primary process thinking.

Some clarification of these issues can be obtained by reference to developmental mechanisms by which the normal state of adult development is attained—differentiation and integration. Theoretically, these are two coordinated vectors of human development (Werner, 1948; Werner and Kaplan, 1963). In Rapaport's view of the Rorschach response process, the aforementioned developmental processes reemerge; perceptual differentiation and reintegration go hand in hand, as do associative elaboration and conceptual specification. Optimally a person maintains these processes in equilibrium with each other and with alternative, developmentally earlier processes (primary process) which have been relegated to altered states of consciousness (such as sleep and dreams). It is indeed the relative autonomy of such equilibria which is taxed by the Rorschach situation, and the reestablishment of such equilibria occurs in miniature in the response process.

The perceptual differentiation-integration process may be seen as pertaining to the identification and representation of internally salient manifestations in objective reality, while the associative differentiation-integration may be seen as the elaboration and conceptual specification, respectively, of the inward meaning of these reality manifestations in ideas and feelings. Combination responses reflect successful differentiation of separate objects and integration among these objects in relation to perceptual reality manifestations, and are the healthy counterpart of condensation, in which the boundary between separate manifestations is violated. Fabulation responses reflect successful differentiation of specific affective and ideational meanings and conceptual integration of them with reality manifestations, and are the healthy counterpart of displacement, in which affects and ideas may be shifted to association with each other or with various reality representations purely in the service of wish-fulfillment, so that logical-aesthetic-social boundaries for communication are violated.

The various pathological modes of thought organization may be seen as involving various degrees and modes of sacrifice of more developmentally advanced for more developmentally primitive processes.

Adaptive Regression

Adaptive regression, or regression in the service of the ego (Schafer, 1958), refers in this context to the emergence of associative or combinatory activity in the form of a fantasy, but in a way which indicates simultaneous awareness of the departure from reality and creatively synthesizes the divergent fantasy and reality contexts. Included among such responses are such subscores of the associative process as impressionism (elaboration of fabulized affect tones into a pervasive atmosphere in the response); symbolism (elaboration of specific ideational meanings of a response whereby it is made to stand, abstractly and simultaneously, for something outside the context of the reality task); and humor as a successful context (in which double meanings or incongruous combinations afford surplus meaning which is intended and perceived as humorous because of the firm distinction between reality and fantasy in which it is couched). Included also among creative responses are such scores of the representational process as W+ and construction responses. M+ responses (in which a percept is accurately seen as if it were alive, but in which the kinesthesis remains symbolic) constitute creative responses of particular significance, since they involve specification of a living human context for the adaptive regression, suggesting that viable object relatedness may develop from, or remain associated with, regressive periods.

Certainly the processes implicated in adaptive regression may call to mind potential reality transgressions of the sort discussed below. Indeed, the risk in creativity is that what begins as adaptive regression may become pathological if the person's representational processes are insufficiently autonomous and/or his unconscious conflicts are sufficiently strong and unresolved to prevent that reestablishment of optimal distance (from his associations) and closeness (to the perceptual and interpersonal reality context) whereby the creative synthesis may be achieved. Thus it becomes important to consider various possibilities—creative potential may (1) occur autonomously with no pathological processes at other points, (2) coexist with concomitant psychopathology which creative elements may be used to excuse or mask, (3) be subverted by increasingly problematic pathology, or (4) represent a sublimation of pathology which "might have been" or "might yet be" except for the person's overall capacity for conflict-free creative synthesis.

Pathological Modes of Thought Organization

The present model conceives of pathological thought organization as an extension of organizing principles within the normal range (fabulation and combination), and considers pathology of thought organization to constitute parallel processes important at different levels of primitive object relations experience. The manner in which tought organization levels may correspond to Kernberg's various object relations paradigms goes beyond the scope of this chapter and warrants detailed future treatment. As regards the boundary deficit view, the present view differs in two ways: (1) thought disorder is not conceived as a unitary dimension of progressive loss of boundary between ideas, but rather as a binary dimension comprised of condensation and displacement, yielding a series of modes of organization which are pathological in various ways; (2) the relationship of pathological modes of thought organization to primitive object relations is not seen as a simple parallel in terms of boundary between ideas or between self and other, but as involving (a) parallels to a variety of boundaries corresponding to progressive differentiation and reintegration, and (b) only a probabilistic set of parallels at that.

Concern over differentiation between self and other (symbiotic fear and/or longing) may emerge without a parallel regression to a level of condensation. While the different levels of pathologically organizational thinking may be seen as steps toward levels of experience involving loss of boundary between self and other, they are offered as a model for understanding in a systematic fashion how for an individual person thought organization regresses toward more primitive levels, and just what boundaries are being violated.

The following pathological thought modes have been conceived as organizational: types of order appropriate to different developmental levels in interrelating subjective and objective reality at certain crucial moments. The various levels and their characteristics are outlined in Table 1, while the transitional processes involved in shifting from one level to another are sketched in Table 2.

As indicated in Table 1, the particular regression involved at any given level for any given response may occur more exclusively in the arena of representational processes (percept identity and combination) or associational processes (affective and ideational specificity and elaboration). This binary view of thought organization is reminiscent of the distinction between structural and thematic views of object relations noted by Spear (1980), but the extent to which they are equivalent or even parallel requires further investigation.

Level 1: insulated idiosyncrasy. At this level, associative and integrative processes have begun to take on a peculiar flavor as reflected in the unusual or unlikely specificity of the thought contents (ideas or affect tones) which emerge in the response. By contrast with fabulation the associations have a highly personalized "ring," as if not all of the person's subjective experience has been brought to terms with the blot reality and/or the task of communicating to the examiner. By contrast with combination responses, the integrations effected reflect a view of reality which introduces improbable events. By contrast with level 2, the patient's ideas do not yet involve dismissal of reality, but only special dispensations regarding it—the combinations are not impos-

TABLE 1

Developmental Continuum of Modes of Thought Organization

Thought Organization Mode	Response Processes: Perceptual-Representational	Response Processes: Associational
Creative Synthesis	W +, Construction	Impressionism, Symbolism, Humor
Normal Modulation	Combination	Fabulation
Primary Process Level 1: Insulated Idiosyncrasy	Peculiar, Arbitrary Combination, Unlikely Combination Awareness of Reality Retained	Peculiar Association
Primary Process Level 2: Circumscribed Reality Rejection	Impossible Combination Circumscribed Abandonment of Reality Awareness	Logical-Affective Contradiction
Primary Process Level 3: Reality Replacement	Fluid Percept Transformation Sustained Abandonment of Reality Awareness	Confabulation, Fluid Association
Primary Process Level 4: Condensation	Contamination Loss of Capacity for Reality Awareness	Verbal Condensation

TABLE 2

Transitional Processes in Mode Shifts

Mode Shift	Violation	Distinction Lost
Normal, Creative Idiosyncrasy	Private context intrudes on public disclosure.	Loss of distinction between intrapsychic and interpersonal contexts due to loss of investment in interpersonal context.
Idiosyncrasy Reality Rejection	Specific intrapsychic context contradicts reality.	Loss of distinction between a specific aspect of reality and a specific fantasy.
Reality Rejection Reality Replacement	Personal associative experience generally overrides reality representation.	Loss of distinction between fantasy and reality in general; beginning loss of distinction between associational and representational processes.
Reality Replacement Condensation	Separate representations condensed	Loss of distinction between essentially distinct representations or representational processes (i.e., association and representation, idea-affect and percept).

sible, only unlikely. By contrast with level 3, the patient has not yet begun building associations apart from justifications in the blot.

This level reflects affirmation of subjective experience which remains both intrinsically alien to the reality cues which evoked it and too close to underlying fantasy elements, though without violating reality outright. Appreciation of reality is maintained, but excessive coloring of associative and representational processes by internal experience has occurred. As contrasted with creative or adaptive regression, no synthesis of subjective and objective reality is attained whereby the underlying fantasy preoccupation might be made public. Rather, reality is adopted to an excessively personalized or subjective point of view which as yet remains apart from objective and interpersonal reality.

Scores included at this level are peculiar responses and verbalizations, as well as fabulized combinations or composite figures in which the patient remains aware of the unrealistic nature of the combination or in which a minor dispensation was assumed by the patient and spontaneously recognized when inquiry was directed to it.[7]

Level 2: circumscribed reality rejection. At this level, a basis for integration is introduced in which those reality considerations (perceptual or logical) which contradict the integration must be ignored. Thus an unresolved clash between fantasy and selective aspects of reality persists in the final response. This reflects the first clear reality violation, wherein an associative process has gained sufficient strength to encourage circumscribed dismissal of reality, but without giving up integrative effort.

By contrast with level 1, reality considerations are dismissed rather than being interpreted in an excessively private way. More is implied here than alienation of part of subjective reality experience: a circumscribed loss of appreciation of reality has occurred at the moment of affirmation of subjective experience. Though reality cues provide the basis for the fantasy, fantasy urges structure the reality interpretation excessively—fantasy and reality experiences become combined in an unrealistic fashion, though without blending with reality (level 4) or generalized replacement of it (level 3).

This level reflects affirmation of subjective experience which requires

[7] Most such fabulized combinations are likely to be of the sort which Holt has termed ''arbitrary unlikely combinations,'' as opposed to ''arbitrary impossible combinations,'' and most such composite figures are likely to be ones which could exist within a certain publicly shareable context (fiction, mythology, etc.). However, the distinction between the combinations at this level and those at the next level rests with the patient's capacity to spontaneously recognize the unrealistic basis for the combination and make it public, not with the content of the response per se. For example, some more regressed patients may give a response at a seemingly more benign level (unlikely fabulized combination) but upon inquiry reveal uncertainty or insensitivity regarding the unreality of the combination.

violation of reality considerations for the subjective experience to be introduced into consciousness or communication, but which remains contained within the context of a specific sort of idea. In brief, the patient has abandoned the distinction between fantasy and reality within a specific ideational or affective context.

Scores included at this level are impossible or bizarre composite figures, impossible combinations, as well as logical and affective contradictions and impossible object-action combinations.[8]

Level 3: reality replacement. At this level, associative processes build upon one another without anchoring to the reality referents of the blot, and/or shifts in representations occur fluidly in such a way as to minimize (without losing) their differentiation, in the service of expressing the associative experience. Associative processes are allowed to fully introduce the subjective fantasy basis for organizing the blot material. By contrast with fabulation, certain affect tones or specific meanings have no justification in the reality of the blot, but are selected only according to their salience to other subjective meanings which have earlier been triggered into consciousness by the blot. By contrast with level 2, the associative process is not contained, attenuated, or implicitly represented in combinatory percept content or in circumscribed affective or logical contradictions. Rather, the associative process emerges as a response in its own right. By contrast with level 4, the sustained immersion in subjective fantasy and abandonment of reality sense does not result in condensations.

This level reflects sustained loss of reality referents during the affirmation of subjective experience so that the patient becomes immersed in fantasy as if it were reality during the course of the fantasy. In brief, the patient has abandoned the distinction between associative and representational processes, though without losing the capacity to distinguish them.

Scores included at this level include classical sorts of confabulation,[9] fluid associations, fluid perceptual transformations, autistic logic, and personalized or bizarre symbolism. In my earlier study (Athey, 1974), such functioning was found prominent in schizophrenic patients with an affect-disordered component and some few patients with major affect disorder.

[8] Inquiry might reveal some such combinations to be in fact those more frequently found at level 1 (see fn. 7), but given the more highly idiosyncratic nature of the combination, the patient must spontaneously offer an acceptable context in which such a relationship might be observed to clearly indicate an appreciation for the unrealistic nature of this context. For example, "a bird with wheels" might on inquiry be clarified as "a toy, like those pull-toys they have for children" (level 1) or as "a fantastic creature like you might see in some science fiction movie" (level 2). Only if the patient were to refer to a specific movie in which a living bird had been depicted with wheels would the latter rationalization indicate level 1 organization.

[9] It is crucial to distinguish true confabulations from associatively elaborated fabulized combinations, which may more likely denote level 1 or 2 primary process.

Level 4: condensation. At this level there occurs loss of differentiation between the various representational processes which, in all other levels discussed above, are retained as basic frames of reality reference. This definition views basic representational processes as the autonomous parallels in cognitive functioning to basic dimensions around which reality and self-nonself (self-other, internal-external) distinctions are organized, in keeping with the notion of cognitive structures proposed by Rapaport (1957). In terms of the basic Rorschach processes, the patient has lost the distinction between associative and representational processes, separate representations (toward which associative or combinatory activity could have been directed), or separate associations. There has occurred a mixing together of reality frames and/or of internal experience and objective reality in ways eradicating external reality apart from internal subjective experience of it. The result is bizarre reconstructions of reality based upon representational processes which are condensed with each other. At the point in time when such responses are conceived, no veridical sense of reality remains represented autonomously in the patient's cognitive functioning.

Scores included at this level are the classical contamination responses as well as verbal condensations between separate thoughts in the absence of overlap among different percepts or percept identities. Loss of boundary between separate ideas does exist here; this sort of functioning was found in the earlier study among schizophrenic patients lacking an affect-disordered component and, in conjunction with level 3 manifestations, among some affect-disordered schizophrenics as well.

The Patient-Examiner Relationship in the Response Process

In general terms, projective psychological assessment is intended to provide a sort of cross-sectional view of personality organization. Fluctuations in the extent of structure intrinsic to the tasks correspond to the extent that a patient is left to rely on the autonomy of internal representational processes in responding to the tasks. On the Rorschach, external structure is minimal and reliance on internal processes maximal. In telling what the blots look like, the patient is implicitly attempting to re-create a veridical sense of the world and to convey his unique internal sense of that world. This restorative aspect of the response process has been spoken to previously by Schachtel (1966). In this process, the patient is left to draw upon all of his experience—the minimal degree of focal structure essentially places the patient in the position of having to reestablish equilibrium between task functioning and unconscious experience (past and repressed). Thus, the Rorschach task involves an unfolding of the patient's preeminent object relations concerns in terms of certain structural levels of representation, which may fluctuate depending on proneness to ego regression.

By contrast with diagnostic interviewing, in the Rorschach situation there is relatively less structure in the sense of opportunities for reliance on an implicit process of personal relationship development. On the other hand, the Rorschach situation appears relatively more structured in terms of the examiner's more or less standard inquiry, though structured in a neutral direction. Thus, specific developments in the patient's sense of relatedness to the examiner, and reactions to these developments, can be masked by the progress of the testing task. In one sense, this is an advantage—the process of unfolding through the medium of the test responses is speeded up in time and becomes less bound to interactive details of the patient-examiner relationship than is the case in a diagnostic interview. It is this "time capsule" element which makes such testing economical in actual clinical practice. One obtains an idea of what may happen in a future clinical relationship over time by virtue of the object relations concerns revealed and the regression in formal thought processes that occurs, while the shared task of the testing may remain intact. A more detailed, microscopic view of the patient's internal functioning is available than if all such processes were to be filtered through the additional task of building a more personal relationship as a base for exploration.

At the same time, there is a relationship involved. Indeed, without some basic rapport around the notion that the tasks require cooperation and are intended for the ultimate benefit of the patient's treatment, the testing could proceed only as an empty exercise. Moreover, much can be lost if nuances of the relationship are not explored. It is precisely in such implicit relationship processes that important confirmations and disconfirmations, and/or supplementary information concerning the patient's functioning, may be found. The elucidation of such relationship processes requires inquiry into the relationship once some significant quality in it emerges. Such inquiry is involved in the case illustrations to follow.

In brief, the Rorschach situation shares processes with clinical relationship development, including that occurring in the psychotherapy situation, although these processes are typically more muted in testing. By contrast with the Rorschach situation, in the treatment situation the elements of transference serve as the focal patient response, so that assessment of formal characteristics may be confounded with the content of transference.[10] Foreknowledge of the pervasiveness and precipitousness of ego regression, the internal object relations conditions for it, and the current relationship conditions ameliorating it, is precisely the sort of anticipatory information that projective testing can

[10] Such confounding may indeed be the reason Kernberg's object relations paradigms, derived as they are from observations within psychoanalytic treatment, blend structural and thematic concerns. Such paradigms are closer to the manner in which sustained transference experiences emerge as an overall gestalt within the treatment situation.

provide. In terms of psychotherapy, *the presence of rekindling of earlier modes of ego functioning (demonstrated in primary process thinking) speaks to the patient's readiness to engage in regressive expression of certain object relations concerns in the moment of their experience. This will pose complications for any highly unstructured or uncovering treatment* (see Horwitz, 1974).

Viewed in this context, the status of the patient-examiner relationship is crucial to assessment for treatment planning, corresponding to the sort of current relationship processes needed for handling various transferential and ego-regressive experiences. There is no assurance that the patient's handling of this relationship will be sufficiently known unless efforts to elucidate it are made by the examiner.

The provisions of the relationship are straightforward. The patient is asked to handle the task on his own while the examiner actively listens, records, and inquires as needed for clarification. The sort of special inquiry required to delineate different types of primary process thinking for accurate scoring may be viewed more readily as judgments about, or even assists to, the patient's ego functioning which may push the patient's experience of the relationship in particular directions. However, clinical experience and the following case illustrations indicate that even very early in the testing process the patient responds to the task with implicit transference feelings and attitudes.

Case Illustrations

The case illustrations provide a view of the parallel processes which emerged in the patients' thinking and in their relationship with the examiner (and which might be expected to emerge in a future treatment relationship) based on an ego psychological understanding of primary process thinking. In this respect, the case material provides encouraging confirmation of the salience of thought organization to the task of anticipating parameters needed for the development and maintenance of a treatment relationship.

In beginning with each of these patients, the same general Rorschach instructions were provided: "I'll be showing you some cards one at a time, and as you look at each card I want you to tell me the things that occur to you about what it looks like." In response to any questions by the patient, certain standard responses were available. If a question concerned what might be seen, the examiner gave a simple paraphrase of the instructions: "What it looks like *to you*." If a question concerned how to approach the task, the examiner said: "You can go about it any way you like." At the end of the inquiry to the first card, the examiner said: "That's the way it will go. After you've given yourself time to tell me the things that occur to you about each card, I'll be going back and asking you some questions about some of the things you saw, to make sure I understand what made it look that way to you."

The approach to test administration followed that of Rapaport: inquiry conducted with the card absent, after free association to each card. No special interventions were necessary with any of the following patients to insure sufficiently long exposure to any card (three minutes if no responses, two minutes if one response, one and a half minutes if two or more responses), or to limit the time spent (six minutes maximum) or the number of responses offered (six maximum) per card.

Each patient responded to the initial task instructions in a noteworthy way, verbally or nonverbally. Such responses were clarified later, sometimes in conjunction with other spontaneous reactions to the examiner. Upon clarification, the patient's reactions may be seen as having been formed and expressed in ways consistent with the patient's predominant mode of thought organization, and as having derived from object relations concerns pertinent to key psychodynamic conflicts.

Case A: Successful Enriching Thought Organization Leading to Transference Disconfirmation and Relationship Potential

Rorschach events. The patient's Rorschach contained no instances of the four levels of primary process thinking. Rather, some of the patient's responses involved denotation of ideas or elaboration of affect tones that were quite specific, at times leading to the sort of impressionistic embellishment illustrated in the following response:

> *Card X*. There is something near the top that looks like two little Martian creatures face to face, maybe having an argument . . . and other parts of it look like different sorts of things . . . these blue things on the side could be crabs . . . overall, it's very colorful and conveys to me a feeling of celebration, even jubilance or flight . . . I guess I'm thinking of fireworks like on the Fourth of July, which some of these colored areas could be, like the burst of color and light of fireworks, and there is an overall feel of lightness and airiness to it as well.

The response traces the fate of strong affect in the patient through the sequence: argument, blue, colorful, jubilance, fireworks, and lightness. The affect was almost expressed in a pure color (c) response, but instead became bound to an affect-laden association ("celebration, jubilance, flight"). The incipient pure c response was not allowed to combine inappropriately with the crabs (such as "blue crabs") and the associative process was not allowed to replace the task set, or to commandeer unrealistic combinatory activity (such as "crabs and Martians, jubilant, because of the colors"). The two arguing Martians was given to an area in which two such creatures may so easily be seen with excellent form level that it seems unlikely that this response represents Level One pathological insulation of experience. Rather, the associative process was reimposed on the colored areas of the blot, allowing expression of a more acceptable color form (CF) response which fit both the associations and the blot areas. Thus, more open emotional expression became represented in the Rorschach response by way of an associative process which served as a creative bridge.

Clinical events. At the beginning of testing, the patient had indirectly asked for increased structure in response to the examiner's instructions: "You mean there are specific things I should tell you about?" Viewed in light of the foregoing impressionistic style, and the patient's spontaneous comment at the end of the test (see below), the patient was probably wondering if more open elaboration such as she made in the above response would be acceptable.

At one point prior to Card X (on Card VIII) the patient looked at the card silently and then gave it back. The examiner indicated he had noticed the patient had paused and wondered if other things had come to the patient's mind. The patient had said, "No, not really, this is a bit frustrating. I feel I should be getting more out of these things."

At the end of testing, the patient expressed a spontaneous transference feeling toward the examiner:

> I don't know if that sort of thing is what you wanted or if you wanted me to stick to specific ideas. (You had a notion you were supposed to do it a specific way?) I remember you saying it was up to me, more or less. There were times I felt I shouldn't have gone on as much as I did, and other times I wanted to say more but felt I couldn't or shouldn't and got frustrated with it. I began to feel you weren't interested in the feelings I had about the card, because you had said, "Tell me what you see." And I felt very frustrated. But you were asking me, seemed interested, to tell you the things that influenced my views and I did and you didn't correct me or anything. (I remember you asking me as we began about being specific or not in what you should tell me and I said, "What it looks like *to you*"—how did you feel about that?) Kind of lost, I wasn't sure how much you wanted me to express myself or just stick to the facts.

The patient's key psychodynamic conflict had concerned an autocratic and emotionally suppressive, distant father, toward whom the patient had experienced strong affectionate yearnings. She had in part identified with her father in seeking achievement in business, and had come to treatment because of inhibitions in expressing intimacy and the development of emotional outbursts toward her husband. Her transference feelings in the patient-examiner relationship repeated her wish to please her father and her fear of his censure. Her affective process in the Rorschach responses repeated her experience of being left with excess inner affect experience in the face of her father's potential censure, and the fireworks which her marriage had inherited.

The patient's Rorschach thought organization reflected her capacity to integrate such surplus feelings with reality in a way enlivening and enriching her responses.[11] Her resolution of the transference feelings toward the examiner reflected this same capacity to continue to deal with a strong feeling and integrate it with her views of the actual conduct of the examiner so as to maintain a sense of shared effort. The working relationship was never overwhelmed, only tinged with temporary inhibition (on Card VIII) and a lingering feeling of frustration (expressed at the end of Card X). The patient autonomously expressed and dealt with the conflict and was able to allow herself to become more expressive in an integrated manner. After sorting out these feelings the patient manifested increased positive affect tone toward the examiner, and this atmosphere continued over several minutes, until the end of the session.

Case B: Idiosyncratic Experience Leading to Failure of Transference-Alliance Integration

Rorschach events. The patient's Rorschach contained primary process thinking restricted to Level One, involving benign arbitrary combinations and composition figures given in a specific fantasy or humorous (often derisively humorous) context, in which the distinction between separate ideas and recognition of the incongruity of the combinations were both possible. Several examples of this approach have been provided to afford a sufficiently clear distinction between this patient and Case C.

Card I. A headless person, evoking, invoking the heavens,

[11] Note that such an integrative process differs from the non–self-critical, excessively associative process which would be expected to accompany a self-indulgent acting-out reaction to excess inner affect. Such acting out might be inferred from a solely dynamic content–oriented sequence analysis of the patient's responses to Card X. The content aspects of the response of course suggest unresolved conflict—argument is followed by jubilation, suggesting a wish for victory over her affect states side-by-side with the continued notion of an argument, with implications for hypomanic defense against conflict.

> in the center. . . . (Invoking the heavens?) Looks like two hands reaching up. (Invoking to do what?) I feel like it's, I get a concept, God help me, that type of thing. Desperate call for help.

Surplus meaning exists within the ambiguous use of the word ''invoking.'' The idea of someone helplessly imploring the assistance of a spiritual power and of someone controlling the delivery of such help are mixed together. The verbal slip ''evoke'' before ''invoke'' momentarily reveals the notion that the other's power must be activated in reaction to the helpless one, but the helpless one must be powerfully evocative or provocative, for help is not simply available. The response blends qualities of both a powerless supplicant and a powerful priest. These concepts were not condensed in the response, but rather were juxtaposed by the verbal slip, suggesting that surplus meaning had been kept in abeyance and left ambiguous in the overt communication.

The headless aspect of the person was something repeated in other responses and suggests an attitude of depreciation. Other responses involved more typical types of level 1 responses:

> *Card V.* A bat going to town on Saturday night, with elegant wings and maybe a cape. . . . (Elegant wings?) Not so much like elegant wings as an elegant cape like Vincent Price would wear as Dracula. (Where would you see something like that, a bat with a cape?) You wouldn't, unless bats go to town on Saturday night. (Patient laughs.) Like going to a bat ball. (Patient laughs.) I've heard of ball bats before but never bat balls. (Patient laughs.)

The combinations allowed to emerge in the response process are the ideas ''elegant wings'' (wings and an elegant cape) and a bat going to town. In his initial response to inquiry, the patient provided a fictional context for the response (Vincent Price would play Dracula). More focal inquiry was directed toward the extent to which bat and vampire had been differentiated as ideas in the patient's thinking. Bat with a cape sounded like a composite of (1) bat and (2) vampire in human form with a cape. Such a composite had not been dismissed by the fictional context. The patient recognized the nature of the incongruity and played with it humorously in a way which demonstrated an appreciation for double meanings (of ''ball''), and the impossibility of something like that in a realistic context (''if bats go to town on Saturday night''). Thus, this was an arbitrary composite of ideas the patient could recognize as separate, and not a condensation or a failure to recognize the incongruous combination.

> *Card X*. This looks like a very unlikely family argument being arbitrated by a piece of celery. (Indicates upper gray detail.) Everybody's arguing, not listening. (How up here?) I was fantasizing, making up a Disney character, something that can't talk but does. Everything was focused up to him, sitting there like a judge, squatty feet, very comical.

Again, a fantasy context clearly guides the combination of celery with other figures and the composite of celery with human features and actions. The patient seems to be deriding a position of leadership and authority, and his derision stands in marked contrast to the power of the unseen, invoked figure on Card I.

Clinical events. In response to the instructions, the patient had responded nonverbally. He flashed an angry look briefly, but then hid his anger and asked the examiner to repeat the instructions. He responded to the examiner's repetition with a mocking smile. He made no further asides nor communicated any spontaneous feelings toward the examiner. This initial behavior may be understood, in light of the foregoing thought organization, as the patient reeliciting the instructions so as to absorb them into a private mocking context in defense against a more direct expression of anger.

At the end of testing, the examiner had been struck by the patient's obvious enjoyment of several of his primary process responses, and asked the patient how he had experienced the test. The patient said:

> At first I was taken aback. I didn't see how this could be relevant to anything. (Did you have any specific feelings as we began? I remember you smiled when I gave you the instructions.) I was thinking how *this was kind of a game, where you are going to leave me blind about what I should do,* but I had a number of thoughts that amused me. You could really let yourself go on this. (How are you feeling about it now?) I still wonder about the value of something like this. What can you tell me from it that will help me? It's hard for me to relate this very much to me as a person, but maybe it's of some use to you. I guess you can get an idea about my daydreams if I let you, but you could be wrong, too. (What were your thoughts about the celery and the family argument?) Those are just some of the types of things that occur to me sometimes, like when I'm trying to get started writing up a story. I do react to people in authority like that sometimes—people who set themselves up to be more than they really are.

There ensued some discussion with the patient about how these feelings had come up repeatedly in his response to treatment thus far. The patient then said, "Well, this has been interesting and maybe it will be helpful in talking with the staff, but I do think you set somebody up here, they can look worse than they are. And I still don't know what you think of me or how you're going to use this information."

In the patient's reaction to the examiner, the idea persisted of help as unavailable unless provocatively "implored," along with a caricature of the examiner as an ineffectual judge, not a true member of the treating staff group, with whom he should speak about his feelings. More importantly, these views persisted despite some disconfirmation in the relationship, to which the patient had been ostensibly receptive. His failure to integrate the transference feeling with some actual aspects of the working relationship paralleled his manner of thinking, whereby he retained private idiosyncratic experiences protected from disconfirmation.

The patient's father had committed suicide, leaving the patient with the family business to run. Before his father's death, the patient had idealized his father and had struggled to meet his standards, but felt he had failed because of his father's excessive, demanding criticism. After his father's death, he went on in his efforts to succeed, but in order to do so he began to devalue his father for having not been all he was cracked up to be. While the content of the patient's views of the examiner repeated certain ongoing feelings about his relationship with his father, the patient's manner of structuring the expression of this inner experience repeated the irretrievably traumatic quality of his father's death—the experience remained as something untouchable by the usual channels of interpersonal contact. The patient had woven this manner of handling feelings into a more general style which in part enforced in the examiner countertransference feelings which echoed the patient's experience of his father—feeling abruptly extruded from the patient's internal world, with one's best efforts rejected and devalued.

Case C: Circumscribed Reality Rejection Leading to Circumscribed Transference Reification

Rorschach events. The patient's Rorschach contained level 2 manifestations, impossible combinations or those unjustified by any mitigating anticipatory context, in which notable contradictions of reality occurred.

> *Card I.* Well, could be two animals on something that rotates 360 degrees, head, feet, tail, feet attached to the 360 degree rotating thing. . . . (Animals?) Nose, ears, head, tail, and their feet, body. (Alive?) Yes. (Rotating thing?) Like a teddy bear or something, bear

> cub or something like that. (How relate to the teddy bear?) Well, there is something central there, like a pole, and naturally I assumed it would be able to rotate 360 degrees if it was cylindrical. (Were the bear and the pole the same thing?) Well, it was attached in some fashion, but being in dark colors it's difficult to discern the nature of the attachment. Like a merry-go-round, something you'd find in a park, amusement park, or something. They're holding on, attached to it, could be bear cubs. (Attached?) Like a ride in an amusement park, so they certainly wouldn't be alive, it would be like horses on a merry-go-round, carved.

Eventually the patient resolved the combination into an acceptable context, but along the way revealed how tenuous his differentiation of the two components had been. At different points in the response and inquiry he saw animals attached to a mechanical object, a part animal/part mechanical object, animals riding a playground merry-go-round, and a true merry-go-round with bears instead of horses. The patient eventually decided upon the last alternative. While his overall response to inquiry suggested a capacity to move in a direction of differentiation instead of condensation, the status of the original response was clarified as a true impossible combination (live bears attached to a mechanical object). Moreover, he retrospectively upgraded the response only in response to inquiry, and revealed further confusion—in response to inquiry about the "rotating thing" the patient answered with details about the animals. This type of combination (impossible, without autonomous recognition) thus involves tendencies toward condensation. The focus of the patient's uncertainties concerns the nature of the attachment—linked versus holding on. The impossible combination derived from his attempt to combine a concrete linkage with living creatures.

Clinical events. The patient initially responded to the instructions in a nonverbal way, becoming somewhat pale, with his facial features immobilized by tension. Then he said, "I'm afraid of the evaluation. What will it tell about me? How am I supposed to do it?" The examiner paraphrased the instructions and indicated there was no right or wrong way to go about it. The patient reluctantly agreed to continue.

Partway through the test the patient said, "I really want to stop. I'm so afraid." The examiner indicated that of course they could stop if it was really too much to go on, but wondered if they might talk about it first. The patient discussed his feelings as follows: "I feel I'm looking silly, and I don't see how you can respect me. I feel like you don't respect me. You are asking me a lot of questions so something must be wrong with my answer." The examiner repeated that he was interested in understanding how the patient had gone about seeing the things as he had, since different people go about it different ways. The patient nodded and said he guessed they could continue.

At the end of testing, the examiner inquired how the patient was feeling about the evaluation. The patient said: "I'm glad it's over. You took away my self-respect and I can't really forgive you for that." The examiner could not dissuade the patient from this feeling. The examiner then pointed out how the patient had seemed afraid near the beginning of the test and seemed to have become more afraid later, and asked the patient what he had felt at the beginning. The patient answered, "You asked me to tell all of my thoughts and I had no way to know what you wanted. I wanted to cooperate but I had no privacy."

The notion of having his privacy invaded by lack of sufficient structure through which to gauge his own progress became the dominant experience of the relationship, to which he could only submit or flee. The transference became fact for him within this specific conceptual frame of reference.

In retrospect, unresolved infantile ego structure had provided such a strong context for the feelings evoked by the task effort that the working relationship and the past relationship became equated. The patient had recently lost his dominating father, who had been the primary source of physical care for the patient in early childhood following the death of the patient's mother, with whom the patient had identified. His father had behaved in a manner the patient had experienced as intrusive in response to the patient's emerging sexuality in adolescence. Before the testing, the patient had haltingly discussed such matters in the diagnostic interview with the psychiatrist, but had not seen the parallel in our relationship sufficiently to sort it out. The patient's experience of loss was so suffused with concern over infantile attachment and his level of ego development so fixated at a correspondingly infantile level that the examiner's exploratory evaluation, like the father's attempts to address the patient's sexuality and similar events in the mother's death, threatened permeation of the patient's ego boundaries.

Case D: Generalized Reality Replacement Leading to Sustained Transference Immersion

Rorschach events. The patient's primary process thinking evidenced several indications of level 3 organization, such as:

> *Card II*. Looks like two continents, sort of on a global map . . . something disastrous about it because of the single splotch, the top center. It looks like these two vast continents . . . as if nuclear war broke out on these two

> things and their only hope is these two separate red marks, which look like embryos, but they're not attached to it. And there is something here that looks like a snake, cobra snake, something for worshiping or something. . . . (Disastrous red splotch?) Yeah, that thing looks like a volcano, a violent splotch here because it was red and I thought of blood and violence, because the red was violent, the way it was splotched down there, like it was animated, had some intensity, red liquid oozing out, not oozing, splashing maybe. It's like the head of the snake, I wouldn't want to go into it but pray to it like an idol, pray to it, praise it, yeah. (Where expect to see?) Oh, maybe in a movie like *King Kong*.

The patient retained some qualities of fabulized combination in his responding, in that things were seen in combination which had size discrepancies and were combined on an unrealistic basis, but the basis became explicit and was built into a full-fledged fantasy without sufficient justification in the blot. Though the patient referred back to blot areas from time to time, the dominant emphasis was on the fantasy process, which went on as though with a life of its own and was not provided a successful context by reference to *King Kong*.

Clinical events. In response at the beginning of the test, the patient said, "Just what I see?" To this the examiner replied with the usual paraphrase. In retrospect, the patient seems to be inquiring as to whether his fantasy processes were to be suppressed or rejected by the examiner.

At the end of testing, the patient said spontaneously, "This reminds me of when I was a little kid and my folks would take me to the movies and I saw Walt Disney and it was real to me. It was another world and I was right there. I wanted Bambi to come to our house and I wanted to go to the forest. My parents told me it was just a movie and I tore hell out of my room, jumped all over the place, they were afraid I was going to hurt myself. Thank you for giving me a chance to tell you about my thoughts." The examiner asked the patient what he had heard the examiner asking him to do as they began. The patient said, "You wanted to know my thoughts and feelings, I guess. That's the reason for this, isn't it? These things just build up in me. I really want to talk, it's like being in another world when no one knows what you're feeling inside. You're the person who is going to help me get my act together, aren't you?"

The patient seemed to have heard the instructions as consistent with his wish, although he had actually seemed at first to have been fearing suppression. His wish specifically was for the examiner to be his therapeutic savior and help him make his fantasies come true. Later he thought because of his having experienced his fantasies openly in the examiner's presence, without the examiner telling him his fantasies weren't real, that the examiner might really be his therapist. Subsequently, the examiner clarified that he had only a diagnostic role with the patient, and the patient accepted this, but later on in the same day again thought that the examiner would probably be his therapist, and asked the examiner if he would be.

Here the fantasy reconstruction of the relationship did not derive from a struggle within a specific conflictual context, as occurred with patient C, but simply overrode the working relationship much as his fantasy expression quickly became for him the dominant motive in his response process. The patient stopped short of delusional conviction that the examiner was his therapist, or that testing had been therapy, but could not autonomously maintain a sense of the reality of the relationship in the face of his fantasy reconstructions about it. The patient's *potential* for transference psychosis (though not fusion) is clear.

Case E: Condensation Leading to Incipient Fusion

Rorschach events. The patient's primary process thinking was characterized by features of level 4. The condensations which occurred were mixed with level 2 and level 3 manifestations, but may be seen as having been the more forceful elements in organizing the more primitive aspects of the patient's transference experience.

> *Card I, Responses 4–6*. [Number 4] Down at the bottom it looks like a vaginal barrel . . . and I see at the top [Number 5] two soldiers. Hats. I also see it as a [Number 6] fragmented bullet, the metal's shattered and pieces are coming out of the card. (Vaginal barrel?) Like pictures of a vagina I've seen in medical books, or a uterus. (Indicating center.) I may have my sexual organs mixed up. (Patient clarifies how he had thought he had seen soldiers with hats on, but had actually seen soldiers' hats, called it soldiers, and then hats, and then could not find the soldiers under the hats.) (Bullet, coming out of card?) Yes, it seems to be some movement as I looked at it. (Actual or suggested?) The structure of it suggested movement, like it had an inner life to it. (Indicating center uterus.) Like perceptual illusions that can take on movement, life.

A subtle contaminatory thought process runs beneath the surface of these responses, not emerging into full simultaneity of meaning in a single percept area until the end. At first, ''vaginal barrel'' seems merely peculiar, but in the context of subsequent associations and the response to inquiry, the phrase appears to have been an infusion of the vagina percept with ideas concerning aggressive destruction (barrel) which were contained in the nascent percepts of soldiers (in a different area) and bullet (in the same area).

The uncertainty of distinction between separate percepts and ideas was revealed in the patient's struggle to differentiate soldiers, hats, and soldiers with hats on. The same area suggested these different but related ideas, and it is unclear how much he ever saw the soldiers and their hats as separate.

The confabulatory, almost hallucinatory vividness of the bullet moving out of the card is linked to the (finally overt) contaminatory thought process—the vividness of the movement is linked to a sense of inner life which he attributes to the uterus, which occupies the same blot area as the bullet.

> *Card V, Responses 1–3*. [Number 1] Flying rabbit. Flying face down over a massive acreage of snow. It has wings of a giant bat and ears like a . . . looks like he has a [Number 2] man's face on top of his head. (Top center rare detail for both.) Dragging [Number 3] two satyrs (side details, same as wings) across cement (same as snow, the white space), an all-powerful rabbit. Like he's presenting them to me, saying, ''Look at these bums.'' Like presenting them to the king or judge saying, ''You're drunk and your sheep have run off.'' (Man's face on top?) It began to appear as I first looked at it, I saw eyes and nose emerging from what at first I took to be the rabbit's head. (Sounded like you saw them together when you said, ''Face on top of his head.'') It changed like if you put water on litmus paper it began to emerge and looked like it was tatooed on the back of his head. That's when he was flying. Then it looked like a rabbit holding the two men. It seems like life occurs within the image and then unfolds. (Unfolds?) It feels like blood coming out of my body, it feels like carving something, having creative juices flowing within me, how I am warming up, coming more alive, interaction with the image. Like blood drained out of me at first, and then it comes back in, like lights being turned on.

The patient allowed himself to see objects in interaction which occupied the same parts of the blot. He attempted to hold off the condensation, describing the transition from the rabbit's head to the man's face as if it were a fluid shift between separate images, but then noting their simultaneity as one emerged within the other as with litmus paper. Some rationalization effort was at work as well, when the patient described the rabbit-satyr relationship as if he had changed the way he had seen the rabbit. The rationalization did not hold, and the patient proceeded to reveal his psychotic experience of the "creative" response process—the projection of his internal experience onto the card was experienced literally like a loss of lifeblood, his "carving" of images becoming suffused by a sense of things being carved out of him, and he must struggle to retain a sense of internal life by maintaining excessive involvement with the projected image. Then it was as if the projected image came back into him and that connection maintained him as alive, the recognition of the projected image being experienced as though lights had been turned back on. It is as though one person projected the response and another recognized it, and as though a threatened symbiotic link existed between these two aspects of himself. The distinction between internal and external, idea and real object, were lost in his experience just as the distinction between separate percepts was violated.

Clinical events. In response to the instructions, the patient nodded and said, "I'm glad you're doing the testing, because I feel more familiar with you, you know me more than the others." At the end of the testing the examiner asked the patient how he had experienced the test, and the patient responded: "I've been wanting to get my creativity going again. I enjoy being able to do more creative work, but my problems have often gotten in the way. I've had conflicts with my supervisor. I guess some of my ideas shock him, so I feel better being able to express myself more freely. I'm already familiar with you to some extent, so I don't feel so afraid. You understood what I was thinking, know what I was thinking and didn't get afraid. You don't lose control when you took that test. You wanted me to do well."

The examiner asked the patient what he had heard the examiner ask for when they began the test. The patient responded, "You wanted me to be creative, to do my best, you know my abilities."

The patient lost the distinction between his motives regarding the test and those of the examiner, and at one point views the examiner as taking the test. He feels familiar with the examiner in the sense that he recognized in him a projected part of himself. There was a need for the examiner to be the positive counterpart of his disapproving supervisor. This seems to be a precursor to a fused self-other state in a positive transference. The supervisor represents the negative aspects of the patient's stern father, from whom he had wanted, but not received, physical care and approval of his imagination. He had received such "approval" from his mother in very early childhood, but in an indulgent and narcissistic way which did not respect the difference between his wishes and hers, nor sufficiently represent the distinction between fantasy and reality. The patient had turned to his father in hopes of diluting what had become an excruciating relationship with his mother. The examiner was asked to be the good father who will not excessively criticize, but who is then invited to subsidize the internal symbiotic, life-preserving bond.

Directions for Further Study

The patients discussed above all expressed some response to the patient-examiner relationship that prompted inquiry. It remains an open question as to whether the same parallels between thought organization and transference handling would emerge in a different group of patients—for example, those with similar primary process and whose experience of the test in the clinical relationship can be pursued by the examiner in an equally systematic fashion, but whose spontaneous reactions do not prompt special inquiry into the patient-examiner relationship. In other words, might the present patients' verbal and/or nonverbal provocation of special attention have been a special condition for the parallels which emerged between their thought organization and their transference feelings? Given the potential importance of information obtainable regarding the patient-examiner relationship, I felt encouraged in more recent diagnostic practice to begin conducting this special inquiry with every patient seen. While the present findings encourage the interpretation of primary process thinking in terms of particular levels of ego regression in transference, study of patients illustrating exceptions to the expected parallels could provide equally useful hypotheses regarding the particular implicit events and processes in the patient-examiner relationship that may serve to prevent ego regression. Such information could be useful in applying test information in planning treatment strategy.

The levels of thought organization delineated above are fairly easy to discriminate in principle, but numerous considerations are required during inquiry to allow for reliable discrimination in actual practice with a particular patient and a particular Rorschach response. While sufficient inquiry is required to clarify the nature of these responses, such inquiry must often be more blatant than one would conduct regarding any other aspect of a response, raising the risk of alteration of the patient's "true" response through suggestion. Also, the different levels of organization may be differentially subject to the influence of suggestion, so that different degrees of directness may be required to maintain a balance of clarity and patient genuineness.

If the present view of primary process thinking does offer some conceptual advantages over previous ones, the ideas warrant further development to facilitate clinical applications. More specifically, the potential meanings of each score type within each level should be examined in great detail to anchor its meaning in relation to the meaning of the overall thought process reflected by the level in which it is embedded. The firm interrelation between specific score types and general levels has been lacking in earlier scoring systems. At various points, such systems have left the categorization of individual score types to face validity only. Differential diagnostic considerations between ostensibly similar score types could then be synthesized with such a conceptual framework and used to guide inquiry, reducing variation among examiners in the crucial process of elucidating the precise nature of any particular response.

The idea of two component processes (representation and association) within which various modes of pathological organization may occur offers a potential bridge from Rorschach functioning to potentially different systems of regulation in brain function. Given the recent improved technologies for assessment of brain response (for example, neurometric and radioactive xenon techniques), systematic research of this sort should soon be possible.

Finally, there is a Rorschach study, begging to be done, in which the structural and thematic approaches to object relations assessment (Spear, 1980) might be carefully distinguished and then compared, with careful attention to the foregoing aspects of thought organization.

References

Athey, G. (1974), Schizophrenic thought organization, object relations and the Rorschach test. *Bull. Menn. Clin.*, 38:406–429.

——— Fleischer, J., & Coyne, L. (1980), Rorschach object representation as influenced by thought and affect organization. In: *Borderline Phenomena and the Rorschach Test*, ed. J. Kwawer, H. Lerner, P. Lerner, & A. Sugarman. New York: International Universities Press, pp. 275–298.

Becker, W. (1956), A genetic approach to the interpretation and evaluation of the process-reactive distinction in schizophrenia. *J. Abnorm. Soc. Psychol.*, 53:299–336.

Blatt, S., Brenneis, C., Schimek, J., & Glick, M. (1976), The normal development and psychopathological impairment of the concept of the object on the Rorschach. *J. Abnorm. Psychol.*, 85:364–373.

——— & Ritzler, B. (1974), Thought disorder and boundary disturbances in psychosis. *J. Consult. Clin. Psychol.*, 42:370–381.

——— & Wild, C. (1976), *Schizophrenia: A Developmental Analysis*. New York: Academic Press.

Holt, R. (1963), Manual for scoring of primary process manifestations in Rorschach responses. Unpublished manuscript.

——— & Havel, J. (1960), A method for assessing primary and secondary processes in the Rorschach. In: *Rorschach Psychology*, ed. M. Rickers-Ovsiankina. New York: Wiley, pp. 263–315.

Horwitz, L. (1974), *Clinical Prediction in Psychotherapy*. New York: Aronson.

Johnston, M., & Holzman, P. (1976), The Thought Disorder Index. Unpublished manuscript.

Kernberg, O. (1975), *Borderline Conditions and Pathological Narcissism*. New York: Aronson.

Rapaport, D. (1957), Cognitive structures. In: *Contemporary Approaches to Cognition*, ed. J. Bruner et al. Cambridge, Mass.: Harvard University Press.

——— Gill, M., & Schafer, R. (1945), *Diagnostic Psychological Testing*. New York: International Universities Press, 1968.

Schachtel, E. (1966), *Experiential Foundations of Rorschach's Test*. New York: Basic Books.

Schafer, R. (1958), Regression in the service of the ego: The relevance of a psychoanalytic concept for personality assessment. In: *Assessment of Human Motives*, ed. G. Lindzey. New York: Rinehart, pp. 119–148.

Shevrin, H., & Shectman, F. (1973), The diagnostic process in psychiatric evaluations. *Bull. Menn. Clin.*, 37:451–494.

Singer, M. (1977), The borderline diagnosis and psychological tests: A review of research. In: *Borderline Personality Disorders: The Concept, the Syndrome, the Patient*, ed. P. Hartocollis. New York: International Universities Press, pp. 193–212.

Smith, K. (1980), Object relations concepts as applied to the borderline level of ego functioning. In: *Borderline Phenomena and the Rorschach Test*, ed. J. Kwawer, H. Lerner, P. Lerner, & A. Sugarman. New York: International Universities Press, pp. 59–87.

Spear, W. (1980), The psychological assessment of structural and thematic object representations in borderline and schizophrenic patients. In: *Borderline Phenomena and the Rorschach Test*, ed. J. Kwawer, H. Lerner, P. Lerner, & A. Sugarman. New York: International Universities Press, pp. 321–342.

Urist, J. (1980), The continuum between primary and secondary process thinking: Toward a concept of borderline thought. In: *Borderline Phenomena and the Rorschach Test*, ed. J. Kwawer, H. Lerner, P. Lerner, & A. Sugarman. New York: International Universities Press, pp. 133–154.

Wiener, I. (1966), *Psychodiagnosis in Schizophrenia*. New York: Wiley.

Werner, H. (1948), *Comparative Psychology of Mental Development*. New York: Harper.

——— Kaplan, B. (1963), *Symbol Formation: An Organismic-Developmental Approach to Language and the Expression of Thought*. New York: Wiley.

Chapter 2

SELF-EXPERIENCE AND REALITY TESTING: SYNTHESIS OF AN OBJECT RELATIONS AND AN EGO PSYCHOLOGICAL MODEL ON THE RORSCHACH

ALAN SUGARMAN

The Shift to an Object Relations Model

Despite the relative social complacency of the seventies, it has been marked by an apparent scientific revolution within psychoanalytic theory. There has been a paradigmatic shift away from the ego psychological model so characteristic of the psychoanalysis of the fifties to an object relations model (Sugarman, 1977a,b). Indeed, it is well nigh-impossible today to open a psychoanalytic journal without having one's eye accosted by the term "object relations" in the title of an article. This shift in models can be traced to the convergence of five different developments within clinical psychology and psychiatry (Sugarman, 1981). These include: (1) dissatisfaction with the logical difficulties inherent in the ego psychological model (e.g. Klein, 1970; Schafer, 1973; Holt, 1975); (2) the development of a "third force" of humanistic psychology disenchanted with the claimed impersonality of ego psychology and psychoanalytic theory in general (e.g. Matson, 1971); (3) more sophisticated studies of early childhood development (e.g. Spitz, 1965; Mah-

A preliminary version of this chapter was presented at the Annual Meetings of the Society for Personality Assessment, Scottsdale, Arizona, March 1979.

ler, Pine, and Bergman, 1975); (4) an increased sensitivity to preoedipal elements of personality organization arising out of psychoanalytic work with children (e.g. Klein, 1932); and (5) the focus on preoedipal elements in psychoanalytic work with patients of weak ego structure (e.g. Fairbairn, 1952; Balint, 1968).

A recent shift to an object relations approach within psychological testing has paralleled this shift within psychoanalytic theory and technique (e.g. Kwawer, Lerner, Lerner, and Sugarman, 1980). Test reports have been refocused to include an emphasis on the patient's experience of self and others (Sargent, 1951; Mayman, 1959; Appelbaum, 1972, 1976) while several new instruments to assess object relations or new scales that assessed object relations on standard instruments have been developed. Colleagues and students of Mayman have drawn on the work of British and American object relations theorists to measure the thematic qualities of the object relations paradigms expressed in the content of Rorschach responses (Urist, 1977), early memories (Mayman and Faris, 1960; Ryan, 1970), and dreams (Krohn and Mayman, 1974; Hatcher and Krohn, 1980). Blatt and his colleagues have assessed the structural dimensions of object representations from a developmental perspective on the Rorschach (Blatt, Brenneis, Schimek, and Glick, 1976; Spear, 1980), in parental descriptions (Blatt, Wein, Chevron, and Quinlan, 1979), and in dreams (Brenneis, 1971).

Conceptual Difficulties of the Object Relations Model

Despite the valuable insights which the object relations model has brought to both therapeutic and diagnostic practice, its advocates seem to have uncritically accepted Kuhn's thesis (1962) that scientific advances involve revolution and an overthrowing of the previous paradigm. Consequently, the perspectives and appreciation of human functioning inherent in the previous ego psychological model seem to have been disregarded or ignored. In our haste to adopt an object relations model we appear to be throwing the baby out with the bathwater. For whatever the limitations of the ego psychological model (and there are many) it represented an effort by the thinkers of earlier days (e.g. Hartmann, 1958; Rapaport, 1959) to escape the "marionette" or "seething cauldron" model of id psychology in which man was conceptualized as motivated solely by biologically derived forces, leaving minimal room for self-direction or self-motivation. The focus on the executive or autonomous functions of the ego was, in part, an attempt to develop a broader model of the individual with a focus on healthy conflict-free experience as well as conflict-laden experience. Implicit in the concept of synthetic ego functioning was a view of man as possessing an innate potential for self-actualization and growth. Although this emphasis eventually led to such mechanistic and reductionistic absurdities as defining the ego as the sum of its functions (e.g. Bellak, Hurvich, and Gediman, 1973) and the other logical problems noted elsewhere (Klein, 1970; Sugarman, 1977a, 1978), the role of cognition, perception, motivation, and impulse regulation must not be ignored in the wish to embrace an object relations model. Unfortunately, most of the theory underlying the object relations model does just that—it ignores the role and importance of these ego functions rather than considering how they relate to the self- and object representations which lie at the heart of an object relations model.

Fairbairn (1952) and Guntrip (1968), for example, ignore the role of cognitive development in their notions of intrapsychic development. Consequently, they postulate a variety of intrapsychic mechanisms such as introjection, projection, and splitting which demand much more cognitive sophistication than is present at the early ages which they emphasize. An awareness of such cognitive elements as boundary differentiation, ego differentiation and integration, and the nature of early sensorimotor thought could explain the same clinical phenomena in a manner which takes cognizance of the complexity of personality development. Their notions of internal object involve similar problems. Again because of a lack of consideration of cognitive development and motivational issues, their model of the psyche begins to resemble too literally their "inner stage" metaphor, populated by homunculi who are undistilled introjects of external figures. Little awareness is shown of the "depersonalization" of such introjects into intrapsychic structures which accompanies the constant assimilation and accommodation to new social schemata inherent in the developmental process. Winnicott's concept (1971) of transitional objects and phenomena is another example of ignoring ego psychology. He intuitively and metaphorically links the attachment to such objects to the attainment of the capacity for symbolic and creative thinking (illusion). Again, despite this valuable clinical and developmental insight, he attributes explanatory status to "good enough" mothering and its impact on the infant's object relations. Little emphasis is placed on the mediating role of cognitive development. Yet careful consideration makes clear the role of the transitional object as a way station to evocative object constancy (Metcalf and Spitz, 1978). Such an integration of cognitive development with object relations development expands the explanatory breadth of the object relations model (e.g. Sugarman and Kurash, 1980).

Testing practice has demonstrated a less polarized and somewhat different problem. Object relations and ego psychological concepts have often become intertwined without their specific relationship being articulated. For example, Mayman (1963) has said that

> an equally tenable approach to diagnosis of character structure and psy-

> chopathology would be to organize the diagnosis around an analysis of the patient's identity patterns. . . . diagnoses of this sort would require a careful content analysis of test productions: contents which in them have traces of a person's object-representations, self-representations, significant introjects, and the relation of all to core neurotic conflicts. The cohesiveness and scope of a person's ego-synthesis will rest heavily upon the synthesis he can achieve of the various partial identities which crystallize out of the various object relationships which in the course of his development have played a central organizing role in shaping the budding ego. [p. 101]

Mayman demonstrates an awareness of the interrelationship between ego development and object relations development but leaves the relationship unarticulated. Arising out of this theoretical unclarity is the emphasis on content over structure. The danger with the thematic orientation of Mayman and his colleagues is the risk of ignoring the diagnostic importance of the structural elements of the test reponse, so carefully worked out by Rapaport in his ego psychological approach to testing. Although the interpersonal paradigms manifested in Rorschach content are crucial for being able to understand and empathize with the patient as a living human being and not an assemblage of ego functions, these ego functions are also important. Affect and thought organization, for example, are crucial in determining the probability that the patient can symbolically represent his wishes and hence contain them or whether he must act on them because of an arrest in cognitive development.

This either/or attitude about the relative value of the object relations and ego psychological models must develop into a synthesis of both perspectives in order to understand personality functioning in all its complexity. Each perspective taps certain intrapsychic variables which are important in personality functioning. In fact, rather than independent theoretical domains, both object relations and ego functioning are better understood as two of several developmental dimensions which become integrated during adolescence into a coherent personality or character structure (Sugarman, Bloom-Feshbach, and Bloom-Feshbach, 1980).[1] These psychological dimensions are "central and salient aspects of human functioning, which change and develop over time and are affected by both maturation and experience" (p. 471). The formulation of a comprehensive psychoanalytic theory will be furthered by an attempt to understand the complex ways in which these dimensions are interwoven in the fabric of the personality and their multiple determination of behavior.

[1] Other developmental dimensions include the psychosocial, the cognitive, the moral, and the psychosexual.

Rather than err on the side of viewing object relations theory and ego psychology as a dialectic, the theorist and clinician must strive for a synthesis of object relations and ego functioning concepts. Such a synthesis must take note of the hierarchical nature of personality functions and not err, as do the ego psychologists, by assuming that all personality functions play an equal role in determining behavior (Horner, 1975). Mayman (1963, 1976) discusses Rapaport's notion of a theoretical pyramid with metapsychological ego concepts occupying the pinnacle, object relational concepts occupying the middle level, and experiential and behavioral concepts making up the base. Horner also places an ego function—the synthetic function—at the top of her hierarchy of personality functions: "The synthetic function seems most clearly related to the innate competency of the organism itself, its ability to assimilate, organize and integrate its experience from the very start" (p. 95).

Although the validity of a hierarchical approach is self-evident, a clinician committed to an object relations perspective must take exception to the superordinate status accorded the ego concept. To be more abstract and experience-distant does not have to imply such superordinate status. Horner herself appears ambivalent about her conclusion. She quotes Wyatt (1969): the "optimum condition for successful language learning in early childhood is a continuous, undisrupted, and affectionate relationship between the mother and child, manifested in frequent and appropriate communication, both nonverbal and verbal" (p. 19). Mahler (1952) also links ego functioning to object relational experiences in her notion that the sense of reality is intimately connected to the relationship with the mother: "the most important transitory step in the adaptation to reality [is the one] . . . in which the mother is gradually left outside the omnipotent orbit of the self" (p. 288).

An integrative object relations perspective does not negate the role and importance of such ego functions as cognition or sense of reality. Rather it subordinates them as secondary functions arising out of the mother-child interpersonal matrix. "If id, ego, and superego have their origins in interactions with the environment that are internalized interactions transposed to a new arena, thus becoming intrapsychic interactions, then psychic-structure formation and individuation are dependent on object relations" (Loewald, 1978, p. 498). Specifically, as self- and object representations differentiate and integrate, psychological boundaries are developed and affects are neutralized which promote the development of cognition, reality testing, etc. These ego functions then promote further development within the self- and object representations in a spiraling fashion. George Klein's reconceptualization of psychoanalytic theory (1976) offers the potential for such an integrative object relations model (Sugarman, 1978). Klein based his model on the "self," which he viewed as an apparatus of control with its own dynamic tendencies focused around the experience of integration (cleavages or dissonance). A cognitive-affective construct of "schema of meaning" replaces the motivational role demanded of the instincts. Both interpersonal and sensual experiences are pleasurable and take on important motivational roles. They do so, however, through the vehicle of being represented cognitively. In fact, it is the breadth of experiences under which their representations can be activated which accounts for their compelling nature. Bursten (1978) develops similar ideas in his diagnostic framework organized around the concept of degrees of firmness of the sense of self. He views the individual's attempt to firm up a cohesive and integrated sense of self as central to the personality structure. These attempts impact subsequently on such ego functions as cognition, perception, and impulse regulation.

Hence, a comprehensive object relations model for both psychotherapy and psychological testing must aim at more than understanding and assessing self- and object representations. It must understand the interrelationships between these representations and ego functions. An excellent example of such synthesis can be seen in Blatt's reconceptualization of Rapaport's major thought disorder indices as representing a continuum of boundary disturbance (Blatt and Ritzler, 1974; Blatt and Wild, 1976). Given Rapaport's interest in thought processes, the contamination, confabulation, and fabulized combination responses had all been considered manifestations of primary process thinking (see Holt and Havel, 1960). The contamination response was the Rorschach equivalent of condensation (Holt, 1970) and the confabulation response was viewed as the Rorschach equivalent of displacement (Shevrin, personal communication). Blatt saw them as representing varieties of disruptions of boundaries which he integrated into a developmental model (Blatt, Wild, and Ritzler, 1975). The contamination response involves the breakdown of the boundary between separate concepts which then become fused. As such, it may be viewed as the test equivalent of a breakdown between the self-representation/object representation boundary. Confabulation responses involve a loss of the boundary between internal subjective reality and external objective reality. A laxness rather than an overt disruption in boundaries occurs in the typical fabulized combination response. There is a second type of fabulized combination response, however, in which parts of two organisms are combined together without the same degree of loss of differentiation as in the contamination response (e.g. a man with the head of a wolf). Such a fabulized combination response should be considered contaminatory in nature and to indicate a brittle and tenuous self-other boundary.

In this chapter I will attempt to follow the lead of Blatt and consider the interrelationship between a specific ego function (reality testing) and a specific experience and structure of the self-representation on the Rorschach. Given the complexity of the conceptual and clinical issues involved, the formulations presented must be viewed as tentative and incomplete. Rather than a comprehensive formulation of a specific test finding, I am attempting to demonstrate the potential utility for both theory development and diagnostic practice to attempt a synthesis of cogent personality dimensions in understanding psychopathological phenomena. It is a manner of thinking about test data rather than an infallible interpretation of a specific Rorschach sign which I am trying to demonstrate. Through a consideration of an unusual pattern of the F+ percentages, I hope to demonstrate that some inferences about the subject's self-experience and self-structure can be made.

The F+ Percentages and the Experience of Self

When scoring the Rorschach, it is relatively standard clinical practice to compute both an F+ percentage and an extended F+ percentage. The first provides an assessment of the subject's form level on responses in which form is the sole determinant, while the second measures form level on all form-dominant responses including ones with other determinants. When these other determinants are primarily color, achromatic color, or shading, the second percentage is usually lower. Such a finding makes sense intuitively when one considers the psychological variables presumably tapped by these responses. The F+ percentages assess reality testing, while the other determinants are thought to reflect how the subject deals with a variety of affects (See Rapaport, Gill, and Schafer, 1945). Thus, most individuals show some decrement in their reality testing when affect must be integrated into the process (extended F+ percentage).

However, clinical experience reveals an occasional reversal of this usual pattern. Some individuals obtain an extended F+ percentage that is greater than their F+ percentage. Only by considering how this peculiar quirk in reality testing relates to the experience and structure of the self can one come to a full clinical understanding of the finding. I suggest that individuals who demonstrate this reversal of the F+ percentages have a particularly unstable or underdeveloped sense of self. In fact, perusal of their Rorschach responses shows a frequent occurrence of responses involving desert scenes, cacti, and other content stressing a barren, arid, poorly differentiated self-experience. These patients are often hollow, empty individuals with few inner resources to brighten or enliven their experiential world. Something about the psychological processes involved in the FC, FCh, FC', and F(c) response impacts on their experience of self and, consequently, on their reality testing. Before elaborating my notions regarding the precise psychological processes at work, I want to explore the relationship between self-experience and reality testing in order to demonstrate the advantages of the integrative approach to object relations formulations that I am advocating.

Freud's earliest formulations of reality testing demonstrate a solely ego psychological approach despite the fact that they antedate his formal structural model. Bellak et al.'s extensive review of the literature (1973) identifies three components to Freud's notions of reality testing: (1) the distinction between ideas and perceptions (Freud, 1895); (2) external perception (Freud, 1911, 1925); and (3) accuracy of perception (Freud, 1925). Other processes linked by Freud to reality testing include secondary process, attention, memory, and judgment. Rapaport (1959) extended this solely ego psychological approach and stressed the differentiation of thought from reality as well as the role of memory.

The major problem with these analyses of the psychological processes involved in reality testing is the lack of awareness shown to the interrelationship between these various processes and the self- and object representations of the perceiving individual. Schafer (1968) expanded this traditional ego psychological approach to reality testing as a perceptual scanning and assessing of the environment to include other processes such as emotion, memory, anticipation, concept formation, attention, and concentration. He concluded that the core process in reality testing is the ability to distinguish what is thought from what is real. Schafer went on, however, to acknowledge a relationship between the experience of the self and the process of reality testing. He noted that logical, objective thinking involves the reflexive or implicit self-representation that a thought is only a thought. Most individuals implicitly qualify their thoughts with an "I think" or an "I believe." For a thought to be taken uncritically as reality, this reflexive self-representation must be suspended. Such a suspension involves regression to a less differentiated mode of functioning.

Lichtenberg (1978) closely approximates Schafer's definition in his description of reality testing as the ability to distinguish perception from inner mental activity. Robbins and Sadow (1974) have similarly defined reality testing as an ego function which allows the discrimination of mental representations stimulated by external events from those arising from internal events, memories, and fantasies. Basic to all of these definitions is a notion of reality testing as a process whereby one distinguishes external from internal reality. A solely ego psychological approach ignores the developmental context of this important developmental boundary. The development of the inner-outer boundary is a crucial one for the formation of more articulated and integrated self- and object representations (Blatt, 1974; Blatt and Wild, 1976). Implicit in the attainment of this boundary is a greater differentiation of self. To know that one's thoughts originate from within rather than from without suggests a clear distinction between self and other. Evocative object constancy is obtained so that thoughts do in fact originate from within. This attainment heralds the depressive position and "whole" self- and object representations.

A developmental model becomes necessary in order to elaborate this relationship between the sense of self and reality testing. The earliest stage of reality testing is based on the intensity of the infant's experience (Lichtenberg, 1978). Within an acceptable threshold range, the more intense the infant's experience, the more vivid perception becomes, and the stronger the sense of reality. Perception, however, remains a passive process, autoplastic and personalized. Reality testing proper does not yet occur. Rather, the intensity of the experience promotes a more vivid sense of reality with little regard for external accuracy. Hallucinations, dreams, and somatic sensations are adult phenomena which exemplify the possible combination of vivid but false experiences. So long as the physical stimuli to which the infant is exposed are appropriately intense, the differentiation and formation of representations of body parts—the precursors of self-representations—are fostered. Either overstimulation or understimulation of the tactile receptors, however, can precipitate a failure to develop normal representations of body parts, with a concomitant craving for or withdrawing from tactile experiences (Shevrin and Toussieng, 1965).

Reality testing proper occurs only with and contingent on self-other and inner-outer differentiation. In the earliest stages of self-object differentiation, self and objects are tenuously distinguished but remain as unintegrated, affectively polarized representations (Kernberg, 1976). At this time the representational world of the infant is based upon experiences of frustration or gratification. Because of the primitive nature of the infant's cognitive functioning, others are poorly differentiated and are experienced as existing solely in relation to the self. Consequently, reality testing is prone to idiosyncratic, personalized, affectively based distortions.

> In primitive mental functioning . . . objects in the external environment are not apprehended as things with separate, fixed characteristics. Rather, objects tend to be understood in relation to their emotional and motor connection with the perceiver, animistic qualities are often imputed to inanimate objects, and there is an inability to distinguish separate parts or to discriminate between essential and nonessential characteristics. [Bellak et al., 1973, p. 87]

Causality tends to be attributed to the outside so that the infant still experiences affects, rudimentary thoughts, and perceptions as coming from without.

If mothering is "good enough," the infant consolidates the inner-outer boundary through the use of transitional objects. Motility allows him to move from a passive, perceptual relation with the world to an active, initiative one. As objects are perceived from many angles and handled in many contexts they come to take on a more full-bodied existence of their own. The development of evocative object constancy marks the emergence of symbol formation. Internal reality takes on a more full-bodied existence of its own which parallels the more differentiated external reality. Self and object become fully integrated and differentiated. Thus the clear distinctions between self and other, inner and outer, contribute to crisp, firm reality testing.

The developmental process goes awry, however, for the subjects I am describing. Here mothering is not "good enough." Early passive experiences are fraught with severe overstimulation, presumably through the mother's symbiotic overattachment and her own subsequent anxiety as tension increases in the child. Thus early perceptual and sensory experiences, characterized by passivity, affectivity, and personalization, become feared as traumatic by the infant. To be passive is to be overwhelmed by affective and perceptual stimulation experienced as originating from both within and without. Passive experience becomes turned defensively into active as affective and personalized experiences are minimized by these individuals. The periphery of the self becomes overstructured while the inner core of the personality remains understructuralized; a "false self" organization is created through pathological development of the ego periphery at the expense of structural differentiation of the self-representation in the ego interior (Kumin, 1978). Anhedonia sets in, accompanied by affect regression and resomatization (Krystal, 1974). Given the inner deadness resulting from the avoidance of affective, personalized experience, the world too becomes lifeless and devoid of personal meaning.

The Case of Joseph

A case example of such a patient will now be presented. This unmarried white male at nineteen was referred for psychological testing by his psychiatric consultant. Toward the end of his first year of college, the patient had become quite depressed. Antidepressant medication prescribed by his physician had precipitated a full-fledged psychotic break characterized by both hallucinations and delusions. Following his remission from the acute psychosis, his parents had sought an intensive psychiatric consultation.

Before presenting his Rorschach, his WAIS performance illuminates some of the points made above. His WAIS scatter is given below. The intersubtest scatter alone suggests an intellectualized detached individual, certainly capable of the inner emptiness and emphasis on formal, detached relating described above. Despite the relative equality of the Information and Comprehension subtest scores, the elevation of Verbal IQ over Performance IQ and the high Arithmetic, Digit Span, Similarities, and Block Design subtest scores all suggest an individual who emphasizes abstract, formal thinking. The extremely high Digit Span, which involved eight forward and eight backward, particularly suggests detachment. By comparison, the Information

Information	13	Digit Symbol	11
Comprehension	12	Picture Completion	12/13
		Block Design	16
Arithmetic	16	Picture Arrangement	9
Similarities	14/15	Object Assembly	12
Digit Span	16		
Vocabulary	13		

Verbal IQ	126/127
Performance IQ	115
Full Scale IQ	123

and Vocabulary scores seem almost modest. Assuming the Vocabulary score to be a measure of his general overall intellectual level, the several scores which surpass it significantly suggest an intellectual overstriving. That is, he seems to have strained his native endowment to its limit. Although his Comprehension score of 12 seems respectably attuned interpersonally, the comparatively low Picture Arrangement score requires a reassessment. It appears that his emphasis on intellect allows him to demonstrate an adequate *knowledge* of social convention, but that he is less capable of *applying* that knowledge in less intellectual contexts. Furthermore, his intact Object Assembly score conceals an erratic, unplanned performance in which parts were randomly juxtaposed until a "fit" occurred. No effort was ever made to ascertain the nature of the object before moving pieces. Thus, hints of a disturbance in body ego occur in the context of overall detachment and intellectual striving.

His Rorschach face sheet amply demonstrates the empty, detached quality described.

RORSCHACH FACE SHEET

Location	*Determinants*		*Content*	
R = 13	FC.m = 1	E.B = 0/2	A = 4	Nature = 2
W% = 69	FC(c) = 1	F% = 77	A-Obj = 1	Explosion = 1
D% = 23	C = 1	Fext% = 85	Blood = 2	Fusion tend = 1
Dr% = 8	FC′ = 1	F + % = 50	Hd-In = 1	
	C′F = 1	Fext + % = 63	Obj = 3	
Thought Disorder			reflection = 3	
Contamination tend = 1				

Human content is lacking except for one human detail–inanimate blend. Three reflection responses speak to a significant degree of narcissism considering the sparse record. The severe degree of constriction (R = 13; no M) in the context of his superior intelligence suggest inordinate detachment. In the two blood and one explosion responses we see the aggression against which he is trying to deaden himself.

As one peruses his actual response record, his need for distance and subsequent experience of barrenness and estrangement become even more clear.

CARD I

Time	*Scoring*	*Protocol*	*Inquiry*
		[doesn't want to take it till I say to]	
V 5 secs.	W_sF_w+ A_{Fab} Deteriorated	1. Looks like maybe the *remains* of some kind of *ancient bird* (What else?) Nothing in particular. (Take a little longer.)	(Q) In the *black image*. (WA) It looks like it might have been a wing-shaped sort of thing but since there were so many *holes* in the wings and it looks kind of *decrepit*. (Anything else about it make it look decrepit?) Yeah.
ΛVΛV 92 secs.		. . . . [moves in to & fro, farther & closer] Nothing else in particular, I don't think.	*Sorta the periphery of the wings don't look perfect. It's more of a sort of a flying reptile instead of a bird. Bird in the sense that it flies but not the kind you see here in the trees.*

Card I becomes a decrepit, ancient bird. Temporal and affective distance is obtained as a warmer, more tactile bird becomes a cold-blooded flying reptile. He is reactive to the achromatic color, but unable to integrate it.

CARD II

Time	*Scoring*	*Protocol*	*Inquiry*
ΛV . . . . . . 1 min., 56 secs.	70 secs. W C′F Obj. D_r FC(c) (Hd-In)$_{w+}$ Blood D C Blood	Looks like some kind of image *of the road from an accident with a car. Blood stains, footprint, you can see through the oil, covered by the oil, bloody footprint.*	(Whole blot?) Yeah. (WA) Well, the inkblot. (WA) Well, it has *both black and red* in it. Gotta be something to it. Mostly to account for the footprint, I guess.

On Card II his detachment becomes manifested in an unusual and gruesome response presented with no affective reaction. It is as though such accidents were observed or noted with no emotion or empathy. His one human response, the oily, bloody footprint, is a blend of human and inanimate qualities, contributing further to his detachment. It is similar to a reflection response in that a footprint is bound inextricably to the foot and person making it. Hence, a narcissistic quality of relatedness also begins to appear. Self-other boundaries become blurred in his contaminatory tendency to fuse the footprint, the oil, and the blood.

CARD III

Time	*Scoring*	*Protocol*	*Inquiry*
		[looks at back and reads it after 2 minutes]	(Q) Well in half the inkblot, the black part. (What made it look strange?)
ΛV > > V > Λ [at back] V > 3 mins., 33 secs.	W F− A Refl.	I don't know. It looks like *some strange animal looking at itself in the mirror.*	*Well it doesn't look like any animal I know so. (What made it look like an animal?) Well, it doesn't give the impression of anything else so might as well make it an animal.* [*able to point out details.*]

Joseph continues to demonstrate his own estrangement, detachment, and emptiness on Card III. The animal is "strange," presumably a self-experience. His internal barrenness and lack of differentiation is demonstrated in the arbitrariness and lack of articulation of the response. The mirror continues the theme of narcissistic relatedness and highlights the need to interpret his responses as self-representations because for him the external world is only a mirror of the internal.

CARD IV

Time	*Scoring*	*Protocol*	*Inquiry*
Λ > Λ	W F_o A_{obj}P Ch avoid	Looks like a rug that somebody's made from an animal skin. You've seen them on the floor where somebody's cut out the shape of the animal. *Since it's one color it's pretty hard to tell what kind of animal it was.*	(What made it look like a skin?) Well, it's symmetric, it has short arms, legs, possibly a head. Both sides of it are the same. [Turns card over to show me] (Anything else?) [Turns it over] Well, no not particularly, not besides the shape.

His response to Card IV demonstrates some capacity to experience the world in a conventional fashion. Again he is struck by the achromatic color but unable to integrate it. His uncertainty about the exact nature of the animal involved or the presence of a head underscores the basic difficulty in differentiation.

CARD V

Time	*Scoring*	*Protocol*	*Inquiry*
V 16 secs. 38 secs.	W F_oC' A P	Looks like some kind of a bat flying, there's two legs (Anything else?) Yeah, the two wings, *funny head* (Anything else besides a bat?). . . .	(Anything else besides the wings?) It's black.

Card V reflects the popular bat but with an elaboration of its head as "funny." Again a sense of himself as different and estranged emerges.

CARD VI

Time	*Scoring*	*Protocol*	*Inquiry*
Λ > V > Λ 42 secs.	W F− Obj. Refl. tend. Fusion tend.	Looks like it's an *aircraft carrier made for outer space. It's launching some kind of* [examiner cannot hear the word] *from the top, small craft.*	(What made it look like an aircraft carrier?) Well, not necessarily an aircraft carrier, but some *sort of launch vehicle that would be traveling in outer space because it was launching sort of like a replica* of itself in front. (What made it look like outer space?)
1 min., 19 secs.			*Well, doesn't look like anything on earth so* (Describe.) [He starts to look at the blot. I stop him.] It was sort of a body with large wings on either side and there was a small replica or a smaller whatever you want to call it, the equivalent of an airplane in outer space, attached to the front of it. It looked like it was about to be launched.

On Card VI, he again shows his sense of distance, detachment, and alienation. The usually animate popular response is turned into a mechanized, inanimate object. This vehicle does not resemble anything on earth. It is alien and estranged. His narcissistic quality of relatedness shows itself in the "replica" of the vehicle.

CARD VII

Time	*Scoring*	*Protocol*	*Inquiry*
15 secs. ΛVΛ 20 secs.	W F− Na	It looks like some kind of *a cactus in the desert.*	(Tendency toward boundary lapse) (Where was the cactus?) *Where was it? In a desert.* (Was it the whole thing?) Yeah. (What?) Well, it had sort of knobby things coming out of it and an irregular shape. (What made it look like a *desert*?) *Well, there was nothing else* in the picture and *where else would a cactus grow*?

Card VII demonstrates his essential inner barrenness and emptiness and his complementary experience of the world as devoid of sustenant others. Thus his basic egocentricity emerges. His concreteness and boundary laxness in answering that the cactus is in the desert to the inquiry about location suggests a marked regression from his usual abstractness. This cognitive regression and distorted perception is clearly linked to the emergence of his core relational paradigm.

CARD VIII

Time	*Scoring*	*Protocol*	*Inquiry*
< Λ	35 secs. W F_o A P Refl. D F_v Obj. D F_w+ Na 75 secs.	This looks like some sort of a *jungle animal looking at its reflection* in a pond, standing on a rock looking in the pond. The blue part could be a rock and maybe there is a tree fallen in the pond.	(What kind of animal?) Uh, possibly a jaguar, some sort of cat type of animal. You could see it had three legs, must have been hiding another leg and a tail. (What else made it look like that?) Well, they were short proportionally in terms of the size of the animal and it had sort of a head. (Why a blue rock?) Well, it would have been coming out of the pond so it must have been a fixed object. Besides, it is the right shape for a rock. (Blue to locate?) Right. (Where was the tree?) Uh, it was in front of the rock in front of the face of the animal sort of coming out of the pond.

Card VIII illustrates what has become a basic theme—his narcissism. Suggestions of a proclivity for experiencing himself and others as duplicitous is apparent in his description of the cat hiding its fourth leg and tail.

CARD IX

Time	*Scoring*	*Protocol*	*Inquiry*
ΛV 31 secs.	W F_{+}C.m Expl.	Looks like maybe an *artist's conception* of an *atomic bomb* with the mushroom cloud at the top and maybe the heat coming down.	(What made it look like heat?) Sort of orange red. (What made it look like a bomb?) The cloud at the top looks like a mushroom-shaped cloud and you can see where it's risen, sort of mushroomed out.

On Card IX, he strives to detach himself from his own explosive rage. The inanimate movement attributed to the heat from the bomb speaks to his passivity toward emotion and proneness to experience it as originating from without.

CARD X

Time	*Scoring*	*Protocol*	*Inquiry*
ΛVΛ 51 secs.	Reject	Looks like *seven inkblots superimposed symmetric to the Y axis*. Because it's symmetric you can tell it's [examiner can't hear word]. Probably couldn't do it all at once distribution of colors. (Anything else?) No. *I test limits for people. He can see them on Card III and in the middle of Card V he sees lips and a pointed tongue.*	(Superimposed) I think there would have been more spilling of colors if they had all been done at the same time. Maybe some of the groups of colors were done at the same time. Looks sort of unusual that some of them don't mix now.

On Card X, the patient retreats to the position of a detached observer describing the supposed production of the inkblot. Associated with this extreme detachment is an impotent reaction to the task at hand. Given the particular importance of the last response to the Rorschach, special significance must be attributed to this card description. With his last communication, the patient underlines his severe detachment and consequent interpersonal impotence.

Based upon this test battery, the following diagnostic understanding and treatment implications were presented in the psychological test report.

Diagnostic Understanding

The patient presents with a borderline schizophrenic core which might be concealed clinically because of his ability to remain organized in structured situations, his extreme interpersonal withdrawal so that others might not become aware of his peculiarities, and his ability to avoid a formal thought disorder despite his poor reality testing and lack of object relatedness. In fact, it is only his absence of a formal thought disorder which makes one uneasy about diagnosing him schizophrenic. But the occasional capriciousness and bizarreness of his perceptions of reality, his seeming indifference to them, as well as the unusually extreme degree of interpersonal detachment speak to a schizoid style that can reach psychotic proportions.

Thus, although his reality testing is adequate in structured situations, he has difficulty even at these times if an interpersonal component is added. In less structured situations, his perceptions of reality can become surprisingly arbitrary and idiosyncratic to the point that at times I could not see his percepts even after he had pointed out the parts. Given his constricted, defended approach to testing, one must weigh the presence of absurd responses even greater. Surprisingly, despite his attempts at ideational and affective constriction, his reality testing does improve under the impact of affective stimulation, particularly unmodulated outbursts of aggression. This reaction to affect over which he loses defensive control is in contrast to its detrimental effect upon his reality testing when he does try to contain his emotions.

This paradoxical finding can best be understood as due to the barrenness of his internal world. The degree of interpersonal detachment is striking in this patient to the point that he was unable to give a human response to the Rorschach. It would appear that his internal world is as devoid of life and substance as the desert he sees on the Rorschach; his self-structure is surprisingly undifferentiated. Consequently, his periodic experiences of anger serve to promote his feeling of self, which then allows for temporary differentiation and hence an improvement in reality testing. At other times, however, he is so withdrawn that he seems almost incapable of empathy and so is unable to perceive the world as others do.

However, it appears that this withdrawal and detachment has also enabled him to avoid a formal thought disorder. Although he does not show the overt disruption of boundaries between separate ideas characteristic of schizophrenic thinking, he does show several signs of boundary weakness. Most noteworthy is his difficulty with human-nonhuman, animate-inanimate distinctions. Around these distinctions his concepts tend to fuse, leading him to compensate by overemphasizing the distinction. It would appear, then, that his withdrawal is for more than dynamic reasons and that it serves to allow him to avoid the situation which could promote a wholesale boundary collapse and consequently a formal thought disorder.

He also showed a consistent tendency to lose distance with the blots or pictures and confuse his internal elaborations of them with their actual reality, reflecting his tenuous self-differentiation. Other disturbances included lapses in metaphors wherein symbols suddenly became interpreted concretely around depressive issues, and he showed occasional combinations of abstract and concrete modes of thought around concerns with anger or body cohesiveness.

Treatment Implications

The patient's paradoxical reaction to affective stimulation suggests that any inhibiting medication will need to be monitored carefully to make sure that it does not dampen his affect and inadvertently interfere with his reality testing. His difficulty at tolerating intimacy will make it difficult for him to form a therapeutic alliance. Given his fears of evaluation and ambiguity, consistent feedback and provision of structure might be more successful at allaying his mistrust than a purely expressive technique. In addition, the patient will need to drop his facade and run the risk of decompensation in order to develop more benign and articulated self- and object representations if he is to accomplish more than sealing over. Such work may well necessitate inpatient treatment.

Conclusion

This case demonstrates well the capability of the Rorschach test to illuminate the relationship between self-experience and reality testing. I will now conclude with an integration of the relationship between the specific test findings and the conceptual model developed earlier. We see the patient's alloplastic rigidity and emphasis on the external world manifested in a somewhat high F percentage, low R, and his subtest scatter on the WAIS. Other determinants are avoided in the same manner as he avoids personal, affective experience. Such pure form responses and cognitive constriction involve what Schachtel

(1966) calls detached form perception. Patients such as Joseph are much too fearful to make form perception and their experience of the world personally meaningful. Consequently he shows a strained, rigid, effortful, and inhibited approach to others and the world rather than a more relaxed, open, receptive, flexible, and playful attitude, which would be manifested in a lower F percentage (Schachtel, 1966). He is left feeling depersonalized, derealized, and estranged from the world. Consequently he is unable to experience and perceive animate and inanimate objects with a full receptive openness. The richness, vividness, and full presence of these objects are subsequently lost. This devitalizing of the external world interferes with the firmness of his perceptual hold, resulting in a lowered F+ percentage and surprising breakthroughs of idiosyncratic concerns given his constriction. Joseph cannot experience the world as accurately as he might because he does not possess a solid and full relationship with it due to his inner estrangement and emptiness. Despite his attempt to overfocus on the external to avoid the internal, he inadvertently interferes with his experience of the external also.

Given this developmental failure it becomes clear why the use of additional determinants improves his F+ percentage and reality testing. The relationship between affect experience and one's experience of color (chromatic)[2] has been extensively documented in the Rorschach literature (e.g. Shapiro, 1960; Schachtel, 1966). Color perception has been equated with passive autoplastic perception. Unlike the activity demanded of the perceiver in order to see form, the perception of color is passive. Color strikes the eye, the eye does not seek color. Color is vivid, personal—it arouses affect. In part, then, the vividness of the experience of the FC response revitalizes and fills the patient's emptiness. As self- and object representations become more vitalized the distinction between them becomes sharper and reality testing improves.

But it is not just this vitalizing aspect of the FC response which accounts for the improvement in the extended F+ percentage. One also has to consider the interrelationship of color, affect, and object relations. Part of the passivity involved in color perception derives from the experience of color as coming from the object. It is "out there"—it "strikes" the eye. The child's early experience of affect is similar in that affect is experienced as emanating from the object (Krystal, 1975). Hence, parts of the body and psyche related to affect expression become experienced by the infant as part of the maternal object representation. If mothering has failed to allow the child to recognize,

[2] The formulations of the psychological processes underlying the C' and Ch responses are not as well articulated. It seems reasonable, however, that the perceptual passivity involved in color perception is also a key ingredient in achromatic color and shading perception. I will therefore assume that the logic presented for the role of color will hold for these other determinants.

tolerate, and verbalize affect, the child is left unable to soothe himself. Affect experience remains tied up in a symbiotic experience of mother. Affect modulation remains part of the maternal representation rather than the self-representation. Color cannot be integrated in a developmentally more advanced cognitive or symbolic fashion because the patient's developmental arrest has precluded sufficient differentiation to internalize important self-regulatory functions. Consequently, self-experience lacks an important component—the vividness and vitality associated with affect mastery. Rather, all feelings and emotions must be warded off to rigidly defend against fusion since emotions are experienced as part of the mother. Such rigidity leads to a developmental impasse in the ability to distinguish between inner and outer reality. Internal phenomena (in this case, affects) remain experienced as arising from and regulated by an external object. Confusion between inner, subjective and outer, objective reality must ensue.

The ability to give an FC response suggests the achievement of a higher level of symbolic thinking for the moment. I would suggest that at that moment the experience of the color and the affective, personalized perception involved marks a temporary advance in the developmental level of object relations. It involves the integration of parts of the self previously attributed to the mother without promoting the feared symbiotic loss of boundaries. For the moment, the inner-outer boundary is coalesced. The temporary integration and enrichment of the self-representation implicit in the FC response allows the attainment of evocative object constancy and whole self- and object representations. The patient is no longer empty. For that moment he has a warm, vital, whole self-representation within. Consequently, the distinction between internal representations and external experience becomes more defined and reality testing improves.

References

Appelbaum, S. (1972), A method of reporting psychological test findings. *Bull. Menn. Clin.*, 36:349–355.

——— (1976), Rapaport revisited: Practice. *Bull. Menn. Clin.*, 40:229–237.

Balint, M. (1968), *The Basic Fault*. London: Tavistock.

Bellak, L., Hurvich, M., & Gediman, H. (1973), *Ego Functions in Schizophrenics, Neurotics, and Normals*. New York: Wiley.

Blatt, S. (1974), Levels of object representation in anaclitic and introjective depression. *The Psychoanalytic Study of the Child*, 29:107–157. New Haven: Yale University Press.

——— Brenneis, C., Schimek, J., & Glick, M. (1976), Normal development and psychopathological impairment of the concept of the object on the Rorschach. *J. Abnorm. Psychol.*, 85:364–373.

——— Ritzler, B. (1974), Thought disorder and boundary disturbance in psychosis. *J. Consult. Clin. Psychol.*, 42:370–381.

——— Wein, S., Chevron, E., & Quinlan, D. (1979), Parental representations and depression in normal young adults. *J. Abnorm. Psychol.*, 88:388–397.

——— Wild, C. (1976), *Schizophrenia: A Developmental Analysis*. New York: Academic Press.

——— ——— Ritzler, B. (1975), Disturbances of object representation in schizophrenia. *Psychoanal. Contemp. Sci.*, 4:235–288. New York: International Universities Press.

Brenneis, C. (1971), Features of the manifest dream in schizophrenia. *J. Nerv. Ment. Dis.*, 153:81–91.

Bursten, B. (1978), A diagnostic framework. *Internat. Rev. Psycho-Anal.*, 5:15–31.

Fairbairn, W. (1952), *Psychoanalytic Studies of the Personality*. London: Tavistock.

Freud, S. (1895), Project for a scientific psychology. *Standard Edition*, 1:281–387. London: Hogarth Press, 1966.

——— (1911), Formulations on the two principles of mental functioning. *Standard Edition*, 12:213–226. London: Hogarth Press, 1958.

——— (1925), Negation. *Standard Edition*, 19:235–240. London: Hogarth Press, 1961.

Guntrip, H. (1968), *Schizoid Phenomena, Object Relations, and the Self*. New York: International Universities Press.

Hartmann, H. (1958), *Ego Psychology and the Problem of Adaptation*. New York: International Universities Press.

Hatcher, R., & Krohn, A. (1980), Level of object representation and capacity for intensive psychotherapy in neurotics and borderlines. In: *Borderline Phenomena and the Rorschach Test*, ed. J. Kwawer, H. Lerner, P. Lerner, & A. Sugarman. New York: International Universities Press, pp. 299–320.

Holt, R. (1970), Manual for the scoring of primary process manifestations in Rorschach responses. Unpublished manual, Research Center for Mental Health, New York University.

——— (1975), The past and future of ego psychology. *Psychoanal. Quart.*, 44:550–576.

——— Havel, J. (1960), A method for assessing primary and secondary process in the Rorschach. In: *Rorschach Psychology*, ed. M. Rickers-Ovsiankina. New York: Wiley, pp. 263–315.

Horner, A. (1975), Stages and processes in the development of early object relations and their associated pathologies. *Internat. Rev. Psycho-Anal.*, 2:95–105.

Kernberg, O. (1976), *Object Relations Theory and Clinical Psychoanalysis*. New York: Aronson.

Klein, G. (1970), The emergence of ego psychology, the ego in psychoanalysis: A concept in search of identity. *Psychoanal. Rev.*, 56:511–525.

——— (1976), *Psychoanalytic Theory: An Exploration of Essentials*. New York: International Universities Press.

Klein, M. (1932), *The Psychoanalysis of Children*. London: Hogarth Press.

Krohn, A., & Mayman, M. (1974), Object representations in dreams and projective tests. *Bull. Menn. Clin.*, 38:445–466.

Krystal, H. (1974), The genetic development of affects and affect regression. *Annual of Psychoanalysis*, 2:98–126. New York: International Universities Press.

——— (1975), Affect tolerance. *Annual of Psychoanalysis*, 3:179–220. New York: International Universities Press.

Kuhn, T. (1962), *The Structure of Scientific Revolutions*. Chicago: University of Chicago Press.

Kumin, I. (1978), Emptiness and its relations to schizoid ego structure. *Internat. Rev. Psycho-Anal.*, 5:207–216.

Kwawer, J., Lerner, H., Lerner, P., & Sugarman, A., eds. (1980), *Borderline Phenomena and the Rorschach Test.* New York: International Universities Press.

Lichtenberg, J. (1978), The testing of reality from the standpoint of the body self. *J. Amer. Psychoanal. Assn.*, 26:357–386.

Loewald, H. (1978), Instinct theory, object relations, and psychic structure formation. *J. Amer. Psychoanal. Assn.*, 26:493–506.

Mahler, M. (1952), On child psychosis and schizophrenia. *The Psychoanalytic Study of the Child*, 7:286–305. New York: International Universities Press.

——— Pine, F., & Bergman, A. (1975), *The Psychological Birth of the Human Infant.* New York: Basic Books.

Matson, F. (1971), Humanistic theory: The third revolution in psychology. *The Humanist*, 20:7–11.

Mayman, M. (1959), Style, focus, language and content of an ideal psychological test report. *J. Proj. Tech.*, 23:453–458.

——— (1963), Psychoanalytic study of the self organization with psychological tests. In: *Recent Advances in the Study of Behavior Change: Proceedings of the American Assembly on Clinical Psychology*, ed. B. Wigdor. Montreal: McGill University Press, pp. 97–117.

——— (1976), Psychoanalytic theory in retrospect and prospect. *Bull. Menn. Clin.*, 40:199–210.

——— Faris, M. (1960), Early memories as expressions of relationship paradigms. *Amer. J. Orthopsychiat.*, 30:507–520.

Metcalf, D., & Spitz, R. (1978), The transitional object: Critical developmental period and organizer of the psyche. In: *Between Reality and Fantasy: Transitional Objects and Phenomena*, ed. S. Grolnick, L. Barkin, & W. Muensterberger. New York: Aronson.

Rapaport, D. (1959), A historical survey of psychoanalytic ego psychology. Introduction to Identity and the Life Cycle, by E. Erikson. *Psychological Issues*, Monogr. 1, pp. 5–17.

——— Gill, M., & Schafer, R. (1945), *Diagnostic Psychological Testing*, ed. R. Holt. New York: International Universities Press, 1968.

Robbins, F., & Sadow, L. (1974), A developmental hypothesis of reality testing. *J. Amer. Psychoanal. Assn.*, 22:344–363.

Ryan, E. (1970), Object relationships and ego coping style in early memories. Unpublished doctoral dissertation, University of Michigan.

Sargent, H. (1951), Psychological test reporting: An experiment in communication. *Bull. Menn. Clin.*, 15:175–186.

Schachtel, E. (1966), *Experiential Foundations of Rorschach's Test.* New York: Basic Books.

Schafer, R. (1968), *Aspects of Internalization.* New York: International Universities Press.

——— (1973), Action: Its place in psychoanalytic interpretation and theory. *Annual of Psychoanalysis*, 1:159–196. New York: Quadrangle.

Shapiro, D. (1960), A perceptual understanding of color response. In: *Rorschach Psychology*, ed. M. Rickers-Ovsiankina. New York: Wiley, pp. 154–201.

Shevrin, H., & Toussieng, P. (1965), Vicissitudes of the need for tactile stimulation in instinctual development. *The Psychoanalytic Study of the Child*, 20:310–339. New York: International Universities Press.

Spear, W. (1980), The psychological assessment of structural and thematic object representations in borderline and schizophrenic patients. In: *Borderline Phenomena and the Rorschach Test*, ed. J. Kwawer, H. Lerner, P. Lerner, & A. Sugarman. New York: International Universities Press, pp. 321–340.

Spitz, R. (1965), *The First Year of Life*. New York: International Universities Press.

Sugarman, A. (1977a), Object relations theory: A reconciliation of phenomenology and ego psychology. *Bull. Menn. Clin.*, 41:113–130.

——— (1977b), Psychoanalysis as a humanistic psychology. *Psychotherapy: Theory, Research, and Practice*, 14:204–211.

——— (1978), Book review of *Psychoanalytic Theory* by G. Klein and *Psychology Versus Metapsychology* by M. Gill & P. Holzman. *Bull. Menn. Clin.*, 42:79–82.

——— (1981), The diagnostic use of countertransference reactions in psychological testing. *Bull. Menn. Clin.*, 45:473–490.

——— Bloom-Feshbach, S., & Bloom-Feshbach, J. (1980), The psychological dimensions of borderline adolescents. In: *Borderline Phenomena and the Rorschach Test*, ed. J. Kwawer, H. Lerner, P. Lerner, & A. Sugarman. New York: International Universities Press, pp. 469–494.

——— Kurash, C. (1980), The body as a transitional object in anorexia nervosa. Paper presented at the Annual Meetings of the American Psychological Association, Montreal.

Urist, J. (1977), The Rorschach test and the assessment of object relations. *J. Personal. Assess.*, 41:3–9.

Winnicott, D. (1971), *Playing and Reality*. New York: International Universities Press.

Wyatt, G. (1969), *Language Learning and Communication Disorders*. New York: Free Press.

Chapter 3

AN OBJECT RELATIONS UNDERSTANDING OF BORDERLINE PHENOMENA ON THE RORSCHACH

ALAN SUGARMAN

Basing her work on Rapaport, Gill, and Schafer's seminal discussions (1945) of overideational and coarctated preschizophrenics, Singer (1977) has enunciated a near-axiomatic rule for the diagnosis of borderline pathology with psychological tests—that borderline patients show a ''normal'' WAIS and a thought-disordered Rorschach. Such a position is consistent with the ego psychological approach of Rapaport et al. (1945) and its application to borderline disorders by Knight (1953), who stressed the ability of these patients to use external structure (e.g. the WAIS) to conceal a profound ego disturbance. This axiom has recently been validated empirically by Carr, Goldstein, Hunt, and Kernberg (1979) in a study which found that schizophrenics could be distinguished from borderlines on the basis of their differential performances on the WAIS and the Rorschach, but that there was no difference in the *amount* of thought disorder on the Rorschach between the two groups. This finding is consistent with Singer's statement that borderlines look dramatically schizophrenic on the Rorschach.

It is my contention, however, that despite the indisputable importance of external structure for the borderline patient, it is incorrect to say that they

---

An earlier version of this paper was presented at a workshop entitled Current Developments in Projective Techniques, New Haven, May 1981, and at the annual meetings of the American Psychological Association, Los Angeles, August 1981.

cannot be differentiated from schizophrenics on the basis of their Rorschach performances. Specifically, I believe that the retention of an implicit ego psychological model and, with it, a conception of borderline pathology as borderline schizophrenia by clinicians such as Singer has obscured important qualitative features of borderline patients' Rorschach performance. The recent paradigm shift within psychoanalytic theory to an object relations model entails an implicit shift from viewing disorders along a quantitative continuum to an emphasis on the qualitatively different developmental level of the object relations characterizing different disorders. Kernberg's model (1967), for example, differentiates the fusion of self- and object representations underlying the schizophrenic disorders from the inability to integrate the affectively polarized self- and object representations of borderline personalities. Consequently, the redefinition and reformulation of Knight's borderline schizophrenia to Kernberg's borderline personality necessitates a more discriminating approach to the diagnosis of borderline disorders with the Rorschach. If the borderline patient is characterized by a specific developmental disturbance in object relations, certain manifestations should occur on the Rorschach which differentiate such patients from schizophrenic or neurotic ones without recourse to the WAIS and the concept of external structure.

It appears to be Knight's, Rapaport's, and Singer's adherence to the ego psychological concept of primary process thinking as the psychological mechanism or personality variable at work that prevents these otherwise astute thinkers from realization of this point. Inherent in their model is the notion that borderlines and schizophrenics differ only in the degree to which they manifest primary process. Schizophrenics demonstrate thought disorder regardless of external structure while borderlines show it only in the absence of such structure. Thus, this emphasis on primary process thinking as the cogent psychological variable leads to a model of borderline pathology as only quantitatively different from schizophrenia, in contradiction to Kernberg's definition of borderline personality organization as qualitatively distinct.

Based on this ego psychological emphasis on primary process, Rapaport distinguished three major types manifested on the Rorschach. The contamination response, in which two percepts are merged into one (e.g. "It's a cat, it's a man, it's a catman), was viewed as the Rorschach equivalent of condensation (Shevrin, personal communication). By contrast, the confabulation response, in which the extensive elaboration of the response lacks sufficient justification from the blot for its specificity and affect loading, was seen as the Rorschach equivalent of displacement (Shevrin, personal communication). An example of one such response, given to Card I, is "Moses parting the Red Sea Waters . . . a man holding his hands up like this and then the two flanking portions appeared to be, you know, banks of water being thrown up, leaving the central portion dry. . . . it was sort of a chaotic mass . . . turmoil . . . there was no line or edge—seeming to break off into infinity.'' Finally, the fabulized combination response, in which two percepts are combined unrealistically on the basis of spatial contiguity (e.g. ''an elephant dancing on a butterfly''), was Rapaport's third major index of primary process thinking. Despite the clinical relevance of these three types of response, the major problem with Rapaport's rationale is the failure to distinguish them qualitatively. Each is viewed as an indicator of primary process, with little consideration of the different psychological processes inherent in each. If this model is taken to its logical extreme, each type of primary process thinking can be viewed as interchangeable—an implicit assumption of the recent study by Carr et al. (1979), in which all primary process responses in borderline and schizophrenic patients were summed and found not to differ in total between the two groups. Furthermore, such an approach leads to vague etiological formulations in which borderline disorders, schizophrenia, and manic-depression are all hypothesized to derive from oral conflicts.

If, however, borderline and schizophrenic psychological disturbances differ in kind rather than in number, a more differentiated approach is necessary. Blatt and his colleagues (Blatt and Ritzler, 1974; Blatt and Wild, 1976) have provided the basis for such an approach through a reformulation of these classical thought disorder indices as involving a developmental continuum of boundary disturbance. In this model, the breakdown of boundaries between separate concepts, as seen in the contamination response, is equivalent to a loss of the self-other boundary. The confabulation response is described as a loss of the boundary between inner and outer reality. And the fabulized combination response is viewed as a laxness of ego boundaries rather than as an overt disruption.

This reformulation adds greatly to the explanatory power of such Rorschach indices because of the ease with which it can be integrated into present-day object relations theory. For example, there is almost unanimous consensus regarding the seriousness of the contamination response as a pathognomonic index of schizophrenia. This clinical fact becomes more easily comprehensible with the reformulation of such a response as indicating a loss of the self-other boundary. Most contemporary object relations theorists have described schizophrenia as involving a developmental failure in the symbiotic stage with a subsequent failure by the infant to develop a firm boundary between the representation of self and the representation of mother.

Even more important for the purposes of this chapter is the added explanatory power of Blatt's reformulations for the borderline disorders. Elsewhere (Sugarman, 1980), I have noted the predominance of confabulation responses in the Rorschach records of borderline patients. At that time I was unclear on why this predominance should occur. With the benefit of this shift in models, however, the meaning of this finding becomes clear and brings with it an increase in the number of clinical inferences which can be drawn from such a finding. To be unable to differentiate inner from outer reality, that is, fantasy from reality, is characteristic of the developmental period marked by the predominance of illusion—the stage of infancy for which Winnicott emphasized the importance of transitional objects. Thus this test finding provides independent corroboration for Modell's contention (1963) that borderline patients show a developmental arrest at the stage of transitional object relatedness.

I will devote the rest of this chapter to developing the implications of this test-derived understanding of the borderline patient in regard to the borderline individual's experience of self and other, the unique cognitive disturbances in such patients, the frequent first occurrence of overt borderline symptomatology during adolescence, and the nature of the transient psychotic symptomatology associated with the borderline condition.

Borderline Experience of Self and Others

This understanding of the prevalence of confabulations in the Rorschach records of borderline individuals is in keeping with the emphasis placed by other clinicians (Rosenfeld and Sprince, 1963; Chethik and Fast, 1970; Fast, 1975; Leichtman and Shapiro, 1980) on the tendency of such individuals to "superimpose fantasies upon reality in ways others may not notice, may tolerate, or may even share . . ." (Leichtman and Shapiro, 1980, p. 439). It has been my clinical experience that the failure to draw a firm boundary between external and internal reality is a more essential clinical feature of such patients than their proclivity for splitting, which has received so much attention of late. Even more striking than his polarization of representations is the borderline patient's reluctance and inability to distinguish between consensually validated reality and his own idiosyncratic interpretations and evaluations of it (Sugarman and Kurash, 1980). Such individuals maintain magical and fantastic views and expectations of themselves and others which are more blatant and impervious to change than their tendency to experience self and others in black and white terms. They avoid or distort the laws of nature and causality to conform to their preconceived and egocentric world view. Their thinking and modes of relating to others have an infantile, childlike quality which is often shocking to the objective observer who espouses a different set of basic premises or axioms than the borderline individual.

Others are experienced as "part" or "self" objects by the borderline patient. That is, they are denied independence or wholeness as separate individuals with their own internal needs, desires, and thoughts. Often this failure to recognize the essential separateness of others is taken to indicate the borderline patient's grandiosity, narcissism, or omnipotent feelings. Such interpretations have a pejorative connotation and reflect the annoyance provoked in the observer or therapist at being treated as only a partial entity. I do not mean to say that descriptively the borderline patient's relationships cannot be described as grandiose, etc. Rather, I wish to emphasize the structural impairment in object representations underlying such attitudes. For the borderline patient has no choice but to appear grandiose or narcissistic, as he has no ability whatever to realize that the objective world, or others' subjective worlds, do not correspond to his own.

It is this failure to realize the distinction between inner and outer reality which contributes to the identity diffusion (Sugarman, Bloom-Feshbach, and Bloom-Feshbach, 1980) and chameleonlike quality of the borderline individual. Because he has failed to develop a firm sense of thoughts, emotions, and other internal states as arising from within, he easily adopts the perceived internal states of others, thereby seeming to adapt to the world of social convention. Yet the easy assimilation of others' ideas is paralleled by the ease with which they are discarded as some other individual's thoughts become valued. That is, there is no real substantive internalization and depersonalization of others' values, philosophies, etc. Wholesale incorporation is followed by wholesale disassimilation. This lack of a substantive inner world is compounded by the borderline individual's failure to develop an active sense of modulation of internal states. Due to his own superego lacunae, he is left dependent on others to control his impulses.

Cognitive Disturbances of the Borderline Patient

This inability of the borderline individual to realize the independence of his own and others' subjective worlds becomes more comprehensible if one examines the cognitive underpinnings of his representational world. Although there is some minor disagreement about the exact timing of the developmental arrest in borderline patients, almost all clinicians are agreed that it occurs somewhere during either the practicing or the rapprochement subphase of separation-individuation (e.g. Kernberg, 1967; Masterson, 1972; Rinsley, 1977). From a somewhat different vantage point, Fast (1975) comments that "the developmental period salient for its establishment appears to be . . . the period out of narcissism into a commitment to objective reality" (p. 397).

At this stage of development the toddler begins to gain a variety of perceptual and emotional perspectives on the mother and to be better able to discriminate her from others. Consequently, perceptual object constancy (Blatt, 1974) or recognition memory (Metcalf and Spitz, 1978) develops. The mother is recognized as an object in her own right, independent of situational context. The mother still remains a "part object" at this stage due to the toddler's cognitive limitations and subsequent inability to recognize the limitations of his powers and the relative independence of others. It is not until sensorimotor stage six that there is sufficient internalization to allow for conceptual recognition of the separateness of the maternal object and an attendant loss of infantile omnipotence (Greenspan, 1979).

The advent of transitional objects during the practicing subphase promotes sufficient boundary differentiation and "disillusionment" to enhance further cognitive development. It is the gradual forgetting of the transitional object and relinquishment of the illusion of symbiotic reunion with the mother that allows the toddler greater internalization and a more realistic, less subjective experience of self and others. The transitional object takes on a bridging function from the illusion of symbiotic merger to an awareness of the mother as someone outside, real, and separate from the infant. "It serves as an external cue to evoke symbolically the illusion of reunion with mother" (Sugarman and Kurash, 1980, p. 6). Consequently, it becomes a steppingstone toward evocative object constancy (Sugarman and Kurash, 1982). Its dual nature as a concrete, external object and also as a symbol for the mother allows the toddler to develop from total dependence on the mother's physical presence to an ability to retain an internalized image of her (Metcalf and Spitz, 1978).

This attainment of evocative object constancy through the advent of the transitional object brings with it a coalesced inner-outer boundary and the beneficial effect of that new degree of differentiation on object relations and ego functioning. Prior to this developmental attainment, self-perceptions remain diffuse because so many inner states are experienced as external. Affect is experienced as emanating from the object, as is the ability to regulate it (Krystal, 1975). With evocative object constancy these self-regulatory functions begin to be internalized so that inner reality becomes a more full-bodied experience. This shift in experience indicates the increasing ability to distinguish the actual maternal object from a mental representation of her (Blatt, Wild, and Ritzler, 1975). Thus these new symbolic capacities involve a progression from symbolic equations wherein symbol and object are undifferentiated to genuine symbolism characterized by abstraction and psychological distance (Segal, 1957, 1978; Sugarman and Kurash, 1980, 1982).

Consequently, the developmental arrest of the borderline patient at the stage of transitional objects has a major debilitating effect on object relations and cognition. For it prevents the attainment of evocative object constancy with its concomitant differentiation of inner from outer experience. It leaves such individuals arrested at a stage of symbolic equations characterized by concreteness and an inability to transcend the immediate. Segal (1957) has noted that "disturbances in differentiation between ego and object lead to disturbances in differentiation between the symbol and the object symbolized and therefore to concrete thinking . . ." (p. 393). Such an arrest leads to the concreteness reported as so characteristic of borderline adolescent test records (Sugarman et al., 1980).

Borderline Symptomatology in Adolescence

In fact, this interplay between developmental arrests in both object relational and cognitive spheres makes the developmental demands of adolescence virtually insurmountable and sets the stage for manifest borderline symptomatology to emerge during this period. The major developmental task of adolescence is synthesis—the integration of a number of heretofore relatively independent developmental dimensions into a coherent character structure (Sugarman et al., 1980). Two major dimensions which must be synthesized at this stage in order to bring about a consistent, stable ego identity are the cognitive and object relations dimensions. But the developmental arrest of the borderline adolescent at a transitional object level of relatedness makes it impossible to successfully traverse this second individuation period.

As mentioned previously, the failure to successfully differentiate the inner-outer boundary reflects the lack of attainment of evocative object constancy and the internalization of self-regulatory functions (Sugarman and Kurash, 1982). Affects and impulses remain experienced as deriving from outside sources, contributing to poor affect modulation and impulse control, and a representation of the self as capable, active, and whole fails to develop. Emotions, sensations, and thoughts become overwhelming to such adolescents, whose infantile experience of such phenomena was characterized by passivity and helplessness. Often such borderline adolescents defensively minimize affective and personalized experiences (see chapter 2). Inner emptiness results, leaving a precariously differentiated self-representation lacking key self-components (affect and affect regulation). A false self-organization ensues, with an emphasis on the more superficial aspects of relationships in order to protect the precarious self-other boundary. Experiences of the self and the other become lifeless and devoid of personal meaning, leaving the borderline adolescent depersonalized, derealized, and estranged. Others are looked to and depended on for guidance, regulation, and confirmation of self. Such adolescents lack a capacity to be alone because to be alone is to be confronted with inner barrenness, emptiness, and helplessness.

Such difficulties in internalized object relations interact with cognitive disturbances. As mentioned previously, the developmental failure to differentiate the representation of the mother from the actual mother leaves the toddler arrested at a stage of symbolic equations. Such a disturbance prevents such toddlers from moving beyond the stage of concrete operations. Instead they remain fixated in the egocentrism of concrete operations—the failure to distinguish representations from perceptual givens. Consequently, such children bring to adolescence insufficient cognitive development to attain formal operations, which presuppose a distinction between representations and perceptions. Formal operational thinking promotes the reversibility of the possible and the real. Symbols become transitional phenomena and facilitate separation from parents through the adolescent's identification with causes, new philosophies, etc. But the borderline adolescent finds such a level of abstraction and symbolism impossible because of the unclear distinction between what is objective and outside and what is subjective and inside. Such lack of differentiation leads to two patterns. The usual pattern involves the occurrence of concretization (Blos, 1971); such adolescents avoid the abstract because of the possibility of their fantasies turning into horrible reality. Another pattern involves the almost defiant abdication of a reality orientation by the borderline adolescent, who clings to magical views of self and others. In this case, grandiose fantasies take predominance over mundane, disappointing reality. Such adolescents often grow into the sort of highly gifted and creative but erratic individuals described by Kernberg.

Psychotic Symptomatology of the Borderline Patient

This developmental understanding of borderline pathology as a failure to consolidate the boundary between fantasy and reality also sheds light on one of the most puzzling questions about such patients—the nature of their short-lived, circumscribed psychotic episodes (Sugarman and Lerner, 1980). Inherent in the formulations of many clinicians is the notion that these patients regress to a schizophrenic psychosis at times of internal or external stress. Such an assumption is expressed most clearly by those who use the term "borderline schizophrenia" (e.g. Knight, 1953; Wender, 1977). Yet what little has been written about their transient, circumscribed psychotic episodes shows a general consensus that borderline patients do not manifest the cardinal signs of schizophrenia. Grinker (1977), for example, declares "there is no borderline schizophrenia. . . . There is, however, a borderline psychosis . . ." (p. 167) characterized by ego-alien, short-lived, confusional, or paranoid states. This formulation is in keeping with the only empirical work in this area—Gunderson's finding (1977) that depressed and paranoid ideation are the two most commonly reported psychotic symptoms.

Gunderson's and Grinker's findings are consistent with my own. Even when loss of external structure, inner pressure, or other stress reveals the poorly developed self- and object representation of the borderline patient, they remain more advanced developmentally than those of the schizophrenic. Although wishes for fusion or other primitive gratifications emerge in relatively unabashed fashion, little in the way of merger of self and other actually occurs. Full contamination responses virtually never appear in the Rorschach records of the borderline patient, although symbiotic content may abound. Although his identity is tenuous and poorly differentiated, the borderline always retains some experience of himself as separate. A simple clinical example of this subtle but crucial distinction suffices. One such patient at a particularly poignant and regressed moment of her treatment wished that she could be inside her therapist, returning to a safe womb. By contrast, a schizophrenic patient, under the pressure of a similar wish, expressed the wish to be one with his therapist. Thus, the borderline patient retained her sense of self as separate even if inside another, while the schizophrenic preferred to lose himself (or find himself) quite literally in the other.

The consistent thread running through both the depressive and paranoid ideation reported by Gunderson is in keeping with the central thesis of this chapter—that the borderline patient is unable to differentiate regularly his inner, subjective reality from outer, objective reality. Common to both depressive and paranoid preoccupations is an emphasis on one's inner concerns to the point that they override and color one's perceptions of external reality. Most striking about both symptoms is the manner in which subjective concerns override and intrude into one's perceptions and interpretations of the objective. Normal slights or other typical day-to-day occurrences take on a subjective, idiosyncratic meaning far from their objective one. In this manner depressive ruminations and the paranoid quasi-delusions of the borderline patient may be viewed as transitional phenomena because of the element of illusion they hold for the borderline individual. When experiencing these states, he is able to avoid his own inner barrenness and protect himself from a more serious regression. That is, the ruminations and delusions serve to highlight the sense of self and distinctness from the other at time of stress, which serves to maintain the self-other boundary. In a sense they can be seen as pathological equivalents of the normal adolescent's love affair with and use of abstractions as transitional vehicles for individuation (see Sugarman and Kurash, 1980, 1982).

The cognitive basis for this symptomatology is also clarified by this developmental formulation. To reiterate, the cognitive underpinnings of the object relational difficulties of such individuals involve an arrest at the stage of concrete operations—wherein representations are not distinguished from perceptual givens. In fact, Elking (1971) reports that at this stage of egocentrism, mental constructions are preferred and assumed implicitly to be more valid than perceptions. This cognitive finding illuminates one of the more puzzling aspects of borderline patients—the countertransference sense that often they choose, quite consciously, to ignore objective reality out of a preference for their idiosyncratic ideas and relational modes.

Conclusion

In conclusion, I have attempted to demonstrate the breadth of explanatory power gained by adopting a developmental object relations model to elucidate borderline phenomena on the Rorschach test. The application of a model which emphasizes the qualitative differences of successive developmental stages on intrapsychic structure formation allows for a far greater number of inferences than does an ego psychological model with its emphasis on quantitatively different stages of ego functioning. Specifically, the object relations approach suggests a more differentiated understanding of borderline pathology as a disturbance in character structure rather than simply a somewhat less severe variant of schizophrenia. Furthermore, this shift in paradigms helps to illuminate four key aspects of borderline pathology: (1) the self- and object representations of the borderline patient; (2) the unique cognitive disturbances in such patients; (3) the first manifestation of borderline symptoms, occurring usually during adolescence; (4) the nature of the short-lived, circumscribed psychotic symptomatology which appears at times of regression in such patients.

An additional goal of this chapter has been to highlight the central role of the Rorschach in respect to the psychodiagnosis of borderline conditions. Such an emphasis has become necessary because of unfortunate statements, particularly in the work of ego psychologically oriented clinicians, regarding schizophrenic performances by borderline patients on the Rorschach. These misstatements stem from an overattention to ego psychological variables and a consequent failure to evaluate the manifestations of object relations. Such clinicians thereby fail to perceive key differences between schizophrenic and borderline Rorschach performance, especially with regard to the importance of the confabulation response.

Such a shift of perspective does not supersede a psychosexual or ego psychological one, however. It is my hope that the model presented can be integrated with these other developmental dimensions in order to clarify the complex interrelationships between ego functioning, psychosexual dynamics, object relations, and cognitive structure. But this integration lies beyond the scope of this chapter, which represents, at best, a step in that direction.

References

Blatt, S. (1974), Levels of object representation in anaclitic and introjective depression. *The Psychoanalytic Study of the Child*, 29:107–157. New Haven: Yale University Press.

——— Ritzler, B. (1974), Thought disorder and boundary disturbances in psychosis. *J. Consult. Clin. Psychol.*, 42:370–381.

——— Wild, C. (1976), *Schizophrenia: A Developmental Analysis*. New York: Academic Press.

——— ——— Ritzler, B. (1975), Disturbances of object representation in schizophrenia. *Psychoanal. Contemp. Sci.*, 4:235–288. New York: International Universities Press.

Blos, P. (1971), Adolescent concretization: A contribution to the theory of delinquency. In: *Adolescent Passage*, ed. P. Blos. New York: International Universities Press, 1979, pp. 278–303.

Carr, A., Goldstein, E., Hunt, H., & Kernberg, O. (1979), Psychological tests and borderline patients. *J. of Personal. Assess.*, 43:582–590.

Chethik, M., & Fast, I. (1970), A function of fantasy in the borderline child. *Amer. J. Orthopsychiat.*, 40:756–765.

Elkind, D. (1971), Egocentrism in adolescence. In: *Readings in Adolescent Development and Behavior*, ed. J. Hill & J. Shelton. Englewood Cliffs, N.J.: Prentice-Hall, pp. 130–137.

Fast, I. (1975), Aspects of work style and work difficulty in borderline personalities. *Internat. J. Psycho-Anal.*, 56:397–403.

Greenspan, S. (1979), Intelligence and Adaptation: An Integration of Psychoanalytic and Piagetian Developmental Psychology. *Psychological Issues*, Monogr. 47/48. New York: International Universities Press.

Grinker, R. (1977), The borderline syndrome: A phenomenological view. In: *Borderline Personality Disorders: The Concept, the Syndrome, the Patient*, ed. P. Hartocollis. New York: International Universities Press, pp. 159–173.

Gunderson, J. (1977), Characteristics of borderlines. In: *Borderline Personality Disorders: The Concept, the Syndrome, the Patient*, ed. P. Hartocollis. New York: International Universities Press, pp. 173–192.

Kernberg, O. (1967), Borderline personality organization. *J. Amer. Psychoanal. Assn.*, 15:641–685.

Knight, R. (1953), Management and psychotherapy of the borderline schizophrenic patient. In: *Psychoanalytic Psychiatry and Psychology*, ed. R. Knight & C. Friedman. New York: International Universities Press, 1954, pp. 110–122.

Krystal, H. (1975), Affect tolerance. *Annual of Psychoanalysis*, 3:179–220. New York: International Universities Press.

Leichtman, M., & Shapiro, S. (1980), An introduction to the psychological assessment of borderline conditions in children: Borderline children and the test process. In: *Borderline Phenomena and the Rorschach Test*, ed. J. Kwawer, H. Lerner, P. Lerner, & A. Sugarman. New York: International Universities Press, pp. 343–366.

Masterson, J. (1972), *Treatment of the Borderline Adolescent: A Developmental Approach*. New York: Wiley.

Metcalf, D., & Spitz, R. (1978), The transitional object: Critical developmental period and organizer of the psyche. In: *Between Reality and Fantasy: Transitional Objects and Phenomena*, ed. S. Grolnick, L. Barkin, & W. Muensterberger. New York: Aronson, pp. 97–108.

Modell, A. (1963), Primitive object relationships and the predisposition to schizophrenia. *Internat. J. Psycho-Anal.*, 44:282–292.

Rapaport, D., Gill, M., & Schafer, R. (1945), *Diagnostic Psychological Testing*, ed. R. Holt. New York: International Universities Press, 1968.

Rinsley, D. (1977), An object relations view of borderline personality. In: *Borderline Personality Disorders: The Concept, the Syndrome, the Patient*, ed. P. Hartocollis. New York: International Universities Press, pp. 47–70.

Rosenfeld, S., & Sprince, M. (1963), An attempt to formulate the meaning of the concept "borderline." *The Psychoanalytic Study of the Child*, 18:603–635. New York: International Universities Press.

Segal, H. (1957), Notes on symbol formation. *Internat. J. Psycho-Anal.*, 38:391–397.

——— (1978), On symbolism. *Internat. J. Psycho-Anal.*, 59:315–319.

Singer, M. (1977), The borderline diagnosis and psychological tests: Review and research. In: *Borderline Personality Disorders: The Concept, the Syndrome, the Patient*, ed. P. Hartocollis. New York: International Universities Press, pp. 193–212.

Sugarman, A. (1980), The borderline personality organization as manifested on psychological tests. In: *Borderline Phenomena and the Rorschach Test*, ed. J. Kwawer, H. Lerner, P. Lerner, & A. Sugarman. New York: International Universities Press, pp. 39–58.

——— Bloom-Feshbach, S., & Bloom-Feshbach, J. (1980), The psychological dimensions of borderline adolescents. In: *Borderline Phenomena and the Rorschach Test*, ed. J. Kwawer, H. Lerner, P. Lerner, & A. Sugarman. New York: International Universities Press, pp. 469–494.

——— & Kurash, C. (1980), The body as a transitional object in anorexia nervosa. Paper presented at annual meetings of the American Psychological Association, Montreal.

——— ——— (1982), Marijuana abuse, transitional experience, and the borderline adolescent. *Psychoanal. Inq.* 2:519–538.

——— Lerner, H. (1980), Reflections on the current state of the borderline concept. In: *Borderline Phenomena and the Rorschach Test*, ed. J. Kwawer, H. Lerner, P. Lerner, & A. Sugarman. New York: International Universities Press, pp. 11–38.

Wender, P. (1977), The contribution of the adoption studies to an understanding of the phenomenology and etiology of borderline schizophrenics. In: *Borderline Personality Disorders: The Concept, the Syndrome, the Patient*, ed. P. Hartocollis. New York: International Universities Press, pp. 255–269.

Chapter 4

PRECONDITIONS FOR INTERNALIZATION: INTROJECTIVE, PROJECTIVE, AND BOUNDARY PHENOMENA IN THE RORSCHACH

MICHAEL K. HARTY

While this chapter describes a particular approach to the interpretation of Rorschach data, and thus may be considered largely clinical and diagnostic in focus, it is intended also as a contribution to research methodology. I am especially hopeful that the approach outlined here will prove useful in the systematic study of therapeutic change processes. In my opinion, certain perspectives derived from psychoanalytic object relations theory can be uniquely valuable in this area, especially in developing an understanding of the phenomena of ''internalization'' cited by numerous authors (Kohut, 1971; Blanck and Blanck, 1974; Kernberg, 1976; Meissner, 1981) who concern themselves with the nature and durability of therapeutic change. An important start in the direction of applying such ideas to research findings has been made by Horwitz (1974), who employs the concept, ''internalization of the therapeutic alliance,'' to account for the unexpectedly stable changes attained in a number of ''nonexpressive'' treatments studied in the Menninger Foundation's Psychotherapy Research Project. Subsequently Horwitz and his colleagues (Athey and Horwitz, 1980; Horwitz and Frieswyk, 1980) have concentrated on developing methods for assessing the therapeutic alliance as it develops over the course of treatment, and their work is paralleled by that in other centers where the therapeutic alliance has become a topic of strong research interest (Hartley, 1978; Luborsky, Bachrach, Groff, Pulver, and Christopher, 1979). The work I am reporting may be regarded as complementary to theirs, in that it focuses not on the alliance as such, but rather on certain aspects of the individual's functioning thought to be crucially involved in the process of "internalization" whereby a therapeutic (or other) relationship comes to have a continuing influence in the individual's life. My aims in this chapter are to outline a theoretical view of internalization which highlights certain component processes, and then to illustrate, through the study of change in a selected case, how these processes may be examined by means of the Rorschach test.

A Conceptual Definition

Processes collectively referred to as internalization have long been recognized by psychoanalytic writers as important in normal development, in the genesis of psychopathology, and in therapy. The most careful theoretical discussion of these processes is that of Schafer (1968), who proposes the following definition: "Internalization refers to all those processes by which the subject transforms real or imagined regulatory interactions with his environment, and real or imagined characteristics of his environment, into inner regulations and characteristics" (p. 9). Schafer goes on to distinguish introjection and identification as distinct types of internalization, and to differentiate these from such related phenomena as imitation, compliance, and so on. These considerations, while crucial to the further study of internalization, are, however, secondary to my immediate purposes. Rather, I wish to focus specifically on a single term of the definition: the word *inner*. This word is consistently used in clinical discussion as though its meaning were self-evident; Schafer points out (1968, p. 10) that this is often the case in theory as well, creating significant ambiguity. In my opinion, the ambiguity consists of the blurring of two perspectives on psychological functioning that ought to remain distinct. I will refer to these as the perspectives of the *observer* and of the *subject* in elaborating the above definition. Schafer preserves both perspectives in his two-part definition of "inner." In some respects, however, such a compound definition is not in the best interest of systematic study of internalization phenomena.

There appears to be little ambiguity from the *observer's* point of view about what is inner and what is not. From this point of view, a regulatory process has become inner if "the stimulation and impact of the regulation does not depend on the actual presence, action, or emotional position of the external object that was one party to the original interactions" (Schafer, 1968, p. 10). (This definition, offered in the context of a discussion of internalization, quite appropriately does not deal with simple maturation.) Thus a regulation is inner, or at least may be, if the subject carries it out by himself. It is evident that this definition, while it provides a ready distinction between inner and outer, is essentially a quite literal physical one. The presumed regulatory processes are occurring *inside the subject's body,* rather than taking place by virtue of the behavior, presence, or characteristics of another person, group, or environmental circumstance. In the context of a consideration of psychological processes, such a notion is at best redundant. It may be *assumed* that, to the extent that the actual location of such processes is of interest, they occur "in" the subject's nervous system. Ordinarily, however, this is not what is intended when we speak of internalization as a psychological phenomenon. Rather, we intend to distinguish from among a variety of processes—all of them occurring "inside" the subject, in the objective sense—those which merit a special designation. Our real interest is in the *process of change* whereby a "regulation or characteristic" formerly associated with a literally external agent comes to be carried out by literally internal means. Thus it is misleading to base a theory of internalization upon such a literal definition, since occurrences that may be appropriately conceptualized in this way—that is, those involving movements through or rearrangements in physical space—are only incidentally involved in the phenomena of interest. Treating the actual inner or outer location of a process or entity as though it were essential to the definition of internalization adds no information, and tends to build into the theory a confusion among literal, metaphoric, and experiential meanings.

The perspective from which "inner" has specific psychological meaning is that of the subject. The part of Schafer's definition dealing with this perspective is as follows: " 'inner' indicates that *the subject locates* the previously external regulatory agent within some self-boundary" (p. 10; italics mine). Schafer goes on to propose that the self-boundary may pertain to the self-as-place, the self-as-object, or the self-as-agent, and further, that internalization in this sense presupposes established boundaries between inner and outer worlds and should be distinguished from the processes by which those boundaries were originally established. Thus, approached from the subject's point of view, internalization is a *psychological* process ("the subject locates" refers to a way of thinking or imagining, not to phenomena in physical space) which can occur under certain psychological conditions (the subject has established a self-boundary). To study internalization is essentially to study an aspect of how people think about themselves, imagine themselves, mentally picture or represent themselves and their interactions with the environment. The relationship between internalization, in this sense, and the evolution of impersonal psychic structure is a controversial issue (Hartmann, 1939; Hartmann and Loewenstein, 1962; Loewald, 1962; Schafer, 1968, 1972; Kernberg, 1976; Meissner, 1981), but one which belongs to another order of theorizing.

Internalization might be described as an aspect of psychic content, were it not for the fact that this usage assumes something that ought rather to be explained—that is, that the psyche has an "inside." Precisely because this metaphor is so much taken for granted by most of us, it is easy to overlook that in fact it *is* a metaphor. To establish a self-boundary is to adopt a particular view of one's activities, not to discover an existing fact of nature. A "self" is a mental construction, not an independently existing entity with the characteristics of physical objects—a fact that in no way diminishes the enormous adaptive advantages of the metaphor. In a sense, internalization is a fantasy (Schafer, 1972), but this term ordinarily connotes phenomena more transient and more expressive of specific wishes or desires than the relatively stable imaginings or quasi-beliefs that are prerequisites for internalization. Perhaps internalization may best be regarded as an aspect of an ongoing representational process—an evolving process in which, under normal circumstances, a self comes to be represented as a bounded entity within a larger field, engaging in various transactions with other elements or "objects" in that field, and gradually changing as a result of such transactions. In general, this representational process serves to provide the person with a cognitive and affective guide to his situation, ideally a guide that combines stability with flexibility as it accommodates the influences of perceptual capabilities, past experience, physiological states, and psychological needs. From this viewpoint, the term "internalization" refers specifically to *the psychic representation of transactions between the self and other parts of the field, in which objects or contents previously outside the self-boundary come to be represented as inside that boundary*. Our chief concern in what follows is with the psychological preconditions for such representational processes.

Development and Psychopathology

The establishment of a self-boundary, referred to above as an essential precondition for internalization, is itself a complex representational process which occurs in the context of the early mother-infant relationship. As outlined by Winnicott (1960), healthy development involves a progressive "disentanglement of maternal care from something which we then call the infant or the beginning of a growing child" (p. 40). The newborn is absolutely dependent on its caretakers, not only for physical necessities but for the "total environmental provision" that sets the stage for all further development. The chief maternal function at this stage Winnicott describes as "holding": the provision of a reliable, protective, need-gratifying environment for the infant, who initially has no means to even know of the existence of maternal care, much less to be aware of needing such care and still less to control its quality. It is only through a process of development that the infant normally becomes aware of its needs for care, gradually develops ways of organizing and controlling their expression, and eventually becomes able to care for itself. Winnicott calls this the attainment by the infant of "unit status"; that is, rather than remaining part of a fused mother-child matrix, the infant comes to have a psychology of its own.

A crucial part of this development is the establishment of "what might be called a limiting membrane, which to some extent (in health) is equated with the surface of the skin, and has a position between the infant's 'me' and 'not-me.' So the infant comes to have an inside and an outside, and a body-scheme. In this way meaning comes to the function of intake and output; moreover, it gradually becomes meaningful to postulate a personal or inner psychic reality for the infant" (p. 45). The progressive organization of this inner psychic reality is the central theme of later development, about which more will be said. It must be emphasized at this point, however, that the important sense in which the infant "comes to have an inside and an outside" is that of *the infant's mental representation of its experience*. In literal physical terms, the infant has of course always had an inside and an outside, but *the transformation Winnicott speaks of is not merely the recognition of this "reality*." Rather, it is the beginning of the infant's experience of itself as a psychological person—the creation of a new "reality," which in an important sense is not a reality at all but a manner of thinking, of remembering, of imagining. From the establishment of the "limiting membrane" onward, psychological development has some degree of independence from physical experience, because the infant now has available a means for organizing the sensations, images, and memory traces generated in its encounters with the environment.

In the beginning, we assume, the infant does not distinguish among these classes of phenomena; physical sensations, perceptions, memory traces, and physical entities are treated equivalently, first according to whether they are "good" (pleasurable) or "bad" (painful), and then, as the "limiting membrane" begins to be established, as "inside" or "outside." Freud referred to this state of affairs when he wrote that the first ego is a body ego. In the present context, however, it is preferable to say that the first self-representation is indistinguishable from body representation, reserving the term "ego" for metapsychological discussion. In what I propose to be their most useful sense, the notions of "membrane," "boundary," "inner," and "outer" are aspects of representational functioning, that is, of the individual's way of picturing his existence in the world and thereby organizing his actions.

This crucial attainment of early psychological development—the ability to represent one's world as divided between an inside and an outside—does not come about all at once, and in fact it is probably most accurate to say that the distinction between inside and outside is at first shifting and unstable.

Only gradually does the infant come to attribute a degree of constancy to the self-boundary, rather than modifying its representation with shifts in affective states. Thus we may outline, for heuristic purposes, three relatively distinguishable stages of "self-boundedness" although in actuality these may shade into each other: (1) *absence or fragmentation* of self-boundary, with experience being represented via unintegrated images which are not clearly localized either inside or outside the self; (2) *instability* of self-boundary, with some distinction between inside and outside but with the basis for the distinction highly dependent on the affective state of the individual, resulting in a lack of continuity in the experience of self; (3) *stability* of self-boundary, in which the self is represented as a single entity with containing properties, which maintains continuity over time while engaging in exchanges of various "contents" with the environment. Interferences with this developmental progression are of course possible from a variety of sources, resulting in disturbances to be considered below.

It is important to note at this point, however, that the phenomena of internalization, as conceptualized here, originate in the early representational equivalence between physical (body) and mental (self). Later development, if successful, can transcend this equivalence, but cannot outgrow it; this is an alternate way of stating the familiar psychoanalytic principle that secondary process ego functioning is superimposed upon and regulates primary process functioning, but does not replace it. In the course of normal development, the "internal world" undergoes extensive elaboration and refinement, enrichment and differentiation, through the inclusion within it of increasingly complex and sophisticated representations of originally "external" figures and relationships. The normal individual becomes progressively able to distinguish unrealistic from realistic aspects of this internal world of representations, and to direct his behavior in accord with the latter. Nevertheless, the basic notion that there *is* an internal world—internal, that is, to the self, a continuous entity with containing properties—is a mental creation, a way of thinking, not an objective fact. The *importance* of the internal world is a fact; the consistencies and deviations of its development are facts; but its *existence* is not a fact of the same order, because its reality is psychic, being created by each individual as development proceeds, rather than having an existence independent of the individual's psychological processes. Thus we arrive at the seemingly paradoxical conclusion that normal psychological functioning is in important respects closely linked to "archaic" fantasy activity, in which the distinction between psychological phenomena (thoughts, feelings, images) and physical phenomena (things, substances, bodies) is not made. Normally, of course, this fantasy activity is for the most part unconscious, although the distinction between inner and outer worlds usually is made *pre*consciously—that is, without conscious awareness, but with the ready capability of directing conscious attention to the distinction if need be. Under specialized circumstances, however, such as in dreams or other "regressive" states, the usually unconscious processes are more accessible to conscious examination. One can then see how regularly, and how pervasively, important psychological occurrences are represented as concrete physical transactions.

The value of this theoretical point of view is of course to be determined by its explanatory usefulness—in this case, for helping to conceptualize the phenomena of observed and reported change over the course of a psychotherapeutic treatment. Before proceeding to an attempt at application, however, it is necessary to consider how the point of view I have outlined applies to psychopathology. The essential principle is this: if normal psychological functioning involves the more or less unimpeded representation of experience in the terms I have outlined, then psychopathology may be partly understood in terms of interferences with, or distortions of, that normal representational process. To be specific, it is assumed that in the normal individual, aspects of subjective experience are continuously, though usually unconsciously, represented in terms of the exchange of contents between the inner and outer worlds. Although inevitable anxieties are aroused in this process—as, for example, when a content that has been "taken in" is experienced as hurtful, or when a loss of "internal" contents is felt as depleting—normally the process itself is not seriously disrupted, and corrective measures are taken with relative smoothness. This occurs through what may be thought of as a normal cycle of projection and introjection. The too-painful inner content may be projected into the external world without excessive guilt or fear, in the expectation that the external world (like the "good-enough mother" from whom it is descended) will be able to "hold" and contain what the individual is for the moment unable to manage internally (this abstract description may refer, for example, to the process of telling one's problem to a friend). When events confirm this expectation, reintrojection may then occur of a less painful version of the previously projected content, thus lessening the need for wholesale reprojection. From a representational point of view, it is this process which makes possible, in normality, the evolution of an internal world that is relatively stable and yet open to continual revision and elaboration as new experience dictates (Sandler and Rosenblatt, 1962).

Interferences with this normal process are, however, possible from a variety of sources. Most obviously, if a self-boundary is not established, an essential precondition for normal projection and introjection is absent. Interferences with the normal cycle may also occur if the individual finds it necessary to reinforce or "fortify" the self-boundary for some reason, or, conversely, if the individual's defensive response to anxiety involves the blurring or attenuation of the boundary. Even in the context of a stable self-boundary, the projective-introjective cycle may be impeded if certain inner contents are felt to be so inimical to each other that they must be kept segregated; or if certain kinds of transactions between inside and outside are both strongly wished for and feared, necessitating exaggerated efforts to control them; or if the objective environment is such as to systematically undermine the individual's expectation that the projective and introjective activities may be carried on in safety.

It will be evident that the above statements refer, in altered terminology, to the same phenomena that are conceptualized in ego psychological terms as ego weaknesses, neurotic or psychotic anxieties, and defense mechanisms of the ego. In the representational frame of reference, as in ego psychology, these phenomena are essential to the understanding of psychopathology. From either point of view, functional symptoms and maladaptive character patterns result from disturbances of a developmental process; they are expressions of the individual's failure (for whatever reasons) to evolve adequate means for overcoming the anxieties encountered in the course of development, and/or of inappropriate and unproductive means the individual *has* adopted for coping with them. By the same token, the aims of psychological treatment from either point of view are to minimize the current and future effects of such developmental disturbances and, where possible, to remove obstacles to the operation of normal processes. The difference in the two approaches is that whereas for ego psychology the developmental process of central importance is the elaboration of depersonified psychic structure, the approach used here stresses the representational processes of boundary formation, projection, and introjection thought to be involved in constructing the inner world and its contents.

Rationale for Rorschach Application

Because the Rorschach technique is often thought of as providing relatively direct access to the subject's inner world, its applicability in a study of this kind might at first seem obvious. However, some qualifications are necessary in the light of the preceding theoretical discussion. To approach a subject's Rorschach percepts simply as expressions of the inner world, without further specification, would be to take for granted the very processes which are here of most interest. *It is preferable to regard the Rorschach response process as a sampling of representational functioning*, which provides an opportunity to assess the processes of boundary formation, projection, and introjection through which the internal world is elaborated and maintained.

With this altered perspective, the Rorschach protocol may be approached with a number of questions in mind. First, what can be learned from the percepts themselves about the way the individual characteristically represents his experience? One important issue is that of *boundedness*. Are the individual percepts clearly defined and distinguishable from each other, or do they have an unstable, shifting quality? Does response content emphasize clearly definable entities, or does it include many vague, amorphous, or insubstantial elements? Are the boundaries of objects unduly emphasized (as for example by mentioning hard shells or protective clothing) in a way that suggests an important preoccupation? Such observations will suggest inferences about the individual's ability and inclination to attribute stable, clearly defined boundaries to himself and to others, and about any special concerns related to maintaining such boundaries. A related issue is that of *containment versus protection,* referring to the functions attributed by the individual to boundaries that characterize his representational world. In the well-functioning individual, one would expect boundaries to be represented not only as protective barriers against painful intrusions from outside, but also as having a "holding" or organizing function: providing a "container" within which a certain amount of conflict may be tolerated as internal stability is sought. Thus we are especially interested in Rorschach percepts of objects with an actual or potential containing function; the *presence* of such responses will suggest something about the individual's ability to represent a "holding" boundary, while the specific qualities of the responses and how they are elaborated will point to difficulties associated with the containing function.

We may also examine the Rorschach responses from the standpoint of the *available contents* with which the individual populates his subjective world. Do the responses reiterate a single affective theme or a very few such themes, such as hunger, the danger of injury, or depression, or do they include more variety and complexity? Further, can we discern imbalances in the ways such contents are *allocated* between the inner and outer worlds—as, for example, by attributing everything painful to the outside? This perspective is complementary to the first, which dealt with boundaries and their functions; the presence of boundaries establishes *whether* there is an inside and an outside, while the range of contents determines *what* may be attributed to either.

Finally, certain Rorschach responses will suggest inferences about *transactions* between inside and outside as these are experienced by the individual. These include especially (1) percepts that implicitly or explicitly refer to the passage of some object or substance from outside to inside, or vice versa; (2) percepts that involve bodily orifices or sensory organs readily experienced as the site of transactions between the inside and outside of the body; and (3) portrayals of relationships between two (or more) figures, on the assumption that transactions across self-boundaries are most likely and most importantly experienced in a relationship context. In examining these responses, we may ask such questions as the following: To what extent and under what conditions do transactions across the self-boundary occur? Are inside-to-outside (projective) and outside-to-inside (introjective) processes equally in evidence, or is there an imbalance? Are such transactions represented as threatening or disruptive to the integrity of boundaries, or can they occur in a relatively controlled and safe manner? Ideally, for research purposes at least, it would be desirable to employ a formal scoring system for the qualities of Rorschach responses just listed. There is in fact considerable overlap between the response qualities considered here and those dealt with by several existing systems, including the work of Fisher and Cleveland (1958) on body image, Blatt and his colleagues on boundary disturbance (Blatt and Ritzler, 1974; Blatt, Brenneis, Schimek, and Glick, 1976), and Pruitt and Spilka (1964) and Krohn and Mayman (1974) on object representation. However, while each of these systems focuses on some aspect of the processes of interest here, none of them approaches self- and object representation explicitly as aspects of a projective-introjective process, or attempts to conceptualize obstacles to such a process. Thus, in the current exploratory phase of this work, it seems preferable to remain at a descriptive level of analysis, reserving more formalized methods for the future.

The preceding paragraphs have dealt with boundaries, contents, projective and introjective processes as they may be inferred from the actual test responses. A second and complementary approach makes use of the response process as a source of inferences, with the test-taking experience itself being viewed in terms of the introjective and projective processes it activates. The subject is asked to ''take in'' the multipotential stimulation of the inkblot, assign to it some meaning on the basis of its correspondence to his internal repertoire of images, and to produce a response which carries this meaning while still conforming to the external reality that has been presented to him. In the optimal situation, a smooth process of checking back and forth between the outer (inkblot) reality and the inner reality of subjective imagery leads to an integrated response which does justice to both; this implies a relative freedom from the kinds of obstacles to the normal introjective-projective cycle that were discussed earlier. When we are interested in examining the response process for evidence of such obstacles, such questions as the following may be considered; What is the subject's reaction to the task as it is presented? Does he respond with avoidance or opposition, suggesting a need to guard against ''taking in'' the stimulus? Does he seem overwhelmed by the task, as if attempting to engage in the required processes has a disorganizing (boundary-disrupting?) effect? Does he seek to redefine the task, induce the examiner to offer further instructions, or otherwise engage in behavior that may suggest characteristic ways of controlling the ''input'' he experiences. Is his approach to the task a global and inclusive one, suggesting an inclination to ''take in'' the whole situation at once, or is it cautious and piecemeal, perhaps seeking to exclude certain stimulus qualities?

Additionally, what is the subject's attitude toward his responses? Does he give them freely or grudgingly, aggressively or timidly? With some indication of pride and pleasure, or with apprehension, disgust, and efforts to dissociate himself from them? Does he remain interested in them once they have ceased to be private, or does he dismiss them as of no importance? Such questions may suggest inferences about how the subject regards his own inner contents, and how he expects them to be received by others. In this regard, the patient-examiner relationship during testing becomes an arena in which conflicts or difficulties associated with introjective and projective processes may be played out, and as such may become a source of additional inferences.

From these somewhat abstract considerations we now turn to a specific case, selected to illustrate the application of the conceptual approach I have outlined to the study of therapeutic change. This material is drawn from a larger, multimethod study of change in patients hospitalized with severe personality disorders.

CASE ILLUSTRATION

The case selected to illustrate this approach is that of a young woman I will call Judy F. At the time of her admission to the hospital she was nineteen years old, having left college early in her second year; she remained hospitalized for twenty-one months and was discharged to an aftercare program just before her twenty-first birthday. Psychological testing, including the Rorschach, was done shortly after her admission as part of the routine examination procedure, and the Rorschach was administered again for research purposes a few days before she was discharged. Thus the two Rorschach examinations to be compared here were separated by about nineteen months of intensive hospital treatment involving participation in regular patient-staff group meetings, a full activities program, regular individual sessions with the "hospital therapist" (the person with overall responsibility for coordinating the treatment), family sessions with the social worker, individual psychotherapy begun soon after the initial evaluation, and other elements as well. I shall not attempt to describe this complex and carefully orchestrated treatment program in detail, as more than a brief description would detract from this chapter's focus. Here I shall only sketch the patient's history and presenting difficulties as a preliminary to the more detailed Rorschach examination and analysis of change which follow.

The patient's clinical diagnoses were "major depressive episode, in an infantile personality organized at a borderline level," and in many ways her history was typical of patients so described. She had experienced severe disruptions of family life in her early years, with the parents in constant conflict and mother frequently absent from the home. At age six Judy went to live with her father when the parents were finally divorced. Both parents remarried within a few years, but although Judy continued to live with her father, stepmother, and stepsiblings, she experienced little stability. The two families competed for parental functions, and at the same time Judy felt excluded by her stepsiblings and harshly treated by her stepmother. For the most part, throughout her childhood she felt herself to be the isolated and alienated misfit within the family group, an experience to be repeated in numerous subsequent contexts.

Despite this unhappy home situation, Judy was able to do well in school. In fact, she seemed to find there some of the satisfaction lacking at home; her high intelligence and the diligence with which she completed her work made her a favorite of many teachers, who gave her special attention and privileges. However, her relationships with other children, always few in number, were awkward and conflicted. At times she acted like a bully, at other times she felt picked on. Apparently it was because of behavioral problems with peers that she was first sent to a psychiatrist, at age eleven; this treatment continued for a few months, without apparent benefit. As she continued through junior high and high school, doing well academically but remaining isolated from peers and in conflict with the family, significant emotional problems were increasingly apparent from her behavior. She began to absent herself from home without permission, abused alcohol and marijuana, and began a sexual relationship with a much older man. Her behavior began to take on a clearly self-destructive quality, and on at least one occasion while still in high school she made a fairly serious gesture at suicide by swallowing a large number of aspirin tablets. The father, now beginning to realize the severity of her problems, arranged for her to live with another family in an attempt to relieve the stress of the home situation. This did bring a temporary improvement, and Judy was able to complete high school and begin college work under this living arrangement.

When she attempted to move to a college dormitory, however, her condition quickly deteriorated. Again feeling picked on and excluded by her peers, unable to concentrate on her demanding studies because of mounting anxiety, and without the support she had received from teachers and advisors, she began to miss classes, wander about at night, spend money unwisely, and eventually to burn herself with cigarets and act in other openly self-destructive ways. Several brief hospitalizations and various pharmacological treatments over the next few months brought only transient improvement, and eventually a referral for long-term residential treatment was made.

The clinical diagnoses quoted earlier were established at a staff planning conference held eight weeks after Judy's admission. Taking note of the patient's abysmal self-esteem, her intense needs for nurturance coupled with rage at being inadequately satisfied, her alternately seductive and coercive attempts to elicit care from others (e.g. through, respectively, idealization and self-mutilation), and her vulnerability to at least brief periods of psychotic regression, the hospital team arrived at an overall treatment plan which was in all essentials followed throughout. This plan emphasized a supportive, antiregressive hospital regime—clear limits on destructive behavior, full activities program, and a firm expectation of responsible self-management—combined with individual psychotherapy aimed at exploring her conflicts over nurturance and her "malevolent and vengeful wish to destroy what she is given out of a sense that it is not enough." Periodic family therapy sessions were also planned, in an effort to help the patient, her parents, and stepparents to alter their intensely conflictual ties to each other.

More will be said about the treatment course later, when changes in the patient are discussed. At this point, however, we turn to an examination of the initial Rorschach protocol, focusing on aspects of the material that suggest inferences about the patient's representation of boundaries, her introjective and projective experiences, and thus, by extension, her readiness to engage in a constructive process of internalization. The protocol as presented here is slightly abbreviated. The patient's responses during the "free-association" period (i.e. following initial presentation of each card) are given verbatim (with numbering added); additional material from the inquiry (performed after each card) is given in edited form, and enclosed in brackets.

Initial Rorschach Protocol

> *Card I*. "(1) A wild cat. More than one? (2) A flying saucer. I guess that's it." [The cat looked wild because "Its mouth is open, its eyes are big, its ears are sticking out, it looks very mean or very scared." The flying saucer was seen with the blot inverted; it looked "kind of flat. Saucer dish, saucer part and there's like a cabin or something sticking out of it."]

Commentary. Neither of these responses refers explicitly to boundaries or to projective and introjective processes, but each suggests issues that later responses may help to clarify. The "wildness" of the cat is an intense affect that involves an unclear distinction between anger and fear. To the extent this response expresses an aspect of self-representation, the patient seems uncertain whether she is a source of danger or is herself endangered—whether the danger is inside or outside. By the same token, it is left unclear whether the mouth, eyes, and ears are "taking in" or "putting out" something dangerous—a frightening external stimulus in the first case, a "mean" glare and perhaps a scream of rage in the second. In either case these organs, which are potential sites for exchange between the inner and outer worlds, seem rigidly fixed in their open position; there is no indication that the patient feels such exchange could occur in a controlled, modulated way.

The "flying saucer" hints at the other extreme, in that it may be designed to operate in an alien environment in which *no* exchange between inside and outside is allowable. The cabin (site of control?) is described as "sticking out of it," as if it were not a fully integral part of the craft. These suggested themes of alienation, insulation, and encapsulation of the inner world, and lack of internal integration will of course require further evidence before their significance and their relation to each other can be determined.

> *Card II*. "(1) A pelvic bone. (2) Very sad man. (3) A missile. That's it." [The pelvic bone was "all of the black." The man is a face; the mouth (center space) and eyes (upper red) are the "most noticeable" features; sad because "The eyes are very long, mouth's open almost like he's screaming or crying." The missile is "the white part in there with the red part being the burning fuel."]

Commentary. While the pelvic bone might be considered a body content, its implications here cannot be determined with confidence. Most notable is the "sad man" response, for it repeats the theme of unclear distinction between affects ("screaming or crying") noted earlier. Again, although this is not explicit, the open mouth seems to serve as a passive channel for the emergence of the scream or cry. This may also be true of the eyes, although the patient's meaning in describing them as "very long" remains obscure; are the eyes somehow distorted by tears emerging from them, is the idea of a "long face" attached to the eyes in a concretistic, part-for-whole manner, or is there some other meaning?

The "missile" response may echo some implications of the earlier flying saucer; a forceful expulsion of contents (the burning fuel) is explicitly mentioned for the first time, but it seems clear that the missile is propelling itself *through* an environment rather than interacting with it. It is also worth noting that this response, which seems to imply a sense of power and direction, is given to an enclosed white area—that is, to the "empty space" within the blot. It also follows a pair of responses likely to have depressive implications. It might be speculated here that the "blasting off" suggested by the missile—perhaps analogous to determined and forceful pursuit of some life objective—represents an attempt to master or transform feelings of inner emptiness. If so, the attempt appears likely to miscarry for either of two reasons. If the patient, like her missile, must rely only on her own "fuel supply,'' she is likely to feel increasingly depleted as she progresses. And secondly, a missile is after all an instrument of destruction—a possible reference to the feelings of rage already hinted at. If the patient views goal-directed activity only in these terms, she is unlikely to allow herself to reach her objectives and may go ''off course'' instead.

Little has been said so far about formal aspects of the responses, and for the most part the commentary will continue to focus mainly on the implications of response content. However, it should be noted that all the responses so far have at least a fair correspondence to the realistic aspects of the inkblot stimuli, and that they are clearly distinguishable from each other as well. Whatever may be inferred about the patient's difficulty in permitting commerce between the inner and outer worlds, she does with some consistency represent her experience in terms of discrete, at least implicitly ''bounded,'' entities which she attempts to make realistic.

> *Card III.* ''(1) Whirlpool. (2) Two men in tuxedos, coming out of a lamp or something, almost like a genie. (3) And two pairs of legs, with half a leg missing. (4) Two bullet wounds. (5) Monster from outer space. (6) And two hearts.'' [The whirlpool is in the lower center, where the ''lighter black'' is described as ''carrying it up.'' Asked to elaborate, the patient refers to ''these circular rings, and there's a hole in the center which makes it seem like it's drawing things in.'' Asked about the men, she says that ''their legs are shriveled up like they're a genie or something''; she is perceiving the usual arms of the popular figures as shriveled legs, with the figures emerging from lamps which are the lower center detail. An apparent uncertainty about their faces prompts the examiner to ask if there is something else, and she then says that the nose ''looked like a rat's nose.'' The ''pairs of legs'' are the legs of the popular figure, but are not seen as connected to the previous image; the protrusion from each leg is seen as a second, ''cut off '' leg. The bullet wounds are the upper red details: ''a hole, and blood is dripping from it.'' The monster (whole, card inverted) ''has a funny-looking nose, and his head has been smashed, and he's kind of fat here compared to here. . . .'' The hearts (center detail) are ''the mirror image of each other.'']

Commentary. The "whirlpool" response refers directly to a voracious sucking force, and to an inner space which is never filled—concerns which could only be distantly inferred from previous responses. One might speculate that their direct emergence here is related to this card's stimulus value for themes of human interaction, although the patient (defensively?) selects a small blot area and nonhuman content for this particular response. The whirlpool, it should be noted, does not truly contain what it appears to consume, for its center remains always empty. Actually, its "boundaries" are in a sense defined by its voraciousness; if it ceased its activity—"unsatisfying" as the activity might appear in terms of filling the inner space—it would also cease to exist as a defined entity. This response, translated into self-representational terms, suggests a painful dilemma, in which the patient takes a sense of inner emptiness to be the necessary price of maintaining a self-boundary. She may appear to "take in" from the outside, but at the same time strongly resists actually "filling herself"; instead, like the whirlpool, she may seek to make everything that comes into her a part of her "outer" boundary or protective barrier.

But a sense of inner emptiness, even if unconsciously felt to be essential, is painful, and calls for defensive efforts in its own right. One such effort has perhaps been touched upon already, in the earlier "flying saucer" and "missile" responses: that is, an attempt to locate the emptiness outside rather than inside, to view the environment rather than the self as barren of needed resources. The next response in the sequence—genies emerging from a lamp—suggests a further elaboration of this attempt. The patient seems to imply with this response, "I need not concern myself with any barrenness within or around me. My lamp contains magical servants who carry out my every command and meet my every need; I can be both empty and filled."

However, the elaboration of this response ("shriveled legs" and "rat's nose," spoiling its potentially good quality), and the subsequent responses even more, demonstrate the failure of this attempted compromise. A sequence of responses now refer directly to damage, injury, and the violent penetration of boundaries, making more understandable the patient's efforts to avoid interaction even as these efforts break down. Only the final response—two hearts that are "the mirror image of each other"—seems to reestablish a kind of peace, but at the cost of a regressive shift to be further considered below.

> *Card IV.* "(1) A giant. (2) Some type of bug. (3) Crab legs. That's all." [The giant "looks like he's from outer space"; the face is small, hands can't really be seen, the hair is "kind of curly and parted down the middle." The bug (lower detail) has legs and antennae;

> ''it looks almost like a mean ladybug.'' The crab legs are ''very small, kind of pinched together.'']

> *Card V.* ''(1) Strange-looking butterfly. (2) Pair of tweezers. That's it.'' [She comments spontaneously that the tweezers ''look like they're embedded in something, you can't see the tail end of them.'' The butterfly looks strange because ''his wings aren't shaped right; there's just one set of them and they're kind of elongated, got funny things on the end of them, too.'']

Commentary. A recovery of sorts is evident in this sequence of responses, although several troublesome themes continue in muted form. There is no explicit violence of the kind just encountered; instead, the potentially powerful giant is portrayed as an apparently passive alien, while overtly aggressive qualities are attributed to small creatures or objects seen in small blot areas. In this way the dangers portrayed earlier are, for the moment, fairly effectively contained, although the responses continue to have a dysphoric quality. The ''embeddedness'' of the tweezers, and the ''funny things'' on the butterfly's wings, are reminiscent of the ''cabin sticking out'' of the flying saucer, Card I; they convey a lack of integration, a sense that things remain a conglomerate of parts rather than a unified whole. In terms of self-experience, this may well represent a consequence of the difficulty of ''taking in,'' discussed above especially in connection with the whirlpool response.

> *Card VI.* ''(1) TV antenna. (2) Two ships, or a reflection of a ship on the water. (3) Head of an antler. (4) Half of a sun. (5) Bearskin. (6) A penis.'' [The antenna is the top detail. Each ''ship'' is half the large lower detail; the card is rotated ninety degrees, so the center line is the water line. She refers to the ''steam tower or whatever it's called, there's the hull, and that's like the cabin and the anchor sticking out.'' Asking about the ''antler,'' she indicates the lower center small hook-like details, which ''look like the pincers . . . off from the head of it.'' Further inquiry establishes that she is referring to an ''antler beetle,'' a ''scary-looking'' insect. The ''half-sun'' is the semicircular inner portion of the upper detail,

> with the projections (often ''feathers'') seen as rays. The bearskin is the large lower detail; the patient points out its legs, then when asked about the specific idea ''bear,'' replies, ''It's just the first thing I think of when I think of skin rugs. I guess its width.'' The penis is the center portion of the upper detail.]

Commentary. A TV antenna is a device for ''taking in'' information from the environment; however, its mechanical, nonhuman, noninteractive character suggests a cautious hyperalertness on the patient's part, and perhaps a quality of detachment as a condition for such ''intake.'' Viewed in this way, the response may represent a way of minimizing or guarding against feared ''intrusions'' from outside. (The fact that a penis is later perceived in the same blot area further suggests a sexual focus for such fears.)

In the present frame of reference, a noteworthy characteristic of the ''reflected ship'' response is its representation of a shared boundary between two identical images, something which also appeared in the ''two hearts'' given to Card III. In the context of the chronic assaults on boundaries experienced by this patient—especially evident in Card III but also in other responses, including some not yet discussed—it is plausible to consider the ''shared boundary'' images as representing a regressive defensive position. That is, a boundary is protected against the surrounding danger by being shared with another (identical) entity; the boundary both divides and links the two halves of the pair, but as a result its adequacy in defining an independent being remains untested. In terms of self- and object representation, such images seem to express a regressive shift toward a form of relatedness that might be described as narcissistic mirroring, or as an incompletely resolved symbiosis. Some safety against projected danger, and some experiences of relatedness, are attained at the cost of partially giving up the sense of individual identity as separate from the object. One might thus expect this patient to develop intense, overly exclusive, ''heart-to-heart'' relationships when she experiences her individual boundaries as too greatly threatened.

More briefly, we may also note the odd verbalization, ''head of an antler,'' suggestive of a lapse in ego functioning as the patient seeks to minimize the grasping, pinching impulses the response expresses; the experience of incompleteness suggested by the ''half-sun,'' perhaps the obverse of the ''mirroring'' form of relatedness; and the by now familiar conglomerate quality of the ship with parts ''sticking out of it.'' The ''bearskin'' may also have implications regarding boundaries and threats thereto, but the response as given does not permit much inference about these.

> *Card VII*. ''(1) Two sisters fighting. (2) The top of a mushroom. (3) A book, open. That could be a

mushroom or a mushroom cloud.'' [The sisters are the usual figures; ''they look like they're sticking their necks out trying to get their point across, their chins are out, they look mean.'' The book is the lower third of the blot. The mushroom, or cloud, is the center space with the card inverted. She thought of a cloud because ''it's white, it doesn't have any real detail. If it had been in the black it would have looked like a real mushroom.'']

Commentary. In some ways the ''two sisters'' response is the ''healthiest'' so far, in that it portrays fully human figures in a realistic interaction. Aggression dominates the relationship, but it is fairly well controlled, and calling the figures sisters seems to imply that their relationship has some continuity. One wonders, however, about the extent to which the fighting is felt to be *essential* to this continuity. ''Sisters'' may also imply ''twins,'' that is, a mirroring form of relatedness; it may be that fighting with such a partner serves the patient as a way to reinforce the ''shared boundary'' between them, and that any lessening of hostilities could be experienced as a threat to her own sense of boundedness and individual identity.

The patient explicitly mentions the lack of detail in the center space as a factor in the response process, leading her to prefer ''mushroom cloud'' to simply ''mushroom'' as a response. Thus, as in the ''missile'' response to Card II, an idea suggesting great power and force is attached to an ''empty'' area. Two complementary inferences are suggested by such responses. It is as if the patient cannot attribute such power and force to ''substantial'' areas, for fear of making their destructiveness too real. At the same time, she seems to *need* to ''make something out of nothing'' by creating powerful images in the empty areas—as if the perception of an inner emptiness cannot readily be tolerated, and must be somehow transformed into the appearance of power.

An ''open book,'' coming at the end of this sequence, may point to an intellectualizing trend as part of the patient's retreat from the danger of aggression. However, thought of in terms of self-representation, it may also continue to express in muted form a sense of being exposed and vulnerable.

Card VIII. ''Oh boy, color. (1) Two lizards or dinosaurs. (2) Another monster or something like that. That's it.'' [The lizards are the popular side details; ''just kind of long, not much features to him at all, just the shape.'' The monster ''wasn't very clear either. You could just see the eyes, its face was skeletal and its hair or helmet stuck way out. . . . It's distorted, and he

> looked mean, like he's out to get you.'' The upper gray is the hair or helmet, the face and eyes are white spaces.]

> *Card IX*. ''I like the black and white ones better. (1) Two fetuses. (2) The head of a giant ant. (3) Two laughing ghouls, monsters of some sort, I don't know what they are. (4) Two witches, with heads cut off right above their eyes. That's all.'' [The fetuses are the lower detail; ''their heads were bigger than their bodies, they were pink, kind of curled up.'' The giant ant (pink and center details, card inverted) ''had eyes that looked like it was mean, like it was trying to eat you, and a big long nose to suck your blood.'' The ''ghouls'' and ''witches,'' apparently different versions of the same response to the upper orange details, are described as ''really distorted, like acid had eaten away at their faces and their heads had been chopped off just before they got to the ears.'' Asked about ''laughing,'' the patient retracts this element and says they looked ''mad or upset.'']

Commentary. The patient's enthusiastic response to the introduction of the first fully chromatic card is not matched by the quality of her subsequent responses. Instead, she seems pointedly to avoid using the color, and instead becomes slightly more vague and constricted in responding to Card VIII. The ''monster,'' one of her more arbitrarily perceived images, repeats earlier themes of distortion and alienation, as well as again suggesting an aggressive danger that is not clearly localized (the monster looks mean, but also may be wearing a protective helmet).

The sequence of responses to Card IX strengthens some earlier inferences, perhaps more clearly as a result of the added affective stimulus represented by the now unwelcome colors. The ''two fetuses'' again suggest an attempt to take refuge in a regressive, symbiotically ''enclosed'' form of relatedness; their large heads may refer to an attempt to substitute private thought and fantasy for activity and interaction. But this attempt is clearly ineffective against the threats portrayed in the following responses, which refer openly to the violent penetration and destruction of body boundaries, and to the loss of vital contents. Perhaps ironically, in view of the patient's apparent attempt to represent the ''head'' as a safe refuge, the most violent assaults are directed precisely there. This latter observation may have special implications for how the patient is likely to experience treatment interventions directed to her ''head''—that is, interventions designed to influence her ideas and fantasies, or to introduce new ones.

> *Card X.* ''(1) Weird-looking spiders. (2) A monster. (3) Two beetles. (4) A wishbone. (5) Two spines. (6) Picture of a nerve cell, two of them. I guess that's all.'' [The spiders are the blue details; the patient comments, ''There's about a million legs. There's no uniformity.'' The monster is the upper enclosed white space, with smaller white areas as eyes. The beetles are the popular upper figures; ''looks like they're pushing on a needle, maybe they're going to jab someone.'' The wishbone is the small center orange detail. By ''spines'' she meant ''someone's curved back,'' referring to the large pink details. ''I don't know why they struck me as spines but they do.'' The nerve cells are the side brown details, which remind her of pictures she has seen. She adds, however, ''They didn't put in the nucleus. It's kind of all spread out. I think nerve cells have nuclei.'']

Commentary. The spiders and the monster seem essentially to repeat themes noted earlier, while inferences about the ''wishbone'' and ''spines'' would be somewhat speculative. The ''beetles,'' however, are noteworthy because they represent two figures in an apparently cooperative activity—the only such instance in the record. It is, however, a manifestly sadistic activity—''maybe they're going to jab someone''—which involves the penetration of a boundary. Bearing in mind that the patient already has made abundantly clear her pervasive fears of such penetration, and also the fact that these Rorschach figures are often seen as arguing or fighting, the following inference is suggested: the patient has dealt with the potential threat to boundaries posed by hostility *in* a relationship by directing the ''jabbing'' action outward, toward an undefined third figure. To the extent that the beetles represent an aspect of self-representation, the response thus suggests an additional aspect of the interpersonal strategy the patient may employ to protect her own boundaries. But the unseen third figure may also represent an aspect of the patient's self-representation—even the very invisibility of this figure in the percept may be linked with the issue of ''empty space'' that seems to concern her frequently. From this perspective, the invisible figure preserves the relationship between the other two, by offering them a joint target for the ''jabbing'' that they might otherwise direct at each other. Without pursuing this line of reasoning further, we may simply note that it suggests an additional way of understanding the patient's experience of having her boundaries constantly assaulted—perhaps even of her need to enact such assaults herself through self-mutilation—and points to a genetic explanation in terms of her perception of parental conflicts.

''Pushing on a needle'' may also be a helping action—that is, a medical injection. This response may thus foreshadow the patient's experience of treatment, and her view of the cooperation between helping figures—but also, in view of the formulation offered earlier, her likely need to regard herself for protracted periods as the ''victim'' of such figures in order to keep them available to her.

Her final response, the nerve cell without a nucleus, seems to condense a number of the themes already mentioned. Referring explicitly to the absence ''inside'' of an essential controlling feature—and thus implying a more general lack of inner organization—the response also carries implications of hypersensitivity at the boundary (''an exposed nerve''). At the same time, the patient attributes the unsatisfactory state of affairs to someone's failure to ''put in'' the nucleus, giving a final emphasis to the externalizing trend which has characterized the entire record.

Summary of initial Rorschach. Focusing on the issues of boundaries, self-contents, and projective and introjective processes identified earlier as crucially involved in normal internalization, the picture that emerges from this initial Rorschach examination may be summarized as follows. (1) The patient lives in a world dominated by violent, destructive forces, to the almost total exclusion of more positive or benign influences. For her, to distinguish between an internal and an external world—to establish a self-boundary—is primarily to determine where to locate the aggression and fear that permeate her experience. (2) She does make the attempt to establish such a boundary, and adheres to it with some consistency; however, she seems to feel unable to ''contain'' the destructiveness within herself, and instead seeks to represent the dangerous forces as belonging entirely to the outside. In consequence, she must then occupy herself extensively with self-protection. The outward-looking protective function of the self-boundary has primacy, and the inwardly directed holding and organizing function is continually slighted. (3) Further, having attributed so much of her ''content'' to the outside, she seems quite literally to experience herself as hollow. There is, however, no safe way of ''refilling'' herself from the outer world; she portrays transactions across boundaries as violent intrusions likely to result only in injury or further loss of contents. (4) She is left with two unsatisfactory and pathological alternatives. Experiencing herself as separate and "bounded," she may achieve a temporary sense of "fullness" by withdrawing from dangerous contact with others and cultivating an inside populated by fantastic magical substitutes. There is evidence, however, that even this stance cannot be maintained consistently. Her other alternative seems to be a more clearly regressive, "boundary-sharing" way of relating herself to others, in which she may participate in some satisfactions and gain some security by partially forfeiting her sense of individual identity.

Based on the foregoing, treatment goals may be formulated with reference to the obstacles to a normal internalization process. This patient should become increasingly able to carry on such a process to the extent that she develops: (1) an ability to "hold" her own aggressive and sadistic feelings—i.e. to locate these feelings, and the images that represent them, inside herself without experiencing disruption of her boundaries, thus reducing her need to attribute them to the outside; (2) an ability to view the outer world in a similar fashion—i.e. as able to contain her projected "bad contents" and to some extent neutralize them, rather than immediately retaliating; (3) as a result, a reduced need to guard and protect her boundaries against assault from outside; (4) an increased ability to experience herself as "taking in" from the outside; and (5) an increased ability to experience herself as organizing and managing her inner contents. Following a brief summary of the treatment course as observed by the participants, the Rorschach record obtained at hospital discharge will be examined for evidence bearing on the attainment of these goals.

Treatment Course

For approximately the first year of Judy's twenty-one-month hospitalization, the treatment plan arrived at in the planning conference was followed without major difficulties. Dr. N., her hospital therapist, met with her regularly to review her hospital program, identify issues calling for special attention, and plan any needed changes. Dr. N. felt early in his work with Judy that they were able to form a good working alliance. An important aspect of this alliance was Dr. N.'s conviction, which he stated directly to the patient, of the necessity that she forgo the self-destructive actions which represented a constant threat to her treatment and physical well-being. Although there were a few occasions when she again flirted with self-destructiveness—for example, planning with another patient (in the sort of regressive partnership foreshadowed by the Rorschach) to put their heads inside a pillowcase and breathe deodorant spray—for the most part she was able to accept the staff's help in limiting this behavior and redirecting her interests.

In another development anticipated by the Rorschach, Judy revealed early in her treatment that she had developed an elaborate "fantasy world" (her term) complete with a cast of imaginary characters and even an imaginary landscape. She described spending increasing amounts of time "retreating within herself " to engage in various adventures and relationships there. While this fantasy world held a compelling fascination for her, she seemed quite aware of its imaginary nature and could acknowledge using her "retreats" to this world partly in the service of eliciting interest and concern from those around her. She was at this point concerned not with her excessive reliance on this mode of withdrawal, but rather with the increasing intrusion of harsh, unpleasant, attacking qualities into the imaginary world which formerly had seemed safe and benign (recall the "rat's nose" of the genies, Card III). However, she did not seem bent on restoring this world at all cost, but on the contrary appeared to involve herself increasingly with interpersonal reality. She participated faithfully in a planned activities program and in patient government, began individual psychotherapy and conscientiously brought up her concerns there, and to all appearances was progressing steadily toward discharge. Concomitant social work with the family—not further described here, but crucial in fostering an improved environment for the patient's treatment—had also begun to bear fruit.

The eleventh and twelfth months of hospitalization, however, were a period of crisis, which both the patient and Dr. N., looking back over the course of treatment,[1] felt had become a crucial turning point. They agreed that the patient's apparent progress toward discharge had masked her intense fears of leaving the hospital, and that in fact her "good behavior" in the hospital had been largely in the service of getting and preserving the approval, encouragement, and nurturant care of the staff. They also agreed that the crucial issue during the crisis period had been whether the patient could give up her wish and demand that this nurturance should be always and unconditionally available to her. There were differences of emphasis, however, regarding how the critical period had come about. For one thing, Dr. N. did not describe the early course of treatment as being smooth and uneventful to the extent Judy did. Aware of the importance of the patient's dependence on the staff from the beginning, he had experienced *his* major dilemma in the treatment as that of balancing the patient's real need for such gratifications against her equally important long-range need to establish greater autonomy. Complicating the picture from his point of view was the difficulty of distinguishing real growth from pseudomaturity, representing an attempt to prolong dependence through compliance. When the patient appeared on the verge of planning her discharge with these issues largely unexamined, Dr. N. felt it was necessary to confront her more strongly than before with her unacknowl-

[1] In the larger study from which this case is selected, patients and hospital therapists were separately interviewed, around the time of discharge, regarding their view of the treatment and the changes that had occurred in the patient.

edged dependency. He thought the crisis in the treatment, which involved the much more direct expression of the patient's fears and her continuing self-destructive wishes, had been largely a result of this shift in his own and the rest of the staff 's approach to the patient.

The patient gave a somewhat different explanation of the same events, although one which in essence confirms Dr. N.'s account. She described herself as adhering to the treatment structure, participating in activities, and taking on added responsibility during the first year of hospitalization, all with little sense of having her own reasons for doing so. All that time, she said, she was afraid to reveal her feelings of uncertainty and "craziness" to the staff, who praised and rewarded her "good" behavior. This continued even as she was planning for discharge and feeling a mounting sense of desperation. In a vocational assessment which she requested as part of her aftercare planning, the psychologist picked up her ambivalence and fear about leaving the hospital and questioned the patient's plan; however, rather than experiencing relief, she felt more upset, and continued to try to keep the fears to herself. Finally, she said, she "fell apart" and could no longer keep her panicky feelings and suicide fantasies from the staff. Retrospectively, the patient felt that her reluctance to trust the staff with her desperate and "crazy" feelings had been self-imposed—that is, their acceptance and caring for her had not in fact been conditional on continued "good" behavior. However, it seems clear that at the time, despite Dr. N.'s and others' awareness of these feelings and their efforts to help her acknowledge them, she felt she had to prevent any access to the "crazy," desperate, destructive parts of herself until she was no longer able to. In her words, she felt for a long time that "there was something I had to get out, but couldn't."

The change in this stance did not happen all at once. Over a period of several weeks, despite now discussing with the staff her suicidal feelings and despite having returned to a much more restricted status within the hospital, she felt increasingly desperate, and eventually made a serious suicide attempt by obtaining and ingesting a large amount of over-the-counter medication. While in a general hospital subsequent to this attempt, she managed to get hold of a knife, and for a time threatened a further attempt. This was prevented, and an even more restrictive regime was set up in an effort to prevent the patient from harming herself, with physical restraints and a round-the-clock special watch. Very soon, however, the patient came to a realization that had not really struck her before: that she now had attained virtually everything she had thought she wanted from the staff—constant attention and concern, even feeding and physical caretaking—and she still felt as empty and desperate as ever. She recalled thinking, "I'm putting so much effort into finding ways to kill myself, taking a lot of energy to figure that out, and having a hard time of it, and in between attempts I'm feeling really miserable; how much energy would it take for me to try to pull it together? . . . It couldn't take more energy, it would take the same amount or less, and I might feel better between [times of crisis].''

All accounts agree that from this point on the patient made steady gains, this time in the context of a more open recognition of the strength of her unsatisfied wishes to be nurtured and cared for. She now manifested a consistent determination to give up the more unrealistic aspects of these wishes, rather than continuing to covertly expect and demand their satisfaction, at the same time punishing herself for doing so. She began to expand her social activities and to again take on added responsibility for herself, with enjoyment of her added mastery now outweighing her fear of moving ahead. Three to four months after the crisis described, she again began to make discharge plans; this time there was no major increase of anxiety, an appropriate plan for aftercare was developed, and the discharge was accomplished without incident. She planned to continue her psychotherapy for an extended period, meanwhile gradually decreasing her involvement in a day hospital program and adding a combination of paid employment and college study.

Despite the promising outcome of this case at the discharge point, the real verdict is of course not yet in. This can come only from an assessment of Judy's functioning over a reasonable follow-up period. We can, however, examine her status at discharge—for present purposes, by means of the Rorschach protocol obtained at that time—and attempt to synthesize an understanding of the changes accomplished through this period of treatment.

Discharge Protocol

In this second Rorschach protocol, the responses during the ''free association'' period are again given verbatim, but the description of inquiry is organized around a card-by-card comparison with the earlier responses. An interpretive discussion follows.

> *Card I.* ''(1) Looks like a cat. (2) And a space ship. That's it.'' [Perceptually, these are the same two responses she gave initially. The cat, which was ''wild'' originally, is now described as ''a Halloween black cat''; ears, eyes, and mouth are mentioned but not emphasized. Asked for further impressions, she says that it looked angry. The space ship, seen earlier as a flying saucer because of its flatness, is now described only as ''standing on its legs.'']

Card II. ''(1) Looks like a sad person. (2) Looks like a bear or something, standing on ice or something, reflected. Guess that's it.'' [The ''sad person'' is the same as the ''sad man'' seen originally, now ''sad'' because ''the face was kind of long, the eyes looked big and sad.'' The open mouth, earlier seen as ''screaming or crying,'' is mentioned but not emphasized. Two responses from the first administration, ''pelvic bone'' and ''missile,'' do not appear. The bear is a new response, seen with the card rotated ninety degrees; the red upper detail is the bear's head; a bear was suggested by ''the body shape, and I guess the blackness too.'' Asked if the bear had seemed to be doing anything, she replies, ''Drinking something.'']

Card III. ''(1) It's a happy person. (2) There's a bow tie in there. (3) Some sort of a creature, looks like an insect or something. (4) The top part of a tree, once again reflected.'' [Only the ''creature'' (whole, card inverted) duplicates an earlier response to this card; seen then as a monster from outer space, with emphasis on its distorted, mutilated qualities, it is now described as having a head, mouth, and eyes, without further elaboration. The ''happy person'' is a face, with the eyes being the usual heads of the popular figures and the ''smile'' being the curving white space outlined by the usual legs and arms on both sides. The smile is ''the only thing very definite about the face.'' The bow tie is the center red detail, with both form and color as determinants. The ''tree'' is the usual popular human figure, but seen with the card rotated ninety degrees; the usual leg and body are branches, with leaves, and the trunk of the tree is not seen. Asked about the unusual arrangement of this ''reflection'' response, she says, ''The only thing I could think of would be a ceiling mirror, above the tree.'' In the course of the inquiry about these responses, she indicates the red side details and says, ''That looks like someone pricked their finger.'' This corresponds to the "bullet wounds" of the first Rorschach; there is no explicit reference to the "whirlpool," "genies," "legs with half a leg missing," or "two hearts" given initially.]

Card IV. "(1) Looks like a weeping willow. (2) Also it looks like some giant, coming toward me with a tree behind him. That's it for that one." [The "weeping willow," a new response, is the whole blot, with a trunk and branches that "came down." The giant, also a whole response, is the same as one given initially, with the foreshortening and large feet again mentioned. Originally the giant was "from outer space"; this time, in response to a question about the "tree behind him," the patient says, "It might have been Paul Bunyan or something, that would mean he's in a forest." The responses which have dropped out from the first administration are "mean ladybug" and "crab legs."]

Card V. "(1) A seagull. (2) An old man with a beard—or rather, a *man* with a beard. (3) An alligator." [The two responses given originally to this card were "strange-looking butterfly" and "tweezers." The seagull, like the butterfly, is the whole blot, but there is now no reference to misshapen wings or "funny things on the end of them"; the gull is merely "flying, its wings spread," and the projections at the outer tips are now seen separately as the common alligator heads. The man with the beard, a new response, is the profile on the upper edge of the side detail. Asked why she changed her impression that the man was old, the patient says, "I guess (that was) just a cliché. You see a lot of young men with long beards."]

Card VI. "(1) Looks like the skin of a cat . . . the head. That's it for that one." [Originally she saw the large lower detail as a bearskin rug, emphasizing its "width"; now she includes the catlike "head," and describes it as a skin because "a cat couldn't lie that way." A number of initial responses now are not mentioned: "TV antenna," "reflected ships," "head of an antler (beetle)," "half of a sun," and "penis."]

Card VII. ''(1) I see two elephant heads. (2) Two Indian women.'' [The elephant heads are the middle details on each side of the blot, seen with the card rotated ninety degrees. This is a new response. The Indian women are the usual human figures, which were ''two sisters fighting'' in the initial testing. This time, however, the patient refers only to the heads, and ''feathers in their hair,'' rather than heads and bodies as initially. Asked for further impressions, she says, ''It looked like they were arguing; their faces, their noses kind of upturned.'' There is no reference to the ''open book'' or the ''mushroom or mushroom cloud'' responses given earlier.]

Card VIII. ''Technicolor! (1) I see two lizards, iguanas. (2) And some big blob out of a monster movie.'' [The iguanas (popular side figures) were ''lizards or dinosaurs,'' in the first testing. Originally they were described as ''just kind of long, not much features''; now they look specifically like iguanas because of the ''stocky head, stocky shoulders—it wasn't slender.'' While she also saw a monster in the first testing, it was then described as having a ''skeletal'' face, with hair or a helmet ''sticking out'' (gray upper detail). Now, referring to the same area, she says, ''It didn't have much shape, but looked like its arms were up (demonstrating), dripping slime . . . looked like his fingers were dripping, holding them out.'']

Card IX. ''(1) Hippopotamus head—two of 'em. (2) And some creature with really big eyes.'' [The hippopotamus heads, a new response, are the green details, seen with open mouths toward the center. The creature with big eyes (eyes are outer parts of pink detail, seen with the card inverted), is perceptually the same as the ''giant ant'' from the initial protocol, which at that time was described as ''mean,'' ''trying to eat you,'' with ''a big long nose to suck your blood.'' Now the creature looks like something ''out of a monster movie. . . . If it had been a natural picture it would have been black, dark. One of those creatures that doesn't look too mean; strange-looking.'' The ''fetuses'' from

> the first protocol are absent, as are the "laughing ghouls or witches" seen then as distorted and mutilated.]
>
> *Card X.* "(1) Two seahorse . . . heads. In fact, most of the body, except the tail. (2) Two hermit crabs crawling on a post. (3) I see two eyes. (4) Two fetuses." [The responses from the first testing that now are absent are "weird-looking spiders," "monster," "wishbone," "two spines," and "nerve cells (without nuclei)." Only the "two beetles" remain, now changed into hermit crabs and merely "crawling on a post" rather than preparing to "jab someone" with a needle. The seahorses are the lower green detail (card inverted), the eyes are the inner yellow—described as "plain-looking, no definite expression"—and the fetuses are the large pink details. With regard to the latter, she says, "The head was pretty well-defined, but the rest of the body was . . . unformed."]

Before proceeding to our own analysis of the differences between these two protocols, it may be of interest to quote the patient's impressions on this score. She said, "I saw a lot of sad expressions; last time they were more angry. Or frightened. I think I saw a lot more anatomy objects last time, and a lot of space ships." She added that she had probably given fewer responses this time, and then was asked if she felt she had approached the task differently. "Last time I was very uninhibited, very loose—letting people know how crazy I felt. . . . [This time] I see what I see—and that's it."

Rorschach Indications of Change

Essentially absent from this second protocol are the images of violent penetration, damage, and mutilation that characterized the first. Clearly the patient experiences her psychological world as less permeated by danger, and it is a less difficult and conflictual task for her to establish and maintain boundaries in it. There is now little or no emphasis on protective coverings, shared boundaries, or other aspects of the earlier responses interpreted as reflecting the patient's need to guard against assaults on her boundaries. At the same time, there is evidence to suggest that her greater security against *outer* danger is sponsored by an increased acknowledgment of inner contents—primarily feelings of neediness and rage—formerly denied or attributed to the outside. Newly present are some fairly direct references to hunger and thirst (bears drinking, Card II; alligator, Card V; hippos with open mouths,

Card IX), in contrast to the first record, in which the only forms of "getting" and "taking" that appeared were both clearly sadistic (pinching, blood-sucking) and ineffectually minimized. In a similar vein, the more matter-of-fact dealing with themes of sadness (Cards II and IV), and the patient's ability to use the blackness of some blots as an integral part of the response process, provide both formal and content indications of an increased tolerance for depressive affect. Also relevant are the indications of a changed role for conscious fantasy, which now serves less as an isolated retreat from unpleasant experiences and more as a means of mastering them by giving them a more realistic and manageable context; note especially how alien monsters and giants (Cards IV, VIII, IX) have become mythical or movie characters.

However, significant difficulties remain. First, it must be noted that the reduction in boundary-threatening and boundary-defending activity is part of a general reduction in activity of all kinds. In part, the patient may be maintaining boundaries more easily by virtue of a degree of withdrawal from others, or avoidance of emotionally laden situations that might present a heightened danger. In fact, this protocol alludes to a new boundary property that may be relevant here: that of the "monster dripping slime" (Card VIII). Here it is as if the boundary itself, though not externally threatened, has taken on disgusting and repulsive qualities of its own that are likely to discourage any more benign approach by others. The fact that this image appears in response to a colored blot suggests that the repulsive substance may represent affective experience. Thus it may be that the patient, under certain conditions of affective stimulation, still seeks to preserve inner comfort by transforming feelings into some form of unappealing outer display at least partly intended to keep others at a distance. (Note also the reference to "hermit" crabs, Card X).

Such maneuvers would tend to perpetuate feelings of neediness, which, although now more clearly acknowledged, represent a continuing problem for the patient. It is evident from this second protocol that the increased presence of recognized need in the patient's world is not matched by the availability of satisfaction. Instead, even when a need-satisfying action involving literal intake—the "bear drinking," Card II—is portrayed, the context is one of coldness ("on ice"). Also, the space ship, Card I, while "standing on its legs," is presumably doing so in a cold, alien environment. The sense of "inner emptiness," which seemed to be both cherished and denied initially, now seems to be experienced more painfully as a longing to be filled—but the *external* world, while less dangerous, is still to a considerable extent experienced as cold and empty. In this vein, it is noteworthy that the single apparent reference to positive emotion—the "smile" given to Card III—involves a forced and quite arbitrary use of white space, and is more suggestive of denial than of genuine pleasure or fulfillment.

Another aspect of the patient's continuing difficulty in managing or "containing" affect is suggested by her emphasis on heads at the expense of the body. This is most evident in her final percept—such percepts are often especially expressive in terms of self-experience—of fetuses with well-defined heads but unformed bodies (Card X). But there are few full bodies of any kind, and those that do appear tend to be somewhat distorted, amorphous, or "monstrous." It is as if "full-bodied" experience remains threatening for the patient, who continues to trust the intellect more than the emotions and attempts to maintain a separation between the two.

In a related but more speculative vein, the "reflected tree" response, Card III, may have special implications for the patient's organization of internal and external experience. The tree, ordinarily an "outside" object, is here transferred by implication to the "inside," since it is thought of as reflected in a ceiling mirror. But it is also seen without a trunk, as if the branches and leaves were somehow floating in space. At the least, the awkwardness and arbitrariness of this perception suggest some discomfort and strain associated with this fantasied internalization. The absence of the trunk (i.e. the lower part) is reminiscent of the paucity of bodies (as opposed to heads) noted elsewhere in the protocol, and suggests that the difficulty may have to do with aspects of internalization touching upon body experiences. The response thus suggests the incomplete integration that may result from an internalizing process carried out in the context of a restriction of introjective and projective fantasy. It is as if the introjected object (and relationship—note the "mirroring" reference in this response) is prevented from "taking root" in the internal world, and remains somewhat disembodied and unassimilated.

At least one aspect of this formulation—the restriction of introjective and projective fantasy—is directly supported by the material. Few boundary transactions of any kind are referred to in this second record, although those that do appear are much less fraught with violence and danger than was seen initially. Sensory organs such as eyes and open mouths, which may represent channels of exchange between outside and inside, continue to receive some emphasis, and the absence of the "paralyzed" quality noted in the first record suggests that the possibility of such exchange is less fearsome and that there is a greater sense of control. But direct references to such exchanges still hardly appear. The notable exception is the "bear drinking," Card II, which does portray a need-satisfying action involving literal intake. However, the context of coldness, and of reflection rather than relationship, in which this action occurs, reinforces the inference that satisfying intake is far from being a well-established feature of the patient's experience, even though wishes for such satisfaction seem to be more tolerable and accessible to her. Gratification associated with output appears even more problematic. The output theme is referred to only distantly in a handful of responses—the belated "pricked finger'' on Card III, possibly the ''weeping'' of the willow and of sad eyes, and the forced smile on Card III as an expression of ''outgoing'' emotion—and none of these convey any sense that contents are being freely released. There are no explosive or eruptive themes as there were previously, but something of a swing to the other extreme has taken place, with the patient now needing to preserve internal ''supplies'' in a rather bleak environment. As suggested earlier, she may be adopting this stance partly in order to defend against the experience that her affective ''contents,'' if allowed expression, would be found disgusting and repulsive.

Application to the Treatment Process

Although the specific details of change in this or any case would require finer documentation than is here available, it is possible to make a general formulation that seems consistent with both the Rorschach evidence and the available reports. Initially the patient's difficulty with internalization was extreme, even though her representational activity had some of the characteristics we would consider prerequisites for favorable internalization. The most significant obstacles appeared to be the following, all interrelated: (1) the patient's inability, in terms of self-representation and self-experience, to contain and successfully neutralize sadistically toned needs and wishes; (2) her attempt to attribute such feelings and wishes—represented as dangerous forces, items or substances—exclusively to the outside, in order to remove this unmanageable inner danger; (3) her resultant experience of herself as empty, and of the world outside herself as permeated by uncontained and unpredictable dangers; (4) her efforts to protect and console herself, especially in relationship contexts, by (a) maintaining an outer ''shell'' and attempting to find her satisfactions in a private inner world safe from intrusion, and (b) conceiving of relationships with real ''external'' figures in a regressive, incompletely differentiated way that compromised her sense of boundedness.

As a result of these factors the patient was unable to comfortably experience either input from others or output directed toward them. She was likely to experience any intervention, no matter how helpfully intended, as an assault, an effort either to further empty her of good contents or to force back into her the ''bad,'' dangerous contents she had attempted to purge from herself. Further, any reminder of her separateness vis-à-vis others was likely to heighten her sense of vulnerability, and thus to provoke intensified defensive efforts. At the same time, the very absence of satisfying intake assured the perpetuation of the cycle of deprivation, rage, projection, external danger, and the attempt to turn inner emptiness into an illusory haven.

In view of these difficulties, all the treatment could realistically provide, for an extended period of time, was the opportunity for the patient to question her assumption of being surrounded by threats to her safety and individual integrity. The ultimate goal of the treatment, almost from the beginning, was to help the patient to "re-own," and constructively master as inner feelings, her rage and deprivation. This could not be done all at once, however, and before she could risk the attempt she had to develop some assurance that others would be able to "contain" these feelings (i.e. to prevent their becoming external dangers to her) even when she could not. Thus the long initial period of compliant behavior in the hospital—which was, however, punctuated by occasional testing of the staff—could be viewed as a preparatory period. As the unreality of the "external" danger was repeatedly demonstrated by the staff's consistent interest and nonintrusive support, the patient began to have a growing sense of danger *within,* even though continuing to conceal this from others.

When the crisis came, the patient had the very literal (and now consciously acknowledged) experience of "something inside that I had to get out," consisting of desperately needy, "crazy," destructive, and suicidal feelings. It will be recalled that whereas Dr. N. and the other staff members had long been aware of and concerned about such feelings, and had agreed that the patient's premature discharge planning necessitated a more active attempt to confront her with them, the patient's memory of the crisis still minimized external precipitating influences and emphasized her inability to contain the feelings any longer. Clearly she had a continuing need to deny the impact of others upon her. But she also acknowledged that a degree of trust in the staff was necessary for her to finally allow them to see how desperate she felt, and that this trust had taken time to develop.

It was only when the patient "broke down," becoming openly needy and demanding, enraged, and actively suicidal, that the "holding" capacities (Winnicott, 1960; Adler, 1977) of the hospital and its staff were fully tested. In the terms of this discussion, the staff's determination to protect the patient, and to continue with her despite their acknowledged frustration, were experienced by her as their successfully containing the noxious material she had allowed to escape, and with which she had assaulted them. She could thus feel relieved of the immediate necessity to protect herself against her own projected contents, and also less convinced of the destructiveness of these contents because others had survived them. At this point a self-perpetuating, destructive cycle of projective and introjective processes had begun to be converted into a benign cycle: projected contents could be reincorporated with less fear; the sense of emptiness resulting from lost (projected) contents could become less compelling; the intensity of rage could be reduced, thereby reducing the danger associated with future projections; and so on. The latter part of the patient's hospital course was consistent with the presence of such a benign cycle. She increasingly was able to "own" (i.e. experience as internal) her neediness and anger, but at the same time was making more efforts to seek realistic satisfaction from external sources.

The Rorschach record obtained at discharge, while documenting to a considerable extent these shifts in the course of treatment—in particular, the reduced sense of external threat, the more secure and less embattled boundaries, and the greater "containment" of troublesome feelings and impulses—also points to persistent obstacles to a normal internalization process. The benign cycle of projection and introjection, while clearly more possible for this patient than formerly, does not yet occur with freedom and spontaneity. She seems to trust her environment not to harm her, but does not trust it to satisfy her needs. Having acknowledged that strong wishes for nurturance, and rage at going unsatisfied, are "inside" herself, she is as yet unable either to give up these wishes comfortably or to actively seek their satisfaction to the extent it is possible. Her continuing tendency to isolation from others, her depressively toned experience of herself (perhaps especially relating to bodily processes or experiences), and her overreliance on the intellect at the expense of affective integration, all appear to be issues calling for further resolution if she is to feel freely capable of rewarding interchange with others.

Conclusion

This lengthy case discussion has been intended to illustrate a point of view, not to serve as a definitive statement of method. Obviously many refinements are both possible and needed if the same approach is to be applied by others. Obviously, too, the analytic approach I have employed is one of many that can be applied to the same material, and no doubt underplays important aspects of the material (the formal aspects of ego functioning, for example) that are emphasized by other approaches. All that having been said, however, I believe this approach represents a beginning toward an important objective: that of incorporating into Rorschach theory, and eventually into systematic research, some of the important insights derived from the object relations view of personality, psychopathology, and the therapeutic process. The essential principles adopted here are, I believe, consistent with the object relations literature, which emphasizes the central role of fantasy, especially projective and introjective fantasy, in personality development, and which formulates the workings of the therapeutic process largely in terms of how those fantasies influence, and are influenced by, the therapeutic relationship. As currently formulated, the guiding assumptions of this study have been: that an essential fact of human personality is a continuous representational process, which in normality is largely excluded from conscious thoughts after early childhood; that an important aspect of this process is the organization of experience, especially interpersonal experience, according to the gradually elaborated conception of the self and of other "objects" as containing (and/or being contained by) various items or substances; that personality change, including normal development, may be formulated in terms of alterations in this representational process; that the normal functioning of the personality requires that this process be carried on in relative comfort; and that individual psychopathology may be understood in terms of inadequacies, distortions, or disruptions of this normal process.

What are the potential advantages of such a viewpoint? In my opinion, there are two that are especially worthy of mention. First, it employs concepts that are closer to observation and to conscious experience than the postulated impersonal forces and structures cited in traditional ego psychological explanation. This is not to deny the importance of the latter type of approach; the enormous impact of impersonal factors (for example, chemical influences or electrical stimulation) on personality functioning is obvious, and it may someday be possible to specify the physical basis for such influences in detail. At least for the present, however, concepts like psychic energy or "system-ego" are limited in their explanatory value by their inferential distance from the data of observation. The concept of a normal representational process provides a nearer point of departure and leads to explanatory formulations that are potentially more parsimonious and more accessible to empirical test.

Second, this viewpoint avoids attributing unique qualities either to psychopathology or to the therapeutic situation. The former is understood in terms of the individual form taken by a universal process; the latter is regarded as a special case of human interaction, which in turn forms part of the broader class of exchanges with the environment. Thus explanations within the frame of reference of change in psychotherapy are intrinsically continuous with explanations of change, and of normal functioning, in other situations. Because of the nature of the concepts employed, the influence on the individual of a mother's care, a leader's example, or a therapist's interpretation would all be formulated in comparable terms—that is, with reference to the individual's current representational activity and difficulties therein.

As the foregoing implies, one might conceivably develop classification schemes for individual psychopathology and for therapeutic interventions based on this frame of reference. However, a more immediate need in exploring the usefulness of this approach is its systematic application to a greater number and variety of cases. This would be best accomplished through process studies, which would provide a more adequate examination of the *course* of change than has been possible in the present study. An accumulation of evidence of this kind, relating representational activity to developments in the treatment process, should help to evaluate the contribution of this point of view to a systematic understanding of therapeutic change.

References

Adler, G. (1977), Hospital management of borderline patients and its relation to psychotherapy. In: *Borderline Personality Disorders: The Concept, the Syndrome, the Patient*, ed. P. Hartocollis. New York: International Universities Press, pp. 307–323.

Athey, G., & Horwitz, L. (1980), Effects of non-exploratory therapy with a borderline patient. In: *Borderline Phenomena and the Rorschach Test*, ed. J. Kwawer, H. Lerner, P. Lerner, & A. Sugarman. New York: International Universities Press, pp. 203–226.

Blanck, G., & Blanck, R. (1974), *Ego Psychology: Theory and Practice*. New York: Columbia University Press.

Blatt, S., & Ritzler, B. (1974), Thought disorder and boundary disturbances in psychosis. *J. Consult. Clin. Psychol.*, 42:370–381.

——— Brenneis, C., Schimek, J., & Glick, M. (1976), Normal development and psychopathological impairment of the concept of the object on the Rorschach. *J. Abnorm. Psychol.*, 85:364–373.

Fisher, S., & Cleveland, S. (1958), *Body Image and Personality*. New York: Van Nostrand.

Hartley, D. (1978), Therapeutic alliance and the success of brief psychotherapy. Unpublished doctoral dissertation, Vanderbilt University.

Hartmann, H. (1939), *Ego Psychology and the Problem of Adaptation*. New York: International Universities Press.

——— Loewenstein, R. (1962), Notes on the superego. *The Psychoanalytic Study of the Child*, 17:42–81. New York: International Universities Press.

Horwitz, L. (1974), *Clinical Prediction in Psychotherapy*. New York: Aronson.

——— Frieswyk, S. (1980), The impact of interpretation on therapeutic alliance in borderline patients. Paper presented to the American Psychoanalytic Association, New York.

Kernberg, O. (1976), *Object Relations Theory and Clinical Psychoanalysis*. New York: Aronson.

Kohut, H. (1971), *The Analysis of the Self*. New York: International Universities Press.

Krohn, A., & Mayman, M. (1974), Object representations in dreams and projective tests. *Bull. Menn. Clin.*, 38:445–466.

Loewald, H. (1962), Internalization, separation, mourning, and the superego. *Psychoanal. Quart.*, 31:483–504.

Luborsky, L., Bachrach, A., Groff, H., Pulver, S., & Christopher, P. (1979), Preconditions and consequences of transference interpretations: A clinical-quantitative investigation. *J. Nerv. Ment. Dis.*, 167(7):391–401.

Meissner, W. (1981), Internalization in Psychoanalysis. *Psychological Issues*, Monogr. 50. New York: International Universities Press.

Pruitt, W., & Spilka, B. (1975), Rorschach empathy-object relationship scale (1964). In: *Handbook of Rorschach Scales*, ed. P. Lerner. New York: International Universities Press, pp. 315–323.

Sandler, J., & Rosenblatt, B. (1962), The concept of the representational world. *The Psychoanalytic Study of the Child*, 17:128–145. New York: International Universities Press.

Schafer, R. (1968), *Aspects of Internalization*. New York: International Universities Press.

——— (1972), Internalization: Process or fantasy? *The Psychoanalytic Study of the Child*, 27:411–436. New Haven: Yale University Press.

Winnicott, D. (1960), The theory of the parent-infant relationship. In: *The Maturational Processes and the Facilitating Environment*. New York: International Universities Press, 1965, pp. 37–55.

Chapter 5

AN OBJECT REPRESENTATION APPROACH TO RORSCHACH ASSESSMENT

HOWARD D. LERNER

Beginning with Rapaport, there has been an historically reciprocal and mutually beneficial relationship between psychoanalysis as a theory of personality and psychological test theory and test usage. While psychological testing within the Rapaport, Gill, and Schafer tradition has served as a source of generating ideas for theory construction and has provided a method for experimentally evaluating psychoanalytic concepts, psychoanalytic theory has provided a foundation of conceptualization which has given clinical testing a remarkable sweep never achieved previously. More recently, however, test theory has not kept pace with contemporary developments within psychoanalysis, and as such there is no greater need in psychological assessment today than the transposing of these theoretical advances into clinically useful, empirical test-related concepts.

Historically, psychoanalytic theory has evolved from a concentration on the identification of the instincts and their vicissitudes during psychosexual development, to a focus on defining the synthetic functions of the ego with particular reference to its defensive organization and role in adaptation, to a current interest in the early mother-child dyad and its decisive impact upon ego development and object relations. This evolution is in concert with a movement away from an ''experience-distant'' metapsychology couched in a mechanistic natural science framework of impersonal structures, forces, and energies to a more ''experience-near'' clinical theory primarily concerned with the representational world as a core focus (Stolorow and Atwood, 1979).

In terms of test theory, emphasis has shifted away from an exclusive consideration of thought processes toward a consideration of the quality and nature of object relations: that is, from a traditional emphasis on "ego structures," "cognitive style," and "impulse-defense configurations" framed in an abstract metapsychological language, to a more phenomenological interest in experiential matters such as "self- and object representations" described in a "middle-level language" (Mayman, 1976) geared toward formulating meaningful clinical generalizations about a patient. The comparatively recent elucidation of modern object relations theory, defined as the psychoanalytic approach to the internalization of interpersonal relations (Kernberg, 1976), coupled with a broadened psychodynamic developmental theory (Mahler, Pine, and Bergman, 1975) are now providing the conceptual foundation for a less mechanistic, more human, and more clinically anchored experiential psychoanalytic theory. Contemporary psychoanalytic theorists and researchers are progressively appreciating the complex interactions among early formative relationships, the level and quality of intrapsychic structures including thought processes and defensive organization, the internal representational world, and the nature of ongoing interpersonal relationships and the ways they are internalized and made part of the personality. Out of this object relations perspective has come a growing interest in the concept of object representation.

Object representations are considered to be complex mental schemata of objects encountered in reality (Sandler and Rosenblatt, 1962; Beres and Joseph, 1970). They evolve from and are intertwined with the developmental internalization of object relations and ego functions (Mahler, 1968); as object relations develop and mature, the schemata become increasingly articulated, differentiated, and integrated (Blatt, 1974). In essence, the development of representations is regarded as the *sine qua non* of ego development and adaptation. Blatt (Blatt, Brenneis, Schimek, and Glick, 1976) has viewed object representations in terms of a developmental process evolving out of an undifferentiated matrix through various epigenetic stages in which at each level of development representations become less concrete and immediate and more abstract and symbolic. Higher-level representations both reflect and provide psychological structure for the modulation of affects and for the capacity to transcend the immediate environment. Implicit in Blatt's formulations is the notion that impairment in the development of object representations can occur at any one of a number of levels (sensorimotor, perceptual, iconic, conceptual), which has important bearing on the underlying structure and organizing principles of different types of psychopathology.

Based on the principle that when a stimulus is consistently ambiguous its image is more readily shaped by the organizing characteristics of the representational world, a proliferating body of empirical research concentrating on the human response on the Rorschach—its content (Mayman, 1967;

Urist, 1973; Krohn and Mayman, 1974) and structure (Blatt et al., 1976; Spear, 1980)—has provided an important source of data for understanding the developmental process involved in object representation and its impairment in psychopathology. Collectively these studies, which utilize a variety of content-grounded and structurally oriented Rorschach scales, lend strong and impressive support to the construct validity of the concept of object representation and indicate the construct to be an enduring dimension of the ego which provides important information about the quality of interpersonal relationships to which an individual is predisposed. When one considers that the capacity for actual object relations depends largely on an individual's internal array of object images it becomes clear that an in-depth assessment of object representations is vital for a clear diagnostic understanding and treatment planning. According to Blatt, Wild, and Ritzler (1975):

> If the internalization of object relations results in the formation of psychic structures during normal development, then the internalizations of significant interactions between the patient and the analyst must play an important role in the therapeutic process. According to Loewald . . . , the analyst becomes available as a new object by eliminating, step by step, the transference distortions which interfere with the establishment of new object relationships. And it is the internalization of new and relatively undistorted relations with the analyst which leads to therapeutic change. The consideration of psychopathological conditions as disturbances in object relations and representations offers the potential for integrating the study of impairments in cognitive processes, interpersonal relationships, and the representation of the self and the object world within a theoretical model which has etiological, as well as therapeutic implications. [pp. 280–281]

While the object representation construct has received the lion's share of research attention as an empirical concept, the clinical usefulness of these research findings remains to be proven. In what follows, the first clinical application of three reliable and empirically validated object representation scales to the systematic appraisal of object representations will be demonstrated in a single case. The capacity of the Rorschach to tap the structure and contents of an adolescent girl's inner representational world will be examined in terms of providing clinically useful information about the perception and quality of interpersonal relationships to which she was predisposed and was later prone to "transfer" into a turbulent therapy relationship and a stormy hospitalization. This will be accomplished by first reviewing the scales to be utilized, providing a brief clinical introduction to the patient to be considered, outlining her psychological test performance with emphasis on her Rorschach, offering an in-depth object representational analysis of her human responses as measured on the Rorschach scales, and finally integrating the object relations analysis based on her Rorschach performance with the subsequent course of her treatment.

Rorschach Scales

The most comprehensive system for assessing the concept of object representation is represented in a Rorschach manual developed by Blatt et al. (1976). Rooted in the developmental theory of Werner (1948) and ego psychology, the system calls for the scoring of human responses in terms of the developmental principles of differentiation, articulation, and integration. Within each area, categories were established along a continuum based on developmental levels. *Differentiation* refers to the type of figures perceived—full human figures, quasi-human figures, human details, and quasi-human details. For *articulation*, responses are scored on the basis of the number and types of attributes ascribed to the figure. Seven types of attributes are specified, including size or physical structure, clothing or hair style, posture, sex, age, role, and specific identity. *Integration* of the response is scored in three ways: degree of internality of action, degree of integration of the object and its action, and degree of integration of the interaction with another object.

In one study presented in Blatt et al. (1976) the scoring system was applied to the Rorschach protocols of normal subjects over a twenty-year period. In this longitudinal study of normal development the investigators found a significant increase in the number of accurately perceived, well-articulated, full human figures involved in appropriate, integrated, positive, and meaningful interaction. In a second study the protocols of the normal subjects obtained at age seventeen were compared with the Rorschachs of a hospital sample of disturbed adolescents and young adults. In comparison with the normal sample, patients offered human responses that were significantly more inaccurately perceived, distorted, and partial, and that were seen as inert or engaged in unmotivated, incongruent, nonspecific, and malevolent activity. The results of both studies lend strong support to the construct validity of the concept of object representation and to the manual designed to assess it.

Based on recent clinical and theoretical advances in the area of borderline and narcissistic conditions, and the conceptual formulations of Kohut (1966, 1971) and Kernberg (1975, 1976), Urist (1973) developed a Mutuality of Autonomy Scale with a view toward assessing developmentally salient aspects of the structure of patients' object relations. This content-oriented scale is based on the assumption that the portrayal of relationships between animate and inanimate figures on the Rorschach reflect an individual's experience and definition of human relationships. The focus of the scale is on the developmental progression of separation-individuation from symbiosis to object constancy. Particular scale points refer to developmentally significant gradations in an individual's relationships—that is, the ability to attribute to others a separate, inherent identity and to cathect them in their own right.

In a construct validation study Urist (1977) correlated Rorschach ratings with independent measures of the mutuality of autonomy dimension consisting of written autobiographies and ratings by a ward staff. Based on a sample of forty adult inpatients covering a broad range of psychopathology, Urist found impressively high correlations among all measures. The results of this study lend support to the notion that there is an enduring consistency to an individual's conception of human relationships and that the Rorschach can be utilized effectively to systematically assess an individual's array of object representations. It appears that Urist's Rorschach scale is a reliable and valid measure of the mutuality of autonomy dimension within a patient's experience of self and others.

A third line of investigation is represented in a Rorschach scoring manual devised by Lerner and Lerner (1980) to assess the specific primitive defenses assumed to underlie as well as organize the internal object world of the borderline patient. Based on the theoretical formulations of Kernberg (1975), the system is comprised of various operationally defined measures of splitting, devaluation, idealization, projective identification, and denial. The basic units to be scored are those Rorschach responses containing an entire human figure, either static or in movement. The manual is divided into sections on the basis of the defense under consideration, and within each section Rorschach indices of the defense are presented and clinical illustrations offered. The sections on devaluation, idealization, and denial call for an identification of the defense as well as a ranking of the defense on a continuum of from high to low order. The human percept is systematically evaluated in terms of the action ascribed to the figure, the way in which the figure is affectively described, and the nature of the exact figure seen.

The first research project (Lerner and Lerner, 1980) planned to assess the scales' reliability and validity and involved a comparison of thirty Rorschach protocols of independently diagnosed borderline and neurotic outpatients. While the Rorschach records obtained from the two groups did not differ significantly with respect to the overall number of responses or number of human responses, the borderline subjects were found to use splitting, projective identification, low-level denial, and low-level devaluation significantly more than did the neurotic patients. The scale measures of splitting and projective identification proved particularly significant in discriminating the two groups. The obtained levels of inter-rater agreement were high enough to indicate that the scale is a reliable instrument. A second study was conducted comparing the Rorschach protocols of hospitalized adolescent and young adult borderline and schizophrenic patients (Lerner, Sugarman, and Ganghran, 1981) on the basis of independent RDC (Spitzer, Endicott, and Robins, 1975) and DSM-III descriptive diagnostic criteria. When borderline and schizophrenic were compared, a number of interesting results and patterns emerged which point to the scale's ability to distinguish the two groups. First, borderline patients are more object-oriented than schizophrenics in terms of generating more human responses of all types, especially of the more developmentally advanced full human and full quasi-human variety (Blatt et al., 1976). In terms of the actual defense scores, borderlines were distinguished from schizophrenics across the board on each defense considered, especially projective identification and denial. Of the various defense scores, the test indices of projective identification were most decisive in separating borderlines from neurotics and schizophrenics. These findings are consistent with the clinical and theoretical formulations of Modell (1963) and Rinsley (1979) that it is the stability of defenses and the degree of differentiation of object relationships which characterize borderline patients and distinguish them from schizophrenics. One of many implications of the data is that borderline patients present a discernible configuration of defenses that can be reliably and validly measured by means of the Rorschach.

Collectively, these empirical studies support the contention that the Rorschach can tap developmentally crucial parameters of the structure and contents of an individual's representational world. Further, these research findings have meaning in terms of one's day-to-day clinical use of the Rorschach. Patients with severe character pathology typically present a contradictory, vexing, and misleading picture to the clinician. In treatment, adverse clinical occurrences such as premature terminations, turbulent transference-countertransference struggles, negative therapeutic reactions, and treatment stalemates are more the rule than the exception. If such occurrences can be predicted in advance, then one can deal with them in a more knowledgeable and constructive fashion. The following clinical example will illustrate the types of treatment forecasts that can be made when one views the Rorschach from a more experiential, object relations perspective.

Clinical Introduction

B., a sixteen-year-old white high school student, presented as an attractive, voluptuous-looking, and distressed adolescent girl. Since the age of twelve, B. was engaged in delinquent behavior that included truancy, drug abuse, running away from home, and prostitution. Prior to her referral for long-term intensive psychiatric hospitalization, B. had become progressively anxious, sad, frightened, and confused, especially around the demands placed on her by a pimp to serve as a prostitute. Upon admission, B. complained, "I need to find out why I keep getting myself into messes—getting involved with people who aren't good for me—pimps and dealers."

B. is the youngest of two children in a decidedly enmeshed family in which generational boundaries were permeable; in which relationships, particularly between B., her brother, and her father, were highly eroticized; and in which communication styles were hostile-dependent. The family was characterized as having "been at war for many years"; intrafamilial transactions were described in terms of "battles," and the typical family affect seemed to be one of anger. B.'s father's family of origin featured extreme marital tension, in which he maintained an intense, enmeshed relationship with his mother. The mother, B.'s grandmother, pressured her children to achieve a great deal as a conduit to social status. B.'s father assumed responsibility for his mother's care even though she was outspoken in her disapproval of his marriage. B.'s mother came from an Eastern European immigrant family. One year prior to B.'s birth, her mother's father had died at age fifty, an event which evoked a prolonged and severe mourning reaction. B.'s older brother had a long history of school difficulties and violent outbursts for which he was seen in psychotherapy for several years.

B.'s birth was complicated by three factors: (1) it coincided with the anniversary of her maternal grandfather's death; (2) the pregnancy itself was confounded by the mother's lumbar disc problem; and (3) the mother suffered a postpartum depression. B.'s early memories revolve around her mother's physical problems and the constant fighting between her parents. She recalls fond memories of her father between the ages of six and ten, but the battle with her parents, especially her father, began when she was eleven and was initiated by arguments around curfews, dating, visiting with boys in her room with the door closed, drug use, and wearing makeup. B.'s explanation for the "war" with her father was that he stubbornly refused to accept the fact she was no longer "Daddy's little girl" or "his little hostess for his friends." According to B., he continually told her "how to live, how to dress, and what to do." B.'s delinquent behavior escalated, and when she was thirteen she and her father engaged in a physical fight which resulted in her running away from home, getting arrested, and being briefly hospitalized. The entire family was referred for family treatment, in which B. attempted to split the family and sabotage treatment by establishing an exclusive need-gratifying relationship with her mother and eventually "dropping out" of family therapy as well as her own individual therapy. At the time, B. contended that her mother could not protect her from the father and brother. B. pleaded with her mother to get a divorce so that the two of them, B. and her mother, could live together alone.

A year later, coincident with her brother's departure from private school, arguments with her father centering around her sexually provocative dress and behavior intensified and culminated in him calling her a "whore." B. became increasingly involved in dangerous activities which resulted in her being hospitalized, fearful that her life was being threatened by a pimp. B.'s understanding of her experimentation with drugs, prostitution, and older men was that it gave her a sense of independence, mastery, and control over her own life and distance from her parents. With an angry sense of disappointment, B. denounced her parents as incompetent and intrusive.

B.'s Rorschach

Apparent on many levels when B. was tested was a seductiveness having an inviting, teasing, "look but don't touch" quality to it. This was evinced in terms of dress, vague allusions to previous experiences, and a marked concern for privacy and secrets. B. exhibited what initially appeared to be an adequate and age-appropriate attunement to reality, albeit a rather benign, childlike, hysterical world view which upon closer inspection, especially detailed inquiry into her Rorschach responses, revealed a frightening and ubiquitous unsureness of her own perceptions, a suspiciousness of others, and a real fear of what she might find in her inner life. Scary and frightening themes of "deterioration," catastrophic destruction, and "sinister," "grotesque" forces uncontrollably emerged when B. was forced to rely on her own internal resources, when she looked inside herself, and when her pleasant, Pollyanaish image of reality was challenged. As long as pathways of action remained open to bind anxiety and forestall self-reflection, B. was able to make her world manageable by perceiving it as small, childlike, and harmless.

The following is a sample of the range and types of responses recorded on B.'s Rorschach. Her first response to Card I was "two dancers," rapidly followed by a second response, "two hands with a body and no head." On inquiry, when asked about the "head," B. snapped "I didn't make the blot." On Card II, B. offered the response "There are two chickens that are dancing," followed by "a butterfly or it could be two chickens fighting." On inquiry, the chickens, whether dancing or fighting, were seen "holding hands." There were seven responses to Card III, all involving small animals and representations of avoidance and flight: "two ants," "a butterfly," "sea horses," "a pair of high heel shoes," "dragonfly," "bow tie," and "two eagles." On Card IV, B. saw two cartoonlike "elks" and then "a monster"; on inquiry, she said "it looks like it's about to step on somebody—it looks like you're looking at it from laying on the ground." This was followed by "two snakes" and, when pressed on inquiry, "those are scary, just looks morbid . . . Jesus, don't get nitpicky. You sound like my grandmother."

Cards V and VI were seen as filled with small animals including ''a bat—sort of gloomy, grotesque,'' a benign ''butterfly,'' ''two alligators with their mouths open,'' a ''dragonfly,'' ''a heart,'' and ''two bears.'' Card VII began with ''Can I go?'' and then ''two little girls with ponytails skipping—stupid,'' followed by ''two heads of a wolf or a vicious dog—they're going to attack,'' which was swiftly followed by ''two bunny rabbits . . . a pair of dirty bunny rabbits,'' and ''a needle, yeah, a shot, you get shots from a doctor.'' After commenting ''This one's pretty,'' her responses to Card VIII were permeated with ''hungry animals—craving something.'' Card IX began with ''two German soldiers fighting . . . they look like the bad guys on Star Wars.'' On inquiry, B. stated: ''They have machine guns, they've destroyed things in the background . . . the colors look like it's deteriorating. Like in war, everything gets destroyed . . . gray looks like a destroyed city or other people they've shot at. Can you see that or am I nuts? . . . Don't tell me to show you!'' In a barely audible whisper B. says, ''I hope my boyfriend's here.'' Card X is broken down into several animal responses ranging from ''two insects having a little fight—don't they look like they're yelling at each other?'' through ''poisonous spine fishes—they'd be poisonous if they touched you, they'd sting'' to a ''person standing on their tippytoes'' and a ''guy's face.''

Object Representation Analysis

Evaluated using Blatt's structural scale, B.'s representations were differentiated on a fairly high developmental level—H and (H)—articulated mostly in terms of lower developmental levels of perceptual attributes (size, physical structure, clothes, and hairstyle), and integrated typically in terms of unmotivated, nonspecific action sequences either extremely malevolent or extremely benevolent. The nature of the interactions described tended to be either active-passive or active-active. B.'s percepts of the human object were for the most part full-bodied and accurately perceived, although skewed toward social stereotypes (populars). Nevertheless, there is relatively little elaboration of either perceptual or functional features; that is, her representations are conventional and lack richness. Further, there is an absence of internality in her representational world; activity is relatively unmotivated and lacking in purpose, intent, and direction. Those responses containing the highest degree of articulation, intentionality of motivation, and congruent integration of object and action were of an extremely malevolent, active-passive nature (e.g. ''monster,'' Card IV, and ''German soldiers,'' Card IX). B.'s representational world appears most appropriately differentiated, accurately perceived, and benign on superficial levels. It is when she is pushed or in any way pressured to explore further into herself or elaborate on her experience that an emphasis on externalizing modalities along paranoid-projective lines may be expected to emerge. Thus B. is capable of maintaining relatively superficial, socially appropriate functioning; but the absence of more positive, more richly elaborated and motivated representations suggests that B. lacks the integrative resources to move beyond superficial behavior to more mature, responsible, and independent levels of functioning. Diagnostically and structurally, this particular object representational configuration, featuring a broad spectrum of representations engaged in a variety of active-passive and active-active interactions as well as benign and malevolent transactions which collectively lack integration, is consistent with a picture of identity diffusion associated with the borderline range of psychopathology (Kernberg, 1975).

According to Urist's scale, B.'s representations portray relations between figures as oscillating between higher-level representations of figures engaged in parallel activity with little stated emphasis on mutuality to lower-level representations of relationships characterized by extreme malevolent control and a severe imbalance in the mutuality of relationships. Again, on representations which appear more superficial and childlike, B. is able to maintain a "live and let live" posture reminiscent of children's parallel play, in which a sense of mutuality is neither highlighted nor abrogated. On the other hand, representations which are more fully elaborated tend to feature a theme of malevolent control of one figure by another; one is seen as powerful and omnipotent and the other as helpless and vulnerable. Themes in B.'s protocol of being stepped on (Card IV) and of apocalyptic destruction (Card IX) may be considered to reflect a serious attack on the autonomy of the object (or a perceived attack on the self). Consistent with the Blatt structural scale, B.'s representations on this content scale depict a range of responses which span higher and lower developmental levels of mutuality of autonomy but lack consistency, consolidation, and integration. While B. can evoke higher, more advanced representations of objects engaged in parallel activity, the mutuality of this activity cannot be maintained under the impact of affective elaboration. As B. gains access, through elaboration, to deeper, less superficial levels of experience, representations portraying a severe imbalance in mutuality emerge, uncontrollably, in full force.

On the Lerner and Lerner scale, B.'s defenses were characterized by splitting, a tendency to perceive and describe objects in terms of overriding polarities, and devaluation, a propensity to depreciate, tarnish, and lessen the importance of both inner and outer objects. In terms of splitting, it appears that B. perceives (1) parts as distinct from wholes, and (2) good and bad part-objects. While B.'s particular polarities convey the division of good versus bad, her affective elaborations take several forms, including frustrating versus satisfying, dangerous versus benign, and friendly versus hostile. B.'s ubiquitous utilization of devaluation, a muted form of spoiling linked to envy

(Segal, 1973), ran the gamut from figures described in more primitive, blatant, socially unacceptable ways (e.g. Card IV) to figures described in negatively tinged but more civilized and socially acceptable ways. In keeping with the range of responses noted on the Blatt and Urist scales, it appears that B. does exhibit the dawning capacity to utilize higher-level, more neurotic defenses (higher-level, more muted forms of devaluation), but that access to these more advanced levels of defensive functioning lack the representational consolidation and integration to forestall or modulate the emergence of affectively charged, polarized representations. It appears that B.'s desperate attempt to make the world small, pleasant, and manageable is ultimately contaminated by the experience of "evil" and "gloom." Significant others have the capacity to be "all-good," but also "ugly" and "poisonous." That these frightening and lugubrious themes are not easily elicited and that B. experiences them as distressing to the point of asking "Am I crazy?" speaks to a strength and a willingness at times to seek others for reassurance and support.

An assessment of B.'s Rorschach protocol utilizing three object representation scales thought to tap separate but not mutually exclusive dimensions of object relations reveals a striking consistency across measures which is predictive of certain transference paradigms likely to unfold during B.'s hospital treatment. Well-differentiated yet superficially elaborated responses such as "two dancers" (Card I), "two little girls with ponytails skipping" (Card VII), and "a person standing on their tippytoes" (Card X) juxtaposed with less differentiated, but more malevolent responses such as "two hands with a body and no head" (Card I), "two heads of a wolf or vicious dog" (Card VII), and "poisonous spine fishes . . . poisonous if they touch you" (Card X) forecast an oscillation between relationship paradigms of a superficially integrated but extremely infantile and orally dependent nature and others that are nonintegrated, split-off, and malignant. Needs for omnipotent control over inner as well as outer objects may be expected to shift with protestations of being controlled, victimized, and left helpless. B. may be expected to flee from deeper levels of feeling, especially when faced with loss, and to seek substitute forms of gratification. The omnipotent control of others, especially parents and therapist, may represent a defensive effort to control her own inner objects, feelings, and impulses, the experience of which rapidly leads to disorganization, fear, and avoidance.

In summary, B.'s tendency to evoke extreme (infantile or malevolent), drive-drenched, nonmutual interchangeable representations of objects in action sequences coupled with content of an orally devouring, destructive, or extreme infantile nature points to a representational configuration consistent with an anaclitic personality structure (Blatt and Schictman, 1980) characterized by an early history of deprivation, unfulfilled neediness, and a profound sense of longing associated with a fear of abandonment and loss of gratification. When B. gains access to these feelings she readily becomes frightened, is easily overwhelmed, and, in attempting to protect herself from further disorganization, is prone to run away or, when blocked, to become subject to paroxysms of anger. It was suggested in B.'s test report that "treatment . . . be focused around a safe, reliable, and supportive relationship that can build on trust and explore B.'s inner world in a slow, sensitive manner appreciating both the stormy quality of her affects and the brittle nature of her defenses." In fact, B.'s hospitalization was permeated with numerous AWOL's, all associated with separations and loss (vacations). These losses appear to have triggered intense feelings of abandonment, pain, and disappointment, which swiftly led to suspiciousness and rage and which could then be contained only by denial, pseudoautonomy, and ultimately flight.

Treatment Course

During the initial phase of hospitalization B. appeared quite anxious and depressed, complaining bitterly to her therapist about her "fate," about her parents not loving her, not being able to protect her, and "dumping" her in the hospital because they did not want her anymore. As feelings of depression, a sense of worthlessness, and low self-esteem began to emerge, B. rapidly befriended a number of other acting-out patients in the hospital and engaged in most of the behavioral patterns, ranging from running away to sexual provocativeness, which were responsible for her admission in the first place. The most pressing issues in therapy at this time were autonomy and control. B. seemed very sensitive to any attempts to explore her behavior in the hospital. She was keenly secretive about her personal history, whether it was within the family or outside the family with friends. Her characteristic way of dealing with strong impulses or negative feelings was to run.

B. attempted to maintain a superficial posture in therapy, polite but distant (parallel activity). Her first AWOL was precipitated by her parents' vacation plans, which she effectively thwarted. Upon return, B. expressed satisfaction about having control over her parents and her own treatment (malevolent control). For several sessions B. presented herself as withdrawn, sad, powerless, and defeated. Then, as her therapist's vacation approached, B. repeated the same AWOL pattern. She returned shortly after the therapist departed and, upon the therapist's return, again absconded, staying away from the hospital for the same length of time her therapist had been away. Upon her return, B. seemed sullen, confused, "too frightened to talk." She mentioned her "crazy father who liked [her] body." She slowly and haltingly began to talk about her needs to be loved and hugged, and discussed how she felt compelled to flee when feeling abandoned and alone. In a poignant moment she stated: "I just wanted to be held and loved." It seemed in her struggle to cope with powerful feelings of loneliness and abandonment, B. attempted to gain a specious sense of independence, control, and mastery. An intrafamilial paradigm emerged in the hospital as B. viewed her therapist as the all-good object and her family therapist as all-bad and depriving—in the very fashion she had seen her father (splitting).

A relatively calm and tranquil period in therapy was juxtaposed upon sexually promiscuous behavior in the hospital as B. engaged in several verbal and some physical battles with patients and staff alike (splitting and devaluation). She talked about her use of boyfriends to gratify intense needs for physical closeness and support. B. began to see herself as a needy child who, somewhat too quickly for her own good, developed an adult body. These realizations evoked painful, anxious, and dysphoric feelings shortly followed by veiled threats to go AWOL, or to get drunk or high on drugs to alleviate the pain. Amid several AWOL's, reported nightmares and hallucinations, and continued battles with staff over limit setting, B. became involved in a torrid romantic relationship with another patient, T., the ex-leader of a motorcycle gang.

The relationship with T. was described in idyllic terms as different from all previous involvements with boys. She referred to him as a very sensitive person, one who cared about her as an individual and not just about her body. She seemed to treasure their ability to talk intimately and to respect each other's feelings. The "honeymoon" was brief, however; arguments stirred and soon B. complained that T. demanded too much of her energies and time, and that he was too intrusive. They fought frequently, and B. refused the staff's offer of help as an intrusion into her freedom and independence. Several violent arguments ensued which led the staff to restrict the couple from each other. B. began to wonder why she ended up in the same "rut" with every boyfriend. Surprisingly, B. became more engaged in hospital activities and quickly became chairperson of the Community Happenings Committee. She gradually climbed the privilege-responsibility ladder to the highest rung. She achieved increased differentiation from her family. These gains also prompted fears of separation and loss. She dreamed about herself baby-sitting for a little girl who almost got hit by a "big pimp car" when she ran out of the house. The dream seemed to be a paradigm of separation, vividly representing her fears of venturing out, of leaving home, and of growing up. Her fears intensified as she initiated plans for future discharge. Her school performance slowly declined as she began to introduce more historical information in therapy, especially data related to her delinquent activities.

As her therapist's vacation approached, B.'s initial reaction was: "Well, it doesn't matter, therapy doesn't do shit for me anyway." She withdrew from her therapist and the hospital community. She spent most of her time in bed, and became reentrenched with T. The staff experienced considerable difficulty keeping them physically apart. B. arrived for the first session following her therapist's vacation clad in black. She complained bitterly and persistently about her parents', especially her father's, disapproval of her impulsive and provocative plans to marry T. following discharge. When the therapist noted that B. experienced difficulty in her absence, B. snapped that her parents were always "screwing" her and it did not matter one way or the other if the therapist were present or absent. Following the session she engaged in a violent fight with T., ran from the hospital, and did not return (active-passive interaction, malevolent control, helplessness, and flight).

Conclusion

It appears that in the intensive hospital treatment of seriously disturbed patients over an extended period of time, the structure and content of the patient's internal representational world is expressed through a limited repertoire of representations of self and other, so that, amid turbulent relationship distortions and chaotic interactions, highly repetitive and enduring patterns of object relations become activated and, indeed, acted out within the transference and hospital setting. Further, it appears that paradigmatic patterns of object relating and experience can be understood through a close examination of Rorschach responses and that these patterns may be particularly evident in the analysis of the human response. Rorschach human percepts may be conceptualized as powerful projections of drive-infused, either conflict-determined or developmentally arrested, imprints of earlier, formative interpersonal relationships and transactions carried forward by the patient's continually assimilating, shaping, and coloring new situations, experiences, and relationships. The present study has attempted to demonstrate how three comprehensive systems for assessing the concept of the object along differential representational dimensions grounded in empirical research can be utilized clinically to enrich our therapeutic understanding of a troubled adolescent's inner representational world by forecasting treatment hazards, transference detours, and avenues of potential intervention and change. Although this case concluded dramatically in a negative therapeutic reaction, one can see how the vicissitudes of intense transference distortions and roadblocks, mirroring crucial developmental impediments in early patterns of object relating, were embedded in the structural configuration, thematic content, and temporal unfolding of a variety of human responses on the Rorschach, and later how these patterns became necessary and essential ingredients manifested and acted out in the treatment process. The Rorschach record and the complex vicissitudes of the therapeutic relationship mutually enrich and illuminate each other prospectively in diagnostic assessment and retrospectively in research. Consistent with Kernberg (1977), it appears that precursors of the therapeutic journey can be gleaned in advance from examination of the Rorschach and that an in-depth analysis of the internal representational world expressed through the human response may make it possible to explore simultaneously (1) the patient's affect organization, (2) the patient's ego organization and levels of defenses, (3) the predominant level of developmental arrest or regression, (4) the level of pathology, and (5) patterns of possible relationship distortions and transference-countertransference impasse.

Since Rapaport's work integrating psychological test theory with psychoanalysis, this field has until recently been comparatively neglected. These new perspectives, based on exciting advances in psychoanalytic theory, do not detract from his contributions, but rather enrich them and hold promise of providing a methodological framework and theoretical foundation for more sophisticated and innovative uses of the Rorschach.

References

Beres, D., & Joseph E. (1970), The concept of mental representation in psychoanalysis. *Internat. J. Psycho-Anal.*, 51:1–9.

Blatt, S. (1974), Levels of object representation in anaclitic and introjective depression. *The Psychoanalytic Study of the Child*, 29:107–157. New Haven: Yale University Press.

——— Brenneis, C., Schimek, J., & Glick, M. (1976), Normal development and psychopathological impairment of the concept of the object on the Rorschach. *J. Abnorm. Psychol.*, 85:364–373.

——— Schictman, S. (1980), Delinquency and personality organization. Unpublished manuscript.

——— Wild, C., & Ritzler, B. (1975), Disturbances of object representation in schizophrenia. *Psychoanal. Contemp. Sci.*, 4:235–288. New York: International Universities Press.

Kernberg, O. (1975), *Borderline Conditions and Pathological Narcissism*. New York: Aronson.

——— (1976), *Object Relations Theory and Clinical Psychoanalysis*. New York: Aronson.

——— (1977), The structural diagnosis of borderline personality organization. In: *Borderline Personality Disorders: The Concept, the Syndrome, the Patient*, ed. P. Hartocollis. New York: International Universities Press, pp. 87–121.

Kohut, H. (1966), Forms and transformations of narcissism. *J. Amer. Psychoanal. Assn.*, 14:243–272.

——— (1971), *The Analysis of the Self*. New York: International Universities Press.

Krohn, A., & Mayman, M. (1974), Object representation in dreams and projective tests, *Bull. Menn. Clin.*, 38:445–466.

Lerner, H., Sugarman, A., & Gaughran, J. (1981), Borderline and schizophrenic patients: A comparative study of defensive structure. *J. Nervous and Mental Disease*, 169:705–711.

Lerner, P., & Lerner, H. (1980), Rorschach assessment of primitive defenses in borderline personality structure. In: *Borderline Phenomena and the Rorschach*

Test, ed. J. Kwawer, H. Lerner, P. Lerner, & A. Sugarman. New York: International Universities Press, pp. 257–274.

Mahler, M. (1968), *On Human Symbiosis and the Vicissitudes of Individuation*. New York: International Universities Press.

——— Pine, F., & Bergman, A. (1975), *The Psychological Birth of the Human Infant*. New York: Basic Books.

Mayman, M. (1976), Psychoanalytic theory in retrospect and prospect. *Bull. Menn. Clin.*, 40:199–210.

Modell, A. (1963), Primitive object relationships and the predisposition to schizophrenia. *Internat. J. Psycho-Anal.*, 44:282–292.

Rinsley, D. (1979), The developmental etiology of borderline and narcissistic disorders. *Bull. Menn. Clin.*, 44:127–134.

Sandler, J., & Rosenblatt, B. (1962), The concept of the representational world. *The Psychoanalytic Study of the Child*, 17:128–145. New York: International Universities Press.

Segal, H. (1973), *Introduction to the Work of Melanie Klein*. New York: Basic Books.

Spear, W. (1980), The psychological assessment of structural and thematic object representations in borderline and schizophrenic patients. In: *Borderline Phenomena and the Rorschach Test*, ed. J. Kwawer, H. Lerner, P. Lerner, & A. Sugarman. New York: International Universities Press, pp. 321–340.

Spitzer, R., Endicott, J., & Robins, S. (1975), Research diagnostic criteria (RDC), *Psychopharmacol. Bull.*, 11:22–24.

Stolorow, R., & Atwood, G. (1979), *Faces in a Cloud: Subjectivity in Personality Theory*. New York: Aronson.

Urist, J. (1973), The Rorschach test as a multidimensional measure of object relations. Unpublished doctoral dissertation, University of Michigan.

——— (1977), The Rorschach test and the assessment of object relations, *J. Personal. Assess.*, 41:3–9.

Werner, H. (1948), *Comparative Psychology of Mental Development*. New York: Harper.

Chapter 6

AN OBJECT RELATIONS VIEW OF THE BORDERLINE DEFENSES: A RORSCHACH ANALYSIS

STEVEN H. COOPER and DAVID ARNOW

Schafer's monograph (1954) on psychoanalytic interpretation of the Rorschach sought to cast defense interpretation within the language and understandings of contemporary psychoanalytic ego psychology. The monograph explored Rorschach content as the primary source for defense interpretation. It is the aim of this paper to examine the reciprocal interaction between defense process and object relations as manifested on the Rorschach especially relating to borderline and other prestructural types of psychopathology (Gedo and Goldberg, 1973). Briefly, we view the development of primitive defenses as derivative from negative representations—defined by Schafer (1968, p. 192) as painful, threatening, and pessimistic—which in turn result from a noxious or unfavorable interpersonal environment. On this view the ego's regulatory, adaptive, and defensive functions interact reciprocally with the representational world. Schafer (1968, p. 195) among others (Hartmann, 1964; Kernberg, 1975) implicitly specifies this reciprocal interaction in stating that "negative representations weaken the incentive for, and efficiency of, adaptive efforts; they contribute to making instinctual and defensive aims all important."

In this chapter the term *borderline defense* is used to refer to the defenses of splitting, projective identification, primitive idealization, devaluation, and omnipotence. However, "borderline" here is not meant to suggest that these defenses are confined to the specific diagnostic category of borderline or are exclusive to any developmental stage. We maintain that the rationale for any specific diagnostic category revolves primarily around the nature of object relationships and an entire defensive organization (Lichtenberg and Slap, 1973). The word "defense" is also controversial as applied to these processes (splitting, projective identification, etc.), in that it generally implies the presence of a well-articulated intrapsychic structure built upon a consolidated representational world. The defenses of the infantile period, such as introjection, projection, denial, splitting, and projective identification, may alternatively be viewed as developmental stages in narcissistic organization (Freedman, 1981) or as "prestages" of defense (Stolorow and Lachmann, 1980) entailing a developmental inability for affirmation of events (denial) or integration of objects (as in splitting).

In the present chapter we will attempt to characterize various manifestations of these defenses on the Rorschach and in certain instances (particularly for splitting) distinctions will be made between developmental failures in integration of object representations and defense process per se, as defined by the effect of intrapsychic conflict on object relations. Sources for Rorschach interpretation of the borderline defenses as suggested in this chapter include content analysis and elements of the patient-examiner interaction.

Content Analysis, Object Relations, and the Borderline Defenses

A central question in Rorschach analysis of object relations and defense interpretation revolves around what constitutes the primary "object relations unit" in the content analysis. A related issue is whether or not a uniform object relations unit may be used to assess varying levels of psychopathology or clinical phenomena.

Lerner and Lerner (1980), in their valuable contribution to the study of "primitive defenses," restrict their analysis to percepts that include human figures static or in motion. In agreement with Smith (1980), we find this circumscription unduly limiting for interpreting protocols in which there is a relative or absolute absence of human figures. More important, however, "borderline" defenses are more profitably examined with a broader data base regardless of the number of human responses. A rationale for broadening the data base to include human, animal, object, and natural phenomena percepts will follow.

From a methodological standpoint, the human figure percept is the most direct way of making inferences about object representations. Most empirical studies (Krohn and Mayman, 1974; Spear, 1980) have, like Lerner and Lerner (1980), employed the human figure as the central unit in content analysis examining object relations. For in using the human figure as an object relations unit one infers a direct relationship, a correspondence of identity, between an individual's interpersonal history and the form of his internalized images of others. Mayman (1967) summarized research examining human figure percepts on the Rorschach and found that such percepts are associated with general capacity for forming object relationships, including specific abilities for empathy and identification. Additionally, Mayman reported correlations between content of human responses and independent clinical appraisals of the quality of interpersonal relationships. Blatt and Ritzler (1974) found that distortions in human responses on the Rorschach increased in frequency as severity of pathology increased. Blatt and his coinvestigators (see Blatt and Ritzler, 1974; Blatt and Wild, 1976) have posited parallels between object relations and thought disorder and in so doing have rated human figure percepts in terms of a continuum of boundary disturbance along three dimensions: differentiation, articulation, and integration. These investigations conceptualize logical incongruities and affective elaboration of percepts (quality of thinking) in terms of the degree to which object representations are differentiated. In their work, the fusion of percepts and ideas is understood as following parallel lines with various potential for boundary distortion.

Summarily, it may be said that the capacity for human figure Rorschach responses that are well-articulated and clearly formed percepts is associated with increasing degrees of psychological health in both clinical (Blatt and Ritzler, 1974) and nonclinical samples (Holt and Luborsky, 1958), capacities for empathy (Pruitt and Spilka, 1964), identificatory relationships (Kelly and Fiske, 1951), and object relatedness.

A number of clinical accounts have highlighted the predominance of part-object relations and representations in the severe pathologies (Klein, 1946; Kernberg, 1966, 1975; Schafer, 1968; Volkan, 1976). While borderline and schizophrenic patients appear to be able to form at least as many human figure percepts as other clinical populations (Exner, 1978), it is not necessarily the only or perhaps even the most conclusive index of object relations or the primitive defenses for such patients. We do not wish to suggest that there is a simple correspondence between fragmentary experiences or part-object relationships and the propensity for perceiving part-human, animal, part-animal, or inanimate objects on the Rorschach. We do propose, however, that the more the patient experiences various levels of integrative failure, the more emergent is a pattern of fluid, disjointed percepts on the Rorschach that requires attention toward all responses in the interpretation of defenses and object relations. Thus Rorschach responses of animal percepts and percepts consisting of parts of objects, animate and inanimate, may contribute vital information to the understanding of an individual's object relations. For example, in the most primitive stages of splitting (prior even to the capacity for defensive splitting) self- and object representations are highly fluid and chaotic, often with whole human figure images alternating with part-human, animal, and inanimate object percepts. On the Rorschach, an individual prone toward using the defense of primitive idealization may fluctuate between whole figure responses such as "a king" or "Willie Mays" and inanimate or part-human responses such as "King's crown" or "It looks like a baseball bat used by a famous baseball player."

Schafer's differentiation (1968) between primary and secondary process representations may be applied to the analysis of object representations on the Rorschach. Schafer objects to the concept of object representation because it has no singular implication for how stable, accurate, external, or reflectively processed the representation may be. He characterizes secondary process object representations as relatively accurate, stable, temporally preserved, and reflectively processed. Primary process object representations within this schema are more unstable, inaccurate, and unreflectively processed. Schafer's proposal of two poles of object representation is not intended to dichotomize but instead to suggest that several forms of object representation may coexist and that the primary and secondary processes interact on all levels of organization. For example, objects that tend toward complex wholeness in secondary process thinking may concomitantly be represented, through primary process ideation, by a malleable array of wholes or parts. Schafer characterizes primary process object representations as "fluid and either simplistically global or fragmentary and uncoordinated." It is difficult to dichotomize between primary and secondary process object representations on the Rorschach as defined by Schafer. There is certainly no direct correspondence between the human figure percept and secondary process object representations on the one hand and animal or part-object percepts and primary process object representation on the other. Nonetheless, applying Schafer's concept of primary and secondary process representations implies the use of a sufficiently differentiated range of content to reflect the underlying characteristics of these contrasting representational modes. This theoretical position is consistent with the clinical observations that severely disturbed patients produce responses that either shift between or combine primary and secondary process. Likewise the fluidity and fragmented content of these responses may often represent highly significant but unintegrated aspects of object relations. The weight of theory and clinical observation both suggest the need for breadth of content in the Rorschach interpretation of defenses and object relations.

SPLITTING

The concept of defensive splitting so central in the object relations theory of Kernberg (1976) and others has been criticized on logical and empirical grounds (Pruyser, 1975; Dorpat, 1979, 1981). Many authors have also pointed to the need for classifying patterns and levels of splitting in developmental terms (Lichtenberg and Slap, 1973; Pruyser, 1975; Freedman, 1981; Stolorow and Lachmann, 1981). We will review various theoretical viewpoints on defensive splitting and propose a method for understanding manifestations of splitting on the Rorschach.

Kernberg (1975) emphasizes the crucial importance of specific defense operations in the diagnosis and treatment of the borderline personality organization. Splitting is seen as a central defense, "an essential mechanism preventing diffusion of anxiety within the ego and protecting the positive introjections and identifications." Splitting, then, for Kernberg, refers to an inability to bring together aggressively and libidinally determined self- and object images and implies the necessity for an individual to actively keep separate object representations, introjections, and identifications of opposite quality; it is the central mechanism for the defensive organization of the ego before object constancy has developed. Subsidiary defensive operations consisting of primitive idealization, devaluation, omnipotence, and denial all function in one manner or another to reinforce splitting and to help the individual compensate for a developmental incapacity to synthesize positive and negative introjections and identifications. Kernberg (1975) views most regressive borderline functioning, including primitive thinking (Urist, 1980) and impaired object relations as derivative from this predominance of splitting.

According to Kernberg (1967) and Mahler (1968) splitting is an adaptive pattern of infantile life dictated by the immaturity of the psychic apparatus. On this view early infantile experience gives rise to the organization of two sets of memory traces consisting of pleasurable-satisfying and punishing-painful stimuli which gradually build up to constitute separate undifferentiated self-object representations, one an "all-good" self-object representation and the other an "all-bad" self-object representation. With increasing abilities to make discriminations between inner and outer, the previously undifferentiated self-object representations become distinct. Under optimal conditions "good" and "bad" become integrated into a whole self-representation which conforms more closely to actual interpersonal experiences; concurrently, positive and negative object images coalesce into a complete object representation.

Stolorow and Lachmann (1980) maintain that defensive splitting—the active keeping apart of oppositely valenced self- and object representations—can operate only after a minimum degree of integration of the object image. On this view splitting operates defensively to dissociate or experientially separate object images in order to reduce early and intense ambivalence conflicts; splitting of object images occurs secondary to intrapsychic conflict. Object representations are split (as within fantasy formations) in order to selectively experience aspects of the representational world that are linked to one side of an internally conflicted view of an object. Stolorow and Lachmann maintain that the fluid and rapid alterations of contradictorily valenced images in connection with the same external object is more likely to reflect an arrest in development at a "prestage" of splitting characterized by an inability to integrate affectively contrasting representations. Defensive splitting is present only in those instances in which contrasting good and bad object images are linked to two or more separate external objects, as in split transferences (in order to ward off pressing ambivalence conflicts).

Lichtenberg and Slap (1973) distinguish between splitting that occurs with reference to the mental contents in infantile life and defensive utilization of the splitting of representations. The former refers to an adaptive pattern in infantile life, as outlined by Kernberg (1967) and Mahler (1968), prior to the developmental stage in which good and bad self- and good and bad object representations coalesce. Lichtenberg and Slap view this splitting of mental contents in infantile life as a more "passive" stage of defensive activity that results from the ego's relative inability to both perceive objects as a totality and to register whole object images in the context of various affective experiences. Lichtenberg and Slap propose that the defense mechanism of "splitting of representations" refers to those instances in which splitting acts to separate strong feelings and urges when these feelings would provoke anxiety if experienced simultaneously toward the object or the self. The defense mechanism of splitting, then, is said to function after the developmental achievement of being able to perceive the object as a totality but at those times when the object has become the source and/or target of intolerable ambivalence. At such times the representation of the object is split so that one set of emotions and accompanying self-representation are experienced toward one object while the contrasting emotional set and its self-representation are attached to another object. Dorpat's admonitions (1979, 1981) regarding the questionable use of the term "splitting" to denote a defensive activity in which psychic contents are split is relevant here. Dorpat suggests that psychic content such as affects and representations cannot be split and that to employ the term "splitting of representations" (Lichtenberg and Slap, 1975) is to commit the "fallacy of reification." While Dorpat's criticism of the term splitting is often astute, we maintain that the nuances of the term as proposed by Lichtenberg and Slap are meaningful in delineating a continuum of integrative failure for Rorschach analysis.

Dorpat has also argued that denial and not splitting is the central defense in the development and later defensive organization of borderlines. He posits, as does Rubinfine (1962), that denial, not splitting, is directed against disturbing percepts of early objects which might stimulate aggression and thus threaten the loss of the object. In contrast, we maintain that the splitting of representations as well as prestages of splitting are separate from denial because they do not rely on the disavowal of entire percepts (in interactions with objects and in the perception of objects on the Rorschach) and substitution of fantasy. Rather, splitting is demonstrated in the tendency to perceive and describe others in terms of polarities (Pruyser, 1975) and to separate representations involved in disturbing percepts.

Grala (1980) proposes a developmental continuum for splitting that might be thought of as beginning with Stolorow and Lachmann's prestages of splitting (1980) and ending with a more advanced developmental level of splitting consistent with the rapprochement subphase of separation-individuation. In this view prerapprochement splitting refers to a developmental limitation on the part of the infant whereby it is unable to form cohesive aggregates in the representational world. At this point in development splitting refers to a constellation of part self- and object representations which are not yet integrated or sorted accordingly to their predominant affective valences; it is synonymous with fragmented organization of the ego, cognitive immaturity, and primitive internalized object representations. With regard to object representations it is the limitation for self- and object impressions to coalesce into cohesive representations that cause even minimal divergences in affective connotations of objects to result in rifts within the representational world. Grala suggests that splitting as a defensive operation is linked with the rapprochement subphase. On this view, splitting becomes a resolution of the fear that the withholding or bad attributes of the mother might override the gratifying attributes; a cleft between opposite representations is sought to hold such a possibility in abeyance.

While splitting always reflects an integrative failure (Freedman, 1981) we attempt to differentiate broadly between two divergent forms or "stages" of splitting. We are in general agreement with Stolorow and Lachmann (1980) that the operation of defensive splitting is suggested in those instances in which contrasting all-bad and all-good object images are associated with two or more external objects in order to ward off ambivalence conflicts. A qualitatively different stage of splitting (referred to as a "prestage" by Stolorow and Lachmann and as a pathological incapacity of the ego to integrate representations of the primary object by Lichtenberg and Slap) involves the developmental inability to synthesize mental aggregates resulting in self- and object representations that are chaotic and highly malleable. We retain the term "splitting" for both of these processes, preferring to conceptualize the differences in developmental terms as stages of splitting.

Kernberg (1975) views both "stages" of splitting as defensive, but in so doing assumes that the appearance of unintegrated representations in a borderline personality stems from attempts to reduce anxiety and protect identifications and introjections: "This division of internalized object relations into 'good' and 'bad,' " he writes, "happens at first simply because of a lack of integrative capacity of the early ego. Later on, what originally was a lack of integrative capacity is used defensively by the emerging ego in order to prevent the generalization of anxiety and to protect the ego core built around positive introjections'' (p. 25). In agreement with Stolorow and Lachmann we see a fundamental difference in terms of type of pathology for patients who seek to protect an object relationship from aggression in contrast to those who demonstrate fluid and rapidly alternating object images and an inability to integrate affectively contrasting object representations. Similarly, defensive splitting of self-representations may serve to maintain positive views of the self while prestage splitting may be associated with less defensively motivated shifts in self-experience. It is our experience that borderline patients with varying degrees of pathology demonstrate both types of splitting on the Rorschach in conjunction with emerging content and particular conflicts.

In contrast with Lerner and Lerner (1980), who restrict evidence of splitting on the Rorschach to human content, we examine all objects—humans, animals, inanimate objects, natural phenomena—in terms of the tendency for such objects to be perceived in polarized terms. As noted earlier in this paper and also by Smith (1980), it is important to broaden the data base for making inferences about splitting and other borderline defenses.

Early or prestage splitting as manifested on the Rorschach is most apparent in instances when a single image is split into disparate parts of opposite emotional or subjective valence. Grala (1980) refers to this Rorschach manifestation of splitting as the ''fragmentation of percepts,'' in which the ability to integrate incompatible percepts is hampered by the tendency to strictly separate representations of opposite emotional valence. This leads to descriptions of objects incongruously combined. With an increased capacity to integrate affectively contrasting object representations, the individual may either be able to screen out disparate or incongruous details of the percept or to integrate such details in a more logical or benign manner. Rorschach percepts demonstrating early stages of splitting include the following response to Card VI: ''That looks like a river with the upper half being majestic and divine and the other half evil and sinister.'' Lerner and Lerner (1980) present similar examples, referring strictly to human figures, in which single human figures are seen in sharply polarized affective dimensions. In both our example and Lerner and Lerner's, images usually seen as uniform are separated into parts having opposite or strikingly different affects. As Grala (1980) points out, the propensity for juxtaposing incongruous details when such incongruities represent oppositely valenced emotions or drives) inherent in many fabulized combination responses suggests a possible strong relationship between splitting and the fabulized combination response. The following is an example of a fabulized combination response to Card VII suggestive of early stages of splitting: ''It looks like a mean, ferocious pig with a peaceful angel sitting on its head.'' This example demonstrates the polarities of aggression and peacemaking with concomitant object images that are depreciated and idealized within the fabulized combination percept. In fact the often cited preponderance of fabulized combinations among borderline patients (e.g. Singer and Larson, 1981) may be the result of a more general integrative failure implicit in the early stages of splitting.

Prestages of splitting are manifest also in Rorschach percepts containing fluid or contradictory verbalizations about objects. Such percepts contain sometimes chaotic and invariably malleable, polarized self- and object representations. The following example is from the Rorschach of a young adult unhospitalized male borderline and reflects extreme fluidity and alternating, radically polarized self- and object representations:

> *Card III.* Those are two hip Boston women at an all-female disco, still carrying their bags (laughter), wearing high heels and in love with each other because they're so identical. Uh, between their breasts is not white, it's red, so that would mean that they're not capable of giving milk to each other, but their hearts have only rage or something. But they have reproduction on their mind, because this is somewhat of a fetus, sort of gangling, hanging fetus with an umbilical cord. And then of course you have the sticky road ahead of them which lies between them which would be this grayish design between them. But they're bitches, because their hands are sort of knifelike pointing daggerlike at themselves. This is also like the dancing, this is sort of like a guitar.

While this response revolves around a consistently depriving and self-absorbed female figure, alternating themes of love and rage and birth and death (danger) are presented in extraordinarily fluid fashion. Experiences split between the wish for nurturance and feelings of rage and destruction appear in shuffling, vacillating fashion. While hypomanic denial is apparent in the magical use of color, there is no interpretation of color in the service of avoidance or minimization of aggressive or dysphoric affective states. Nor is the presence of hostile percepts of themes accompanied by apparent oppositionalism or anxiety and then substituted with frankly Pollyannaish or euphoric thematic content. Instead what emerges is what Freedman (1981, p. 269) has called the earliest and most basic form of splitting, "fragmentation," in which the individual experiences disconnected and simultaneous experiences of images, thought fragments, and contradictory verbalizations. Milder forms of this use of splitting are demonstrated in Rorschach percepts supplied during free association: initially described as benign, these become transformed into hostile or aggressive images during inquiry, with little resolution as to the affect or intentions of the object. For example, on Card IV the response, "It looks like a friendly man,'' becomes on inquiry: ''Now he looks angry, like he's coming at me; first he's friendly, then he's murderous, I can't tell.'' The response suggests that self- and object representations are fluid and bespeaks an inability to integrate affectively contrasting representations.

Later stages of splitting, or the ''defense mechanism of the splitting of representations'' (Lichtenberg and Slap, 1973), are manifest in Rorschach percepts containing all-good and all-bad object images linked to two or more separate perceived objects. Lerner and Lerner (1980) provide an excellent example of a Rorschach percept consisting of two human figures representing opposite emotions or ideas: ''Two figures, a man and a woman. He is mean and shouting at her. Being rather angelic, she's standing there and taking it'' (p. 260). This response suggests the operation of defensive splitting aimed at mitigating or warding off an ambivalence conflict and possibly the need to protect an object relationship from aggressive feelings. Primitive idealization, apparent in the description of the female figure as angelic, further suggests a defensive effort to fortify the object (albeit through masochistic or martyrlike resolution) in the face of considerable aggression. We do not restrict the notion of polarization to affective or drive dimensions (libidinally and aggressively tinged object representations). Rather, splitting is also suggested when sequences of responses include objects that differ along dimensions such as strength, power, honesty, and durability. For instance, on Card VIII the response, ''Two animals, one is a scavenger, a parasite, the other is strong and beautiful,'' suggests that splitting may be viewed as the process whereby opposing conceptions and affective descriptions of the object are dissociated and kept apart in order to alleviate ambivalence conflicts. This percept contains polarities of oral dependency versus self-sufficiency and depreciation versus idealization, suggesting dissociated elements of a potential conflict revolving around a conception of the self as needy or dependent (or the wish to eschew the reliance of the self on objects). In either case, the predominance of split images—split in terms of affective coloration, intention of the object, or drive qualities—seeks to protect the self from intolerable ambivalence.

The same interpretive principles about splitting apply to response sequences (Lerner and Lerner, 1980) which entail rapid shifts from libidinally to aggressively determined objects or other polarized concepts. For example, the following response to Card V involves a sequence of percepts in which an animal described with one affect is followed by another animal percept of opposite affective coloration, physical description, and intention: ''A bat, an ugly vicious bat'' followed by ''A beautiful butterfly in flight, it's harmless, just flying.'' Another example of defensive splitting demonstrates the patent shift from a libidinally tinged object representation to a more aggressive one: (Card III) ''A woman with large breasts'' followed by ''A mushroom cloud from an atom bomb.'' This percept indicates an interest in receiving nurturance and love only to be immediately invaded by rage: defensive splitting seeks to separate these two feelings in the service of protecting the longed-for object from overriding anger and rage.

Projective Identification

Melanie Klein (1946) initially described projective identification both as a primary mode of object relating and a defense involving sequential projection and reintrojection of both good and bad split-off parts of the self. This leads both to a blurring of self-object differentiation and to an identification with the object, now regarded as part of the self:

> In so far as the mother comes to contain the bad parts of the self, she is not felt to be a separate individual but is felt to be the bad self. . . .
>
> Much of the hatred against parts of the self is now directed towards the mother. This leads to a particular form of identification which establishes the prototype of an aggressive object relation. I suggest for these processes the term 'projective identification'. When projection is mainly derived from the infant's impulse to harm or to control the mother, he feels her to be a persecutor. [p. 8]

Also included in Klein's original concept are fantasies of forcefully entering the object (via an act of projecting a part of the self ''into'' an object) and destroying it from within or taking possession of the object. Significantly, an object image is then introjected which includes the object's real or fantasied reactions both to the specific content of projections and to the projective process itself. Though including both good and bad parts of the self, Klein focuses primarily on the dangers associated with excessive projective identification in the sphere of bad self- and object representations. Here the individual is prone to experiencing strong retaliatory anxiety coupled with fears of retaliation in kind for specific projections or fantasies surrounding the projective process, e.g. expectations of being hurt, controlled, possessed, or aggressively penetrated from without.

Clinically, the concept of projective identification has been utilized to illuminate transference phenomena in work with schizophrenic patients (Rosenfeld, 1952; Bion, 1956; Searles, 1963) and with paranoid characters (Heimann, 1957). More recently, Kernberg (1975) has viewed it as an important defense used by borderline patients; he believes that projective identification is a primitive or unsuccessful kind of projection which leads the patient to ''continue to experience the impulse as well as the fear of that impulse while the projection is active'' (p. 31). This leads to a ''fearful empathy'' with the target of the projected aggression and a need to control that object to avoid counterattack. The need to avoid counterattack may also mobilize hypervigilant scanning of the environment for potential sources of danger (Sugarman, 1980). Kernberg distinguishes between this defense and simple projection in that the latter involves a more complete if not exaggerated differentiation between the drives and affects experienced by self and object, with projected impulses tending to be perceived as clearly ego-alien. This is a distinction shared by Ogden (1979): "In projection one feels psychological distance from the object; in the projective identification one feels profoundly connected with that object" (p. 359). Sugarman (1980) points out that while projection often leads simply to hyperalertness to attack from a threatening object, projective identification involves the presence of hyperalertness in conjunction with expressions of primitive rage and aggression directed at the object containing hated parts of the self.

Much confusion surrounding the concept of projective identification stems from the fact that many contributions to the literature have tended to emphasize either its defensive, pathological aspects or its adaptational aspects (Ogden, 1979). For example, in contrast to Kernberg, Malin and Grotstein (1966) conclude:

> It is one of the most important mechanisms by which growth and development take place through object relations. This mechanism can be described as one in which objects and associated affects are re-experienced on a new integrative level so that further synthesis and development can take place within the ego. . . . In our view projective identification seems to be the way in which human beings are able to test their own inner psychic life by projecting psychic contents out into the environment and perceiving the environment's reaction to these projected parts of oneself. [p. 31]

Further contributing to the complexity of this concept is the fact that, even when viewed primarily as a defense, projective identification, in contrast to other defenses, involves a cycle of multistep processes occurring between self and object. Built into this defense are notions concerning both a psychological event, splitting off a part of the self and projecting it into another, and the multifaceted intrapsychic and interpersonal ramifications of the projection.

Ogden (1979) integrates numerous aspects of projective identification, describing it as "a psychological process that is simultaneously a type of defense, a mode of communication, a primitive form of object relationship and a pathway for psychological change" (p. 362). He describes projective identification as a process composed of three phases. The first involves fantasies of the wish to rid oneself of self-representations that are threatening to the larger configuration of self-representations or are in danger of being destroyed from within. In fantasy, parts of the self are projected into others to safeguard them from dangerous internal attack or for the purpose of controlling others. "This type of fantasy is based on a primitive idea that feelings and ideas are concrete objects with lives of their own" (p. 358). The second, or "induction," phase involves the projector forcing or pressuring the recipient to "experience himself and behave in a way congruent with the projective fantasy" (p. 359). Finally, and less directly relevant to this discussion, is a reinternalization phase, which depending on the recipient's degree of psychological integration (in the area of the specific projection) determines whether the process will have a pathological or a growth-facilitating outcome.

On the Rorschach we assess, as do Lerner and Lerner (1980), the presence of projective identification by looking for manifestations of the components of this complex process, key elements of which include (1) fantasies of concretely putting a dangerous or endangered part of the self into another object in order to control or harm the object or to safeguard part of the self (Klein, 1946; Ogden, 1979); (2) fearfully empathizing with objects bearing projections of aggressive self-images (Kernberg, 1975); (3) hyperalertness to external threat or attack coupled with expressions of primitive rage (Kernberg, 1975; Lerner and Lerner, 1980; Sugarman, 1980).

The presence of projective identification is suggested by responses in which a figure puts a substance or a feeling into another object for the purpose of controlling or destroying the recipient. The following response illustrates this theme through a highly concrete image:

> *Card X*. These tarantulas are injecting their poison into these grasshoppers.

While the response does involve projection and the concomitant preoccupation with external threat and victimization, projective identification is inferred by the theme of actively (and with aggressive intent) projecting a part of one object into another. Fantasies of placing hated or dangerous parts of the self into other objects, in contrast to simply ridding self of those parts, is an important distinction between projective identification and projection. As will be seen throughout, projective identification involves fear of an object and the establishment of a particular type of relationship based on that fear.

> *Card III*. These are the forces and energies that are controlling what these two people are doing. The force is going to make them have a bloody flight.

Classically, the above response would be interpreted as a projection of aggression leading to fears of being controlled (Schafer, 1954). This interpretation is true, but fails to adequately consider an underlying fantasy which involves a concrete transplanting of feelings from one object to another. This kind of response includes both fears of external threat and fantasies involving the active transfer of toxic feeling states from one object to another.

The fantasy of causing harm by placing dangerous substances (representing hated parts of the self) into an object is not always expressed explicitly. Implicitly, this fantasy underlies the following group of responses: animals or insects capable of injecting poisons; parasites; and poisonous plants or substances. We infer the presence of projective identification in all such responses.

The dynamic of projecting a good but internally threatened part of the self into an object to protect it from destruction by other parts of the self is suggested by responses in which a valued but vulnerable object is protected from danger by placing it in another object.

> *Card X.* These little innocent, weak-looking creatures seem to be trying to get inside these pink things. Maybe they are trying to find refuge from this world of vicious-looking crabs and insects.

Here splitting, which for Klein and Kernberg is a prerequisite for the operation of projective identification, is also suggested by the extreme polarization of innocent creatures versus vicious crabs and insects. As with the other responses discussed, this kind of response crosses the boundary from projection to projective identification in that the experience of external threat (mirroring the state of the internal object world) is accompanied by fantasies in which a self-representation is placed into an object for the purpose of establishing a particular type of "relationship" with that object.

Kernberg's description (1975) of the fearful empathy that accompanies projective identification focuses on the fact that an individual simultaneously fears attack from an object (due to the projection of all-bad, all-aggressive images) and yet identifies or feels a bond with the object as a result of experiencing the same feelings as those which have been projected onto the object (as a result of weakened ego boundaries in the face of aggression). It is the presence of this bond which locks the individual into a relationship with an object, albeit a relationship defined by an aggressive need to control and to ward off attack.

On the Rorschach, fearful empathy between the subject and a recipient of particular projections is often observed in the subject's own reactions to his responses:

> *Card VI.* This looks like an evil cat that's been run over. Poor thing. It really makes me mad that people do things like that all the time.

First, this response includes a statement of feared attack from an object, i.e. the cat, having become evil as a result of the projection of aggressive self-images. The dangerous object is then attacked, run over. At this point, when the self and object (following projection) are both felt to be aggressive, the basis is established for a fearfully empathic bond and the subject expresses concern and later anger ("It really makes me mad") over the object's fate. Note how the subject's anger represents a further identification with the presumably angry object (the run-over cat), a victim of the subject's own aggression. Commiseration, as it were, with the victim of one's own aggression, in the face of likely retaliation, is the hallmark of fearful empathy and is a good indication of projective identification.

In conjunction with the expression of aggression, fearful empathy may also be expressed through direct statements of identification with an object who, as the result of projection, is now seen as hostile: "An angry man. I'm angry now too"; "A face full of hatred, just how I feel sometimes." This type of response also points to the impairment of ego boundaries. Secondarily, this kind of identification with the aggressor involves an effort to control or minimize the threat from a now dangerous object by saying in effect, "Don't hurt me, we're really on the same side."

We also suggest that the texture determinant, when occurring with indications of external threat or overt aggression, also provides likely evidence for the type of "ongoing empathy" (Kernberg, 1975) resulting from projective identification. In the context of aggressive responses, the texture determinant may signify the need to feel assured that one is safe from the danger of retaliation.

> *Card I.* Kind of an ominous picture. Just like those eyes are staring out through some sort of mask. It looks almost like cloth, furry around the edges, like those woolen masks that bank robbers sometimes use.

Texture is present with a clear indication of external threat (ominous, eyes staring). The response is suggestive of the tendency to project aggression and of a need for a nurturant, approving response from objects. Fear of the now dangerous object, accompanied by a need for its approval and thus a degree of rapport with the object, represents an important element of fearful empathy.

The final element of projective identification is the copresence of hyperalertness to attack or external threat and expressions of primitive rage (Lerner and Lerner, 1980; Sugarman, 1980). While basically agreeing with Lerner and Lerner, we seek to extend their formulations. It is our view that hyperalertness can be manifested in either of two general ways: through the articulation of specific content or formally, through the use of certain locations and determinants. Schafer's outline (1954) provides the basis for a content-oriented assessment of hyperalertness to attack: "fierce, threatening, sinister, evil, approaching or hovering figures, faces or global physiognomic qualities may be conspicuous, also with traps, webs, pits, poison, electrical or radio waves, concealing darkness, and hidden or partly concealed or obscured figures" (p. 288). To these we would add responses overtly manifesting vigilance to external threat, e.g. frightened faces, figures awaiting attack, and the like. However, as mentioned earlier, we believe that images of poison and controlling forces independent of other content bespeak the presence of projective identification.

With regard to formal scores, the use of Dr locations when combined with the F(C) determinant is indicative of a paranoid awareness of potential danger (Schafer, 1954; Lerner and Lerner, 1980; Sugarman, 1980). While this combination of scores constitutes the firmest evidence of wary environmental scanning, the F(C) determinant alone, especially when occurring with primitive rage may well express the same tendency. Rapaport, Gill, and Schafer (1945) link this determinant with a "watchful, affective display, adaptation with little freedom or flexibility and dictated by anxiety, rapport of a calculated and speculative character . . ." (p. 402).

Finally, turning to the assessment of primitive rage, Holt's primary process scoring system (1963) provides some excellent guidelines. His two-level classification of aggressive drive manifestations, reflecting the degree of integration, control, and intensity represents an extremely careful drive analysis of Rorschach content. Excluding some of the less intense drive manifestations (e.g. rotten plants or objects, broken objects, defensive objects, etc.), we would propose using both levels of aggressive content (including oral aggression) to assess primitive rage.

Summarizing, a significant aspect of projective identification may be inferred from the copresence of hyperalertness to external threat, as articulated by specific content or determinants—F(C)—and the expression of primitive rage as outlined by Holt. Two brief examples follow.

> *Card II.* A face with a cut and bleeding tongue. The differences in the shades of pink make it look like a tongue, with the light part in the center. These parts are the dripping blood.

Here the F(C) determinant appears in conjunction with primitive rage. The next response provides evidence of both hyperalertness to attack ("headed . . . toward me") and rage.

> *Card IV.* A giant who has crushed this animal to death. He's headed this way, toward me.

Primitive Idealization, Omnipotence, and Devaluation

Omnipotence, primitive idealization, and devaluation are closely linked to splitting and are prominent aspects of the object relations of the borderline patient. Patients employing these defenses identify in various forms with all-good idealized objects in the face of potentially destructive persecutory objects. Often all three of these defenses work in concert to protect the experientially precarious vulnerable representational world. Primitive idealization is characterized by the individual's creation of all-good and powerful images so that they may be insulated and protected against bad objects or against their own anger. Defensive omnipotence often entails an omnipotent identification (Kernberg, 1975, p. 30) with an idealized object so that the individual may share in the greatness of the object and in so doing stave off envy or frustration. Omnipotence and primitive idealization are linked in so much as the need to direct and autistically monitor idealized objects implicitly rests on the assumption that such objects owe their existence to the individual and thus must serve him against potentially bad objects. Such idealized objects are construed to be owned and possessed by the individual (Modell, 1968). Defensive devaluation may have one of several determinants. Devaluation may represent negativistic aggressive impulses directed toward frustrating objects (or the withholding parts of the rapprochement maternal object). Kernberg describes devaluation entailing the individual's deeming an idealized object no longer gratifying, so that the object can now be discarded. Devaluation of the self may be, but is not necessarily, related to devaluation directed toward objects. Self-devaluation that is depressive in nature involves criticisms of the self as a resolution to guilt over one's own frustration or anger toward objects. More "primitive" devaluation revolves around an implicit assumption that the individual is entitled to possess more talents or capabilities than in fact are observed by the individual. In order to make this differentiation in Rorschach analysis with certainty, it is necessary to examine whether self-depreciatory remarks are present together with defensive primitive idealization, omnipotent trends, or grandiosity.

Lerner and Lerner (1980) have ably delineated a number of Rorschach manifestations of primitive idealization. They focus on human figure percepts described in blatantly positive terms, objects of fame or strength, and human forms that are praised, explicitly or implicitly, through an enhancement of human form: angels, idols, famous figures. Examples of human figure percepts that are suggestive of primitive idealization include figures who are described as exceptional with regard to attributes such as intelligence or beauty. Percepts involving distortion of human forms (Lerner and Lerner, 1980) include famous political, religious, or athletic figures: e.g. Jesus Christ, Willie Mays.

Due to the fragmentary and fluid perceptual process that often accompanies patients who employ primitive idealization, we suggest that all percepts (and not only those of human figures) be examined in defense interpretation. For example, we interpret percepts that include objects that are possessions of or part of the apparel or tools of figures of adoration or strength as germane to primitive idealization. Thus percepts such as "a crown, a king's crown" or a "crest of royalty" are suggestive of a tendency to employ the defense of primitive idealization.

Another data base for examining primitive idealization lies in the analysis of the relationship between patient and examiner. We suggest that primitive idealization may be evident in the patient's references to the examiner, the testing procedure, or testing materials in blatantly positive terms. Responses such as "You really know how to listen," or "These tests were really amazing—you must have learned so much about me. I know you could help me," are highly suggestive of primitive idealization. Such responses stand in contrast to reaction-formation in that in the latter the patient attempts to be particularly servicing toward the examiner. Reaction-formation is characterized by the patient's attempts to prove to the tester that he is dutiful, obedient, and good and this is usually accomplished through dramatically zealous attempts to be helpful during inquiry or productive in generating percepts. Thus reaction-formation is less often accomplished through laudatory remarks to the examiner and more often through conscientious behavior in the service of appeasing the examiner and staving off feelings of passivity and hostility. Primitive idealization in which the examiner is praised is generally carried out in order to ensure the individual's protection against a "bad" object (the examiner). So too, the tester when aggrandized is made so powerful that he or she cannot be destroyed or marred by the individual's aggression. Another variation on the theme of primitive idealization of the examiner lies in the defensive aim of vicariously sharing in the power and greatness of the idealized tester and thereby accomplishing a gratification of one's own narcissistic needs. This is illustrated most clearly when laudatory remarks to the tester are accompanied by grandiose remarks about how both examiner and patient are privileged and special by virtue of knowing one another and engaging in the testing process.

Like Kernberg (1975) and Stolorow and Lachmann (1980), we view omnipotence as an idealization of the self in which there is an unconscious conviction that one deserves to be lauded by others and treated as privileged. Omnipotence may also involve an inner conviction that objects (often idealized objects) may be used or manipulated to deter aggression or projected aggression. Often, omnipotent fantasies are apparent in the individual's perception that objects exist in order to serve his needs.

Modell's (1963, 1968) discussion of transitional phenomena in relation to the transferences of borderlines and schizophrenics is relevant here. According to Modell borderline and some schizophrenic patients are prone toward viewing the therapist as possessing unlimited power and unlimited and protective capabilities for the patient. The therapist like the transitional object in development is created in accordance with the need (Winnicott, 1953). In such a relationship the therapist is construed as existing for the patient alone with only a limited appreciation for the separate qualities of the object. The results are what Modell refers to as a kind of exploitive tendency in which the object serves only to gratify the needs of the individual. Objects are omnipotently construed to be a result of a creative illusion that denies or downplays the sense of separateness between the self and object. Modell's analysis may be seen as hinging on a more specific type of paradigm than Kernberg's view of the object relation inherent in defensive omnipotence. According to Kernberg both omnipotence and devaluation represent stages in an identification with an "all good" (1975, p. 33) idealized object. Whether, as Kernberg suggests, the uses of primitive identification and introjection should be conceptualized as exclusively defensive in nature is an important theoretical question outside the bounds of this chapter.

On the Rorschach, omnipotence is most clearly seen in direct descriptions of self in blatantly positive, adulating terms. This often takes the form of laudatory remarks by the individual as to special abilities, be they test-taking abilities or special capabilities outside the testing situation. The following response immediately preceding the first percept on Card I of the Rorschach illustrates grandiose fantasies of magical omnipotence. "I think you are going to hear some very distinctive responses. My vocabulary is incredible." On the Rorschach often grandiose fantasies of omnipotence may be viewed as reparative or compensatory in the face of various injuries (both past injury and contemporary injury incurred in the testing situation) to the self-representation. Sometimes Rorschach remarks such as the one above are preceded by difficulties in forming percepts on a given card.

Omnipotence is also demonstrated on the Rorschach by responses in which the individual perceives himself in the actual blot and elaborates this with aggrandizing remarks as in the following response to Card I: "Looks like a beautiful woman with a full, formal gown, that looks like me when I was dressed to go to the prom. I was the prettiest girl at the prom that night." Such a response is suggestive of loss of distance in the self-object boundary as well as of vulnerability for loss of a reflective self-representation, as shown by the transition from perception to a verbal excursion into personal experience. What is notable, however, is that the stimulus for such a loss of boundary lies in the area of the idealization of the object and the self. Defensively, this example may illustrate what Kernberg refers to as defensive use of primitive introjection and identification—that is, the tendency to vacillate between the need to establish relations with idealized objects, on the one hand, and fantasies of magical omnipotence, on the other. Rorschach correlates of this process may be seen in percepts of idealized, gifted, or special objects accompanied by a likening of the self to such objects. Omnipotence, as manifested on the Rorschach card by identification with highly idealized, magically powerful objects may also underlie use of the "editorial we" in responses (Schafer, 1954, p. 241), e.g. "We will say it looks like a snake assuming we are asked to see such things." Such remarks may be suggestive of a tendency toward defensive intellectualization in which the Rorschach is transformed into a guided tour or art history analysis. But often such intellectualization belies imperious, grandiose tendencies. The editorial we may be understood as an implicit alliance with an idealized object that through omnipotent fantasies insulates and protects the individual from a number of possible threats, including a scrutinizing examiner. As suggested by Modell's formulation of the transitional object (1968), the need to control idealized objects and the omnipotent pride in possessing them may be revealed by the use of "we" on the Rorschach.

Devaluation serves to mitigate both unfulfilled longings for objects as well as the fear of persecutory action on the part of others. Kernberg (1975) suggests that one of the motives underlying the disparagement and rejection of objects is revenge—the individual frustrated by the withholding aspects of objects seeks retaliatory destruction toward the frustrating object. In essence, devaluation and primitive idealization may be viewed as defensive correlates of the tendency, during the rapprochement subphase of separation-individuation, to alternately express dependent behavior toward the gratifying (idealizable) mother or aggressive, oppositional behavior toward the frustrating (potentially disparaged) mother.

Lerner and Lerner (1980) have rated Rorschach manifestation of devaluation on three dimensions, including degree to which humanness of the figure is retained, a spatiotemporal dimension, and finally severity of depreciation. Our criteria for examining devaluation include percepts in which a tarnishing of the object world (humans, human parts, humanlike organs, animals, animal parts) is apparent. Included in this disparagement of the object world as evidenced on the Rorschach are derogatory remarks directed toward the testing enterprise, the construction of the blot, the examiner, or the self. Since we view distancing of objects in time and space as the operation of obsessional defenses (often isolation, intellectualization, or rationalization), we do not necessarily view the aggression expressed within the devaluing percepts as quantitatively less. Rather, the individual's repertoire of defenses is sufficiently broad to allow for an adaptation to frustration and aggression toward objects. Devaluation is often reflective of a view of oneself as flawed or lacking. It is most commonly evidenced on the Rorschach by human or animal figure percepts described in pejorative terms such as "an ugly-looking face" or "a bird without wings," in which the flaws or injuries imputed to the object bespeak anger or envy that is retaliatory in nature or that serves to minimize wishes for gratification from the object. Disparagement of masculine and feminine identifications as described by Schafer (1954) is viewed here largely in terms of defensive devaluation. For instance, devaluation is seen in the following hostile characterizations of women: "an amazon," "an old hen," "two women gossiping away." Various forms of hostile portrayals of men that Schafer terms "symbolic castration" (p. 136) may also be seen as devaluation—these include percepts such as gnomes, dwarfs, or men viewed as having flaws. It is difficult to ascertain the defensive motivation of this devaluation out of the context of a complete Rorschach record. But it is clear that a percept such as "two women gossiping away" may speak either to an individual's attempts to debase and retaliate against a preoccupied, unfulfilling female figure, or to an attempt to minimize the degree to which such a figure could fulfill affectional longings and to thereby minimize the longings themselves. Such percepts clearly have important reference to the individual's self-representation. Percepts containing disparaging portrayals of objects may serve also to minimize persecutory or retaliatory fears of objects (e.g. fears of castration). Remarks which reflect a derogation of the testing enterprise or the examiner are often aimed at minimizing the feared scrutinizing or other potentially persecutory actions of the examiner. For example, the remark, "I cannot believe that this is the way you spend your time—how boring," may serve to minimize the potentially destructive effects of interpretation by the tester as well as to express revenge toward the examiner for placing the individual within the testing situation (this may also represent anger toward the therapist displaced onto the examiner). So too, rejecting remarks to the examiner may attempt to minimize regressive longings stimulated within the testing situation.

Self-deprecatory remarks may also indicate defensive devaluation. It is useful to differentiate between self-deprecation that appears to be part of a characterological resolution of the individual's anger or frustration toward objects and defensive devaluation. Self-deprecation may derive from disappointing experiences with objects and involves a self-representation replete with images of a flawed, undeserving, and rejectable self. On the Rorschach this may be manifested by remarks such as, "I don't know how to do things like use my imagination." Defensive self-devaluation as seen in the Rorschach of many borderline patients is evinced by remarks that bespeak a more entitled and grandiose self-representation. In essence such remarks bemoan the perceived discrepancy between their perceived ability on the Rorschach and their fantasied, grandiose self-representation. In these instances self-deprecatory remarks may be followed by reparative statements that aim toward restoration of a grandiose self-representation: "I'm unable to do a test like this, I sound so mundane" followed later by "It's always been like this, my imagination being hemmed in by people like you." Here self-derogation, projection of responsibility, and devaluation of the object coexist in attempts to alternately protect the object from the individual's anger and preserve the self from the object's painful scrutiny.

Clinical Illustration

To provide a more coherent context for the interpretation of borderline defenses we will examine the excerpted Rorschach of a fifty-year-old borderline woman. Because our analysis focuses primarily on a content-oriented approach to defense interpretation, we have omitted the assessment of formal scores. We do not wish to imply disregard for this approach and believe the two sources of data should be used as complements to one another. Inquiry was conducted following the completion of free association for the entire ten cards. Inquiry was conducted with cards present, and included the examiner's repetition of initial responses.

The patient's response to Card I involved themes of primal aloneness, helplessness, and profound depression: "Looks like my life, all broken pieces, empty spaces, no direction . . . a figure trying to reach for help but couldn't get it, feelings of despair."

CARD II

Free Association	*Inquiry*
1. A creature with fire raging.	Fire coming out of his mouth right here. (Could you outline that?) Right here. (Points to bottom.) It's coming out. No here. (Points to top.) It's coming out raging. (Could you show me more of the creature?) This whole thing. (What makes it look like fire?) The red. (Location—W)
2. Also looks like somebody praying.	Two hands up here. (Location—center D)

3. Looks like two dogs showing affection for each other.	Here and here. Trying to show affection, but there's like a barrier there. (What makes them look like dogs?) Two ears. (Anything else?) The way they are shaped. (Location—entire black D)
4. I can see no people, but bloodshed.	Some blood coming out of their heads. (Can you show me the people?) (Blood?) Is coming out down here. (Location—W)

Here, in the presence of a strong pull for interactional themes, borderline defenses emerge. The first response, nearly confabulatory and reflecting poor form, comes close to Lerner and Lerner's first component of projective identification (1980)—the presence of aggression with the capacity to blur boundaries (confabulation). In the next response we see a striking shift from raging aggression to the theme of praying. Given the free expression of aggression in the first response, the latter one is indicative of a poorly integrated and probably harsh superego. The image of prayer also includes an oblique reference to the need for an idealized all-powerful object (see Card VIII) both to protect the patient from dangerous objects bearing projections of her rage and to forgive her for her aggression. The response ''dogs showing affection for each other'' suggests that libidinally toned but immature relationships are associatively linked to an implicitly idealized object. This may suggest that idealized objects stimulate affectional yearnings and needs for contact. Within this percept dogs are engaged in mildly incongruous, humanlike activity, ''showing affection,'' indicating the need to minimize and deny the intensity of these yearnings. The perception of ''a barrier'' during the inquiry raises questions about the patient's concern with the frightening merger that might result from sustained or excessive closeness with a longed-for object. The final two responses to Card II point to the presence of disintegrated affective experiences with primary objects. In direct contrast with the affectional longings expressed in the third response, the final response is replete with destructive hatred that may derive from abortive, frustrating attempts to receive nurturance. Defensive splitting is inferred from the dramatic shift from libidinal to aggressively toned representations. At the same time the aggression expressed in the final response suggests rage toward an engulfing mother whose neediness prevented her from fostering the patient's separation-individuation: in this context, ''the barrier'' perceived in the third response and the ensuing aggression in the last response may serve to fend off potentially engulfing objects.

CARD III

Free Association	*Inquiry*
1. Two ladies, like they're ready to fight. Parts missing from the bodies.	Two ballet dancers. I can see fire between them. They can't get at each other, they're too far apart. They want to be friends but they can't get to each other to make up. (Ballet dancers?) Pointed shoes. (Fire?) (Location—P with center D)
2. A butterfly in the middle.	No inquiry conducted.
3. Two swans at the top. That's all.	These look like two devils. (What makes them look that way?) The length of the neck and the teeth. (Anything else?) They look like they want to attack these two women. My first image was swans but I changed them. Swans are a sign of peace, devils are a sign of hell, trouble. (Do they look like swans anymore?) No. (Location—upper red D's)

This card includes a clear statement of the patient's unresolved rapprochement issues, a theme hinted at in her reference to the barrier on Card II and more clearly indicated by the primitive defensive structure. The initial devaluation of women (parts missing) in inquiry gives way to a somewhat idealized image of ballet dancers, an image which points also to isolation of affect. This higher-level defense quickly gives way under the stress of aggression and conflicted wishes for closeness. As if to purge this relationship of aggression and yet still preclude the possibility of frightening fusion, the dancers are beset by attacking devils. This leads to the hypothesis that the patient may try to establish a relationship with one object in order to ward off attack from other objects. The transformation of swans into devils bespeaks both a primitive polarization and a fluid oscillation of affect states congruent with the earlier prestage of splitting in which a single object fluctuates between experiential extremes. This contrasts with the type of splitting found on Card II, as does the shift from devaluing to idealizing the women. Intensification of rapprochement issues (e.g. loss, abandonment, frustration, or excessive closeness) may stimulate the emergence of a more primitive kind of splitting. That the butterfly is this patient's first neutral response further attests a virtual absence of object constancy. Instead, as on the previous card, this woman vividly presents us with the intensely drive- and affect-laden fragments of her object world.

CARD IV

Free Association	*Inquiry*
1. A creature with large feet. I can see eyes and looks like he's hanging in air. Ears are large. Unhappy. Looks very unhappy. That's all.	(Points out feet, ears, eyes.) Afraid, a frightened look. Looks like he's sitting on a powder keg, ready to explode, but is stuck. Can't move. (Hanging in air?) In thin air, can't get his feet on the ground. (Anything else make it look like air?) Nothing down here to support his feet to rest on. (Location—W)

This response includes an example of projective identification; hyperalertness to attack ("frightened look") is combined with primitive rage (the powder keg ready to explode). The percept also conveys the patient's fear of her own aggression, which no doubt activates projective processes. Helplessness (hanging in air, stuck, can't move) may play a specific role in the nature of projective identification. This woman may try to rid herself of these painful feelings by aggressively attempting to make others act as if she had successfully projected her helplessness into them. Concern with the creature's unhappiness suggests the presence of an empathic bond with the victim or her sadistic efforts to induce helplessness.

CARD VIII

Free Association	*Inquiry*
1. This looks like someone's very happy, very colorful.	Very colorful. Happiness is here. (Someone?) The colors are colorful, except there is a cloud that's falling over the happiness. (A cloud?)

	Here, the gray cloud. (Location—W)
2. Two dogs trying to climb, but they are falling, trying to grab on to something, but . . . crying out for help. Trying to reach the top. Slipping, keep slipping. They can't get up there.	These look like two dogs. They are grabbing on to two hands. But they don't have a grasp. (Points out dogs and hands.) Going to fall 'cause can't get a grasp on the hands. (Location—P with upper D)
3. A knight in shining armor. That's all.	The way this is. His coat is formed right here. (Points to blue.) (Can you show me more of the knight?) He's broad across here. His head is not there. It's gone. (Anything else?) He's splitting his coat right here. He's falling apart. (Armor?) The gray part, but it's not that shiny. (Location—gray and blue D's)

The response process begins with hypomanic detail ("Happiness is here"), the instability of which is highlighted by the cloud as well as the helplessness in the following response. Desperation fosters the creation of a libidinally toned idealized object (the knight). Inquiry for this response, especially the piece-by-piece dismantling and dissolution of the knight shows the striking transformation of an idealized into a devalued object. This patient's overwhelming sense of helplessness stimulates the need for rescue by idealized objects. In consequence, however, feelings of envy toward the idealized object as well as fears of merger provoke the need to devalue the once-idealized object. Defensive splitting is inferred in the shift from a self- and object representation of helplessness and futility to one of power and salvation. Self- and object representations of this patient are certain to be characterized by rapid fluctuations between affective extremes.

Conclusion

The Rorschach provides fruitful material for the interpretation of borderline defenses and the object relations with which they are inextricably linked. Valuable data can be gathered from examination of a broad range of content, raising questions about the validity of limiting the analysis of these defenses to human figure responses. Important information about these defenses can be gleaned also from aspects of the patient-examiner interaction. Specific criteria are offered for the assessment of splitting, devaluation, primitive idealization, omnipotence, and projective identification. Clinical use of these criteria can shed light on a patient's defensive structure and can stimulate meaningful hypotheses about the individual's object relations.

References

Bion, W. (1956), Development of schizophrenic thought. *Internat. J. Psycho-Anal.*, 37:344–346.

Blatt, S., & Ritzler, B. (1974), Thought disorder and boundary disturbance in psychosis. *J. Consult. Clin. Psychol.*, 42:370–381.

——— Wild, C. (1976), *Schizophrenia: A Developmental Analysis*. New York: Academic Press.

Dorpat, T. (1979), Is splitting a defense? *Internat. Rev. Psycho-Anal.*, 6:105–113.

——— (1981), Basic concepts and terms in object relations theories. In: *Object and Self: A Developmental Approach*, ed. S. Tuttman, C. Kaye, & M. Zimmerman. New York: International Universities Press, pp. 149–178.

Exner, J. (1978), *The Rorschach Comprehensive System*, Vol. II. New York: Wiley.

Freedman, N. (1981), Varieties of splitting. In: *Object and Self: A Developmental Approach*, ed. S. Tuttman, C. Kaye, & M. Zimmerman. New York: International Universities Press, pp. 267–289.

Gedo, J., & Goldberg, A. (1973), *Models of the Mind: A Psychoanalytic Theory*. Chicago: University of Chicago Press.

Grala, C. (1980), The concept of splitting and its manifestations in the Rorschach test. *Bull. Menn. Clin.*, 44:253–271.

Hartmann, H. (1964), *Essays on Ego Psychology: Selected Problems in Psychoanalytic Theory*. New York: International Universities Press.

Heimann, P. (1957), A combination of defense mechanisms in paranoid states. In: *New Directions in Psychoanalysis*, ed. M. Klein. New York: Basic Books.

Holt, R. (1963), Manual for scoring of primary process manifestations in Rorschach responses. Unpublished manuscript.

——— Luborsky, L. (1958), *Personality Patterns of Psychiatrists*. New York: Basic Books.

Kelly, E., & Fiske, D. (1951), *The Prediction of Performance in Clinical Psychology*. Ann Arbor: University of Michigan Press.

Kernberg, O. (1966), Structural derivatives of objective relationships. *Internat. J. Psycho-Anal.*, 47:236–253.

——— (1967), Borderline personality organization. *J. Amer. Psychoanal. Assn.*, 15:641–658.

——— (1975), *Borderline Conditions and Pathological Narcissism*. New York: Aronson.

——— (1976), *Object Relations Theory and Clinical Psychoanalysis*. New York: Aronson.

Klein, M. (1946), Notes on some schizoid mechanisms. In: *Envy and Gratitude and Other Works, 1946–1963*. New York: Delacorte Press/Seymour Lawrence, 1975, pp. 1–24.

Krohn, A., & Mayman, M. (1974), Object representations in dreams and projective tests. *Bull. Menn. Clin.*, 38:445–466.

Lerner, P., & Lerner, H. (1980), Rorschach assessment of primitive defenses in borderline personality structure. In: *Borderline Phenomena and the Rorschach Test*, ed. J. Kwawer, H. Lerner, P. Lerner, & A. Sugarman. New York: International Universities Press, pp. 257–274.

Lichtenberg, J., & Slap, J. (1973), Notes on the concept of splitting and the defense mechanism of the splitting of representations. *J. Amer. Psychoanal. Assn.*, 21:772–787.

Mahler, M. (1968), *On Human Symbiosis and the Vicissitudes of Individuation: I. Infantile Psychosis*. New York: International Universities Press.

Malin, A., & Grotstein, J. (1966), Projective identification in the therapeutic process. *Internat. J. Psycho-Anal.*, 47:26–31.

Mayman, M. (1967), Object representations and object relationships in Rorschach responses. *J. Proj. Tech. Personal. Assess.*, 31:17–24.

Modell, A. (1963), Primitive object relationships and the predisposition to schizophrenia. *Internat. J. Psycho-Anal.*, 44:282–292.

——— (1968), *Object Love and Reality*. London: Hogarth Press.

Ogden, T. (1979), On projective identification. *Internat. J. Psycho-Anal.*, 60:357–373.

Pruitt, W.A., & Spilka, B. (1964), Rorschach empathy and object relations scale. In: *Handbook of Rorschach Scales*, ed. P. Lerner. New York: International Universities Press, pp. 315–324.

Pruyser, P. (1975), What splits in "splitting"? *Bull. Menn. Clin.*, 39:1–46.

Rapaport, D., Gill, M., & Schafer, R. (1945), *Diagnostic Psychological Testing*. New York: International Universities Press, 1968.

Rosenfeld, H. (1952), Transference phenomena and transference analysis in an acute catatonic schizophrenic patient. *Internat. J. Psycho-Anal.*, 33:457–464.

Rubinfine (1962), Maternal stimulation, psychic structure and early object relations. *The Psychoanalytic Study of the Child*, 17:278–282, New York: International Universities Press.

Schafer, R. (1954), *Psychoanalytic Interpretation in Rorschach Testing*. New York: Grune & Stratton.

——— (1968), *Aspects of Internalization*. New York: International Universities Press.

Searles, H. (1963), Transference psychosis in the psychotherapy of schizophrenia. In: *Collected Papers on Schizophrenia and Related Subjects*. New York: International University Press, 1965.

Singer, M., & Larson, D. (1981), Borderline personality and the Rorschach Test. *Arch. Gen. Psychiatry*, 38:693–698.

Smith, K. (1980), Object relations concepts as applied to the borderline level of ego functioning. In: *Borderline Phenomena and the Rorschach Test*, ed. J. Kwawer, H. Lerner, P. Lerner, & A. Sugarman. New York: International Universities Press, pp. 59–87.

Spear, W. (1980), The psychological assessment of structural and thematic object representations in borderline and schizophrenia patients. In: *Borderline Phenomena and the Rorschach Test*, ed. J. Kwawer, H. Lerner, P. Lerner, & A. Sugarman. New York: International Universities Press, pp. 321–340.

Sugarman, A. (1980), The borderline personality organization as manifested on psychological tests. In: *Borderline Phenomena and the Rorschach Test*, ed. J. Kwawer, H. Lerner, P. Lerner, & A. Sugarman. New York: International Universities Press, pp. 35–57.

Stolorow, R., & Lachmann, F. (1980), *Psychoanalysis of Developmental Arrests: Theory and Treatment*. New York: International Universities Press.

Urist, J. (1980), The continuum between primary and secondary process thinking: Toward a concept of borderline thought. In: *Borderline Phenomena and the Rorschach Test*, ed. J. Kwawer, H. Lerner, P. Lerner, & A. Sugarman. New York: International Universities Press, pp. 133–154.

Volkan, V. (1976), *Primitive Internalized Object Relations*. New York: International Universities Press.

Winnicott, D. (1953), Transitional objects and transitional phenomena. In: *Collected Papers*. New York: Basic Books, 1958, pp. 229–242.

Part II
Other Tests

Chapter 7

OBJECT RELATIONS ASPECTS OF HUMAN FIGURE DRAWINGS

MORTON KISSEN

The inference process utilized to interpret psychological test responses has recently shifted from the metapsychological model so carefully and logically developed by ego psychologists such as Hartmann (1939) and Rapaport (1959) to a more phenomenological and essentially experiential model of clinical communication. This shift is documented in the writings of a number of psychologists who have been grappling with issues around the testing process (Mayman 1967; Athey, 1974; Krohn and Mayman, 1974; Allen, 1977; Sugarman, 1977). These psychologists are essentially involved with the task of applying the concepts of Jacobson (1964) and the British school of object relations theorists (Winnicott, 1951; Fairbairn, 1954) as well as the more recent work of Giovacchini (1975), all developed as a means of conceptualizing the intrinsic curative properties of the psychotherapy interaction, to a keener understanding of particular features of the psychological testing process.

From a somewhat different vantage point, Schafer (1976, 1978) has been engaged in the development of an ''action language'' approach to the communication of insights derived from both the testing and the psychotherapy interactions. His basic argument hinges upon a critique of early Freudian and subsequent ego psychological metapsychological models; these he feels have left us a legacy of clinical conceptions that imply an essentially passive and almost impotent organism buffeted about in helpless, puppetlike fashion by impersonal objective forces beyond its control. Thus, in his recent reassessment of Freud's contributions to the clinical theories of free association and dream interpretation, Schafer (1978) makes the following remark:

> What I am saying is congruent with what Freud said on the question of responsibility for one's dreams. Who else, he asked, dreamed the dream? In other words, Freud took the position that a dream is a mental act like any other and that attributions of responsibility for mental acts must be made across the board. In this view, responsibility emerges as a defining feature or constituent element of mental acts and not as a logically independent causal factor. [p. 45]

Schafer emphasizes the need to stay closer to the active, experiencing, and organizing *self* of the patient in our clinical formulations. Thus, the individual who describes his feelings of depression causally, as stemming from a frustrating collision of his own deep emotional needs with an extremely frustrating external environment, needs to explore some of the active choices involved in his depression. The individual who reacts in a detached, helpless fashion to the supposedly chance features of his dream (or free-associative slip of the tongue) needs to consider the possibility that he has somehow *arranged* to creatively produce them.

The action language model of communication recommended by Schafer implies a shift in emphasis away from the static and relatively mechanistic concepts of impulse-defense configurations derivable from the dynamic, economic, and structural levels of inference to more phenomenological observations conveyed in clear-cut and articulate object relations language. Although object relations conceptions can be unduly dense and abstract, as exhibited in Kernberg's complex descriptions of transference paradigms (1975, 1976, 1980), they nevertheless offer what Mayman (1963) has called a uniquely efficient and nonmetapsychological *middle* language for communicating clinical understandings in an experientially useful manner.

A basic object relations model can be derived from a melding of the more complex concepts contained in the writings of the object relations theorists with the framework for action-oriented and more phenomenological inference developed by Mayman and Schafer. This model requires only three operationally definable clinical concepts and can be easily applied to both the psychotherapy process and to a broad variety of psychological test data.

The three object relations terms to be operationally defined and exemplified through projective test responses in this chapter are those of *self-representation, object representation,* and *ego state*. A number of authors (Mayman, 1963, 1967, 1976; Jacobson, 1964; Kernberg, 1966; Horner, 1979) have offered definitions of these clinically relevant constructs. The following definitions, presented in the introduction to this volume, are simple enough to be operationalized in both psychological testing and therapeutic experience.

Self-representation. The various physiognomic modes by which the individual symbolizes an experiential image of himself and its associated affects. The individual may utilize nonverbal or verbal means for expressing these internalized units of self-perception. Although these self-perceptions may be experienced at a relatively conscious, preconscious, or even unconscious level, they are most likely to be consciously available.

Object representation. The various physiognomic modes by which the individual symbolizes an experiential image of a significant other and its associated affects. These units of object perception may be expressively captured either verbally or nonverbally. They too may be experienced at a relatively conscious, preconscious, or unconscious level, but are most likely to be consciously available.

Ego state. More complex and relatively differentiated units of self- and object representation and their associated affects. The composite of these experiential states defines essential aspects of an individual's self-organization. When viewed using a *structural* mode of observation and inference, they define the individual's central sense of identity. From a more *adaptive* vantage point, these experiential entities define the individual's characterological style. At a very personal and experiential level these ego states may be felt as undesirable and foreign to the individual's core sense of identity and more idealized strivings, but on the other hand they may be felt as intimately essential aspects of the self-concept. Foreign-seeming and experientially unpleasant ego states may be operationally defined as *introjects*. More intimately comfortable ego states may be operationally defined as *identifications*.

Mayman has suggested the possibility of observing these three object relations constructs in sentence completion, Rorschach, TAT, and Early Memories Test responses. Mayman's work with early memories has been particularly productive in this regard. His analysis of the memories of a childless married woman of forty-five who decided to seek therapeutic assistance due to spells of tiredness and incipient depression contains a truly lucid and therapeutically useful description of this patient's inner experiential states.

According to Mayman (1963) this patient's early memories, when analyzed into component themes, could be sorted into three distinct thematic clusters:

> One cluster fits well the austere, highly principled and stoically long-suffering way of life which characterized this woman at the time she presented herself for treatment. Her very earliest memory tells of being unjustly coerced, threatened and then punished by her father, who wanted her to confess to something she hadn't done; she stoically and with

> stubborn adherence to principle accepted all of the punishment rather than tamper with the truth. [p. 112]

Mayman goes on to describe a second cluster of memories depicting a somewhat warmer, softer, and related young girl:

> One incident, which according to the patient is the memory in which she felt herself to be 'most fully herself,' was a time when the sister went off to camp. The patient tells not of taking advantage of the sister's absence to enjoy mother's full attention—a response one would normally expect—but rather says this provided the opportunity to make three new dresses for her sister to surprise her with on her return. [p. 113]

In a similar vein, the patient described a memory of being read to in bed by her mother together with her sister. The mother suddenly broke into tears and she herself (although the younger of the two children) had to finish the story for the three of them.

The third cluster of memories was the most surprising of all and depicted a youngster eager for spontaneous new experiences. She recalled once wandering into a store where she saw a woman's hat lying on a counter. She picked it up, put it on her head, and walked home dressed in style. Another time, instead of going to the movies as she was supposed to do, she stayed out in the rain, took off all of her clothes and was found dancing around in the nude. Mayman concludes from this cluster of memories:

> These incidents were told by the patient with wry amusement, but without any recollection of a time when she was such a vigorous, outgoing, zestfully hedonic and self-sufficient person. This third self is now so thoroughly repressed as to seem to her wholly ego-alien. It is part of herself with which she has lost all empathic touch. [p. 114]

In terms of the object relations model being developed in the present chapter, each of these three clusters of anecdotes contains a relatively integrated series of self-representations, object representations, and associated affects. Thus, the first cluster can be focused on from a *self-representational* viewpoint as depicting a harsh, overly constricted, controlled, and almost anhedonic sense of self. From an *object representational* viewpoint, on the other hand, the patient's father can be seen as a cruelly oppressive, intimidating, and demanding sort of figure. The basic linking affect state comes across in the form of an unpleasant sense of responsibility and inner burden.

Early memories thus offer us a rather unique opportunity to projectively explore relatively differentiated and complex *ego states*. In subsequent sections of this chapter a new projective approach to human figure drawings will be described which highlights their similar object relations implications.

Human Figure Drawings

The figure drawing test is unquestionably one of the most popular projective instruments available to clinical psychologists. Sundberg (1961) noted that the Draw-A-Person test is the second most frequently used psychological test (the Rorschach being first) in outpatient clinics and hospitals throughout the country. This popularity continues despite a number of empirical reviews which have raised questions with regard to the reliability and validity of inferences drawn from the various discrete and more global physical characteristics of human figure drawings (Swensen, 1957, 1968; Roback, 1968). Interestingly, the more global characteristics (i.e. overall physical quality and expressive characteristics) seem to be more reliable and useful for purposes of deriving personality inferences.

A method will now be described which capitalizes upon these more reliable global characteristics and which enhances the psychodynamic potential of the figure drawing test—particularly with regard to the generation of therapeutically useful object relations inferences. A specific format for the administration of the figure drawing test and a formal inquiry procedure will be delineated, and a clinical case example will be presented which highlights the usefulness of this approach. The method consists, in part, of an invitation to the patient to psychologically explore some of the salient expressive characteristics of the human figures he has produced. A certain attitude of naivete and psychological curiosity is encouraged in the patient with regard to his own figure drawings. The paradigmatic technique of "joining the resistance" (Sherman, 1961) is subtly involved in this methodology, in that the patient is invited to become a consultant to the examiner (Strean, 1970). Such a role reversal allows the patient to become more spontaneous and open to inner experiential states.

The figure drawing test possesses certain natural characteristics which make it an ideal "ice-breaker" for most patients. In my own practice I introduce patients to the testing experience by asking them almost immediately for human figure drawings. No informal chat or interview with the patient has been found necessary for purposes of establishing spontaneity and rapport. The figure drawing test itself, properly administered, helps establish a spontaneous and experientially open testing atmosphere. Over many years of testing experience, I have found that almost all patients (child, adolescent, or adult) have responded in a receptive and self-revealing fashion to the structured interview format to be described. Occasionally, of course, an oppositional patient would be encountered who refused to comply with the test instructions, but such occurrences were very rare. Extreme difficulty or inhibition in response to the figure drawing instructions was occasionally confronted in markedly schizoid patients. Even so, such patients were able to successfully complete the task when allowed to physically turn away from the examiner, during both the actual drawing and parts of the structured interview.

Many patients initially respond to standard forms of inquiry on the drawing test by making a statement to the effect, "Why don't you ask me about myself, if you would like to know me?" Such relatively sophisticated statements frequently mask an underlying anxiety about the object relations aspects of the test and a wish to somehow be in control of the self- and object representational projections that unconsciously are sensed as being elicited by this test. Typically I respond to such queries by encouraging the patient to take a much more naive and objectively curious posture toward his drawings. The patient is asked to look at his drawings as though they were produced by someone other than himself. In most cases, a properly naive attitude (at a *subjective* level) and yet an extremely psychologically curious attitude can be produced in patients confronted with their own figure drawings.

The Method of Test Administration

Figure drawings have traditionally been viewed as an ideal means of exploring the body image of a given individual. Machover (1949) formulated this hypothesis as follows: "The human figure drawn by an individual who is directed to 'draw a person' relates intimately to the impulses, anxieties, conflicts and compensations characteristic of that individual. In some sense, the figure drawn is the person, and the paper corresponds to the environment" (p. 35). Machover's statement, however, is rather vaguely formulated and is not articulated in object relations terms. An object relations approach to the figure drawing test must highlight its potential for eliciting significant internalized self- and object representations that offer clinically useful insights into the psychodynamic and characterological functioning of a given individual.

As in the standard test procedure, the patient is first asked to draw a human figure. Unless there is some suspicion of organicity or intellectual retardation, he is told that stick figures are not acceptable. If he asks about the sex of the figure, he is given his choice. Whatever the sex of the figure drawn first, the patient is next asked to draw a figure of the opposite sex on a different piece of paper. (Unlined paper is most desirable for this test.)

Once both figures have been completed, the patient is asked to look at his first drawing, with the following instructions: "I would like you to look at your drawing as though it were drawn by somebody else. From the physical and expressive characteristics of the drawing (facial expression, posture, style of clothing, etc.), what sort of person comes through to you? What personal characteristics come to mind?''

Inquiry of an open-ended and naturally evocative nature is used to encourage the patient to clarify particular personality traits or to elaborate upon additional traits that seem characteristic of the person depicted in the drawing. An attitude of naivete is encouraged with regard to personal projections implicit in the drawing. Such a suspension of disbelief is surprisingly easy to achieve with most patients. The patient is encouraged to begin to describe an almost stereotyped image of a certain sort of person that comes to mind as he scans some of the expressive and physiognomic features of his drawing.

Next the patient is asked how he would picture the person in the drawing relating to same-sexed peers. Should a more elaborate inquiry be necessary, the patient is invited to imagine the sort of interpersonal image that the person in the drawing might have within the peer group. A similar question is then asked about relationships with opposite-sexed peers.

After obtaining responses with regard to peer relationships, the patient is asked to describe the animal that seems most like the person in the drawing. Here again, a physical or physiognomic feature of the drawing or some personality trait alluded to in response to the previous questions can be fed back to the patient as a means of priming a properly imaginative response. Should the person say ''dog,'' he should be asked what breed of dog he has in mind. After eliciting this response, the characteristics of the person or the physiognomic attributes of the drawing that suggested such an animal should be explored.

Finally, the examiner draws a cartoon balloon emanating from the mouth of the figure drawing and says: ''I would like you to write in the balloon a statement that you can imagine the person you have described making. Write in a *typical* statement characteristic of this sort of person.'' Should the patient seem confused with regard to the task, he can be primed with the following statement: ''Sometimes it helps to imagine the person in a particular social situation. What would you picture this person saying in a social situation?''

The same structured interview questions are addressed to the patient with regard to the second figure drawing. The essential goal is to create in the patient an attitude of subjective naivete and yet, paradoxically, an attitude of psychological curiosity toward the various expressive characteristics of his figure drawings. Surprisingly, most patients will be quite comfortable in suspending their more sophisticated notions with regard to the self-projections contained in figure drawings if the examiner directly or indirectly encourages such a reduction in self-consciousness and awareness. On almost every occasion, a rather stereotyped and yet complexly differentiated expressive portrait of the person in the drawing can be obtained using the structured interview procedure outlined here.

The inquiry format for the figure drawing test should be very similar to that typically used on the Rorschach test. Thus, with regard to a particular inkblot percept, the patient might be asked, as an initial line of inquiry, "What makes it look like a butterfly?" The purpose of this format is to ask the patient, nondirectively, to explore some of the salient physiognomic characteristics of the inkblot being considered. A very similar directive is given to the patient who is asked to peruse his own human figure drawings for salient expressive characteristics. The outward form of the question on the figure drawing test, however, is somewhat different from the typical inquiry on the Rorschach. The person is asked, more directly, to look at the various physical and expressive characteristics of his drawing and to use them as cues and as a means of forming a stereotypical impression of the person depicted in the drawing.

This format lends itself rather aptly to a clinically valid and useful delineation, in modern object relations terms, of the body image and personality dynamics alluded to by Machover (1949). Thus, internalized self- and object representations can be inferred in a smooth and cogent fashion from the patient's verbal associations to his drawings. No speculative inferences need be made with regard to possible psychodynamic meanings of the specific physical attributes of the drawings themselves (i.e., physical size, placement on the page, stance, line quality, shading, erasures, etc.). The patient himself, however, is invited to utilize these specific characteristics as well as the overall global and expressive features of his drawings as a means of depicting the various attributes of a particular sort of person.

The following clinical material may serve to concretize the specific testing procedures being recommended and their relevance for an object relations approach to the figure drawing test.

Clinical Case Example

The following two drawings and verbal captions (see Figures 1 and 2) were obtained from Mrs. W., a thirty-five-year-old housewife. Rather than developing inferences with regard to the physical and expressive characteristics of the two drawings, Mrs. W.'s verbal associations in the structured interview will be presented.

Figure 1 (Woman). (What sort of person do you picture?) A professional woman. . . . Someone who is very efficient and pretty. . . . I'm not supposed to criticize the drawing, am I? (You may if you choose to.) Her hands are out of proportion. . . . Someone who is stylish, a conservative dresser. (Here the examiner attempts to slow down Mrs. W.'s rapid verbalizations a bit by saying, "Let me keep up with you, I record what you are saying verbatim.") I'm sorry. . . . Someone who applies makeup very well, puts it on well. . . .

I. Woman
I have a few
ideas about that
and I plan to
put some idea
into action
tomorrow

It looks almost like the kind of picture a successful person, somebody who feels together. . . . She is probably not super-friendly, but she is always nice. (How do you mean that?) I just think that she is on another plane, she's a very successful person. She probably has business on her mind. (Could you talk a bit slower?) You should have a dictaphone. . . . She's not common. . . . Probably economically well off. Just not like your housewife. . . . In fact, I don't even think she is a mother. (How would you picture her relating to other females?) Oh, she's looked up to by other women. (And with males?) Certainly not flirtatious, but she is sophisticated enough to show an interest, if somebody catches her eye—if she feels she would like to get to know him better. . . . I think men genuinely like her. (What sort of animal does she remind you of?) That is hard! . . . The thing that comes to my head is a cat, but I don't mean a tigress—my feline vision of her is different than someone who is on the prowl. . . . I think it's the independence of a cat. (What sort of statement can you picture her making?)

Figure 2 (Man). (What sort of person do you picture?) A nice guy, but not very handsome. . . . Probably a helpful person. . . . He is probably industrious and successful, somebody you can rely on and trust. . . . He's very friendly, but he's a private person. You just don't know what is going on for him in his day-to-day life. . . . Because he is so mild-mannered and even-tempered, you get the idea that he can handle anything that is happening to him. In fact, if he appears to be down, it's really upsetting because you think that it must really be something bad. . . . He's very well-educated. (Said in a very serious tone.) He has a lot going for him. (What other personal traits do you picture?) Just real friendliness—he's a pleasure to be with. (How do you picture him with his male peers?) Very well liked. . . . And, he probably plays paddleball or tennis or something. . . . And I bet he skis in the winter. Money is no problem, but he's not exceptionally wealthy. (How do you picture him relating to females?) I think women would really like him. He's the kind of person for an office setting. He's the person you'd say "hi" to and a few conversational words. Women would think he's very cheerful. He'd always be up for an office party. Oh, he has a great sense of humor—I guess that's why men and women would like him, he can really make you laugh. . . . (What sort of animal do you picture him as being most like?) That I find very hard, I really do. . . . I guess like a German shepherd dog—a reliable, strong companion. . . . (What sort of statement can you picture him making?)

Object Relations Tendencies in the Verbal Associations to the Two Drawings

The test protocol obtained from Mrs. W. is no more elaborate and imaginatively embellished than those typically obtained from other patients with

II. Man
Hey! How's it going? Take it easy.

this structured interviewing procedure. Certain object relations formulations with regard to Mrs. W.'s internalized self-representations, object representations, and ego ideals can be inferred from her verbal associations to her two drawings. What follows are a few such inferences.

Mrs. W.'s verbal statements about the female drawing depict a rather efficient and capable professional woman. The emphasis in her associations is upon ego attributes of effectiveness, business acumen, and disciplined self-control. Certainly, the existence of latent perfectionistic ego ideals are suggested by these associations. Interestingly in this regard, Mrs. W.'s mother (as gleaned from her responses to the Early Memories Test) was seen as an "organization" woman whom Mrs. W. could not imagine as a housewife and mother. "I am curious," she said, "now that I have children of my own, what kind of mother my mother was. . . . I can't imagine. . . . She seemed like a real committee type. . . . I can't imagine her going through the experiences of toilet training we mothers all have to go through." One possible reason for Mrs. W.'s uncertainty with regard to her mother's maternal behavior is the fact that her mother had died when Mrs. W. was nine years of age. Mrs. W. has an almost total lack of recall for specific experiences with her mother during her first nine years of life.

In addition, her statement about the female drawing, "I just think she's on another plane," suggests, in part, her experiential dilemma with regard to her mother. On the surface, such a comment would appear to indicate a view of the mother as superior. At a deeper level, the statement can be interpreted as conveying a quality of ethereal unattainability. Her inability to recall, on either a purely cognitive or a more deeply affective level, specific experiences with her mother suggests an acute emotional disengagement from the traumatic experiences associated with her mother's death and hence, quite possibly, a failure to fully mourn the loss. Mrs. W.'s depressive symptoms may, in part, be associated with this process of decathexis and repression of both traumatic and nontraumatic memories associated with her mother. Giovacchini (1975) has described a similar process of failure to mourn in certain character disorders, a failure he views as associated with a *frozen introject* of the lost love object. Such an introject, according to Giovacchini, can have a damaging and intrusively inhibiting effect on normal executive functions such as memory, ego identity, and the development of normal adaptive identifications with the lost object.

Indeed, the stereotypically idealized quality of Mrs. W.'s verbal associations to her female drawing suggests a fragmented ego that must rely, at least occasionally, on the primitive defenses of splitting and idealization that Kernberg (1975, 1976) has emphasized as characteristic of patients manifesting borderline personality organization. The mother must be viewed in exaggerated idealized terms and protected from critical or angry feelings.

Mrs. W.'s question to the examiner—"I'm not supposed to criticize the drawing, am I?"—suggests a wish for external admonitions against her potentially critical and not so idealized feelings toward her mother.

Thus, without probing very much deeper or more speculatively, it can readily be seen that Mrs. W.'s verbal associations to her female drawing reflect both self- and object representations of a very significant nature. The object representations are probably related to partially dissociated memory fragments and early experiences with her mother. The self-representations largely take the form of unrealistic ego ideals that are hard to live up to; smoothly integrated identifications with her mother's organizational skills and assets are not in evidence. A failure to fully mourn the loss of the mother can be inferred as the psychodynamic responsible for at least part of Mrs. W.'s depressive tendencies and ego impairment. Her inability to attain the status of a competent professional woman (this was one of her presenting complaints) may stem from the frozen and excessively idealized nature of her maternal introject. One therapeutic goal would therefore be the interruption of this process of maternal idealization via a recathexis and recollection of the critical and angry feelings toward her mother that have been largely dissociated as a result of traumatic loss.

Mrs. W.'s associations to her male drawing convey a similarly idealized pattern ("he's a pleasure to be with. . . . Very well liked," etc.), except for the hints of slightly less idealized qualities ("he's a private person. You just don't know what is going on for him in his day-to-day life"). Her recollections of her father on the Early Memories Test are interesting in light of this last statement. She recalls her father as a very capable physician and caring sort of person whose career and loving relationship to Mrs. W. and a younger brother were interfered with by his second wife, who is depicted as an explosively angry and rejecting sort of person. Mrs. W.'s early memories of her father contained the following statement: "He was very well respected for most of those years. He was successful and very, very dedicated. But, you know, he was not an easy man to get to know. I never knew quite what to say to him." Mrs. W.'s father eventually became addicted to drugs and was unable to practice medicine effectively. Mrs. W. blames her stepmother for most of her father's career decline and personality difficulties later in life.

Thus Mrs. W.'s associations to her male drawing further indicate her heavy reliance on the defense mechanism of idealization. In addition, she appears to utilize a form of projective identification that can be labeled *proxy-evocation* (Wangh, 1962; Kissen, 1978, 1979). This maneuver involves a partial dissociation of latent critical, angry, or aggressive feelings and their projection onto suitable environmental figure (i.e. her father, her husband, or men in general). Thus, rather than accept her angry or aggressive feelings, Mrs. W. may disown them by inciting them in male figures in a subtly interactive manner. Her depiction of the male figure as a German shepherd, despite her minimization of any aggressive characteristics of this animal ("a reliable, strong companion"), suggests a tendency to view males in idealized, aggressive terms which may occasionally be reflected in a disowning of her own potentially aggressive feelings and a consequent subtle evocation of them in males in her outer environment: her aggressive proxies. This defensive maneuver is often associated with a tendency to experientially disown inner feelings of potency and aggressive resourcefulness while simultaneously interactively projecting them upon external environmental figures (Kissen, 1979).

Her depiction of the male figure as "mild-mannered" and likable, of course, conflicts with her statement that he resembles a German shepherd. This discrepancy may be associated with a view of the father as outwardly unaggressive and a wish that he would have been more aggressive. Or it may be associated with an awareness of split-off angry feelings that the father was unable to openly experience or behaviorally express. At some level, she seems to have internalized a self-representation involving feelings of even-temperedness and a general inability to experientially get in touch with more potent critical and angry feelings.

Her associations to the male drawing, then, involve both object representations (i.e. actual recollections and perceptions with regard to her father and, possibly, with regard to her husband) and self-representations (i.e. introjects and identifications stemming from her relationship to her father which have been internalized in the form of self-perceptions). Her reliance on various neurotic and more primitive borderline defensive maneuvers against the experiential aspects of these object relationships may also be gleaned from her verbal associations to her male drawing.

The present analysis is by no means exhaustive; it is intended to suggest only a few of the object relations tendencies and associated defensive maneuvers that can be gleaned from this patient's verbal associations to her two figure drawings. These clinical inferences have of course been facilitated by viewing the patient's associations in the context of her other test responses, especially those on the Early Memories Test, as well as her current symptoms and presenting complaints. The main purpose of this analysis is to suggest the evocativeness and therapeutic usefulness of this testing procedure and formal inquiry structure, particularly with regard to the illumination of significant object relations tendencies. These inferences must of course be validated in the convergent fashion appropriate to any other type of test inference. They must be judged in the context of inferences derived from other projective and nonprojective tests administered in the test battery. Hopefully, their predictive validity will be assessed in terms of their applicability and usefulness in the therapeutic setting.

Conclusions

The approach to the figure drawing test described in this paper goes beyond the early recommendations of Machover (1949), in that it highlights and is more sensitive to the object relations aspects of this test. The structured interview format involves a self-interview technique in which the patient is asked to peruse his own test productions in a curious and psychological-minded fashion. This procedure is particularly compatible with the methods I have outlined for using psychological tests to explore therapeutic parameters (Kissen, 1977), as well as with a number of contributions to the formulation of a systematic art and science of testing for the psychotherapist (Appelbaum, 1969, 1970, 1972; Kissen, 1971, 1973).

This methodology is not open to the empirical criticisms leveled at the standard approach to drawing inferences from figure drawings (Swensen, 1957, 1968; Roback, 1968), in that the unreliability of direct correlations between specific physical aspects of drawings (physical size, placement on the page, line quality, erasures, etc.) and specific inferences is of no consequence. The present method allows the patient to highlight the significant physiognomic features of his own drawing and hence utilizes the patient as a consultant (Strean, 1970). The verbal associations of the patient are then used to develop inferences with regard to object relations tendencies (i.e. self- and object representations), as well as specific defense mechanisms used to cope with these object relations projections.

The case material presented is exemplary of the sort of object relations perspective that can be developed with the Draw-A-Person test. The test offers a particularly sensitive instrument for exploring object relations tendencies that are of great significance to the ultimate psychotherapy needs of the patient. When utilized in connection with other projective instruments —particularly the Early Memories Test, which Mayman and Faris (1960) have developed from a similar object relations perspective—the figure drawing test can produce quite valid and therapeutically useful insights into the inner experiential world of a given patient. Whereas the figure drawing test largely illuminates individual units of an individual's self- and object representations, the Early Memories Test tends to produce the more complex units that have in the earlier portion of this chapter been labeled *ego states*.

References

Allen, J. (1977), Ego states and object relations. *Bull. Menn. Clin.*, 41:522–539.

Appelbaum, S. (1969), Psychological testing for the psychotherapist. *Dynam. Psychiat.*, 2:158–163.

——— (1970), Science and persuasion in the psychological test report. *J. Consult. Clin. Psychol.*, 35:349–355.

——— (1972), A method of reporting psychological test findings. *Bull. Menn. Clin.*, 36:349–355.

Athey, G. (1974), Schizophrenic thought organization, object relations and the Rorschach test. *Bull. Menn. Clin.*, 38:406–429.

Fairbairn, W. (1954), *An Object Relations Theory of the Personality*. New York: Basic Books.

Giovacchini, P. (1975), *Psychoanalysis of Character Disorders*. New York: Aronson.

Hartmann, H. (1939), *Ego Psychology and the Problem of Adaptation*. New York: International Universities Press, 1958.

Horner, A. (1979), *Object Relations and the Developing Ego in Therapy*. New York: Aronson.

Jacobson, E. (1964), *The Self and the Object World*. New York: International Universities Press.

Kernberg, O. (1975), *Borderline Conditions and Pathological Narcissism*. New York: Aronson.

——— (1976), *Object Relations Theory and Clinical Psychoanalysis*. New York: Aronson.

——— (1980), *Internal World and External Reality*. New York: Aronson.

Kissen, M. (1971), The status of psychological testing in current clinical practice. *J. Clin. Iss. Psychol.*, 2(3):20–22.

——— (1973), The importance of psychological testing for the psychotherapy process. *J. Clin. Iss. Psychol.*, 5(1):11–13.

——— (1977), Exploration of therapeutic parameters during psychological testing. *Bull. Menn. Clin.*, 41:266–272.

——— (1978), Meshing characterological structures in marriage partners. *ASPP Newsletter*. Adelphi University, Dec., pp. 4–7.

——— (1979), A note on two defense mechanisms against feelings of power. Unpublished manuscript.

Krohn, A., & Mayman, M. (1974), Object representations in dreams and projective tests. *Bull. Menn. Clin.*, 38:445–466.

Machover, K. (1949), *Personality Projection in the Drawing of the Human Figure*. Springfield, Ill.: Charles C Thomas.

Mayman, M. (1963), Psychoanalytic study of the self-organization with psychological tests. In: *Recent Advances in the Study of Behavior Change: Proceedings of the Academic Assembly on Clinical Psychology*, ed. B. Wigdor. Montreal: McGill University Press, pp. 97–117.

——— (1967), Object representations and object relationships in Rorschach responses. *Internat. J. Psycho-Anal.*, 31:17–24.

——— (1976), Psychoanalytic theory in retrospect and prospect. *Bull. Menn. Clin.*, 40:199–210.

——— Faris, M. (1960), Early memories as expressions of relationship paradigms. *Amer. J. Orthopsychiat.*, 30:507–520.

Rapaport, D. (1959), A historical survey of psychoanalytic ego psychology. Introduction to Identity and the Life Cycle, by E. Erikson. *Psychological Issues*, Monogr. 1. New York: International Universities Press, pp. 5–17.

Roback, H. (1968), Human figure drawings: Their utility in the clinical psychologist's armamentarium for personality assessment. *Psychol. Bull.*, 70:1–19.

Schafer, R. (1976), *A New Language for Psychoanalysis*. New Haven: Yale University Press.

——— (1978), *Language and Insight*. New Haven: Yale University Press.

Sherman, M. (1961), Siding with the resistance in paradigmatic psychotherapy. *Psychoanalysis and the Psychoanalytic Review*, 48(4):43–59.

Strean, H. (1970), The use of the patient as a consultant. *New Approaches in Child Guidance*. Metuchen, N.J.: Scarecrow Press.

Sugarman, A. (1977), Object relations theory: A reconciliation of phenomenology and ego psychology. *Bull. Menn. Clin.*, 41:113–130.

Sundberg, N. (1961), The practice of psychological testing in clinical services throughout the United States. *Amer. Psychol.*, 16:79–83.

Swensen, C. (1957), Empirical evaluation of human figure drawings. *Psychol. Bull.*, 54:431–466.

——— (1968), Empirical evaluations of human figure drawings: 1957–1966. *Psychol. Bull.*, 70:20–44.

Wangh, M. (1962), The "evocation of a proxy": A psychological maneuver, its use as a defense, its purposes and genesis. *The Psychoanalytic Study of the Child*, 17:451–469. New York: International Universities Press.

Winnicott, D. (1951), Transitional objects and transitional phenomena. In: *Collected Papers: Through Paediatrics to Psycho-Analysis*. London: Tavistock, 1958, pp. 229–242.

Chapter 8

COMBINED USE OF HUMAN FIGURE DRAWINGS AND THE EARLY MEMORIES TEST IN ASSESSING OBJECT RELATIONS PHENOMENA

MORTON KISSEN

Over the past few years, there has been a tremendous increase of interest in the implications of object relations theory for both psychological assessment and psychotherapy. The pervasiveness of the paradigm shift from the earlier ego psychological model to a more phenomenologically oriented object relations theory is noted by Sugarman (see chapter 2) in the following statement: "Indeed, it is well-nigh impossible today to open a psychoanalytic journal without having one's eye accosted by the term 'object relations' in the title of an article." Standardized approaches to psychological testing have recently shifted to an object relations model, both methodologically and inferentially. New projective tests have been added to the existing armamentarium, and revised procedures have been developed for the standard battery of tests, in order to better assess object relations phenomena.

Most projective tests have traditionally, in line with the early creative contributions of Schafer (1948) and Rapaport, Gill, and Schafer (1945), been administered and analyzed from a structural perspective with inferences being generated in terms of impulse-defense configurations. Schafer (1978) has more recently begun to argue that the ego psychological model has a rather blatant deficiency, in that it implicitly conceptualizes a very *passive* individual buffeted about by his various impulsive strivings on the one hand, and his more restrictive needs for control and order on the other. While such conflicts certainly do exist for most individuals, Schafer feels that the more active, volitional aspects inherent in the individual's dilemma are essentially overlooked when this ego psychological model becomes the sole perspective from which clinical inferences are generated. He recommends, as an alternative, an *action language* approach which he argues is far more faithful to the conscious choices implicit in most forms of psychopathology. From this newer perspective a patient is not merely depicted as depressed, for example, but rather as choosing to be unhappy as a means of attaining certain secondary gratifications and goal states. Schafer's approach accentuates those phenomenologically discernible and active self-representational states that are so intrinsic to the object relations conceptual model.

The Rorschach Test Viewed from an Object Relations Perspective

The Rorschach test was one of the first projective instruments to be utilized from an object relations perspective. Mayman (1967) underlined the clinical significance of those object representational states that can be inferred from a series of inkblot perceptions. Schafer, in a brilliant clinical tour de force (1960), offered an illustration of the manner in which a Rorschach protocol can be viewed solely from the perspective of body image and self-representational states. Kwawer recently analyzed a series of Rorschach test protocols of borderline patients and arrived at the following conclusion: "The Rorschach imagery I have discussed indicates that borderline psychopathology encompasses several modes of object relatedness including *narcissistic mirroring, symbiotic merging, separation and division,* and *metamorphosis and transformation*. Within these interpersonal modes, boundary disturbances reflect difficulty with developing selfhood" (1979, p. 524).

Blatt (1974), from a more empirical perspective, has developed a number of systematic and quite reliable procedures for scaling object representations in inkblot perceptions. His studies across a broad variety of patient psychopathology have contributed to the construct validation of the concept of object representation on the Rorschach.

Athey (1974), in a very significant contribution, offered a demonstration of how the schizophrenic's thought processes, as reflected in Rorschach responses, essentially parallel the way he experiences object relations in the transference during psychotherapy. Thus, the continuum of *thought disorder indicators* (fabulized combinations, confabulations, contaminations) was found to correlate quite closely with certain transferential paradigms observable during treatment. Athey argues that the quality of self- and object representations underlying each thought disorder indicator is responsible for this sort of parallel object relations process.

Object Relations Aspects of the Early Memories Test

Mayman has made some of the more important contributions to the burgeoning interest in utilizing projective tests other than the Rorschach to explore object relations phenomena. Mayman's interest in collecting early memories from patients culminated in his development of an instrument for obtaining such early recollections in a highly standardized fashion (Mayman and Faris, 1960). Mayman essentially obtains a series of chronologically earliest recollections and then goes on to ask for specific memories involving relationship experiences with each significant parent. Memories reflecting particular affect states (happy, sad) are also requested, as well as family stories about the patient's early childhood; these may be about events of which the patient has no recollection.

For each memory, Mayman asks for a phenomenological picture of the significant object representation depicted (e.g. "How do you picture your mother in the memory?") and a description of the affect state prevalent in the memory. He inquires also into the self-representational aspects of the memory (i.e. "How do you picture yourself in the memory?")

I have devised for my own clinical use additional structured items that can be used either to augment the Mayman test or together with a truncated version of it. I ask the patient, "What memory comes to mind that captures the sort of person you picture your mother to be?" Upon obtaining the memory, I ask for the object representational and self-representational recollections in the manner recommended by Mayman. I next ask, "What memory comes to mind that captures the sort of person you picture your father to be?" Upon obtaining that memory, I follow up with inquiry into how the patient perceives his parents in the two memories and then how the patient perceives himself. For both memories, I ask about the patient's feeling state at the time of the remembered event.

Mayman's systematic procedure for gathering early memories, together with my own augmented version of that test, allows for a projective testing process that is truly object relational. The patient is invited to produce a series of object relational experiences very parallel to the units described by Kernberg (1966) in his now classic conceptualization of object relations phenomena. This basic unit consists of a self-representation, an object representation, and an associated affect state. Kernberg places his conceptualization within a developmental perspective and differentiates the developmentally most primitive units, which he calls *introjects,* from the more sophisticated units he calls *identifications* and, finally, from the most differentiated and complex organizational unit, which he calls *ego identity.*

Kernberg goes on to describe the concept of mutually dissociated ego states so predominantly seen in the split-off identification processes observable in borderline personalities: "there exists [in borderline personality organizations] what we might call mutual denial of independent sectors of the psychic life. Actually, we might say that there exist alternating 'ego states,' and I use the concept of 'ego state' as a way of describing these repetitive, temporarily ego syntonic, compartmentalized psychic manifestations" (p. 236). Kernberg's notion of the dissociated ego state, so pervasively reflected in the pathological processes of borderline patients, meshes quite well with Mayman's description (1963, 1976) of the complexly differentiated ego states discernible in early memories.

The Early Memories Test, then, is a very sensitive clinical instrument with a rather unique potential for assessing the self-representations, object representations, and ego identity states of a given individual.

Object Relations Assessment Through Human Figure Drawings

The human figure drawing test is unquestionably one of the most popular projective instruments available to psychologists. For many years, this test has been administered and analyzed largely from the interpretive perspective recommended by Machover (1949) in her volume on the figure drawing test. The methodology recommended by Machover relies almost completely on the discrete (as opposed to global) physiognomic attributes and spatial characteristics of the drawings. A number of research studies (Swensen, 1957; Roback, 1968), however, have questioned both the reliability and the validity of this methodology. In chapter 7 I presented a rather different methodology which capitalizes instead on the far more reliable global physiognomic attributes of the drawings, and which uses a structured interview format to assess, in a highly systematic fashion, the self-representations of a given patient. This methodology allows for a more clinically valid and useful delineation, in modern object relations terms, of the body image and personality dynamics alluded to by Machover (1949). Thus the patient's internalized self- and object representations can be inferred in a smooth and cogent fashion from the patient's verbal associations to the drawings.

It is the central premise of this chapter that the figure drawing test, used in conjunction with the Early Memories Test, accentuates the object relations potential of the standard test battery. The clinical illustration to follow reflects the interlocking object relations inferences that can be derived from these two tests.

Clinical Case Example

The patient, Miss M., is a twenty-three-year-old woman who came to an outpatient clinic with symptoms of depression. Rather than seek help for herself, however, she requested conjoint family therapy interviews for herself and her parents, with whom she resides.

Early Memories

A modified version of the Mayman inventory was administered. The patient's responses will be reported verbatim. The examiner's inquiries appear in parentheses.

(Think back and recall your earliest memory.) I remember the first time I threw a tantrum. It was over a haircut. Maybe I was two or three years old. They held me down. (Who did?) My mother and father and some lady. (What did you feel?) Angry, I felt controlled. I remember always feeling controlled.

(What is your next earliest memory?) In the kindergarten, getting made fun of . . . I felt hurt, very hurt. I felt that I was good. I didn't do anything to hurt anyone. . . . Then, in the first grade, I remember my teacher yelling at me. (What were your feelings?) I felt hurt again, humiliated for no reason. I didn't do anything wrong. She was frustrated with me. (Can you picture her?) She had red hair and a deep voice . . . I felt that she didn't like me. It may have been my imagination. . . . It probably was my imagination.

(What is your next earliest memory?) In the fourth grade, I remember being the teacher's pet and accelerating in school. (Was your teacher a man or a woman?) He was a man. I had it easy because he liked me and told me I was good. (What were your feelings?) Now, I don't think he was fair. (Why not?) He treated some people better than others. (What were your feelings then?) Uncomfortable—like I didn't deserve it.

(Do you have an early memory involving you and your mother?) When I was in the fourth grade and threw the tantrum. My mother said everything would be all right. My mother held my arm with another person. I was so angry that I twirled around. (Can you picture your mother?) I really wanted to get her attention and to have her understand what I was feeling. (Can you picture the expression on her face?) Smiling, laughing, as if it was some sort of joke . . . I'm making my mother sound terrible. She really isn't.

(Do you have an early memory of you and your father?) I remember him yelling at all of the children on the street. They were playing baseball and he wanted them to get away from our street. (What were you feeling?) Embarrassed. (Can you picture him?) Just angry . . . I was embarrassed because I felt they would hate me. (Did they?) Yes, they made fun of us.

(Can you recall a memory that captures the sort of person that you picture your mother to be?) I don't know. I picture her as very warm, very caring. My father is the same way. Both are very overprotective, extensively, extensively. (What memory captures your mother?) I remember coming home crying. I wanted her to tweeze my eyebrows. People were making fun of my eyebrows. (How do you picture your mother?) Caring. She said that she would do it. I see her holding my face and tweezing my eyebrows. (Did it hurt?) A little bit. (Was she gentle?) She was very gentle and tried not to hurt me. (Did she succeed in not hurting you?) As much as she could.

(What memory captures the sort of person you picture your father to be?) The way he used to joke around. Talking to him about math a lot. He helped me with my math. Also playing the piano. We used to play together. He always wanted me to be successful and smart. He looked up to me, I *guess*. (You seem unsure about this.) I'm not sure. He looked at me in a certain way. I'm not too sure what he was feeling. . . . Sometimes he would criticize me when I did badly. But he also encouraged me a lot in those years. (How did you feel when he criticized you?) I usually felt that it was true. (How did you feel when he encouraged you?) I felt it was true, also, I think—I'm not too sure. (You seem less sure about his encouragement.) Probably, my inner feelings are that I'm not that sure about his good statements.

(Are there any stories that the family likes to tell about you?) My mother said that I locked myself in the closet. I was very young, about two years old. They didn't know where I was. My father turned red, he got scared. (What were you feeling?) I don't know. I thought it was funny that I could trick him. . . . Also, they say that I used to take my clothes off and throw them in the garbage, whenever I made in my pants. (What were your feelings?) Funny—my parents were laughing about it.

Human Figure Drawings

Two drawings and verbal captions (Figures 1 and 2) were obtained from Miss M. The following verbal associations were obtained in response to the structured interview format described above.

Figure 1 (Woman). (What sort of person do you picture?) I didn't mean for her to look that way, but she looks angry . . . a women's libber, aggressive, I guess, a go-getter. A career woman. (Any other traits come to mind?) Very, what's the word when you keep going after something, what's the word? (Determined?) Yes, determined, she has probably been hurt in the past (anxious laugh). . . . People have stepped on her. . . . They looked at her as a dumb broad. Now, she's fighting to get a prestigious job, for some kind of freedom, I guess. . . . She's basically content with what she has achieved. (How do you picture her relationships with women?) She would probably be a kind of boss. I see her ordering other women around on the job. . . . In other relations with women, she seems happy, full, and complete. Happy with her close friends. She probably would only have close friends. (Why is that?) She wouldn't have women friends who aren't close with her. (?) She has been hurt before. . . . She is careful in picking her friends. (What

I'm happy I finally got this job after being told how I could never make it by everyone

I. Woman

Ma, why did Johnny & Louis do that to me?
II. Boy

are her relationships with men like?) She is flirtatious (anxious laugh). She goes after anything she wants—even if she can't get it, she will try. (At this point, she looks somewhat seductively at the examiner.). . . . (What sort of animal comes to mind that she seems most like?) Something the way I picture myself—a friendly dog. (Any particular breed?) All right, mine is a small collie. . . . I didn't mean to make her look angry . . . a small shy poodle—a very small dog. (What parts of her does this animal capture?) The part of her that is very shy and sensitive.

Figure 2 (Boy). (How do you picture him?) A young boy, he's shy . . . naive, I guess—for the boy part. He thinks that everybody is a very good person and tries to please people. I'm just saying anything that comes to mind. (That's the idea.) He likes to please people. (Any other characteristics?) Polite, very polite. He is quiet and doesn't stand up for his rights. He is afraid of being hurt by people. (How do you picture his relationships with other boys?) He is very well liked, but is often taken advantage of and hurt by other people. . . . He hurts himself a lot because of other people, gets very hurt. Although they like him, they take advantage of him. They are not afraid of him, but he is afraid of all his peers. (How does he relate to girls?) He has many friends that are girls, but not sexually attractive girls, just loser girls. He doesn't talk to girls that he really likes. (What sort of animal does he remind you of?) A little tiny toy poodle (anxious laugh). This is terrible, poor boy. (Are you feeling sorry for him?) Yes.

Object Relations Analysis of the Test Data

M.'s severely self-disparaging and self-critical tendencies are evident in both test protocols. Her early memories are replete with incidents in which her parents and authority figures such as teachers behave in a critical or seemingly cruel fashion toward her and yet she questions her right to an angry or critical reaction.

Thus, after producing a series of memories in which her parents and teachers are depicted in object representational terms as indifferent to her needs, as controlling and oppressive in their mode of interaction, and as humiliating and essentially hurtful figures, she comments around a specific memory of her mother in the process of restraining her outburst in the presence of another person: "I'm making my mother sound terrible. She really isn't." This is the response that is so typically obtained from inhibited patients with severely restrictive superego structures. It is as if the object representations, self-representations, and associated affect states that have been generated by her memories are too harsh and unpleasant. They seem also to link up to potentially explosive feelings of anger and resentment, and hence she attempts to utilize her favorite defense mechanisms of denial and reaction-formation to camouflage these affect states.

Her characterological style quite clearly involves a series of mechanisms for effectively maintaining a masochistic status quo and for cutting off any potential she might have for more aggressive or assertive forms of behavioral reaction. She thus produces a consistent series of memories repeatedly depicting herself as being humiliated or controlled by cruel and sadistic authority figures. There is an almost exhibitionistic quality to the flair with which she is able to produce and deliver this series of childhood memories, and one wonders if she is obtaining subtle sadistic gratifications by thus depicting her internal authority figures. She cannot, however, allow herself even the subtle and essentially passive sadistic gratifications that might be obtained from such depictions. She attempts instead to divert her angry reactions and to maintain her internalized ego state of the long-suffering and essentially martyred little girl who must passively suffer the cruel and uncaring ministrations of others, while at the same time she rationalizes, maintaining that these individuals certainly know better than she does what is good for her. Thus she protects these authority figures from her angry feelings, which instead are turned against herself. She proceeds in this process to idealize her parents and teachers while at the same time producing a series of memories that place them in a very harsh and cruel light.

Many patients with severe character problems use a similar mechanism in association with a form of projective identification that can be labeled *proxy-evocation* (Wangh, 1962). Essentially this maneuver involves the induction of angry feelings in another person. Thus M. prefers to idealize her parents and to rationalize and minimize any noxious attributes implicit in her memories. As I was recording her memories, I found myself feeling angry toward her parents, who seemed so coldly oppressive and controlling. M. herself, on the other hand, never gave even the hint of any angry feelings toward them. She seemed able to *disown* such feelings and to interactively project them into me. I would assume that this is a mechanism she feels quite comfortable in utilizing as a means of preserving parental idealizations and of denying feelings of anger.

Her preference for proxy-evocation maneuvers to cope with angry feelings was also reflected in her associations to the female figure drawing, which she described, at least somewhat consistently, as depicting a hard-nosed, ambitious, and success-driven sort of woman. The aggressiveness and liberated qualities of assertiveness implicit in such self-representations evidently made her feel uncomfortable and she therefore proceeded to depict the female figure as a "small, shy poodle." Thus she disowns her latent ego ideals and aspirations toward a more assertive and aggressive self-image. She might very well seek out more aggressive women friends who are capable of expressing anger in the assertive fashion she herself eschews. It would not be surprising if she actually had such a friend, one who perhaps criticized her own parents (or even the patient's) in a more energetic and angry way than she herself is capable of. It would also not be surprising if she eventually chose a very aggressive mate, a man quite different from the shy, passive boy she drew, who can only go out with girls he does not find attractive and who fears and is picked on by everyone.

Indeed, her associations to the male drawing reflect both her slightly masculine identification with her father (who is seen as shy and a bit castrated like herself) and her own internalized self-representations, which clearly are not very ego-syntonic. She is not very happy about her self-critical, shy, and easily intimidated expressive demeanor and can only indirectly express such discomfort—in the camouflage of her association to the male figure drawing.

I have previously described (Kissen, 1979, 1981a,b) the proxy-evocation mechanism as a means, often utilized by patients suffering from character disorders, of disowning inner feelings of competence, assertiveness, and power. M.'s characterological difficulties are certainly involved in her reliance on this projective identificatory defensive mechanism. It helps her maintain idealizations of her parents (object representations) and her self-representation as the long-suffering, martyred little girl who is too powerless and timid to defend herself in a more assertive manner. Her need to protect her parents from her angry feelings almost certainly has the reparative, guilt-ridden aspect alluded to by Searles (1979), who holds that the wish to cure and therapeutically help the parents is unconsciously contained in many forms of characterological difficulty. M.'s need to protect and perhaps cure her parents overshadows her latent ego ideals and aspirations to become a more powerful, emotionally spontaneous, and aggressively capable sort of woman. The early ego identity states associated with such aspirations are suggested in the family stories about her that she recalled. It is interesting to note that these stories reflect a very feisty and emotionally spontaneous child (note her enjoyment in observing her father turn red in fright after she locked herself in the closet, and her throwing her clothes away after she made in her pants) who certainly evinced a degree of spunkiness and provocative potential. But somewhere in her development she began to split off these ego states. They became essentially unavailable at a conscious expressive level and were available only through largely dissociated and preconscious modes of expressive activity.

The self-representations contained in both her early memories and figure drawing associations thus cluster into two mutually dissociated but reciprocal sorts of ego states. On the one hand, her most pervasive and characterologically consistent pattern is to play out the role of an inhibited, timid, and utterly powerless little girl who is totally dominated and controlled by powerful and potentially sadistic authority figures. On the other hand, she possesses certain very dissociated and not very consciously available strivings toward assertiveness and a more actively aggressive mastery of those in her outer environment. She, like her female figure, would like to aggressively show off her potential for success. She would like to boss and control others and, at a sexual level, would like to successfully flirt with men she finds attractive—in contrast to her timid male figure, who can seek out only women he finds unattractive.

The inferences being drawn from M.'s two test protocols are not meant to be comprehensive. They are intended merely to suggest the productive potential of these two projective tests when utilized together in a test battery. All the inferences are tentatively offered and would need to be coordinated through inferences drawn from other tests as well as from such sources of behavioral and situational data as the initial referral and social history. The present analysis merely offers some inferences that can be generated from an essentially object relational perspective and is a contribution to the object relations potential of the Early Memories Test and human figure drawings.

References

Athey, G. (1974), Schizophrenic thought organization, object relations and the Rorschach test. *Bull. Menn. Clin.*, 38:406–429.

Blatt, S. (1974), Levels of object representation in anaclitic and introjective depression. *The Psychoanalytic Study of the Child*, 29:107–157. New Haven: Yale University Press.

Kernberg, O. (1966), Structural derivatives of object relationships. *Internat. J. Psycho-Anal.*, 47:236–253.

Kissen, M. (1979), A note on two defense mechanisms against feelings of power. Unpublished manuscript.

——— (1981a), Inferring object relations from human figure drawings. *Bull. Menn. Clin.*, 45:43–54.

——— (1981b), Therapeutic use of self- and object representations in the treatment of character disorders. Unpublished manuscript.

Kwawer, J. (1979), Borderline phenomena, interpersonal relations and the Rorschach test. *Bull. Menn. Clin.*, 43:515–524.

Machover, K. (1949), *Personality Projection in the Drawing of the Human Figure.* Springfield, Ill.: Charles C Thomas.

Mayman, M. (1963), Psychoanalytic study of the self-organization with psychological tests. In: *Recent Advances in the Study of Behavior Change: Proceedings of the Academic Assembly on Clinical Psychology,* ed. B. Wigdor. Montreal: McGill University Press, pp. 97–117.

——— (1967), Object representations and object relationships in Rorschach responses. *Internat. J. Proj. Techniques and Pers. Assessment* 31:17–24.

——— (1976), Psychoanalytic theory in retrospect and prospect. *Bull. Menn. Clin.*, 40:199–210.

——— Faris, M. (1960), Early memories as expressions of relationship paradigms. *Amer. J. Orthopsychiat.*, 30:507–520.

Rapaport, D., Gill, M., & Schafer, R. (1945), *Diagnostic Psychological Testing.* New York: International Universities Press, 1968.

Roback, H. (1968), Human figure drawings: Their utility in the clinical psychologist's armamentarium for personality assessment. *Psychol. Bull.*, 70:1–19.

Schafer, R. (1948), *The Clinical Application of Psychological Tests.* New York: International Universities Press.

——— (1960), Bodies in schizophrenic Rorschach responses. *J. Proj. Tech.*, 24:267–281.

——— (1978), *Language and Insight.* New Haven: Yale University Press.

Searles, H. (1979), The patient as therapist to his therapist. In: *Countertransference and Related Subjects: Selected Papers.* New York: International Universities Press, pp. 380–459.

Swensen, C. (1957), Empirical evaluation of human figure drawings. *Psychol. Bull.*, 54:431–466.

Wangh, M. (1962), The "evocation of a proxy": A psychological maneuver, its use as a defense, its purposes and genesis. *The Psychoanalytic Study of the Child.* 17:451–469. New York: International Universities Press.

Chapter 9

AN OBJECT RELATIONAL THEORY OF AFFECT MATURITY: APPLICATIONS TO THE THEMATIC APPERCEPTION TEST

ANNE E. THOMPSON

Clinicians acknowledge that emotion is central to our notions of psychopathology and the process of therapy, yet it has been difficult to conceptualize affects in a clinically useful way. This chapter sets forth a theoretical view of affect development and maturity and describes the application of these ideas to clinical material from the TAT.

In recent years converging trends in a number of diverse fields—psychoanalytic theory (Schur, 1969; Brenner, 1974; Ross, 1975), cognitive and developmental psychology (Sroufe, 1979; Averill, 1980), and philosophy (Pitcher, 1965) have supported a conceptualization of affect in *cognitive* and *intensional*[1] terms (Thompson, 1980). By a *cognitive* view of affects I mean one in which affect has cognition as an intrinsic component, that is, one in which affects are, in part, cognitive structures. By an *intensional* view of affects, I mean one in which emotions are intrinsically directed to objects. If one is angry, one is angry *at* someone or something; if one envies, one is envious *of* someone or something. While such ''objects'' as conceptualized in the philosophical literature should not be equated with the ''ob-

[1]This term stems from Brentano (1874), who saw intensionality as the defining characteristic of mental processes. The spelling follows Kenny (1963), in order to distinguish this concept from the sense of intentionality that refers to agency or goal-directedness of actions.

jects'' as conceptualized in the literature on object relations (the philosophical term is to be taken more generally to refer also to situations, states of affairs, and so forth), it nevertheless seems that the most important subclass of such objects comprises other persons. Thus the internal representations of self and other within the realm of affect experience and the extent to which these representations are individuated form an important aspect of the ability to experience emotion in its mature form.

In describing emotions as intrinsically cognitive and intensional in form, I am speaking of adult, mature, standard cases of emotion—cases which we can take as central, and in terms of which we can understand derivative cases. For example, it is not claimed that emotions in children are directed to an object or that their emotions have cognitive components in the same sense that those of a mature adult do. I suggest that a conceptualization of emotion in cognitive and intensional terms will provide a basis for understanding affective clinical phenomena, as well as allowing us to bring to bear recent findings in cognitive and developmental psychology on clinical psychoanalytic theory.

The Developmental Line of Emotion

I am suggesting that emotions can be seen as having a developmental line (A. Freud, 1963) of their own. (Schmale, 1964; Krystal, 1974, 1975; and Yorke and Wiseberg, 1976 are among those who have expressed a similar view.) The view of emotional maturity presented here assumes that a general characterization of the line of development of emotion can be given independent of the emergence of any particular emotion. Thus the same affect, anger for example, may be manifested at an earlier or later developmental level, but its organization and structure would differ at the two levels. That is, the same emotion may be manifested at different levels of affect maturity, from the most primitive to the most mature.

By developmental line, Anna Freud (1963) means a conceptualization of the development of some aspect of functioning (in this case, affect) that itself is not a function of the development of any unitary facet of biological or psychic development but involves interaction among numerous facets (pp. 245–246). This view is close to the view currently predominant in developmental psychology regarding development of the emotions—the organizational or systems approach (Sroufe, 1979). On the organizational or systems view, any one differentiated response or capacity (for example, object permanence) can become organized into a number of different systems, of which affect may be one. The line of development of affect, then, will involve complex hierarchization and systematization, and may overlap with other lines of development (for example, the development of cognition, the development of self-other representations), without thereby being reducible to such systems.

It has become relatively commonplace, within both the psychoanalytic and the developmental psychological literature, to say that infantile or primitive affects are "global" and that they then "differentiate" (Schmale, 1964; Krystal, 1974; Kernberg, 1976; Sroufe, 1979). I have tried to give a more precise sense to this notion (Thompson, 1981), drawing on Werner's conceptions (1948) of the "dynamic event" and "things-of-action" (which he elaborates especially with respect to the development of perception and cognition), and also on Piaget's description (Inhelder and Piaget, 1958) of the development from sensorimotor to conceptual, nonegocentric thought; here I shall sketch briefly the direction that such a conceptualization may take.

According to Werner, primitive thought may sometimes be undifferentiated, in the sense of being global, but perhaps more important, such elements as have been differentiated are *unintegrated,* that is, not organized into hierarchical systems. In the vocabulary of systems theory, such elements are highly *segregated* (Bertalanffy, 1968; Hall and Fagen, 1968), where a highly segregated "system" refers to one in which the elements are not hierarchically organized, but rather are loosely connected and independent. I am assuming that the elements of primitive affect experience are unintegrated and segregated rather than systematized.

Paradoxically, these relatively independent and unsystematized elements are thus rendered wholly dependent upon the total affect-event in which they are embedded, and have psychological reality for the subject only so long as the affect-event exists. I have used the expression "thing-of-affect" (by analogy with Werner's "thing-of-action") to refer to such segregated, unintegrated, event-dependent elements of affect. As Werner says (of "things-of-action"), they are "intrinsically formed by the psychophysical organization of which they constitute an integral part, by the whole vital motor-affective situation" (p. 59). In other words, the event may involve "things"; however, these have no existence independent of the event: they have not been differentiated (via integration into hierarchical systems) *from* the event. As Werner suggests, "things as constituent elements of a dynamic event must necessarily be dynamic in nature" (p. 67). In terms of primitive affect experience, a particular self-representation, for example, may be associated with and wholly dependent upon a particular affect-event and so be a "thing-of-affect."

The present model proposes that early affect states have this character of events, such that any elements that have been differentiated are segregated (unsystematized) "things-of-affect." Such eventlike[2] early affect states are (in Werner's terms) both "rigid" and "ephemeral": no changes within the affect event are possible, and any change results in the total disappearance and replacement of the current affect state.

[2]Here and elsewhere in the chapter I am indebted to many classes and discussions with Dr. Irene Fast.

That such a primitive affect state may be experienced by the subject as "global" and even overwhelming is understandable on the basis of its being, temporarily, *all there is:* when the subject is "in the event," all experience of self and reality takes on the dynamic coloring of the affect-event and is dynamically dependent upon it; when the affect-event changes, it takes with it the cognitive representations of reality, self, and object that are associated with it. On this view, affect regression involves not merely a "dedifferentiation," but a "resegregation," that is, a release of elements in the affect system from hierarchical control, and a reinstitution of eventlike, unsystematized affect states.

We would certainly expect such eventlike affect states to hold sway during the Piagetian sensorimotor period of cognitive development (birth to two years), which heralds the establishment of physical object constancy (see Gouin-Decarie, 1965), and during which the child's rudimentary concepts are dependent upon the sensorimotor (or, in terms of the present model, sensoriaffective) event in which they are embedded. However, there is no reason to believe that eventlike affects would disappear around age two. The preoperational child (age two to seven years) remains largely under the sway of sensorimotor representations (see Flavell, 1963, p. 151). The child is still egocentric, that is, cannot conceptualize things independently of his or her own perspective. The preoperational period is also characterized by "centration," that is, one isolated feature of the objective situation may determine the child's entire conceptualization of the situation. The child also has little or no conception of inner, psychological reality. Most important, preoperational thought is "irreversible," that is, the child cannot carry out transformations in thought (e.g. as represented in the perceptual realm, by conservation of volume, and so forth). These features have many implications for the nature of the affect states experienced by the preoperational child. I suggest that the concept of reversibility has direct and central application to the development of affects. In the affective realm, we may call an affect irreversible when, while in one affect state, the child cannot conceptualize his or her relation to other affect states or other evaluations of the object. As Cowan (1978) points out, the preconceptual child will say "I hate you" but is really just conveying "hateful feeling now," without any implication of the enduring feeling state and evaluation of the object that adult hatred implies. Also, the child cannot conceptualize what the cause, target, or object of the emotion is like when he or she is not in the grip of the affect. In other words, a hated object is a hateful object and cannot be evaluated independently of that feeling.

A further implication is that the preoperational child cannot experience "mixed" or "contradictory" emotions; rather, the introduction of a new feeling represents instead a new and irreversible affect-event. The quality of centration suggests that one isolated feature of the objective situation can determine the whole affect-event for the child. The lack of a concept of psychological reality makes for an inability to differentiate between "inner feelings" and their expression, so that a smiling child "must" be a happy child and a crying child a sad one. The continuing eventlike character of affects, the resulting dependence of self- and object representations upon the affect-event, and the lack of a concept of inner psychological reality all converge to make genuine attribution of affect to self (or other) impossible—the self may be "in" the feeling or "have" it somehow, but the feeling is not seen as a psychological state of a differentiated self.

The period of concrete operations (extending from about age six to early adolescence) has the development of reversibility as a central aspect (Inhelder and Piaget, 1958). In the affective realm, the present model assumes that the child acquires reversibility of affect and begins to realize that an emotion, experienced now, can change, and begins also to evaluate the object of the emotion independently of the affect being experienced. In other words, the object of the affect and the affect itself are now differentiated from each other, allowing the distinction between "how one feels about the object" and "how the object really is" to begin. This allows for the beginning of the reality testing of emotions themselves, that is, judging emotions to be appropriate or inappropriate, as justified by the real characteristics of the object or not. This allows also for the experiencing of mixed and contradictory feelings toward the same object. Similarly, the self is differentiated from the affect, and we have the beginnings of the understanding of affects as internal psychological states. With this development, affects become more differentiated from, and independent of, their expressive aspects, so that the child can imagine inhibiting, exaggerating, or feigning the expression of affect. With "decentration," more complex evaluations of objective affective situations become possible. As such integration of the elements of affect into independent, hierarchically organized systems proceeds, the eventlike character of affect diminishes.

Later, in adolescence, in the period of formal operations (Inhelder and Piaget, 1958) widening time perspectives are incorporated into the structure of affects and the adolescent will develop "reflectiveness" about affects similar to what Flavell (1979) describes as "metacognition" in the cognitive realm; that is, the adolescent will begin to develop a fuller understanding of the relationships among affects, situations, and self and others as affective experiencers.

The Concept of Affect Maturity

In brief, then, the achievement of mature affect involves progression through this line of development.[3] The view presented here assumes that individuals

[3]Although in this paper I focus on the cognitive and object relational elements of affect, my discussion elsewhere (Thompson, 1981) refers also to the differentiation of action, expression, and somatic components out of the original affect event, and to the integration of these elements into the affect system.

progress through the line of development with varying degrees of success, and that fixations and regressions occur within the developmental line, so that individuals display different levels of affect maturity as adults. However, it does not assume that levels of affect maturity in the adult necessarily reflect in a one-to-one fashion the levels of development of affect in children. If there has been regression or even loss of previously attained structure, some traces of the higher level of functioning may remain (see Werner, 1948; Martindale, 1976). Neither do the lower levels of functioning completely disappear even with the highest levels of maturity. Also, for an individual at any given level, the beginnings of organization at a higher level may be present. For all these reasons it seems unlikely that an individual will show consistent and persistent performance at a given level. Rather, it is assumed here that individuals differ in *characteristic* level of functioning.

Thus affect maturity forms a fundamental *capacity*, one that determines how an individual will experience and cope with his or her feelings. In particular, this capacity underlies the ability to tolerate affects (Krystal, 1975) and the ability to subject them to reality testing. Affect maturity is here seen as a necessary (though not sufficient) condition for affect tolerance. In therapy it will be difficult to work with defenses against particular affects if the patient is operating at such a low level of affect maturity that the primitive form of the affect will itself pose a problem in tolerating it. For example, an affect in the form of an event may well be terrifying and disintegrating to the patient, who experiences a loss of fundamental cognitive distinctions, of executive functioning, and of an integrated sense of self. Or, for someone who has not yet attained reversibility, an affect may be frightening because it seems as if it will never end, or because it brings with it an all-or-none change in the experience of the object (for example, the therapist). The process of therapy with such individuals requires helping them develop a more mature affect system. (For a discussion of such a process with drug-dependent patients, see Krystal, 1975.) For patients with more mature affect systems, therapy can proceed via the process of interpretation of defenses against particular affects.

The ability to reality test affects is also fundamental to the process of therapy, and depends on affect maturity. Once we have conceptualized emotions in cognitive and intensional terms, it becomes possible to speak of emotions as appropriate or inappropriate, "well-founded" or "mal-founded" (Pitcher, 1965). Ascertaining this appropriateness or inappropriateness, that is, reality testing emotions, involves such operations as accurately assessing the cause of the emotion, knowing whom the emotion is directed toward, what the emotion is, and whether it is justified in relation to its ostensible cause. Reality testing of emotion also involves the ability to make accurate attributions of emotions to the self and others. For example, someone who wildly attributes emotion globally to the surround, such as a borderline patient who would cry, ''What is making all this anger happen?'' (A. Krohn, personal communication), will be seriously handicapped in the ability to reality test emotion.

The Affect Maturity Scale

The purpose of the research to be described is the development of a scale to measure affect maturity, based on the conceptualization outlined so far, for application to the TAT and similar materials. However, the use of the word ''scale'' is somewhat misleading, as it was in no sense a simple rating scale. Rather the aim was to set forth on the basis of theoretical views five hypothesized complex levels of affect maturity, and then to use the process of scale construction to refine these levels, as a beginning step in the construct validation of the conception of affect maturity. (The refinements of the levels go beyond the scope of this paper and are reported in Thompson, 1981.) This process involved the use of a method adapted from Loevinger, Wessler, and Redmore (1970) for the construction of a scale of levels of ego development involving an interactive rating process that requires complex input from clinical judges. This process, though time-consuming, has been found to yield acceptable interjudge reliability (Redmore and Waldman, 1975), and allows clinical judgments, usually so difficult to systematize, to be incorporated into the scale. The emphasis was not so much on a psychometric process of scale construction as on the collection of process data about the judgments made at every step of the raters' task, as a record is made of a judge's justifications of each rating as well as an indication of what aspects of a story provide the evidence for each rating. That judges can carry out such a process provides not only information about the reliability of the scale, but also some preliminary support for its validity, since the exactness of the supporting remarks provides some justification for asserting that the dimension in question—affect maturity—is indeed what is being rated, and not some other dimension such as global health-sickness (a common problem in diagnostic rating scales).

The scale levels were defined in a highly complex manner, in an attempt to integrate as many aspects of the conceptualization as possible. In this chapter, only a brief description of each level will be presented, focusing on the cognitive and object relational aspects of the scale definitions (for a complete description of the scale see Thompson, 1981).

Level One

Here emotions are purely eventlike in character, and there is little differentiation within the affect-event. As such, the emotion is attributed more to the situation as a whole (which includes self, object, the surround, etc.)

than to any individual facet of the situation. (For example, the whole scene may be described as "sad," with everything in it having an undifferentiated quality of sadness.) Emotions may thus have an "atmospheric" or moodlike quality. Rather than being the psychological subject of an emotion, a character may seem more to be immersed in the affect-event. While a character is "in" the affect-event, it colors all reality for him or her, but as the event is ephemeral, it may pass away leaving little trace, and its occurrence is not integrated as part of the self's history.

Level Two

While emotions are still predominantly eventlike, there is now some rudimentary attribution of the emotion to self and others, although not on the basis of their being individuated selves with inner psychological reality. The emotions are attributed rather indiscriminately on the basis of external features of the characters; as expressions and expressive actions are not yet differentiated from the affect, they constitute an important basis for attribution of the emotion. The storyteller may even attempt to "read" the emotions from the expressive appearances. (For example, a smiling face *must* indicate some sort of happy situation.)

The affect-state is still not seen as a psychological state, and it retains eventlike properties, although the role of the self or other is now more predominant than in Level One. Thus, the affect may seem as if it is a happening emanating from outside the self, perhaps moving toward or away from the self, or it may be lodged "inside" the self, in a manner analogous to the physical location of a substance. The implication may be that the person "has" the emotion rather than "being" happy or whatever. There may be the implication that the affect can be warded off, expelled, or eliminated in some way.

The affect-state is still irreversible, with the event coloring all reality and self- and object representations. However, while mixed or contradictory feelings still are not possible, in some stories there may be rapid alternation of affects, attributed to part-selves or part-objects (so that the storyteller may switch the subject's emotions several times in succession without any integration of these affects into a single organization). That is, several different affect-states may be evoked, but successively rather than simultaneously, and as each state is eventlike, it redefines the situation, the representations of self and other, and the evaluation of the target or object of the emotion.

Level Three

Emotions are now attributed to persons, but not in a fully independent way. Self and other may be enveloped in the same emotion (or in not very well differentiated ones) with no understanding that two people may experience the same emotion but for their own individual reasons. If some explanation is given, it is the same for both, or is rather trite. For the single subject, feelings are attributed to the self, but rationalizing feelings is done in a simple way more or less concordant with the immediate situation.

With slightly more differentiation, self and object may be assigned complementary affects, but these are still not rationalized in an individualized way. The affect of the other, although it may differ from that of the self, is still assigned in a highly egocentric way, so that it is the expected response to the self's own feeling. Reversals of affects may occur between self and other (for example, first one is feeling guilty, then the other) so that it becomes unclear who is experiencing the affect, or whether both are.

Mixed or contradictory emotions now make their appearance in that they are simultaneously attributed to the subject rather than presented in succession. However, these affects remain largely independent of each other, do not interact, and are not integrated into a hierarchical, reversible structure. The situation and the target of the emotion are still redefined in a manner coordinate to the emotion for each of the simultaneous affect-states. (For example, "he's happy that she loves him; he's depressed because he wants to join his unit.")

Although the affect-state is now seen as a psychological state to be attributed to a subject, it is still largely irreversible. The situation, causal object, target of the emotion, and self- and object representations still take their coloration from the affect-state, and are conceived in a manner coordinate to it. For example, the object of the emotion is still evaluated in terms consistent with the affect state (for example, good feelings are caused by a good object; bad feelings by a bad object), with no recognition of the object's independent existence, complex characteristics, and so forth.

There may be some hints of the realization that affects have to be dealt with by the self; they will not simply pass away. However, this is often expressed through a magical, even Pollyannaish resolution ("He'll get over it" or "He'll be happy again"). This suggests strongly the substitution of another affect-event, which is attributed to the self but not integrated with the previous one. Nevertheless, it seems as if this new event is being evoked in order to counterpose the original feeling, so that there is some relationship between the two rather than a simple replacement of one event by another.

Level Four

Affects are now clearly attributed as psychological states to individual persons, and the affect is a more individualized expression of the person's characteristics. However, because extended temporal integration is still not carried out, the attribution of individualized affect-states tends to be not so much in terms of the subject's enduring personality and dispositions as in terms of relatively superficial, "external," or somewhat stereotyped ways of individuating a person, such as role, sex, or occupation, or of relatively immediate features of the person's reaction to a situation.

Mixed or contradictory emotions may be attributed to the subject at this level, and these are brought in juxtaposition to each other so that there may be some recognition of the contradiction and conflict, and some attempt to resolve it. This level is a way station in the development of reversibility, in that mixed emotions are not wholly independent conceptually, but full reversibility—which requires the integration of mixed emotions into a hierarchical scheme so that they may modify each other—has not yet been achieved. One possible solution to the conflict is still to minimize or eliminate one side of the contradiction (for example, "He's pulled in two directions—he loves her but he wants to get away. He finally leaves and manages to forget her.") Similarly, the cause, object, or target of the emotion may now have mixed attributes, causing conflict and attempts at resolution, although these are not fully resolved in a hierarchical scheme allowing a complex view of a fully independent object.

At this level, affects, although still determining some of the evaluation of reality and self- and object representations, have lost their predominantly eventlike character. As such, there is now some sense that affect-states do not "pass away without a trace," and that they may change the self and themselves undergo modification.

Level Five

At this level, reversibility has been fully achieved. The self and the other are perceived as individuated affective beings with enduring inner dispositions that affect their emotional responsiveness. This does not mean that specific reference to a person's enduring character structure has to be made, but rather that the affects he experiences are clearly modified by and stem from his uniqueness as a person (as compared to others). Thus self and other are assigned affects in terms of their uniqueness as persons, and are individuated uniquely even when they react in terms of their roles (or sex, etc.).

Mixed and contradictory emotions may often be experienced, but the conflicting emotions now modify each other and may be placed in a wider perspective. (For example, "He's torn between his love for her and his wish to join his unit. Duty is stronger than love, so he leaves, but lives with regret over what he has lost.") With this organization of emotions into hierarchical organizations conflict is not eliminated and in fact may sometimes be intensified, since simple defenses against affects such as denial and minimization are no longer facilitated by the affective organization, as they were before reversibility was achieved. The cause or object of the emotion may now be evaluated independently of the affect, and states of the self are seen as contributing to the affect.

Affects are clearly seen as needing to be integrated into the self's history, rather than passing away, being replaced by other affects, or being "undone" through forgetting or action. There is a sense that the person can tolerate this and that the emotion will be integrated, and some realistic sense of how long this will take and how it will take place, and that the self may be modified by the feeling (especially if it is a very important one).

The person may show evidence of reflective self-awareness concerning affects. However, this need not be an explicit self-reflective statement. Rather, he may experience a reaction to his feeling, or show awareness of how he is reacting, or of what effect he may have on others. (For example, "He's depressed over how angry he is, and wishes he could be more tolerant.")

Research Findings

Preliminary results concerning the ability of clinical judges to use the scale to evaluate the levels of affect maturity represented in TAT stories are available from a study reported in more detail elsewhere (Thompson, 1981). In that study, two advanced (postinternship) female doctoral students in clinical psychology rated TAT stories from sixty patients (half men, half women). Forty patients for whom TAT protocols were available were selected from the files of an outpatient clinic. Although these patients covered the range of psychopathology from psychotic to neurotic and adjustment reactions, to ensure coverage at the extremes the sample was supplemented by protocols from ten psychotic patients from hospital files and ten nonpatients from an introductory psychology class. Although it was not possible to equate the added cases exactly with the main sample, an attempt was made to remain within the same range of IQ, educational level, and age.

Five stories—from TAT cards 4, 3BM, 15, 13MF, and 6BM—were rated for each subject (for a total of three hundred stories). These cards have been found typically to elicit affect-laden stories (Murstein, 1972). For the purposes of rating, each story was typed in identical format, coded by number, and all identifying marks removed. The stories were arranged by card, in random order (for example, sixty stories given to card 4), and judges rated all stories given to one card before going on to the next set of sixty stories, in an attempt to avoid halo effects. The judges reported the basis in the scale descriptions for their ratings as well as the relevant data in the story. Differences between judges were reconciled by discussion for the purpose of arriving at a single score per story. Thus each subject received a set of five item ratings. For each subject the mean of these scores constituted a mean affect maturity index (AMI), and this, along with the associated standard deviation, summarized the scores of each subject on the item ratings.

The judges also rated the protocols (consisting of five stories) of each subject, which yielded a total protocol rating (TPR).

Although high reliability was not a central aim of this study since the discrepancies between the judges comprised one aspect of the data to be used to refine the scale, nevertheless the results with the preliminary scale seem encouraging. For item ratings (IRs) and total protocol ratings (TPRs) respectively, the judges agreed within one scale point 89.3 percent and 93.3 percent of the time, and reached absolute agreement 53.3 percent and 50 percent of the time. Many of the disagreements concerned the relative salience of evidence for two adjacent scale points (for instance, one judge would rate the item "level one, with secondary two," while another would rate it "level two, with secondary level one," while they agreed on the assignment of a given piece of evidence to a scale level).

The question arises as to the extent to which subjects tend to respond consistently in their affect maturity level across cards, as opposed to responding idiosyncratically to the individual cards. A coefficient of concordance (*W*) was calculated to determine the consistency of ordering of subjects within each card-group. This test yielded a coefficient of concordance (*W*) (corrected for ties; see Ferguson, 1959, p. 188) of .2936. This was used to obtain an $X^2 = 86.612$ with 59 degrees of freedom (Ferguson, 1959, pp. 188–189), which is highly significant statistically ($p < .001$). *W* represents the proportion of the obtained variance of the sums of ranks across subjects to the variance of the sums of ranks that would be expected if the subjects were ranked identically within each card group (the case of "perfect concordance"). In this case, the rankings show about 29 percent of the maximum possible concordance. This result suggests a modest but significant tendency for subjects to respond consistently across the individual items.

The study also provided some preliminary support for the discriminant validity of the scale (Campbell and Fiske, 1959). There is always the possibility that raters will agree, but on the basis of something other than the concept ostensibly represented by the scale. In particular, as Loevinger et al. (1970, p. 52) point out, many artifactual personality variables have been created by the researcher's neglecting to measure verbal fluency (which turned out to be the variable actually being measured). This is obviously a potential problem in using TAT materials, as subjects tend to vary widely in fluency. For the purposes of this study, verbal fluency was measured for each subject by the average length of his or her stories, and verbal ability by the verbal IQ and vocabulary subscale of the WAIS. The correlations[4] between these

[4]Since it was not possible to match exactly the two small subsamples on the discriminant validity variables of IQ and vocabulary subscale scores, these correlations were based on the main sample of forty clinic patients.

variables and the two overall affect maturity indices (AMI, TPR) were small (ranging from .028 to .273) and none were statistically significant, providing some evidence for the conclusion that affect maturity is not contingent upon verbal ability or fluency.

Levels of Affect Maturity in TAT Stories

Examples of the five levels will be presented here, all drawn from card 6BM. (Each story reflects some, though not every, characteristic of its level.)

Level One

> Looks like they are either waiting for . . . there looks to be a pensive mood. Maybe filled with some anxiety, could involve an interrelationship between them or a third party. He's telling her something hard for her to . . . it's hard for him to confront, or they're confronting a third issue together. Or maybe it's hard for her to tell him or vice versa, maybe it's hard for her to tell him. (Goes on in similar vein.)

Here the emotion seems to be eventlike in form—it is experienced as a global occurrence that envelops the characters and is attributed more to the situation as a whole than to the characters as persons. The cause seems not to be differentiated from the affect-event; rather, the storyteller attempts to come up with a cause that seems dependent upon, and consequent to, the definition of the affect-event.

Level Two

> This young man has just come to see his mother, an elderly woman. He has a very troubled and disturbed look on his face because the news he's just confronted her with was not at all pleasant. What perplexes me is exactly what kind of news he brought her, because I can't tell from her expression what prompted that reaction. She looks like she's wringing a handkerchief, at most she looks like she has some expression of grief on her face, but I don't think it's very profound. (Goes on in similar vein.)

This story illustrates a number of aspects of Level Two. The storyteller attributes the affects to persons but in a rudimentary way: he or she tries to "read off" the affect from the appearances, which are taken more or less to stand in one-to-one relation with the emotions experienced. The cause is taken as coordinate to the affect-event—if the storyteller could only read the expressions accurately enough, he or she feels that the cause could be inferred from it. In this story affects are still eventlike, but there is a beginning of attribution of affects to persons, though in a rudimentary, undifferentiated way that is still highly dependent on the affect-event.

Level Three

> This sounds (sic) like two people worried about something. I don't know what it is . . . (Led up to?) I don't know, something happened. (What?) Something happened. They figured somebody was hurt? . . . (Thinking and feeling?) Thinking about whether he's okay. And the guy is really concerned and so is the lady. (Outcome?) He'll be all right. Whatever happened will fix itself.

In this Level Three story, affects are attributed to persons in a simple way, and both persons are enveloped in the same (or a very similar) affect. The causal object is still seen in a simple, coordinate way. There is some hint that affects may have to be dealt with by the self, although this is given a magical, Pollyannaish resolution. This suggests strongly the substitution of another affect-event, which will be attributed to the self but not integrated with the previous event. Nevertheless, it does seem that to a limited extent this new affect-event is evoked to counterpose the original feeling, so that there may be some relationship between the two rather than a simple replacement of one event by another. The cause still seems coordinate to the affect-event and defined in terms of it.

Level Four

> The man looks like some official and he's brought news to the woman about her son . . . he died in a car crash. And then he'll go about his business. She's feeling sad because she lost her son . . . and she'll continue to gaze out the window. (His feeling?) He's feeling uncomfortable because he's a stranger and he has to bring such bad news and he isn't sure how to comfort her. (Outcome?) He'll go back to his job, maybe relieved that he got it over with. (Her?) She is shocked, she didn't have any idea this would happen. She's thinking about how much he meant to her and now she's lost all that.

In this story, the characters are assigned individualized emotions, although somewhat in terms of their roles rather than individualized motivations and character. The individuals are assigned affects that are appropriate to their different roles. Affects are seen as having some enduring effects on the self rather than being replaced by a new affect-event.

Level Five

> Let's see . . . just came in and told his mother that um . . . told his mother that his brother died in the war and she's pretending not to hear

> him or not to believe. . . . She's not pretending . . . she doesn't want to hear, she's not facing up to it. He's very sad so he's trying to be gentle with her and trying to think of a way to tell her so that she'll understand. Um I think maybe . . . she'll come through . . . I don't think she is going to face it for a few months and that's going to cause him a lot of pain.

In this story the affects are attributed to persons in a highly individualized way—in terms of their enduring inner dispositions that affect their responsiveness. There is a clear distinction made between the inner and outer manifestations of affect, and what the reactions *to* affects may be (showing a level of reflective self-awareness). The son shows awareness not only of the mother's emotion, but also of how it will affect her as an individual.

Discussion

The concept of affect maturity seems particularly relevant to the issues of prognosis in therapy and the ability of an individual to profit from a certain type of therapy or another. It also presents itself as a concept relevant to the measurement of progress in therapy. Especially, on the cognitive-intensional view of emotion transference can be seen as an intrinsically affective phenomenon. One often hears of the ''as if'' quality of the transference in the case of neurotic patients, whereas a ''psychotic'' transference is said to be one in which this quality is lost so that the patient takes how he feels about the therapist to indicate what the therapist is in reality. However, this does not do justice to how *real* the emotions generated in the transference seem to the neurotic patient; indeed, that they seem real and do not have an ''as if'' quality is necessary to the progress of therapy. Rather, the present view suggests that the distinction between neurotic and a psychotic transference lies on a continuum and reflects relative levels of affect maturity. At one extreme the patient has acquired reversibility, the ability to maintain a concept of what the therapist is like independent of the affect state, and can reality test the emotion. In a psychotic transference, on the other hand, the eventlike character of the affect determines the quality of the object, which is a ''thing-of-affect,'' so that reality testing of the appropriateness of the emotion is not possible. The affect maturity scale offers one way of locating a patient's affective capacity along this continuum.

If one looks at the scale points from a normative point of view, it may be noted that the level of affect maturity represented by the midpoint on the scale is still quite ''low'' when measured by the theoretical standard of mature affect as involving reversibility, attribution of affect as individualized internal states, affect tolerance, and the ability to reality test the affect itself. Subjects at Level Three, for example, still attribute affects to self and other in a relatively undifferentiated way. Even though they do have some concept of affects as psychological states of a person, they do not see these states as very individuated, or as being related to the inner continuity of the person. At this level reversibility has not been obtained, and outer reality and the affects of others will be taken as a reflection of one's own inner state. To borrow Sartre's felicitous expression (1948), affect at this state of emotional development still involves a "magical transformation" of the world. This severely limits the reality testing of emotion because the distinction between the real characteristics of the object and how one feels about the objects is not clearly made. Emotions may also lack fine distinctions at this level because the kind of corrective feedback from the environment that promotes the grasping of emotional nuances is not possible when the environment itself is taken as reflecting the affective state. Objects are still "things-of-affect" in the sense that their characteristics are determined by the affective state.

Affect tolerance at this level will be limited by the fact that the person has limited resources at his disposal to deal with an emotion, except to try to replace it by another affect-event or to try to sustain the current one. If an unpleasant emotion is experienced, it will color all reality for the moment and the perception of self and other within the reality. This may be one reason why some borderline patients, who are frequently angry, find the experience of anger so painful. If they are operating at this level of affect maturity the experience of anger entails not only the loss of the "good object" but also the loss of the "good self." One must make a differentiation within the affect-event between the state of the self and the other before one can be angry *at* the other without conceptualizing both self and other in terms coordinate to the affect.

Overall, the quantitative and qualitative findings provide support for the concept of affect maturity delineated. Naturally such a claim remains tentative until the concept is subjected to further studies of its reliability and validity. It is hoped that further research with the concept of affect maturity will clarify its generalizability, its relationship to various forms of psychopathology, its developmental basis, and its relationship to prognosis and the process of therapy.

References

Averill, J. (1980), A constructivist view of emotion. In: *Theories of Emotion*, ed. R. Plutchik & H. Kellerman. New York: Academic Press, pp. 305–339.

Bertalanffy, L. von (1968), *General System Theory*. New York: Braziller.

Brenner, C. (1974), On the nature and development of affects: A unified theory. *Psychoanal. Quart.*, 43:532–556.

Brentano, F. (1874), *Psychologie von empirischen Standpunkte*. Leipzig, 1924.

Campbell, D., & Fiske, D. (1959), Convergent and discriminant validation by the multitrait-multimethod matrix. *Psychol. Bull.*, 56:81–105.

Cowan, P. (1978), *Piaget with Feeling*. New York: Holt, Rinehart, and Winston.

Ferguson, G. (1959), *Statistical Analysis in Psychology and Education*. New York: McGraw-Hill.

Flavell, J. (1963), *The Developmental Psychology of Jean Piaget*. Princeton, N.J.: Van Nostrand.

——— (1979), Metacognition and cognitive meaning. *Amer. Psychol.*, 34:906–911.

Freud, A. (1963), The concept of developmental lines. *Normality and Pathology in Childhood: The Writings of Anna Freud, Vol. 6*. New York: International Universities Press, 1965, pp. 62–92.

Gouin-Decarie, T. (1965), *Intelligence and Affectivity in Early Childhood*. New York: International Universities Press.

Hall, A., & Fagen, R. (1968), Definition of system. In: *Modern Systems Research for the Behavioral Scientist*, ed. W. Buckley. Chicago: Aldine.

Inhelder, B., & Piaget, J. (1958), *The Growth of Logical Thinking from Childhood to Adolescence*. New York: Basic Books.

Kenny, A. (1963), *Action, Emotion and Will*. London: Routledge & Kegan Paul.

Kernberg, O. (1976), Structural derivatives of object relations. In: *Object Relations Theory and Clinical Psychoanalysis*. New York: Aronson.

Krystal, H. (1974), The genetic development of affect and affect regression. *Annual Psychoanalysis*, 2:98–126. New York: International Universities Press.

——— (1975), Affect tolerance. *Annual Psychoanalysis*, 3:179–219. New York: International Universities Press.

Loevinger, J., & Wessler, R. (1970), *Measuring Ego Development, Vol. 1*. San Francisco: Jossey-Bass.

——— ——— Redmore, C. (1970), *Measuring Ego Development, Vol. 2*. San Francisco: Jossey-Bass.

Martindale, C. (1976), The grammar of altered states of consciousness: A semiotic reinterpretation of aspects of psychoanalytic theory. In: *Psychoanalysis and Contemporary Science*, 4:331–354. New York: International Universities Press.

Murstein, B. (1972), Normative written TAT responses for a college sample. *J. Personal. Assess.*, 36:109–147.

Pitcher, G. (1965), Emotion. *Mind*, 74:326–346.

Redmore, C., & Waldman, K. (1975), Reliability of a sentence completion measure of ego development. *J. Personal. Assess.*, 39:236–243.

Ross, N. (1975), Affect as cognition: With observations on the meanings of mystical states. *Internat. Rev. Psycho-Anal.*, 2:79–93.

Sartre, J.-P. (1948), *The Emotions: Outline of a Theory*. New York: Philosophical Library.

Schmale, A. (1964), A genetic study of affects. *The Psychoanalytic Study of the Child*, 19:287–310. New York: International Universities Press.

Schur, M. (1969), Affect and cognition. *Internat. J. Psycho-Anal.*, 50:647–653.

Sroufe, L. (1979), Socioemotional development. In: *Handbook of Infant Development*, ed. J. Osofsky. New York: Wiley, pp. 462–516.

Thompson, A. (1980), Emotion, Cognition and Object: Philosophical and Psychological Views. Unpublished manuscript.

——— (1981), A theory of affect development and maturity: Applications to the Thematic Apperception Test. Unpublished doctoral dissertation, University of Michigan.

Werner, H. (1948), *Comparative Psychology of Mental Development*. New York: International Universities Press.

Yorke, C., & Wiseberg, S. (1976), A developmental view of anxiety. *The Psychoanalytic Study of the Child*, 31:107–135. New Haven: Yale University Press.

Chapter 10

BIONIAN INTERPRETATION OF THE WECHSLER SCALES: PARANOID-SCHIZOID OPERATIONS

RICHARD M. BILLOW

Expanding on certain of Freud's and Klein's conceptualizations, W.R. Bion proposed a structural theory of thinking based on object relations. He also described, although not systematically, a series of primitive ego defenses which could add greatly to the clinician's understanding of normal and pathological thought processes. These ego defenses, and their accompanying constellations of affect, fantasy, and anxiety, manifest themselves on psychological tests, as exemplified in this chapter concerning the Wechsler Scales. Whereas the treatment of the Wechsler test in its various forms as a projective instrument is not new (see Mayman, Schafer, and Rapaport, 1951; Waite, 1961; Rabin, 1965; Blatt and Allison, 1968; Rapaport, Gill, and Schafer, 1968; Matarazzo, 1972; Zimmerman and Woo-Sam, 1973; Schafer, 1980), this contribution represents what seems to be the first attempt to offer psychodynamic interpretations from a Kleinian-Bionian viewpoint.

Bion saw man's greatest struggle neither as between instinct and civilization, as did Freud, nor between love and hate, as did Klein, but rather, between the emotional experience of thinking and the human tendency to avoid pain. The human being needs "food for thought." However, thinking hurts. The human being suffers from needing something painful. But fearful of pain, even the strongest evades what he or she needs, and often chooses instead ways of avoiding thinking.

The Painful Nature of Thinking: Overview of Bion's Theory

Freud (1911a), in "Formulations Regarding the Two Principles in Mental Functioning," considered in some detail the problem of pain in relationship to thinking. The failure of primitive repression or of hallucinatory gratification to dissolve unpleasant aspects of external reality leads to the development of thought and thinking functions. As trial internal action, thought contains but only partially modifies pain rather than discharging it. Freud conceived of fantasy as the mode of thought activity subordinated to pleasure and not dependent on reality or real objects. Psychotics, and to some extent neurotics, continue to evade pain by evading thinking, by living in fantasy, or by discharging mental stimuli through action-discharge, as in direct bodily expression of affects.

Melanie Klein (1930, 1946) and her coworkers (e.g. Heimann, 1952; Isaacs, 1952) added the following to Freud's formulations. Thinking is painful because it must deal with the unpleasant aspects of internal as well as external reality, those pertaining to the dynamics of the paranoid and depressive positions. Klein emphasized that when thinking would be too painfully anxiety-provoking, both psychotics and neurotics, as well as "normals," evade thinking not only by hallucination or repression, but by three other basic defenses. These are (1) withdrawal of the introjective-projective processes which underlie thinking; (2) splitting of the self, the object, the mental apparatus and its functions; and (3) projective identification, through which the self disowns split-off elements and places in another (or in a dissociated part of the self) that which upon consideration would lead to mental pain. Klein challenged Freud's formulations by positing fantasy as a central unconscious mental activity, one accompanying all other forms of mental activity, including those dealing with the painful aspects of internal and external reality as well as the pleasurable. Thinking and ego defenses may be experienced as fantasies, such as of internal or external objects, or of relations between objects, or of primitive developmental experience (Isaacs, 1952).

Bion continued to emphasize the importance of fantasy in normal and pathological development. He came to understand that primitive fantasy and other precursory forms of mental activity were important in infancy (and perhaps prenatally), as they expressed an instinctual drive to use experience for thinking. The "hunger" for thought-content to satisfy the mental organ he compared to the physiological hunger for food to satisfy the stomach. While both sources of hunger are rooted in instinctual need, their aims and objects are located within a psychological, initially maternal, context. It is the mental region particularly which is disturbed when material, but not psychological provisions, are offered in infancy.

The importance of what Klein called the "epistemophilic instinct," or the curiosity or exploratory motive, led Bion to revise Freud's instinct theory.

Freud postulated two basic instincts, Eros and Thanatos, the "destructive instinct." Bion designated these instincts L and H, Love and Hatred, and notated a third basic instinct as K, Knowledge. Freud (1938, p. 148) postulated that the aim of Eros was "to establish ever greater unities and to preserve them thus—in short, to bind together." The aim of the destructive or "death instinct" was "to undo connections and so to destroy things."

Freud (1905, p. 194) had also called attention to "the instinct for knowledge or research," and related it to "obtaining mastery" and to scopophilia (voyeurism). He did not, however, consider the curiosity motive as among the "elementary instinctual components," that is, as part of the infant's basic constitutional equipment. Freud dated its onset "at about the same time as the sexual life of children reaches its first peak, between the ages of three and five" (1905, p. 194).

The addition of K allowed Bion to bridge affect theory to cognition theory, and these to personality development and functioning, as well as to psychopathology. Neither Freud nor Klein conceptually differentiated adaptive aggression from maladaptive destructiveness, seeing their difference in the respective proportions of fused libido. According to Freud (1938, p. 149) healthy aggression, which is seen in the mature sexual act, for example, is dependent on the "proportions of the fusion between the instincts." But the sexual act, while successfully accomplished physiologically, may be meaningful, meaningless, or perverse. In the human context, love and sexuality (L), as well as hatred and destruction (H), are self- and species protective responses when modified or fused with each other, as Freud held, but only when also "linked" to K, that is, when motivated meaningfully. When the L, H, and K elements are unlinked from each other, which may stimulate or be the outcome of anxiety situations, normal personality functioning is disrupted. The individual becomes or remains preoccupied with expressing and defending against maladaptive love (greed), hate (destructiveness), and curiosity (omniscience).

Predating Bion's revision of instinct theory (1962a) as well as his theory of thinking (1962b), his collection of early papers, *Experience in Groups* (1959b), adumbrates the interaction of unlinked elements of L, H, and K and various primitive mental states. Bion's discovery of the "basic assumptions" existent in group life clarified how the predominant oral aggressive and incorporative fantasies, anxieties, and defenses elaborated by the Kleinians affect mental operations to preclude the possibility of learning from experience. In the *Fight-Flight* state of mind, paranoid-schizoid anxieties, hatred, and aggression (unlinked H) predominate. In the *Dependency* state of mind, intense, immature idealization (unlinked L), accompanied by melancholic worry and guilt, become central. Finally, in the *Pairing* state of mind, manic "hope" spurs an omnipotent mental system (unlinked K) to protect the individual from painful feelings of hatred, destructiveness, and despair, feelings stimulated by paranoid-schizoid and depressive anxieties and fantasies.

Each of us contains these basic assumptions, representative of the Kleinian paranoid-schizoid, depressive, and manic positions. Each of us maintains therefore a perverse, primitive, or psychotic "twin" (Bion, 1950) of our normal personality. Bion (1957) came to call this element "the psychotic part of the personality." Bion does not mean that one is necessarily clinically psychotic when evincing this aspect of personality, but rather that to the extent one evades or perversely transforms symbolization, each personality contains a psychotic component.

Freud's definition of the aim of the destructive instinct Bion relegates to the definition of the psychotic part of the personality. This personality element, dominated by the unfused (unlinked) destructive instinct, seeks "to undo connections and so to destroy things." Bion emphasizes that "things" may be understood as "mental things" or "meaning" (Freud, 1938, p. 194). Hence, pathological thought organization emanates from that personality element which seeks to undo, halt, destroy, or negate meaning, replacing K with −K.

Developmentally, to the extent that the infant's drives and related anxieties remain excessive and uncontained, because of constitutional or environmental factors or their interaction, an evolving aspect of the individual becomes fixated on expressing and defending against primitive feelings. Three psychopathological organizations of personality and defense, by no means mutually exclusive evolve alongside the developing normal personality organization. These correspond to pathological versions of Klein's paranoid-schizoid and depressive psychotic positions, and her elaboration of the manic defense. Because they function to negate the meaning-making processes, these pathological structures may be conceived of as antiego or −K organizations.

Each psychotic suborganization exhibits characteristic minus transformations of L and H, as well as of K. For example, −L may be characterized by control of others, lust, greed, fusion, protective withdrawal, and narcissistic self-expansion. −H involved intense envy, triumph, contempt, violence, wanton destructiveness, pseudohelplessness, and placation. −K, the focus of this chapter, may be characterized by perverse or bizarre constructions having no meaning, by thought withdrawal, by disordered, blocked, or ruptured thinking, by purposive, confusing ambiguity, or by omnipotence: arrogant curiosity, arrogant stupidity, and stereotypy.

While ego psychological theory posited a unitary self-ego with fixations, arrests, regressions, and adaptive and maladaptive defenses (strengths and weaknesses in its structural organization), Bion posited a fundamental, vertical split in self-organization which begins during the first three months of infancy. Two major subselves evolve, Bion's normal and psychotic "twins," each maintaining its own motivational and structural organization of defense, id, ego, and superego (Grotstein, 1980).

Let us consider further the concept of splitting, which is so central to Kleinian psychology. Freud (1938, p. 204) differentiated splitting from repression in that splitting avoids painful demands from the external world "by means of a *disavowal* of the perceptions which bring to knowledge this demand from reality" (Freud's emphasis). Whereas in repression, realistic thought may proceed, in splitting, reality attachment and reality detachment coexist simultaneously. Freud (1938, p. 204) notes that "whenever we are in a position to study them [disavowals], they turn out to be half-measures, incomplete attempts at detachment from reality. The disavowal is always supplemented by an acknowledgement; two contrary and independent attitudes always arise and result in the situation of there being a splitting of the ego."

Grotstein (1981) has traced psychoanalytic conceptualizations of splitting to their roots in Breuer and Freud's earliest work to Kohut's recent contributions. Anna O. herself observed the phenomenon of dissociated normal and psychotic parts to her personality. Breuer reported that "even when she was in a very bad condition—a clear-sighted and calm observer sat, as she put it, in a corner of her brain and looked on at all the mad business" (Breuer and Freud, 1895, p. 46). According to Freud (1938, p. 204), as well as to the Kleinians, splitting is a feature not only of psychosis, but also "a universal characteristic of neurosis." Freud described splitting within the ego, and between the ego and the id and superego structures. Bion showed how the id and superego structures also may be split into normal and pathological variants, each variant contributing to a particular type of personality suborganization, paranoid-schizoid, melancholic, manic, or normal-neurotic.

Freud (1938) held that the dominance of a particular personality element depended on economic factors, i.e. on which structure "can seize hold of the greater [psychical] intensity" (p. 204). Bion clarified that the economic principle applied always to mental pain, as well as to factors of innate aggressivity and love, envy and empathy, etc. The nature of mental pain, how mental pain interacts with primitive fantasy as described by Klein, and the individual's structural, defensive, and constitutional capacities to bear mental pain—these determine the propensity to disavow realistic mental activity and the intensity and extent of splitting.

When frustration and ensuing mental pain is intolerable, the mental apparatus may function like a muscle and discharge stimulation directly, as suggested by Freud (1911a) rather early. Bion elaborated how, in addition, the individual may split himself and his mental apparatus and evacuate thoughtful aspects of the self along with the painful stimulation. To the extent that pathological splitting and mind evacuation via pathological projective identification is fantasized as successful, the psychotic part of the personality establishes itself concurrently with the developing normal part of the personality.

Since splitting and projective identification occur on a mental plane, i.e. on the dimension of thinking versus no-thinking, Bion's theory is well-suited to the dual focus of clinician-tester. The clinician draws inferences from the Wechsler both about intellectual functioning and about intellectual malfunctioning, i.e. both the thinking and no-thinking aspects of test performance. Such inferences are also about object relations, since Bion conceived of thinking as an emotional experience based on, and unconsciously expressive of, object relations.

An Object Relations Theory of Thinking: Normal: Thought Organization

Bion, like many contemporary psychoanalytic thinkers (Mahler comes immediately to mind), called attention to the effects of normal versus premature and hence intolerable absence of or separation from the loved object. He thereby stressed the role of separation anxiety in both normal and pathological development. The infant, as well as the adult, becomes quickly frustrated by the failure to possess its object, be it the mother or, later, an object of knowledge such as one's feeling. Nascent thought always is of a persecutory nature, since it alerts the individual to a painful "missing," a "no breast state."

Freud (1911a) had observed that in maintaining thought the individual supports "increased tension during a delay in the process of discharge." Bion (1962a) refined this to mean that the tension which needs discharge arises from unpleasant stimulation resulting from maternal insufficiency or absence—sensations of hunger, coldness, boredom, uncertainty, etc. The absent good breast is first felt as a bad breast concretely present. Realistic thought involves a beginning recognition of a good object which is absent. Frustration becomes a "problem to be solved" by generating thoughts rather than simply "something to be evacuated." On this view, the first thought is the idea of the absent good breast.

Thought represents accomplishment of the ability both to delay action and to replace a thing with its representation. Thinking thoughts involves the toleration of painful frustration, of nonpossession. In tolerating the absence of a breast, the "no breast" emotional experience may be named as an idea and further thought about. The toleration of pain leads to its eventual modification by thinking and contributes to the maturing of a thinking apparatus which remains, however, woefully inadequate to the task of translating experience into thought. The task is further complicated by potential disturbances in the following essential processes.

The Container-Contained Relationship

Freud established that the infant gives up hallucination and omnipotence because of the buildup of love and need for the real mother. Klein (1946) emphasized what the grateful infant does for love. The infant reorganizes its personality, shifting from the paranoid-schizoid to the depressive position. Aggression and projection are modified in favor of reparation and symbol formation. Bion called particular attention to the latter, and suggested that symbols and thoughts, since they contain anxiety and establish meaning, serve functions once provided by the mother.

The relationship to the breast forms the infant's first representation of reality and of an object relationship. It forms then the first representation of an emotional-cognitive interchange. This takes place with a thinking mother with intact ego functions. The mother provides not only material comforts, but also psychological comforts. By thoughtfully modulating her availability, she prepares the child to self-modulate the psychological discomforts of frustration of immediate satisfaction and of absence. She prepares the infant to think its thoughts, which sooner or later arise in her absence.

The normal part of the personality introjects the good breast's "containing functions." The infant projects undigested raw experience (which Bion calls "beta elements") such as a fear of dying into a receptive mother. Via an empathic, receptive process of "reverie," she gathers and deciphers experience, divesting it of its disintegrating impact, and returns it in a form manageable for thought. She thereby modifies the "autistic" part of the infant's personality (Tustin, 1972; Meltzer, Bremner, Hoxter, Weddell, and Wittenberg, 1975), which seeks to eject frustrating sense experience rather than thoughtfully transform it.

The mother satisfies the child's curiosity not only by teaching him "about" emotional experience, but primarily by having emotional experiences with him. By being with the infant in this way, the mother fosters the development of the normal part of the personality, which comes to predominate. The infant introjects a model of the thinking couple: the dynamic container-contained relationship, which Bion (1962a) symbolized as (♀ ♂).

The introjection of the thinking couple develops concurrently with toleration of the mother's absence. Because the infant has introjected the mother's containing function, he is able to contain good feelings and bad feelings while in her absence, and to transform them into images and prototypes of more sophisticated thought. The child places in conscious and unconscious symbols and thoughts—the containers—that which previously was split off and/or projected into the containing other. In other words, the child thinks, rather than fusing with an hallucinatory good object and/or evacuating the hallucinatory bad object.

Alpha Functioning

Influenced by the major epistemologists, Bion considered the question, How does the human being come to know the world? Following Kant, Bion accepted the premise that experience (the world) remains an unknown quality (eventually to be notated "O") known only to the limited extent that it impinges on the sense organs to become a psychological event. This limited knowledge derives from the "mating" of external "facts" (called "realizations") with internal ideational structures of processing experience ("preconceptions"). These internal structures are not necessarily physiological. They are dynamic structures based on the operation of an underlying process of the normal part of the personality which Bion named "alpha functioning." Alpha functioning operates on the sense impressions and on emotions, producing "alpha elements." What ego psychologists refer to as "autonomous ego functions" and repression-based "ego defenses" depend ultimately on the workings of alpha functioning. This hypothetical process establishes and maintains a contact barrier between consciousness and unconsciousness. Alpha functioning makes storage in the unconscious possible and produces elements suitable for unconscious as well as conscious waking thoughts. That is, alpha functioning assures normal primary as well as secondary processing. Experience may be processed further through both unconscious and conscious mental structures, through fantasy, dreams, art, science, mathematics, etc. The essential quality of the normal part of the personality is to create elements for thinking via alpha functioning, ultimately verbal symbols, containers in which experience (the contained) may be organized and reorganized symbolically. The normal part modifies pain by developing thoughts and the thinking apparatus, which thereby contributes to the development of the thinker.

Under the impetus of alpha processing, the LHK links, in conjunction with maturing forms of mental activity, foster integration of minus feeling and thought. Tasks of adaptation and self-preservation include understanding (K) the destructive −L, −H, and −K elements in our personality and in civilization, forgiving them (L), but also overcoming them (H) through thoughtful action. When alpha processing is disturbed, L, H, and K become unlinked and simultaneously negated.

The Oscillation Between the Paranoid-Schizoid and Depressive Positions

Bion held that thinking inherently involves an exchange of painful, primitive feelings. This exchange involves a recapitulation of the earlier developmental shifts from paranoid-schizoid to depressive positions (Klein, 1946) into moment-to-moment processes of oscillation between disintegration and reintegration, which Bion (1962a) symbolized as $Ps \longleftrightarrow D$. As patterns of painful emotional-cognitive experience, Ps$\longleftrightarrow$D oscillations participate in all other learning experiences, in conjunction with container-contained processes. Let us see how this works.

Learning involves partial disintegration of what is known until a state of absence is regained. The process, or even the prospect, of absence subjects the thinker to the "no breast" anxieties of infancy. The amalgam of feelings of loss, anxious insecurity, persecution, and depression is analogous to the "bad breast present" feelings. The container-contained relationship, based on the model of the good breast, is momentarily disturbed. Because of his history of good object relations, the thinker has developed the patience and security to bear absence and impingement by unorganized sense and emotional stimuli without feeling unduly persecuted or depressed. As the mother once did for him, the thinker contains undigested experience, transforming it into alpha elements. Experience thereby coheres into potentially meaningful patterns, allowing for the growth of thought.

Reintegration entails symbol formation, which inherently acknowledges absence and loss, one's frailties and limitations, one's envy as well as love, hence again pain.

Bion emphasized that creative mental activity is not characterized solely by the incremental buildup of manageable experience. Thinking is inherently painful in that it involves intense episodes of emotional turbulence in which meaninglessness prevails. Hard-won new understanding continues the process of persecution and depression, for understanding brings greater clarity to the vast areas of ignorance, which is frightening. The achievement of a mental attitude of openness or naivete is also painful, for one must give up orienting memory and deprive oneself of the desire to "possess" knowledge (Bion, 1965, pp. 158–159). Words and "facts" may constrict the thinker to conventional ways of knowing "about" experience, and prevent him from freshly experiencing his experience.

If experience is food for thought, one "becomes" what one eats and no longer is what one was. Thinking changes one's identity, and hence also disorients and reorients the thinker to past, present, and future. The person who bears to think and to learn risks ever greater separation from established, conventional relations with others, as well as with one's previous ideas. Freud and Klein emphasized that self-knowledge brings forth the primacy of self-integration over repression and splitting; hence self-knowledge brings inner peace and social harmony. Bion (1970) emphasized that integration entails also the capacity and the courage for even greater levels of emotional turbulence, existential risk, personal and social disharmony.

Paranoid-Schizoid Organization

Due to limitations of space, I will concentrate in this chapter only on the paranoid-schizoid organization and its antiego or $-$K defenses, how these defenses appear in the testing situation, and how they are manifested on the Wechsler Scales.

The most severe form of pathological organization occurs in response to the greatest failure in maternal containment of the infant's projection of its drives and related anxieties. The infant's hatred of frustration comes to dominate, unmodified by sufficient introjective experiences with a loving, containing mother capable of reverie. Hatred (H) overwhelms other basic emotions of love (L) and curiosity (K). The infant also develops a hatred of hatred (− H versus H), so that feelings of intense hatred, along with primitive internal representations of what caused such feelings, are split and projected rather than understood meaningfully (− K versus K). The mother—her absence as well as her frustrating ministrations—are experienced as purposefully persecutory. The infant seeks to evade an emotional relationship with her (− L versus L). Projective-introjective exchanges become progressively unbalanced, with projective mechanisms predominating. When splitting and projective identification fail to bring psychic relief, the infant may feel forced to rely ever more singularly on them as modes of ridding the self of psychic stimuli. These mechanisms become pathologically overused and intensified, eventually adapted perversely to attack, fragment, and eject painful stimuli and whatever is related to pain and frustration. The mental apparatus and the normal part of the personality, those self-elements which perceive and feel reality, also are split. Along with painful anxieties, the mental apparatus is then relinquished, ejected into an outer sphere which also is fantasized as disintegrating. The normal part of the personality, as well as the curiosity-satisfying good breast and each of its ego functions, are fantasized as lost forever.

Upon the model of a fragmented bad breast which recombines for the purpose of retaliation, the infant constructs an internal and external object world. Normal projective identification is replaced by pathological, violent splitting and projective identification, so that the external world is perceptually unfriendly and dangerous. In the place of normal introjection there exists implosive fusion (splitting in reverse) and violent projective identification in reverse. Disavowed self-experience is felt to forcibly enter the personality and take over again. The individual feels attacked and subjugated by controlling, reintrojected projections. He becomes exceedingly uncomfortable within himself. The three major processes described above are then pathologically transformed as described below.

Paranoid-Schizoid Transformation of Symbol-Making Processes

Parasitism of the Container-Contained

The child develops a fear of the intolerable, unsatisfying container-contained learning process and of his first teacher, the unempathic breast-mother, who becomes envied and hated. The child also identifies with his mother, and hence comes to fantasize that an aspect of his own personality which should empathically contain experience and contribute to the growth of thought is instead envious and obstructive. An internal and obstructive maternal object (Bion, 1962b) contributes to the structural organization of the psychotic part of the personality. The psychotic self relates to the normal self and to others in a manner to strip of goodness and meaning all that it gives or receives. The antiempathic, minus container-contained relationship Bion notates as − (♀ ♂).

Transformation of Alpha Elements Back into Beta Elements

Bion maintains that the psychotic part of the personality works actively to make emotional experience meaningless or perverse. By reversing the meaning-making process, the psychotic self attacks and splits alpha elements. The alpha elements, to refresh the reader's memory, which Bion postulates as the building blocks of thought, are split into bits of meaningless sensation: beta elements suitable for ejection. For example, semantic elements which normally comprise what is perceived as language are "reversed" into mere phonemes, with a resultant lapse of meaning. Ignorance is hardly bliss. Emotional reality continues to impinge, but the individual attacks and ejects simultaneously the mental products by which he can make sense and meaning from it. Hence, experience becomes ever the more frustrating and bewildering when it cannot be talked about or even understood. Experience is literally "sensational" but also dreadful when unsymbolized as beta elements. This process of reversal of meaning may be notated as $\alpha \rightarrow \beta$.

Deterioration of the Ps ↔ D Exchange into → Ps

What remains of the normal Ps ↔ D exchange which leads to meaning are fragmented, fragmenting antisymbols, which Bion (1963) notates as → Ps. The psychotic hatred of things cohering contributes to the failed Ps ↔ D interchange, which results in confusion and mental chaos. In normality, a gentle disintegration of "fact" may lead to new fact, a fresh coherence, growth and development. These gains make pain and frustration bearable. In primitive disturbances, mental elements disintegrate violently and cohere violently. What results are bizarre, persecutory "black holes" (Stoeri, 1981, 1982) which greedily seek "saturation" by absorbing anything good, anything alive. That is, → Ps antisymbols seek to take out rather than extend meaning, growth, and development. The fragmenting response on the WAIS-R of the acute schizophrenic, for example, may destroy whatever may pass meaningfully (the "links") among tests, tester, and subject. The patient then may feel frightened and persecuted by the failed communicative exchange in which all constructive meaning has been removed and which is saturated with intense confusion. The pathological workings of the three processes of $-(♀ ♂)$, $\alpha \rightarrow \beta$ and $\rightarrow$ Ps may be observed in the testing situation.

The Testing Situation in → Ps: Oedipus versus the Sphinx

Let us consider the testing situation when paranoid-schizoid anxieties, fantasies, and defenses predominate. According to Bion, the Oedipus myth (along with such myths as the Garden of Eden and the Tower of Babel) may be understood as an unconscious fantasy which links thinking to loss and destruction of good objects. Thought is a tantalizing, but untrustworthy object which, like the monstrous Sphinx herself, must be evaded or outwitted. The patient fears being controlled, humiliated, annihilated, driven into a netherworld of catastrophic but unnameable dread, and may therefore experience examination as something purposefully destructive.

The examiner, for example, may be personified as someone hostile to curiosity, a minus container ($-$ ♀). As did the Sphinx, the examiner tantalizes with riddles or "trick" questions. Some questions seem too easy not to be instances of devious minus questions ($\rightarrow$ Ps). For instance, a patient may wonder quite sincerely how answering an item regarding the names of four recent presidents will help him get out of the hospital and away from the testing situation. Perhaps there is some as yet not understood connection between presidential power and the patient's impinged-upon freedom of movement. He may wonder whether answering the item will be constructive or destructive in deciding his fate.

At other times the items are perversely riddling because they are stimulating questions not immediately gratifying but rather provoking a host of possibly treacherous associations. Becoming frightened and then confused by an item, the subject may feel that this was the examiner's purpose. In reality, the examiner takes in the subject's understanding, and does not usually facilitate or offer further understanding. In $\rightarrow$ Ps organization, the examiner may be experienced as devouring the testee's understanding, returning sensationally unpleasant confusion in its place ($\alpha \rightarrow \beta$). Should the subject succeed in mastering such a riddling item, the examiner, like the Sphinx, may explode in envious fury, annihilating the subject in some unforeseen way.

In solving riddling external reality, the subject may be tricked into "naming" dreaded internal reality. This is by far the greatest fear in intellectual functioning. To many deeply disturbed patients, premature knowledge of the envious, aggressive—or loving—elements in their personality causes a panic reaction and may precipitate deepening fissure between K and $-$K, with the latter persisting. The patient may become momentarily "insane" to avoid knowledge of his psychology, fragmenting his intellectual functioning to evade the testing situation.

Given the intensely aggressive nature of the patient's fantasies, and the extent to which he may rely on violent splitting and projective identification, the examiner may experience intense countertransference reactions. These occur even when the patient offers little or no behavioral resistance to testing and may appear genuinely friendly. After recording one or two fragmenting responses, for instance, the examiner may feel suddenly isolated, exiled with forbidden, criminal knowledge about the patient (e.g. regarding the prevalence of primitive elements in the patient's personality). Or, the examiner may proceed overcautiously. His undue concern about further disintegrating his subject with K may reflect unconscious fears regarding his own integrative powers. Watching and listening to the subject struggle against disintegrative forces stimulates primitive fears of similar cognitive disintegration in himself. In both instances, the examiner has made concordant identifications (Racker, 1968) with the examinee, who also feels isolated and fearful.

With overtly paranoid but not necessarily hostile patients, the examiner may project back the patient's split-off violence and rage, and become cold, controlling, disinterested, etc. Acting out his complementary identification (Racker, 1968), the examiner treats the patient in a manner similar to the latter's harsh treatment by primary objects, now represented in the patient's and in the examiner's sadistic superego. Thus both examiner and subject are deprived the opportunity to understand empathically the latter's lack of understanding.

In contrast to certain personality instruments, such as the Rorschach or the TAT, the Wechsler constrains a retreat into omnipotent fantasy and projection. That is, the task requires that the patient think and face not only the examiner, but also feared, even hated, reality. For these reasons, the Wechsler may be exceedingly provocative. Both members of the testing dyad may be relieved when testing proceeds from the intellectual evaluation to, ironically, less anxiety-arousing projective tests.

General Characteristics of → Ps Ego Defenses as They Appear on the Wechsler

What follows is an abbreviated description necessitated by space limitations of some of the characteristics which distinguish paranoid-schizoid pathological (→ Ps) ego defenses on the Wechsler Scales.

Overwhelming Impact of Aggressive and/or Persecutory Anxieties

Grotstein (1977a, b) has linked the paranoid-schizoid position to the predator-prey series of defenses observed in both human and animal species.

The psychotic part of the personality (or, as Grotstein prefers, the "primitive" part) remains alert to potential danger. The normal or mature part of the personality evaluates how realistic are the particular internal and external manifestations which lead to paranoid anxiety. This mature part evaluates whether a configuration of impinging stimuli is enemy or friend, harmful or helpful, and then responds meaningfully in thought and action.

Evidence on the Wechsler of the failure of such modulation or transformation of experience appears structurally, formally, and thematically. The clinician traditionally assesses when, and the extent to which, major and minor sources of anxiety dominate and obstruct thinking. This is done by examining the adequacy of the accompanying Wechsler response (intra-item variability), as well as the pattern of subtest (intra-test) variability and inter-test variation. Encroachment by underlying psychotic as well as neurotic anxiety may be evidenced by the erosion of full score responses, as when the patient earns one point instead of two, or fails to receive otherwise achievable bonus points, or makes an excessive number of seemingly impulsive or careless errors. Schafer's Mr. V. (1980, pp. 218–232), a schizophrenic character, conveyed a sense of persecution thematically when he exhorted "Oh God!" on commencing Digit Span Backwards. We may hypothesize that the patient's structural inability to work through persecutory anxieties and fantasies contributed to his early failure on the task, a formal indicator of the grossly inefficient thinking characteristic of → Ps organization.

Underlying fantasies of persecution are suggested in the following verbalizations, which may be offered with accompanying affects varying from terror to mild sarcasm: "You got me on that one"; "Okay, I give"; "Oh no, not another one, I can't take this anymore"; "Fire away, I'm ready!"; "What are you doing to me?" The examiner's communications are experienced not as alpha or thought elements stimulating further mental processing, but as confounding beta elements (projective evacuations) stimulating defense.

The predator-prey theme, transformed into a bullied-bully motif, with transference implications directed toward the tester (and the referring therapist), is suggested in the verbalization offered by an excessively friendly eleven-year-old. After putting together the FACE item on Object Assembly, the boy commented, "Give face a black eye for fooling him." The relatively simple intellectual challenge offered by involvement with the puzzlelike task is experienced as something which humiliates (– ♀), and consequently, as a stimulus for counteraggression.

The failure of adequate transformation and concomitant fixation on persecutory fantasies appears in the following from the WISC-R protocol of Janey, a thirteen-year-old hospitalized adolescent. She answered the Information question as to who invented the electric light bulb with "Electricity is useful, but has to be watched, Edison" [2].[1] To the item regarding the

[1]Bracketed numbers refer to Wechsler score.

function of a barometer, the adolescent responded, "Measures brain waves, electricity" [0]. On Similarities, she declared that a telephone and radio were similar because both "Give off electricity, are furniture, don't stand in front of because you get zapped" [0]. On Comprehension, she found it important to hold elections by secret ballot "so people won't influence your vote . . . people may influence your vote with brainwaves" [0].

Janey's responses suggest the failure of her electrical or "primitive" forces to be adequately contained, first by an empathic mother, later by her own normally maturing thought processes. Inadequately insulated from the primitive element in her personality, she gets "zapped" or unduly "influenced" by excessive and intense anxieties and fantasies of persecution which overwhelm the coexistent thinking part of her personality. Hence, structural failure appears formally and thematically on her Wechsler.

Items illustrative of untransformed aggressivization of experience taken from other protocols are as follows:

INFORMATION

How does yeast cause dough to rise? "Some explosive power within it" [0] (WAIS; in Weiner, 1966, p. 438).

COMPREHENSION

In what ways is a house built of brick or stone better than one built of wood? "Stone and brick don't go on fire. (Q) No termites in brick. They'd get their teeth knocked out" [2] (WISC-R).

What does this saying mean? "Strike while the iron is hot." "When have iron, throw water on it to see if hot, then strike when hot. Men, when they fight wars, throw water on grenades" [0] (WAIS-R).

What does this saying mean? "Shallow brooks are noisy." "Well, means that someone makes a lot of noise because rocks are noisier. Throw rock to kill fish" [0] (WAIS-R).

What does this saying mean? "One swallow doesn't make a summer." "I've been told this by a psychologist before, and it means that if a man hit me once, it doesn't mean that every man I see will hit me all the time" [0] (WAIS; in Zimmerman and Woo-Sam, 1973, p. 212).

SIMILARITIES

Cat-mouse. "One eats the other, both part of animal race" [2] (WISC-R).

A *knife* and a *piece of glass* both "Kill" [0] (WISC).

VOCABULARY

Knife. "To kill people" [0] (WISC-R).
Prevent. "To invent ways of hurting people, torture" [0] (WISC-R).

PICTURE COMPLETION

Dog tracks (picture of man and dog in snow). "He doesn't have a gun" [0] (WAIS). Same patient:
Stacks (picture of ocean liner). "The guns on top" [0].
Screw (bolt) (picture of scissors). "The bloody thorn" [0] (WISC-R).

Attacks on Links

In analyzing Schreber's autobiography, Freud (1911b, p. 49) concluded that "paranoia resolves once more into their elements the products of the condensations and identifications which are effected in the unconscious." Freud explained the "decomposition" of mental products in psychotic states as resulting from the withdrawal of psychic energies (cathexes) from reality concerns. Bion (1959a), emphasizing that the psychotic hates reality, suggested that the psychotic not only withdraws energy from reality, but also attacks energetically the links that bind mental products together to represent reality.

The dawning realization that things go together, as in the sound-sequence of Mommy's footsteps and her eventual visual reappearance, excites curiosity and spurs symbol formation in the normal part of the personality. The psychotic self, however, feels excluded, tantalized, and depressed by the singular object, event, or process that becomes defined by such togetherness of elements, and to avoid such feelings hatefully attacks what brings the elements together, as well as the elements themselves. It is this primitive envy of cohesion which underlies what Bion calls, with the pun seemingly intended, the psychotic failure of "common sense."

The decomposition of mental products under the aegis of the psychotic part of the personality may be shown to encompass (a) the categories of thinking (e.g. time, space, and dimensionality); (b) mental operations (e.g. attention, association, memory, reasoning, and judgment); and (c) the objects of thinking (e.g. perceptions, verbal thought, and language).

Attack on the categories of thinking: massive temporal discontinuity and disorientation. The mother's presence, absence, and eventual reappearance is a sequence which occurs over time. The psychotic part of the personality does not tolerate the sense of time passing when the object is absent, or a meaningful sequence of presence of the object which might lead to or include periods of absence. To avoid awareness of these aspects of reality, the sense of time—taken in Kant's meaning, as an a priori mental category—is attacked and fragmented. Also treated to such attacks are the linking mental operations such as attention, memory, reasoning, etc. which establish sequence and continuity and cause and effect. Reliable boundaries separating past, present, and future are made to no longer exist. Time becomes something which does not pass in an orderly, reasonable manner, but a disjointed series of "nows"; the *concept* of a series, however, is absent, as this would entail awareness of sequence.

When a clinically psychotic patient fails on Picture Arrangement, for example, he may evidence understanding of each picture as a segregated instance of "now," but not how several pictures go together in a sequence over time, comprising a past, present, and future. One patient attentively followed the examiner as he laid out the pieces of the first item and then conveyed instructions: "These pictures tell a story about a bird building a nest, but they are in the wrong order. Put them in the right order so they will tell a story" (Wechsler, 1955, p. 49). After a moment's hesitation, the patient volunteered the following story, without attempting to rearrange three of the cards. "There are some eggs waiting to be hatched. A bird is getting twigs for its nest. A bird is feeding her babies."

The patient "decomposes" (Freud, 1911b) the task by physically withdrawing from the materials and mentally evading the requested sequencing operations. The story acknowledges the mother's provision of material comforts (nest building and feeding). But elements which compose mother-infant psychological reality remain dissociated. The story pointedly neglects the eggs' growth and development into babies, and the mother's innate or empathic participation in that process, which begins before or shortly after conception.

The patient stubbornly maintains the fantasy that he was born without the necessity of prior psychological maternal and paternal provision. He accomplishes this by attacking the sense of time and related operations establishing sequence and cause and effect. If left unimpaired, these mental operations would lead to recognition of the mother bird's (and his internalized mother's) participation in the psychological task of mothering which precedes, and is independent of, the actual physical presence of the mother-infant dyad.

Even under optimal conditions, the early, immature ego of the paranoid-schizoid position experiences maternal ministrations as a discontinuous, disjointed series of "nows." The continuously empathic, containing mother reinforces and secures the maturing ego's faith (see Eigen, 1981) in its innate mental categories, through which the experience of continuous time is gradually made meaningful.

Let us return to another example from Picture Arrangement. The subject may arrange the cards in correct sequential order, unlike the previous instance, while conveying a bewildered story. The WAIS-R FISH subitem describes the following. A king fishes, accumulating an increasing number of fish in his basket. He then calls into the water. The concluding frame depicts a servant rising in diving gear, fish in hand. The patient's story is as follows: "The king is fishing. He catches a small fish, then a large fish. He then calls into the water. Interesting, now his chauffeur appears" (ANGLER) [2]. (The "chauffeur" refers to a previous subitem.)

The servant's appearance attracts curiosity ("interesting"). Yet, the patient dares not retrospect to the "then" of the earlier cards, to make the inference that it must have been the chauffeur to whom the king was calling, and who supplied the king's catch. Maternal causal signification, the relationship of the provider (the servant) to what is provided (the fish), hinges on an acceptance of absence, the past, and the capacity to retrospect. By evacuating these representations and mental processes establishing temporal human relationships, the patient creates a story in which oral supplies are recognized but segregated from their human emotional context.

The attack on time may be illustrated in the response to the proverb, *One swallow does not make a summer*. The patient answered: "I don't know. It is not summer now" [0]. The patient unreasonably asserts that she will think about the verbal referent, summer, only if it is also concretely present. To think about summer while it is winter promulgates the thought of seasonal variation, with the embedded concept of absence. Such time concepts are arrogantly negated.

By insisting that only what is "now" may be known, the patient also maintains a fantasy that she exists without knowledge of her past, of her personal history and its attendant pain (see Lovett and Wolf, 1981). But the evasion of pain is only temporary, since the past returns oppressively, to be lived out over and over again, without understanding.

Santayana once commented that "those who cannot remember the past are condemned to repeat it." The failure to learn from what time teaches dooms one to live in an endless, meaningless, repetitive "now." For this reason, time reduced to the moment is experienced as time expanding to boundless infinity. Thus, a patient reported to the relevant Information item that there were eighty-four weeks in a year" [0]. The answer conveys both the psychotic experience of time expanding beyond its natural boundaries, and the pathetic ignorance which results from time's ahistoric distortion.

The boundless quality of destroyed time is illustrated also when a patient matter-of-factly amalgamates disparate elements from the Wechsler, as if the test were one continuous item, expanding infinitely. For example, a patient referred to "the lady's eyebrow" from the relevant Picture Completion item as he contemplated the FACE item on Object Assembly. The verbalization asserts that it is the same eyebrow, on the same task, in the same time frame of the present. The perseverative hallucination may be understood as an example of psychotic repair. The perseveration represents an unyielding mental "hold" on what otherwise would be "lost" to thought. This is accomplished by the evacuation of temporal reality. The halting and hence destruction of the temporal elements of beginning and end, accomplished through splitting, attacks, and projection, is denied through the condensation of mnemonic and perceptual images more appropriate to the infancy stage of hallucinatory gratification.

Another subject spent five to ten minutes on each of the one to two minute Block Design items with no realization of the passage of time. Time is not passing; hence the subject need not anticipate further questions. He feels no reason to anticipate, control, or delay what is left of his desire to make meaning. Meaning here is endlessly *not made*, neither destroyed outright nor created, but forever caught in the breach of an endless present.

The psychotic self may come to feel trapped in an endless intellectual examination while feeling simultaneously without enough time. On Digit Symbol, for example, the patient may feel weighed down by a concretely oppressive sense of time, illustrating how → Ps time may be experienced as a persecutory object. Weiner (1966) described the performance of one patient, diagnosed as chronic schizophrenic, on this task: "The patient worked very unevenly on this subject, and his manner of coding suggested considerable preoccupation and limited ability to maintain focus on the task. He would code several numbers rapidly, then abruptly cease working and gaze fixedly at the page for several seconds, seemingly distracted, only to resume his efforts just as abruptly with a sudden burst of efficient coding" (p. 280). The patient acts out the role of a dawdling slave who periodically is driven into submission by an internal reproach from the harsh taskmaster of time. Time is evacuated, only to return with a retaliatory counterattack.

While the examinee evades temporal meaning, it is the examiner who persecutes by destroying non-meaning. He affronts the patient with the unbearable reality of beginning and end, present and past. The patient claims to be "too tired" to continue. Yet the same individual conveys a sense of mortification when the examiner says reassuringly, "We can stop." The examiner has killed the time of preverbal merger, bliss, and reunion (see Billow, 1980). By requiring the subject to think or by ending the testing session, the examiner threatens to usher in the dreaded "now" of merger-absence and abject aloneness.

Attack on mental operations: the failure of correlation. Reality is reliably perceived when a correlation is established within and between sensory and cognitive modalities, as in vision and tactility, or audition and memory. Bion also refers to this as the establishment of common sense, through which reality is tested. Bion held that envy may extend to a hatred of the sensory, perceptual, and cognitive subsystems' capacity to work harmoniously. Via dissociative processes, various sensory and cognitive modalities are experienced as competing rather than cooperating, to mislead and exhaust the thinker.

An interesting description of the accompanying confusion is supplied by Weiner (1966, pp. 438–439) in his discussion of dissociation. A patient diagnosed as schizoaffective disorder answered the Information item of *Who was Longfellow?* with "He was a poet; maybe I better put on my glasses" [1]. Weiner commented that "nothing in the apparent nature of the test or the examiner's behavior provided reasonable basis for such a conclusion; in fact, she had at this point in the examination completed a visual test (the Bender-Gestalt) during which she had not worn her glasses" (p. 439).

In this example, the patient appears to lack common sense because she calls for a cooperative relationship between verbal-cognitive and perceptual modalities when none is required. There is nothing in the test protocol to suggest that she improves her thinking by the use of glasses, nor by a partial reliance on visual or visual-motor organization. Of the five subtests which she completed, the visually oriented Performance pair was significantly below the Verbal triad (Information, 11; Comprehension, 13; Similarities, 13; Picture Completion, 8; Block Design, 9).

Two other examples involving sensory disharmony are as follows. To the Information item regarding why light-colored clothes are cooler than dark clothes, a patient responded: "Light colors are more porous, let in more air" [0] (Weiner, 1966, p. 475). Weiner commented that the patient "illogically implies a necessary relationship between the color and porosity of a fabric." I may add here that, to the psychotic self, relationships are based anthropomorphically on parasitic competition for ultimate domination and destruction. In this example, the properties of color are fantasized as in a dominating relationship with those of fabric, taking over the latter's functions, which become enlivened (light colors "let in" air).

To the Comprehension item regarding why deaf children usually do not speak, another patient responded, "Because their equilibrium is gone, the sense of balance that controls their speech" [0] (Weiner, 1966, p. 281). The auditory apparatus is fantasized as "controlled" by the sense of balance. In reality, these receptors work in harmony but are not dependent upon one another.

The failure to maintain correlation negates the maintenance of reality-bound concreteness, the sensory-perceptual foundation upon which certain types of abstract categorizations are based, such as in similarity tasks and in proverb comprehension.

To the WAIS-R Similarities item regarding how two different directional perspectives, North and West, are alike, a patient responded, "Both directions, but one North, other West, like Northwest passage" [0]. Different perspectives first are brought together creatively to give birth to the superordinate category of "directions." However, the psychotic part of the personality enviously uncouples the linkage between the elements North and West ("but one North, other West"), undoing the abstract answer of the normal part of the personality.

"Northwest" deprives both "North" and "West" of their characteristics as concrete directional entities. The new word blurs boundaries between the terms, creating an amalgamation of split directions fused together. "Passage" is an additive term, a new concrete entity, rather than an abstraction which leaves preexisting entities with their identities intact. Thus, the answer serves to destroy the appropriately concrete, while substituting an inappropriately concrete term for the abstraction.

"Northwest passage" functions, on a cognitive level, as a displaced unconscious symbol rather than as realistic thought. The mutually interdependent elements from which commonality is to be drawn while difference is maintained and respected is analogous to a thoughtful and hence abstract relationship. In contrast, here the two terms, "North" and "West," are destructively joined (as, earlier, infant and mother may have been), to the detriment of intellectual functioning. The answer in which distance between terms is collapsed symbolizes the invasive maternal atmosphere in which claustrophobic fusion halted the movements in the normal direction of separation. No longer signifying what the terms share in common, the answer also signifies meaning's evacuation, its "passage."

To the Comprehension proverb, *Strike while the iron is hot*, a patient responded, "I wouldn't." On inquiry he explained, "If I knew it was hot, I wouldn't strike"; further inquiry elicited, "It could mean that when you're mad you strike, because you have quick reflexes" [0] (Weiner, 1966, p. 259).

As Bleuler (1911) emphasized, the associational network of such a patient is disturbed by her primary concerns. Aggressive fantasies and anxieties quickly come to dominate her associations. But also, when attacks on links are instituted, aggressively hypercathected associations as well as mental operations serve to split apart potentially interactive levels of meaning, both psychological and verbal.

The nature of the proverb task, which requires the suspension of a literal attitude to consider metaphorical possibilities, is itself anxiety-producing. The process of separation from previously established, or literal, meaning is crucial to the development of the moral or metaphoric solution of a proverb. This is analogous to separation from the real object, which initially was crucial to the establishment of primitive representational thought (see Searles, 1965; see also Billow and Lovett, 1984). We may understand, then, that not only may objects alternate between presence and absence, but levels of meaning also. In this instance, the cooperative oscillation between concrete and abstract, knowledge and its lack, upon which metaphorical thinking and proverb interpretation is based, is not tolerated.

To evade falling prey to a test item made persecutory by its evocation of abandonment as well as of aggressive fantasies, the patient first attempts to withdraw her thinking operations. While miscomprehending the proverb, she also comments symbolically on her refusal to think abstractly: "I wouldn't."

The effect of the examiner's initial prod is to confirm the existence of splitting attacks on the links between literal and metaphoric referential activity. The words "strike" and "hot iron" share a common context referring to benign, smithing associations, as well as possibly unsublimated aggressive associations relating to hitting and to intense heat. By also splitting the links between the associations and evacuating the sublimated semantic elements, the remaining aggressive associations are reinforced and exaggerated. The homily becomes transformed into a perverse enticement to self-destruction: Strike a hot iron. The patient informs the prodding examiner that she is not enticed and would not succumb: "If I knew it was hot, I wouldn't strike it."

The examiner's further intervention is met with renewed attack, now on the sensory level of correlation. The words "hot iron" are split apart and the "iron" term dispersed. The proverb's realistic reference—the link which could supply an "objective correlative" to the metaphor and to the moral abstraction—is now destroyed. All that remains is an idiosyncratic semantic viewpoint in which "hot" equals "mad" ("It could mean that when you're mad you strike, because you have quick reflexes"). The self, the mental apparatus, and the products of thought become dominated by aggressive, unthoughtful emotion. As in the previous example, the realistically concrete (the references to smithing) are preempted by an additive term ("mad") which serves as a displaced symbol misleadingly reconcretizing the stimulus.

Angry feelings may be discharged directly without fear of retaliation when no other viewpoint is internally represented, whether that of the other or that of the normal part of the personality. By destroying multiple viewpoints which provide common sense, the patient may succeed in reversing her position from prey to mindless predator. Before, the patient revealed a fear of unknowingly hurting herself ("If I knew it was hot, I wouldn't strike"). Presently she may reveal her wish to mindlessly hurt another. The proverb becomes newly transformed into a war cry of the primitive, discharge-seeking self: Strike when mad.

Revealed in this answer is the fantasy of the mind as a muscle with "quick reflexes" rather than as a thinking organ which tolerates delay in order to modulate mad feelings with thoughtful action ($-$H versus H linked with K). Such a fantasy was, hypothetically, a reality during the earliest months of infancy. As Freud (1911a) postulated, prior to the development of realistic thought, motor discharge "had served to unburden the mental apparatus of accretions of stimuli" (p. 16).

When attacks on links are instituted, sensory, emotional, and ideational stimuli "accrete" for discharge rather than meaningfully integrate in abstract verbal thought leading to common sense. This process is revealed in the following response to the TAXI item on the WAIS-R Picture Arrangement subtest. This stimulus set depicts a man transporting the torso of a manikin. He hails a cab, then discovers with blushing embarrassment that from the perspective of onlookers into the rear window, he appears romantically "compromised" by the proximity of the manikin's head to his own. In the last frame, the man has placed himself and the manikin at opposite corners of the back seat.

One patient arranged the cards in the proper sequence, earning full credit, while also verbalizing something of the interpersonal turmoil of the protagonist: "He's embarrassed because he is with a woman or a dummy, it's definitely a woman or a dummy." To empathically comprehend the sequence, the patient would have had to adopt a mental apparatus similar to that of the neurotic but sane protagonist. The latter tolerates the conflict caused by the correlation between two perspectives, experiencing the manikin both as itself and as its human representation. The blushing protagonist is also aware of the possible perspective of the onlookers. In fact, he is painfully aware of it, but he manages to take constructive action.

The patient's action seems empathic, since the cards are arranged correctly and he mentions that the protagonist seems embarrassed. But his intellectual performance also reveals a partly successful incursion from the psychotic element such that action has a manic quality to it (see Segal, 1981). The patient's verbal story reveals a paucity of inner feeling and emotional understanding, which seems both to result from and be a cause of the failure of converging perceptual foci.

The patient, like the protagonist, takes "proper" action. But unlike the protagonist, he is in effect dominated by intense anxieties. Such anxieties and fantasies are stimulated, presumably, by the pictures of the damaged maternal figure (the manikin torso), and the pictorial necessity to compromise between unacceptable regressive closeness and equally untenable total separation. Thinking represents a compromise between opposing feelings and actions, a compromise that contributes to realistic acceptance of human ambivalence. The psychotic element obdurately refuses these human qualities of compromise and ambivalence. Left without adequate common sense, that part of the personality experiences emotional, and often perceptual, confusion as to whether or not the self and others are human or manikin. Such confusion appears in the anxious repetition of the phrase, "a woman or a dummy." The visual stimulus is identified with two names, but the relationship between terms which abstract thought may provide has been attacked. Thus the words do not further conceptual sense but function merely to discharge "accretions of stimuli." Langs (1978) has called attention to this communicative style, whereby language is used primarily to discharge tensions and affects.

Common sense on the level of identity or of social comprehension is achieved when self or other is simultaneously perceived via two different emotions, e.g. in this sequence, desire and shame, which are then integrated in thoughtful action (see Conklin, 1981; Stoeri, 1981). Such cooperation between receptors of emotional stimulation, and between reception and action, would bind ambivalence and hence usher in what Klein (1935, 1940, 1946) referred to as the depressive position. At this level of mental organization, realization of separation and of attendant feelings of anger and guilt are tolerated. To avoid depressive realizations and depressive pain, the psychotic part of the personality reduces correlations to zero, which is randomness. The patient's verbalizations reveal the either/or approach of prevalent splitting operations; the figure is randomly "a woman or a dummy." Dominated by primitive defenses which split apart common sense, the patient verbally evidences social and perceptual perplexity and "stupidity" while behaving in a dissociated but appropriate and directed manner. He earns full credit for intellectual functioning, and full credit for intellectual malfunctioning.

Attack on the objects of thinking: psychotic language. Freud (1915) wrote that "by being linked with words, cathexes can be provided with quality even when they represent only relations between presentations of objects and are thus unable to derive any quality from perceptions. Such relations, which become comprehensible only through words, form a major part of our thought-processes" (p. 202). Words, by contrast to perceptions or perceptually based imagistic symbols, are an essential prerequisite to the advanced thought processes which lead to understanding of one's feelings toward others. Verbal thought advances awareness, therefore, of ambivalence, the negative pole of which is linked unconsciously with painful fantasies of destruction and loss of good objects (Klein, 1930, 1935, 1940). Bion (1959a) held that to evade unconscious painful experience, verbal communication is treated to the same envious and violent attacks the person once launched in fantasy against parental intercourse, verbal or sexual.

One weapon used against language is language itself. The psychotic part of the self holds a linguistic theory that misunderstanding is superior to understanding, since pain may thereby be temporarily evaded. The patient uses language inappropriately as a mode of hostile action, rather than as a means of furthering depth of meaning (see Grotstein, 1978; Langs, 1978, 1980, 1981; Billow and Lovett, 1984). Verbal communication is used to split the thinking processes of the normal part of the personality, which link one to inner and outer objects, and to split as well the verbal elements which form the building blocks of such thinking processes. Antilanguage is promulgated in order to create confusion and miscommunication with self and others.

I have chosen eight items from the WAIS protocol of Mr. G., a twenty-four-year-old outpatient at a university clinic, to illustrate the complex manner in which psychotic defenses obtrude willfully to defeat the linguistic organization of the normal part of the personality. Mr. G. achieved a full scale score of 111, with a verbal score of 112. The items, and Mr. G.'s responses and scores, are as follows:

COMPREHENSION

Shallow brooks are noisy. "A lot of dirt being where you least want to find it" [0].

One swallow does not make a summer. "Don't hitch your hat to a shooting star, 'cause your hat will go and you'll stay behind" [0].

VOCABULARY

Domestic. "A huge umbrella kind of word to show what goes on in one's shelter; accidental rites; also a maid" [2].

Remorse. "A mellowed-out, hollowed-out regret, more domestic overtones, regret is personal" [1].

Calamity. "Social catastrophe, Calamity Jane; anagram is 'calm,' Caliban, clam" [2].

Tranquil. "Very calm, inspired calm, I don't know the reason for it" [2].

Encumber. "Cucumber, plumber; load down, bother, interfere unnecessarily" [2].

Impale. "To lessen the effect of, interfere, impeach, impala, lessen honor and respect due" [0].

I will begin with Mr. G.'s response to the proverb, *Shallow brooks are noisy*. His answer is: "A lot of dirt being where you least want to find it." The response conveys a primary motivation activating attacks on language. As mentioned above, this is to evade the realization of unbearable depressive experience attendant upon verbal comprehension. Mr. G. does not "want to find" and thus to experience the "dirt," i.e. the truth about himself, which is linked to dirty, self-devalued depressive feelings. To evade verbal comprehension of the depths of his personality, he seemingly maintains a shallow semantic level of mental organization. His refusal to move from concrete to abstract or shallow to deep serves to dirty or spoil the semantic elements of the proverb.

Mr. G.'s response is not merely concrete, however, for it cryptically retains some of the links to the abstract meaning of the proverb. These links are maintained via metaphor (see Billow, 1977; 1981; Billow, Rossman, Lewis, Goldman, Ross, and Palermo, 1983a,b). Nature imagery ("dirt" replacing "shallow brooks") continues to serve as the figural descriptor for verbal communication. But the metaphoric replacement is oblique and therefore misleading. It is antimetaphor, useless in terms of contributing to the proverb's comprehension, but useful in creating self-protective confusion and ambiguity (see Billow and Lovett, 1984). Metaphor as antimetaphor is language used primarily for destructive action rather than language used for communication about destructive wishes, feelings, thoughts, etc. The effect of the aggressive scooping out of meaning from the metaphoric bed in which the proverb rests is to make the clinician as well as the patient perplexed and unsure as to the latter's comprehension and intended communication.

The tester cannot be sure whether the patient has merely interpreted the proverb concretely. Nor can the tester be sure whether the patient has provocatively filled the emptied figure with new metaphor. For one senses in this and in the following responses that Mr. G. has self-knowledge that he wishes ambivalently both to communicate and to obfuscate, knowledge about his psychotic character structure, about his hostility, and about his pain and loneliness. The patient personalizes the question and identifies with the stimuli. His veiled, sarcastic comments subtly alert the listener to this process to evoke but also to confuse understanding. Like the Sphinx, Mr. G. dares the tester to solve the riddle of his response and to "find" the dirt or truth about his twin personality.

Part of the effectiveness of psychotic obfuscation is to make difficult clear differentiation between the two parts of the personality. Psychosis blurs the boundaries between itself and reality by depriving the communicator of the liquid medium of verbal thought, through which differentiations may be established. In this way the self becomes like a brook which, deprived of water, suffers eventual attrition and deformation of its boundaries, misleading the confused traveler.

The patient warns those who travel with him about his treacherous misuse of language in the response to the next proverb, *One swallow does not make a summer*. He answers: "Don't hitch your hat to a shooting star, 'cause your hat will go and you'll stay behind" [0]. Mr. G. advises the tester not to connect his thinking cap to the patient's words. As one swallow is not a reliable sign of summer, so Mr. G.'s language is not a reliable sign system. Semantic meaning is split or implosively fused, dispersed so that words become like shooting stars, brilliant, seductive, and effervescently disappearing. For the shooting star has a chimerical reality. What one perceives is delayed information regarding an imploded astronomical container (– ♀) which is no longer reliably representing itself.

Paranoid-schizoid operations reduce words into deceptive phonetic images of themselves, elusive remainders of a mental apparatus which has triumphantly destroyed itself. As with the previous item, reliable boundaries between knowledge and ignorance, fantasy and reality have been willfully exploded, making the tester's job of accurate assessment exceedingly difficult. Certainly, an intelligence is at work in Mr. G.'s responses to the proverbs, although no Wechsler credit is achieved. In fact, "twin" intelligences are at work. The psychotic twin destructively acts out a theory of language which states that misunderstanding is superior to understanding, by making language provocatively ambiguous and confusing. As with Anna O., a "sane" but devitalized twin passively watches (and symbolically comments on) "all the mad business" of the "crazy" twin.

The double misuse of language, for protection and for autistic privacy, as well as its proper use for communication, is suggested in Mr. G.'s three definitions of *domestic:* "A huge umbrella kind of word to show what goes on in one's shelter; accidental rites; also a maid." Mr. G.'s word-umbrella does not always collect consensual meaning under it, although this is what the patient's first definition implies. The adjacent definition ("accidental rites") suggests rather that the patient's umbrella at times fails to adequately envelop or contain communicable verbal meaning. "Accidental rites," like the use of "dirt" or "shooting stars" in the proverb interpretations, becomes an ironic but ambiguous play on words. A rite is not accidental, but formal and deliberate. Entrapped within the introjective antishelter of paranoid-schizoid operations, linguistic rites are purposefully "accidental." The domestic or mother tongue's seemingly accidental conjunction of disparate verbal elements forms a bizarre umbrella protecting the patient, if only temporarily, from uncontrollable elements of reality.

Mr. G.'s Vocabulary performance is like the impala in his leaping associations to *impale:* "To lessen the effort of, interfere, impala, less honor and respect due." Language becomes primitivized in its reduction to action, a wild antelope which agilely takes flight from pursuit by feared reality. Paranoid-schizoid operations impale language to lessen its effectiveness in containing the abstract relations between objects to which Freud called attention. The success of –K operations in lessening abstraction, reason, and common sense appears in Mr. G.'s definition of *tranquil:* "Very calm, inspired calm, I don't know the reason for it." Although Mr. G. achieves full credit for the item, the accompanying verbalization ("I don't know the reason for it") suggests that the psychotic part of the patient's personality has attacked and drained him of the knowledge behind the concept.

Mr. G. has lost the verbal knowledge or "reason" which is necessarily linked to the vocabulary item. The calming sound of "calm" proliferates as an auditory afterimage, the ear's version of a shooting star. The phonological level dominates the semantic level. Auditory sensation is self-soothing, while meaning, reason, and advanced thought represents not calm, but calamitous pain (see the patient's definition of *calamity,* as well as the discussion below).

"Calm" becomes an empty container in search of meaningful content. Under the impetus of an aggressivized, hypercathected auditory channel, the naming process operates in reverse, i.e. meaning is reduced to sensation or beta elements ($\alpha \rightarrow \beta$). Symbolic representation, recalling a time when the absent mother was named and abstracted, is attacked and dispersed. One may hypothesize that the thought of an available mother is not secured adequately enough to be calming. "Calm" serves as a fetishistic (not transitional) auditory object, a precursor to regressive clanging. Sound replaces the mother's concrete presence, an hallucination which threatens to become a painful reminder of unreasonable absence. Here is an example of (Ps $\leftrightarrow$ D) $\rightarrow$ Ps.

These inferences are supported by the definition of *encumber:* "Cucumber, plumber; load down, bother, interfere unnecessarily." The word is first broken down to auditory sensation, to which other words become added according to their phonological rather than semantic properties ("cucumber, plumber"). Here Mr. G. relieves anxiety by overt clanging, perversely using auditory perception and association to attack word meaning. Mr. G. then returns to the semantic level in which audition harmonizes rather than competes with other cognitive processes. He ultimately earns full credit for his response. From the viewpoint of the normal part of the personality, the psychotic self had "bothered unnecessarily" with verbal objects of thought. But from the psychotic viewpoint, massive underlying anxieties necessitate the temporary escape and relief offered by psychotic word trickery.

Such anxieties and defenses appear in the definition of *calamity:* "Social catastrophe, Calamity Jane; anagram is 'calm,' Caliban, clam." The patient associates calm with calamity of catastrophic proportions. Hence calm creates intense anxiety and must be made meaningless. The defensive use of language to confuse and defeat communication, as through such word trickery, is implicated in the association to the synonym for word game, "anagram," and also in the association "Caliban," slave to the poet-trickster, Prospero.

As previously noted, at times Mr. G. does not "know the reason for" an "inspired" or mental calm. A sane calm is unreasonable to the part of his personality which believes that verbal mentation tricks one into social calamity. This is because the primitive superego links the realization of anger and hatred directed toward absent or insufficient loved objects with a concrete sense of actual wrongdoing to them, and to fantasies of retaliation by these objects (Klein, 1935, 1940). The thought is equated with the act, and with consequences to the act.

The fantasy of calamitous, concrete emptiness attendant on the realization of depressive feelings is suggested in the patient's definition of *remorse:* "A mellowed-out, hollowed-out regret, more domestic overtones, regret is personal." When remorseful, Mr. G. feels hollowed-out, emptied of the maternal and paternal ("domestic") inner objects which have been themselves scooped out ("mellowed out") by the patient's mental onslaughts. When Mr. G. feels his feelings, their painful intensity contributes to a disinclination to think about them. The realization of feelings may stimulate further defensive word trickery to circumvent further realizations. But the word magician risks becoming forever lost within his own destructive spell.

When the psychotic theory of miscommunication predominates, it is not only inner human objects which are grossly damaged, but any objects capable of verbal thought. Functional intelligence is reduced to self-parody. Destructive wordplay, as in reversing the "a" and "l" in "calm," contributes to both social and mental withdrawal. The characterological deformation of language into a shield to hide behind, rather than communicate with, contributes to the "accidental rite" of psychosis. The sane personality loses the tools to translate the action-oriented messages from the psychotic self into usable verbal symbols. When in the world of $-K$, Mr. G. functions like the deformed, ineducable Caliban, while his sane self withdraws into its clammy shell, having lost faith in verbal objects which could eventuate mental calm.

Bizarreness

In → Ps, fragmented elements of internal and external experience, to the extent to which they cohere, often form perverse, unnatural agglomerations of pathological fantasy and reality. Such "bizarre objects" are constructed on the immature ego's model of a fragmented breast which has come together motivated and animated by the force of envy and hatred of the child's vital needs (LHK). Bizarre objects are not only unnatural, but also antinatural. They exist solely to destroy existence, and accomplish this task by first exciting interest and curiosity.

According to the myth, the Sphinx, an agglomerate, unnatural object with the head of a woman and the body of a lion, tantalizes Oedipus with riddles. Her monstrous hatred of knowledge and of things alive extends to a hatred of hatred. She fragments herself into irreparable bits rather than bear an envious hatred of Oedipus, who confronts her with the riddle of reality "solved," i.e. represented in verbal thought.

I have chosen a single item from a Wechsler-Bellevue protocol discussed by Schafer (1980, pp. 218–233) to illustrate how categories, operations, and objects of thought may fragment and amalgamate into bizarre objects. The response is to the TAXI item of Picture Arrangement: "It doesn't make any sense whatsoever. He hailed a taxi, had a dummy with him. It starts to lean over to him in the car and he's rather surprised and gets out.'' The patient's verbal production, while incorrect, is also the obverse of the equally incorrect solution offered in his ordering of the stimulus materials: MLEUAS [0]. In the patient's verbal sequence, the protagonist separates from, in effect flees from, the manikin; while in his visual sequence, the protagonist concludes walking with his arm around her.

Schafer analyzed the response as suggesting ''generalized blandness'' and ''careless discrepancy'' between verbal and pictorial versions (p. 228). But the total response time of 55 seconds, the longest of any of the subject's Picture Arrangement responses, suggests intense interest in this final item rather than careless disinterest. The time, in seconds, of all the responses, starting with the initial stimulus, was 5, 7, 7, 20, 47, and 55; all but the last two items earned partial or full credit. Since the items are arranged in ascending order of difficulty, the increasing amount of time per item suggests that the patient appropriately met the task with increased attention and energy. Further, the emotionally charged verbal elaboration reflected bizarre enlivening—the inanimate dummy comes to life—rather than a generalized bland deanimation, as in Schafer's interpretation.

The response and the discrepancy between verbal and pictorial versions may be understood alternatively. The patient's words described unrealistic flight, separation, and isolation, while the pictorial sequence expressed the predominance of the wish for preverbal fusion over reality testing. The verbal story is fueled by the prevalence of the complex of anxieties and fantasies described by Klein (1946) as ''paranoid-schizoid.'' Such anxieties, pertaining to endangerment by others, stimulate a need for safety, one which is felt to be unrealizable by maintaining reality contact through need-delaying thought. Internal and external good objects cease to represent adequately protective and nurturant functions, and are overwhelmed by persecutory, obstructive representations. In groups, such anxieties stimulate the Fight-Flight mentality described by Bion (1959b).

The pictorial construction is fueled by the anxieties and fantasies labeled ''depressive'' by Klein (1946). Unrealizable wishes for dependency and adhesion to a good object accompany fantasies of impending abandonment and resultant harm. Fear for the object's safety and fear of separation replace fear of the object and fear of closeness. Bion (1959b) described a Dependency mentality in groups as related to the depressive anxieties.

A hypothetical phenomenological analysis of the patient's response follows. As Oedipus to the Sphinx, the patient is attracted to the riddling stimulus materials. The visual arrangement attests to how the patient is drawn particularly to the compelling, attention-gathering manikin. The protagonist, with whom the patient is projectively identified, begins seated head to head, and in the last sequence remains physically connected. A regressive state of concrete, physical presence is sought. This state is similar to the stage in early infancy (see Freud, 1911a) during which disruption of the mother-infant dyad via meaningful conflict or absence is denied mentally, whenever possible, via hallucination or evacuation.

The reality which is denied visually is partially acknowledged on the level of verbal thought. Freud (1938) observed that splitting of the normal ego does not fully achieve the disavowal of reality which motivates this primitive ego defense: disavowals "turn out to be half-measures, incomplete attempts at detachment from reality. . . . two contrary and independent attitudes always arise and result in the situation of there being a splitting of the ego" (p. 204).

It is the partial acknowledgment of an intellectual problem rather than its disavowal which intensifies anxiety and the series of Fight-Flight paranoid-schizoid operations. Thus, on the verbal plane, fight is illustrated as the patient immediately fires a barrage at the materials: the test (not himself) "doesn't make any sense whatsoever."

The patient's momentary construction of reality—"He hailed a taxi, had a dummy with him"—is followed by paranoid retransformation. Realistic thought is experienced as further entrapping a self already endangered by aggressive fantasy that is confused with reality. Hence, thought is evacuated along with other aspects of the personality. We see an example of this projective process when, via projective identification, the manikin torso becomes invigorated with disowned oral-incorporative motivation: "It starts to lean over to him in the car."

The effect of the evacuation of mental elements is to weaken the experiencing itself, making it more prone to manipulation by un-understood conflations of inner and outer experiences represented symbolically by the manikin. As the manikin turns against the protagonist, the patient finds thinking turning frighteningly against an overwhelmed self.

Indicated in this sequence is, hypothetically, the psychosis-destined individual's most pervasively traumatic early maternal relationship. A potentially regulative dyadic interchange involving presence and absence became a source of intolerable "surprise," such that the idea of the unwanted-wanted mother is experienced as persecutory. It is Bion's formulation that when this occurs all ideas are "surprising," i.e. unwanted and persecutory. The mind becomes a claustrophobic bad object, one which the self must fight or take flight from. The latter is indicated in the patient's verbalization: "and he's rather surprised and got out." Like the taxi, the mind is not a safe inner place for transport when it contains an introjected obstructive maternal object. And like the protagonist from the taxi, the patient belatedly "gets out" from the entrapping "container" (Bion, 1962a) of thinking, but not successfully. Pathological splitting does not accomplish the "disavowal of reality," a point Freud emphasized. But in addition, splitting and concomitant projective identification do not accomplish a disavowal of painful *unreality*. Rather, these primitive mental operations bizarrely magnify and distort reality's most frightening and bewildering emotional aspects. What the patient verbally dissociates from proliferates pictorially. The patient's nonverbal construction, representative of the asymbolic, action-oriented primitive self, reconnects the protagonist with the ambivalent (and now bizarre) object.

Let me summarize and review briefly the dynamics of this response. The normal personality attempted to bear anxiety and began to construct and solve reality by the creation of mental elements. But the dominant psychotic element countered via the institution of defenses of pathological splitting and projective identification. Two −K suborganizations recohered along different perceptual dimensions. Such recoherence further polarized rather than bound emotional ambivalence, since each suborganization was the recipient, via projective identification, of emergent primitive paranoid-schizoid and depressive personality trends of the patient.

Under the impetus of persecutory anxiety, a −K verbal suborganization described a repellent bad object and the protagonist's reactive flight and withdrawal. Under the impetus of depressive anxiety, a −K visual motor suborganization described a magnetizing "magus" object (Grotstein, 1981) and the protagonist's dependency and physical adhesion. Neither story represented a realistic synthesis of the pregenital, much less the genital, mental (or alpha) elements. They formed twin amalgamations, equally barren of realistic meaning, and equally bizarre. The predominant primitive defenses of splitting and projective identification manifested themselves in the cleavage between the verbal and the pictorial versions. Each version is projectively identified with unintegrated split-off paranoid-schizoid or depressive self-object elements, similar to what Bion has referred to as "beta elements."

In this item, the patient appeared to be using words correctly in describing bizarre perceptual and cognitive processes. But the words are also deceptive, for they unexpectedly empty themselves of representational meaning and become full of misrepresentation (−K), i.e. they deny what the visual elements describe. In effect, the words themselves form bizarre objects, being tantalizing but treacherous amalgamations of semantic truth and falsity, capable of hostilely misleading the testing clinician.

In psychotic states, often the syntax as well as the semantic content of language may become bizarrely agglomerated. Bizarre or deviant language (Weiner, 1966, pp. 41–45; see also Holt and Havel, 1960) may be composed of pieces of conventional words or phrases amalgamated with fragmented words, concrete images, and inchoate feelings and memories. The semantic elements work in disharmony to create perversions of the metonymic and metaphoric bases of language expansion (Billow and Lovett, 1984).

From a different perspective, the construction of bizarre objects, in this example as well as others, is an attempt to *repair* fragmentation, although such constructions are also the products of active efforts toward fragmentation. Freud (1911b) called attention to the "secondary reconstructive" efforts of psychotic language and thought in his analysis of the Schreber case. Freud held that although attempting to resymbolize reality, secondary reconstruction retained the pathogenic element emanating from the narcissistic, reality-decathected self. That is, secondary reconstruction emanated from a psychotic suborganization which structurally and defensively presented but did not represent normally the world of destroyed representation. The bizarre world of −K may be resymbolized and understood by the sensitive interpreter, just as Freud was able to clarify Schreber's world for us, but not by the personality (or part of the personality) dominated by psychosis.

Ironically, attempts at repair in psychotic states may increase a tendency to create bizarre objects. The normal mental elements which come together are reconnected cruelly, since reconstructive efforts are thwarted by continuing attacks by the part of the personality which fears and hates resymbolization. The relative strength of destructive versus reparative trends in the personality may be inferred from the degree of violence to coherence presented in a particular response. To the extent that a response is bizarre but also interpretable, the clinician may have confidence that he or she has contained, resymbolized, and understood something of both the destructive and reparative parts of the patient's personality.

Hallucination

Freud (1920, p. 11) observed that "most of the unpleasure we experience is *perceptual* unpleasure." The receptive apparatus, rather than receive and further integrate unpleasant reality, may work in reverse to disperse, eject, and misperceive reality. In this manner, unpleasure may be momentarily evaded. What is classified on a Wechsler as animation, or loose association, dissociation, etc. (e.g. Weiner, 1966, pp. 39–41) may be phenomenologically an instance of a pervasive process which Bion (1965) called "transformation in hallucinosis." Sense impressions may be split and expelled, along with other aspects of personality, creating negative hallucination. Or, via projective identification, such evacuations may penetrate and encyst the external objects to create the bizarre objects described in the previous section. In this situation, fragmented external objects, upon which are superimposed projected pathological fantasies, may serve as the basis for visual, auditory, olfactory, or tactile distortions, illusions, or positive hallucinations.

An example of hallucination, technically an illusion, was offered in the preceding section. Schafer's patient reported that the manikin "starts to lean over to'' the protagonist. An example of visual distortion appeared in an adolescent's response to the WISC-R Picture Completion item depicting a mild-looking man missing a nostril: ''Looks like a monster, looks strange, looks like a football player'' [0]. The solution of expelling nascent experience into an hallucinatory external world backfires, as in these responses with their sense of premonitory violence. The person becomes endangered by an external world of unfriendly, animated test stimuli, while the inner world is depleted of a mental apparatus on which to rely. Upon seeing the WAIS-R Picture Completion item of a raised pitcher without visible human support, a regressed hospitalized patient exclaimed ''What's holding the pitcher up?'' as if she were responsible for this ghastly levitation, having negatively hallucinated a supportive external figure on which the pitcher and her equally mindless self depended.

Transformations in hallucinosis are frequent in → Ps. They are subtle and difficult for the clinician to assess as to the extent to which they are transitory and simultaneous with normal perceptual processes. Hallucinations also are difficult for the patient to assess, since they remain unreliably segregated from nonhallucinatory reality, a factor which adds to their potential to produce pain rather than pleasure (see next section). The personality has no confidence that an hallucination is not a fact, or vice versa (Bion, 1959a, p. 100). The sudden superimposition of dreamlike experience over reality contributes also to the confusion and blurring of boundaries between sleeping and waking, inner and outer, projection and perception. The clinician may be alerted to the possibly literal message intended through the use of such verbalizations on the Wechsler as ''I'm dreaming, this couldn't be real!'' ''My eyes deceive me!'' ''I don't believe my ears!'' ''This feels strange!'' and ''My memory is playing tricks on me!''

When a patient asks to have an item repeated, it may be to ascertain whether the tester in reality said what the patient heard, or whether the patient experienced a momentary auditory distortion. After having the examiner repeat the WAIS Comprehension item regarding why one should avoid bad company, a patient volunteered, ''Oh, I thought you had said that you were bad company.'' The patient is relieved to discover that he had distorted auditory reality, because the reality of his hallucination was too frightening to bear. Hallucination stimulates feelings of persecution from an internal and external world of bad company.

Often patients do not share spontaneously their misperceptions, and need to be asked to do so. As Weiner (1966, p. 41) has observed in a different context, the examiner may receive the mistaken impression that he merely has been misheard or misunderstood. The patient may reveal what ego psychologists have referred to as ''failures in repression.'' I would suggest, additionally, that the salience of the patient's unrepressed and intrusive thoughts and fantasies have transformed the instructions and/or the stimuli so that elements of the external task become amalgamated, via hallucination, with inner preoccupations. Because this pathological process occurs along with normal intellectual functioning, it is sometimes informative to ask the subject to describe what he has heard or what he sees, even when he has achieved full credit.

The patient may fear seeing, hearing, or touching Wechsler stimulus materials when they have become infused and confused with hallucination. A hospitalized patient responded catastrophically to the first item of the WAIS-R Picture Completion, which depicts a door left ajar and missing a knob. The patient exclaimed, "Oh my God! I don't want to see what is behind the door!" Since it is in reality impossible to "see" behind the door, the remark conveys the subject's fear of his hallucinations, which are experienced as frighteningly out of his control, and quite real. The patient fears the Picture Completion task, which has become confused with his projected inner mental contents. Such contents are fantasized as hidden behind the "door" of each succeeding page.

Another patient reported that the figures on the WAIS Picture Completion items would "change shape" as she looked at them. Her predilection for projection over perception animated the stimuli. The picture of the PIG, for example, while correctly identified as missing a tail, looked "like it is beginning to snarl." The same patient involuntarily shivered while correctly identifying the missing dog tracks in the picture of a MAN AND DOG walking in the snow. The snow, she explained, "felt cold," a reaction which may be classified as a thermal illusion.

The same patient reported becoming dizzy from the red and white cue cards of Block Design because "the designs spin around." Such dizziness seemed not to affect her superior performance. The patient experienced a loss of distance and became entrapped perceptually with the enlivened stimuli while remaining separate on the verbal, semantic level. She perceptually acted out the fantasy that thinking is hostile, cold, and mentally painful, finding release neither in thinking nor in hallucinatory transformation.

On the contrary, a patient feels endangered and entrapped when suddenly confronted with a stimulus made worse through violent projection. Further, because of the confusion between hallucination and perception, a patient may become insecure in his belief that he is *not* experiencing hallucination but is correctly perceiving the stimulus items. Many of the stimuli may seem to foster confusion by appearing fragmented, violent, and bizarre.

The task on Picture Arrangement, for instance, may seem to require refragmenting and reamalgamating hallucinatory sequences of senseless violence or greed. In the WISC-R version (Wechsler, 1974, p. 76), for example, the child is faced with three cards and told, "These pictures tell a story about a fight—a boxing match. The pictures are in the wrong order now. See if you can put them in the right order so they tell a story that makes sense'' (FIGHT). A disturbed youngster may wonder about his own auditory and visual senses when a grown-up seems to be telling him about jumbled pictures of other grown-ups hurting each other. The child is next shown pictures of what the grown-up calls a picnic, but the child seems to see a dog stealing the food (PICNIC). In the next item, a fiery nightmare appears before the child's eyes (FIRE).

The patient may feel humiliated by hearing or seeing something that he fantasized he had covertly ejected into the test or the tester. The normal paranoid-schizoid state involves the introjection of part objects. In → Ps, these part objects are then fragmented and reprojected. Thus the patient may habitually take in aspects of a person and quickly expel them. The presentation on Object Assembly of parts of a part object, as on PROFILE (the face) or HAND, may frighteningly confirm the patient's fantasy of his oral-visual aggressivity. What has occurred is an unexpected, unnerving correlation between hallucination of fragments and perception of fragmented external reality.

On the WAIS Picture Completion, as well as on these other pictorial tasks, the patient is confronted with symbolic representations of the paranoid-schizoid inner world. These include depictions of damaged humans e.g. a woman's noseless profile (#3); a woman with no arms (#16); eerie, desolate scenes, e.g. the personless rowboat, adrift in an empty sea (#9); the schizoid male figure in the shadowy landscape (#18); and ''castrated'' animate and inanimate objects, e.g., respectively, the crab without a claw (#15) and the ocean liner with no smokestacks (#14).

In → Ps organization, such stimuli are experienced not as representations with potential symbolic meaning, but as real, haunting apparitions of that which has been destroyed mentally (see Segal, 1957, on ''symbolic equations''). This may partially explain the catastrophic reactions sometimes encountered from disturbed patients presented with Wechsler pictorial stimuli.

The Wechsler becomes a task to make realistic what appears surrealistic in a palpably concrete manner. But to make realistic what appears otherwise would ''trick'' the patient into receiving back what was ejected along with hallucination, i.e. the normal part of his personality. Under the auspices of alpha functioning, the normal part clarifies boundaries between momentary hallucination and test stimuli, and between test stimuli (the representations) and reality itself (the represented). This normal element is ''the most important part missing'' when the hallucinating subject considers Picture Completion. Similarly, to assemble fragmented objects on Object Assembly necessitates reassembling the patient's mind. The Wechsler requires, then, the maintenance of a boundary between autistic, hallucinatory transformation and reparative, imaginative introspection.

Although the psychotic element may temporarily comply with this requirement on individual items, it may quickly reassert its dominance by creating in the patient the expanding experience that the examination in toto is an unbounded hallucination. The Wechsler becomes a bad dream from which the patient can awake only by gross physical and mental action. I believe that the subtle reestablishment of convincing, unbounded hallucinatory "reality" coincident with adequate intellectual functioning accounts for the sudden decathexis of interest and attention encountered so often when testing disturbed patients. The patient seems to be complying with the examination, then suddenly becomes tired, fearful, silly, violent, etc. In these circumstances, the tester must delay or terminate the intellectual examination and, along with the normal part of the patient's personality, submit to defeat.

I might add here that remnants of hallucinatory dominance remain in more integrated personalities as well. While at the same time appreciating the cooperative efforts of examiner and examinee, many subjects find or report in retrospect that the IQ examination is unpleasantly "unreal." Even without blatantly derealizing or depersonalizing the interaction, most individuals do not experience such a task as friendly, and they remain uninsulated from the exam's painful, humiliating, and persecutory aspects, which color and distort their perception and memory. The intellectual examination arouses prominent affective and cognitive schemata from childhood, when one had to "answer" to authority figures. It may stimulate regressive feelings and fantasies in some patients, as well as primitive ego states.

Pathological Elaboration

Psychotic organizations, by their very nature, lead to underdiscrimination, so that the individual cannot easily distinguish between these states and higher-level functioning. In addition, psychotic processes, although pervasive in disturbed individuals, are neither consistent nor consistently pervasive. These facts contribute to the fantasy that perceptual and thinking processes are deliberately confusing and misleading, as was the experience in childhood of the mother's inconsistent ministrations. Negative ego functions may reverse or negate themselves, supplying the self with correct reality assessment when this is not wanted or expected, as well as with an unexpectedly false one. In this way among others, the −K systems personify obstructive objects by being tantalizingly unloyal. −K ego processes not only destroy purposive mental activity, but by also destroying purposeless mental activity, i.e. themselves, disallow comfortable adaptation to reality evasion. The person becomes unable to live with or without hallucination, feeling, or thought.

The unreliability of K and −K ego functions contributes to the phenomenon of pathological elaboration, which is a major contribution to intra-item, intra-test, and inter-test scatter (Rapaport, et al., 1945, ch. 2; Weiner, 1966, pp. 51–54). The patient experiences great difficulty in checking the accuracy of an item or of his responses with further reality testing. When he produces to a question both a bizarre response and a correct response, he may be confused as to where the bizarreness lies, in one of his answers, in the question, or in the situation which requires him to think. He experiences equal difficulty in ascertaining that what he perceives or produces is sufficiently inaccurate for his purposes, as he may find himself burdened suddenly with unwanted mental clarity. The request "explain further" creates a double-bind, no-win situation, since the subject in doing so can be assured neither of intellectual success nor of its evasion.

Even the simplest of mental tasks may be overladen with conflict between coincident but dissociated parts of personality, and may produce responses signifying such conflict. Elaboration extenuates conflict, and as such emboldens the part that hates internal conflict and the resultant pain.

For example, to the WAIS Picture Completion item involving a picture of a violin with a peg missing, a patient responded "peg, bow." When the examiner asked the patient to choose between the two responses ("But which is the most important thing missing?"), the patient wrinkled her brow and offered a third response: "hole in violin" [0]. Frustrated by the conflict represented in a choice between a more and a less appropriate response, the patient submits wholeheartedly to the psychotic element and attacks rather than repairs the stimulus item. She puts a hole in the violin and thereby further damages her response as well.

Possibly associating genital castration (symbolized visually by the pegless violin) with brain castration, the patient acts out a fantasy of internal mental damage. Instead of describing the absent object (the peg), she perversely describes the absence itself (the hole), i.e. "missing" rather than "thing missing." However, the patient cannot rely on −K operations to remain without, for the frustrating pairing of correct and incorrect responses continues on subsequent items.

The following elaborated WAIS-R response, revealing unreliably alternating K and −K processes, is from a thirty-four-year-old hospitalized nurse, a college graduate. When asked the number of senators in the U.S. Senate, she responded:

> I don't know. One from each state. Two, I'm sorry, two. (So how many altogether?) Uh, I think it's changed since I've been out of school. I'll say 102. Or is it 100? I'll say 102. No, 100. There are 51 states. Alaska. Hawaii. I'll say 100. Something else was. . . . You writing all that down? (Yes.) I'd better keep my mouth shut. You writing *that* down! [2]

The patient first attempts not to remember (''I don't know''). The subsequent answer suggests that the correct memory, retrieved by the normal part of the personality, is then split in half by the psychotic part. The patient responds that there is a single senator per state. The intact memory of twoness unexpectedly returns (''Two''). Unconsciously recognizing her hateful splitting, the patient experiences momentary depressive sorrow, and a temporary reaffirmation of re-pairing (''I'm sorry, two''), temporary because she remains resistive to thought, and needs to be pressed to do further pairing (''So how many altogether?''). The temptation to think is undermined by the suspicion that what she once had learned as fact no longer can be relied upon (''Oh, I think it's changed since I've been out of school. I'll say 102''). The patient has lost confidence in her history and hence in the constancy of internal objects and the relationships among objects. The relationship of ''two'' to ''100'' in this context is that of part (♂) to whole (♀). The psychotic element disturbs the ♀ ♂ relationship, forcing together the subordinate and superordinate to form the pathologically super-superordinate (− ♀ ♂) ''102.''

The idea of a governing body—the Senate—is conflictual when one feels that a part of oneself is out of control and ungovernable. Ambivalence contributes to pathological elaboration, as one part of the self wants to ''get it wrong,'' regress into ignorance, and fuse with preverbal, dictatorial internal objects, while the other part wants to function democratically in lawful, literate society. Pathological elaboration accomplishes the doing and undoing of this ambivalence but lacks conviction and therefore resolution. The patient may regain confidence and security in neither right nor wrong versions of reality, and remains at the mercy of these conflicting versions, which are experienced as alternating infinitely, out of her control. Hence, the correct response of 100 reappears on elaboration (''Or is it 100?'') only to be erased by the reasserted amalgamation (''I'll say 102''). When, in the next sequence, the correct response reappears (''No, 100''), the patient launches a further attempt to reason incorrectly, producing a faulty memory of 51 states. (''There are 51 states. Alaska. Hawaii.'') But the −K operation abruptly cancels itself, as the patient dubiously returns to the correct choice (''I'll say 100'').

Getting the right answer as well as the wrong answer makes the examinee in → Ps anxious and dissatisfied. The lack of mental satisfaction when one can think neither correctly nor incorrectly leaves one hungry for thought. It contributes to the often desperate continuation of elaboration, and the appearance of numerous ''spoilages'' and/or intrusions of related associations. In this example, the patient searches for something else to think about, but hesitates uncertainly (''Something else was . . .''). She becomes afraid that out of her desperate hunger for food for thought she has exposed too much of her sanity or her insanity. The examiner, like the mental apparatus, functions as a minus container, entrapping exposed thoughts but not clarifying or supplementing them ("You writing all that down?"). The patient resorts to her opening defense, and attempts not to involve herself further ("I'd better keep my mouth shut"). The examinee's expressive apparatus (her mouth), like her receptive and integrative apparatuses, is treacherous and unreliable, and may lead her into further pain. By keeping her mouth shut, she will keep thoughts from getting out or getting in.

The enforced silence and withdrawal from elaboration serves to evade the problem of choosing between conflicting, underdifferentiated elements in the personality, as well as the problem of right and wrong. But noncommunication and nonelaboration succeed only temporarily in evading these issues of internal and external reality. The primitive means of mental evasion the patient uses to defend herself are not beyond greedy absorption by obstructive mental objects. When the patient threatens not to talk, she finds that too being observed and taken in ("You writing *that* down!").

But neither nonelaboration nor pathological elaboration removes the patient from the persecuting "uncertainty cloud" (Bion, 1963) of $\rightarrow$ Ps mental organization—a phenomenological state of heightened anxiety in which dreadful, vague and unnameable aggressive fantasies are experienced as palpably real and pervasive. The patient cannot be sure that nonelaboration is respected, and fears that elaboration may be pursued by the examiner without her willing it. Confusion, psychosis, and withdrawal are made more painful when intruded upon and judged harshly by persecutory reality in the form of the examiner. This aggressive figure observes, questions, and writes down the seemingly most inconsequential verbalizations, follows leads as well as pauses, right responses as well as wrong ones, and, worst of all, threatens to meet again for further testing, further elaboration.

Concluding Remarks

This chapter is an introduction to a Kleinian-Bionian interpretation of the Wechsler Scales, and by extension, of other cognitive as well as projective instruments. I have focused on paranoid-schizoid organization and have concentrated on the following types of pathological test phenomena: pervasive aggressivity; attacks on links; hallucination; bizarreness; and pathological elaboration. I should again emphasize that $\rightarrow$ Ps organization may be coincident not only with normal and neurotic organization, but with depressive ($\rightarrow$ D) and manic-omnipotent $-$(Ps $\longleftrightarrow$ D) organizations as well. A similar typology may be established regarding the other psychotic positions, with characteristic variations in the form of pathological test phenomena. These findings will be presented in subsequent contributions.

References

Billow, R. (1977), Metaphor: A review of the psychological literature. *Psychol. Bull.*, 84:81–92.

——— (1980), On reunion. *Psychoanal. Rev.*, 67:253–270.

——— (1981), Observing spontaneous metaphor in children. *J. Exp. Child Psychol.*, 31:430–445.

——— Lovett, J. (1984), Psycholinguistic phenomena of the bipersonal field. In: *Listening and Interpreting*, ed. J. Raney. New York: Aronson, pp. 303–322.

——— Rossman, J., Lewis, N., Goldman, D., Ross, P., & Palermo, D. (1983a), Metaphor comprehension in schizophrenia. Unpublished manuscript.

——— ——— ——— ——— ——— ——— (1983b), Metaphor production in schizophrenia. Unpublished manuscript.

Bion, W. (1950), The imaginary twin. In: *Second Thoughts*, London: Heinemann, 1967, pp. 3–22.

——— (1957), Differentiation of the psychotic from the non-psychotic personalities. In: *Second Thoughts*. London: Heinemann, 1967, pp. 43–64.

——— (1959a), Attacks on linking. In: *Second Thoughts*. London: Heinemann, 1967, pp. 93–109.

——— (1959b), *Experiences in Groups*. London: Tavistock.

——— (1962a), *Learning from experience*. London: Heinemann. Reprinted in: *Seven Servants: Four works by Wilfred R. Bion*. New York: Aronson, 1977.

——— (1962b), A theory of thinking. In: *Second Thoughts*. London: Heinemann, 1967, pp. 110–119.

——— (1963), *Elements of Psycho-Analysis*. London: Heinemann. Reprinted in: *Seven Servants: Four Works by Wilfred R. Bion*. New York: Aronson, 1977.

——— (1965), *Transformations*. London: Heinemann. Reprinted in: *Seven Servants: Four Works by Wilfred R. Bion*. New York: Aronson, 1977.

——— (1970), *Attention and Interpretation*. London: Tavistock. Reprinted in: *Seven Servants: Four Works by Wilfred R. Bion*. New York: Aronson, 1977.

Blatt, S., & Allison, S. (1968), The intelligence test in personality assessment. In: *Projective Techniques in Personality Assessment*, ed. A. Rabin. New York: Springer, pp. 421–460.

Boris, H. (1976), On hope: Its nature and psychotherapy. *Internat. Rev. Psycho-Anal.*, 3:139–150.

Bleuler, E. (1911), *Dementia Praecox or the Group of Schizophrenias*. New York: International Universities Press, 1950.

Breuer, J., & Freud, S. (1895), Studies on hysteria. *Standard Edition*, 2. London: Hogarth Press, 1956.

Conklin, J. (1981), Empathy and Bion's clinical theory: Psychotherapeutic progress or stalemate. Paper presented at the Annual Meeting of the American Psychological Association, Los Angeles.

Eigen, M. (1981), The area of faith in Winnicott, Lacan and Bion. *Internat. J. Psycho-Anal.*, 62:413–433.

Freud, S. (1905), Three essays on sexuality. *Standard Edition*, 7:130–243. London: Hogarth Press, 1953.

——— (1911a), Formulations regarding the two principles in mental functioning. *Collected Papers*, 4:13–21. London: Hogarth Press, 1950.

——— (1911b), Psycho-analytic notes on an autobiographical account of a case of paranoia (dementia paranoides). *Standard Edition*, 12:9–79. London: Hogarth Press, 1958.

——— (1915), The unconscious. *Standard Edition*, 14:166–215. London: Hogarth Press, 1957.

——— (1917), Mourning and melancholia. *Standard Edition*, 14:243–258. London: Hogarth Press, 1957.

——— (1920), Beyond the pleasure principle. *Standard Edition*, 18:7–64. London: Hogarth Press, 1955.

——— (1938), An outline of psycho-analysis. *Standard Edition*, 23:144–207. London: Hogarth Press, 1964.

——— (1940), Splitting of the ego in the process of defence. *Standard Edition*, 23:275–278. London: Hogarth Press, 1964.

Grotstein, J. (1977a), The psychoanalytic concept of schizophrenia I: The dilemma. *Internat. J. Psycho-Anal.*, 58:403–425.

——— (1977b), The psychoanalytic concept of schizophrenia II: Reconciliation. *Internat. J. Psycho-Anal.*, 58:427–452.

——— (1978), Gradients of analyzability. *Internat. J. Psychoanal. Psychother.*, 7:137–151.

——— (1980), A proposed revision of the psychoanalytic concept of primitive mental states: Part 1. *Contemp. Psychoanal.*, 16:479–546.

——— (1981), *Splitting and Projective Identification*. New York: Aronson.

Heimann, P. (1952), Certain functions in introjection and projection in early infancy. In: *Developments in Psycho-Analysis*, ed. M. Klein, P. Heimann, S. Isaacs, & J. Riviere. London: Hogarth Press, pp. 122–168.

Holt, R., and Havel, J. (1960), A method of assessing primary and secondary process in the Rorschach. In: *Rorschach Psychology*, ed. M. Rickers-Ovsiankina. New York: Wiley, pp. 263–315.

Isaacs, S. (1952), The nature and function of phantasy. In: *Developments in Psycho-Analysis*, ed. M. Klein, P. Heimann, S. Isaacs, & J. Riviere. London: Hogarth Press, pp. 67–121.

Klein, M. (1930), The importance of symbol-formation in the development of the ego. In: *Love, Guilt and Reparation*. New York: Delacorte, 1975, pp. 219–232.

——— (1935), A contribution to the psychogenesis of manic depressive states. In: *Love, Guilt and Reparation*. New York: Delacorte Press, 1975, pp. 262–289.

——— (1940), Mourning and its relation to manic depressive states. In: *Love, Guilt and Reparation*. New York: Delacorte Press, 1975.

——— (1946), Notes on some schizoid mechanisms. In: *Envy and Gratitude*. New York: Delacorte, 1975, pp. 1–24.

Langs, R. (1978), Some communicative properties of the bipersonal field. *Internat. J. Psychoanal. Psychother.*, 7:89–136.

——— (1980), Truth therapy/lie therapy. *Internat. J. Psychoanal. Psychother.*, 8:3–34.

——— (1981), Some communicative properties of the bipersonal field: Postscript. In: *Do I Dare Disturb the Universe?*, ed. J. Grotstein. Beverly Hills: Caesura Press, pp. 441–488.

Lovett, C., & Wolf, J. (1981), Bionic reconstruction. Paper presented at the annual meeting of the American Psychological Association, Los Angeles.

Matarazzo, J. (1972), *Wechsler's Measurement and Appraisal of Adult Intelligence*. Baltimore: Williams & Wilkins.

Mayman, M., Schafer, R., & Rapaport, D. (1951), Interpretation of the Wechsler-Bellevue Scale in personality appraisal. In: *An Introduction to Projective Techniques*, ed. H. Anderson & G. Anderson. New York: Prentice-Hall, pp. 541–580.

Meltzer, D. (1978), *The Kleinian Development, Part III: The Clinical Significance of the Work of Bion*. Perthshire, Scotland: Clunie Press.

——— (1979), *Sexual States of Mind*. Perthshire, Scotland: Clunie Press.

——— Bremner, J., Hoxter, S., Weddell, D., & Wittenberg, I. (1975), *Explorations in Autism*. Perthshire, Scotland: Clunie Press.

Rabin, A. (1965), Diagnostic use of intelligence tests. In: *Handbook of Clinical Psychology*, ed. B. Wolman. New York: McGraw-Hill, pp. 477–497.

Racker, H. (1968), *Transference and Countertransference*. New York: International Universities Press.

Rapaport, D., Gill, M., & Schafer, R. (1945), *Diagnostic Psychological Testing*. New York: International Universities Press, 1968.

Schafer, R. (1980), *The Clinical Application of Psychological Tests*. New York: International Universities Press.

Searles, H. (1965), The Differentiation between concrete and metaphorical thinking in the recovering schizophrenic patient. In: *Collected Papers on Schizophrenia and Related Subjects*. New York: International Universities Press, pp. 560–583.

Segal, H. (1957), Notes on symbol formation. *Internat. J. Psycho-Anal.*, 38:319–397.

——— (1973), *Introduction to the Work of Melanie Klein*. New York: Basic Books.

——— (1981), Manic reparation. In: *The Work of Hanna Segal*. New York: Aronson, pp. 147–158.

Stoerl, J. (1981), Envy and Bion's clinical theory. Paper presented at the Annual Meeting of the American Psychological Association, Los Angeles.

——— (1982), The assessment of envy and its relationship to personality and therapeutic outcome. Unpublished doctoral dissertation, Adelphi University.

Tustin, F. (1972), *Autism and Childhood Psychosis*. New York: Science House.

Waite, R. (1961), The intelligence test as a psychodiagnostic instrument. *J. Proj. Tech.*, 25:90–102.

Wechsler, D. (1955), *WAIS Manual*. New York: The Psychological Corporation.

——— (1974), *WISC-R Manual*. New York: The Psychological Corporation.

Weiner, I. (1966), *Psychodiagnosis in Schizophrenia*. New York: Wiley.

Zimmerman, I., & Woo-Sam, J. (1973), *Clinical Interpretation of the Wechsler Adult Intelligence Scale*. New York: Grune & Stratton.

Part III

The Testing Process

Chapter 11

THERAPEUTIC EXPLORATION OF OBJECT RELATIONS PATTERNS OBSERVABLE DURING THE TESTING PROCESS

MORTON KISSEN

In recent years object relations principles have been formulated which have very significant ramifications for therapeutic work with highly resistant or borderline individuals—the "difficult" patients alluded to in the psychoanalytic writings of Balint (1968), Giovacchini (1975), and Kernberg (1975). In a recent work (Kissen, 1980) I have explored the implications of the concept of projective identification for the development of object relational strategies in work with difficult, characterologically impaired patients. All of these more recent contributions are elaborations of the earlier work of Jacobson (1964) and the British analysts Fairbairn (1954), Guntrip (1969), and Winnicott (1965) toward development of an object relations model for conceptualizing the psychotherapy interaction.

Object relations theory has also had a very pervasive impact upon psychological testing and has expanded and deepened the process of diagnostic communication. A number of recent writers have begun to explore the use of object relations constructs as an alternative to the more reified and rather lifeless diagnostic test report language implicit in the earlier ego psychological, dynamic, and structural models. Mayman (1976) has noted this conceptual shift from an ego psychological to an object relational approach and has characterized it as a movement toward a more phenomenologically valid mode of conceptualization which is closer to actual clinical occurrences and which involves a movement away from the more experience-distant and metapsychological abstractions of the earlier dynamic and structural models.

Schafer (1976), in an essentially similar vein, but from a somewhat different vantage point, has recently begun to explore the *actional* and *non-actional* implications of the language used by clinicians to communicate both diagnostic and therapeutic understandings. His emphasis upon action language as essential to a phenomenologically valid process of clinical communication dovetails quite nicely with the object relations approach. Schafer envisions an active, choice-making individual, even at moments of seeming pathological regression, neurotic ambivalence, and characterological rigidity, and asks clinicians to capture such psychic activity, at all times, both in their diagnostic reports to colleagues and in their therapeutic communications with patients.

Interestingly, in his early work Schafer (1954) took a great deal of interest in the transferential aspects of the tester-patient interaction. In formulating certain parallels between the psychoanalytic therapy and diagnostic testing situations, he focused extensively upon a number of transference and countertransference patterns discernible in that interaction. In the present chapter, Schafer's psychoanalytic model of the testing process will be elaborated from a more modern object relational perspective. Two basic, therapeutically relevant parameters (Wolstein, 1964)—transference-countertransference and resistance-counterresistance—will be focused on through a study of the ways in which they can be discerned in the tester-patient relationship. This interactional focus will highlight certain object relations processes, particularly the significant self-representations, object representations, and ego identity states of patients, in a fashion that has practical implications for the psychotherapy process.

The Tester's Personal Reactions

Transference-Countertransference

While a countertransference reaction is essentially a subjective reaction on the part of either tester or therapist, it nevertheless has certain "objective" features. These stem from its replicability and from the fact that it can be discerned via parallel modes of observation and empirical verification. For instance, if a particular self- or object representation inferred from a patient's early memory involving a parent figure (e.g. a tendency to come across as oafish before a rigidly authoritarian father figure) is paralleled in the testing session via a subtle proneness to play out the role of bumbling fool with the tester (thereby provoking the latter's countertendency to respond in a slightly more harsh or judgmental manner than might otherwise be the case), then it can safely be assumed that an objective countertransference reaction has been induced and may well be a significant interactive dimension of the psychotherapy.

The experienced tester, operating within a standardized format, can use his own attitudes and emotional reactions during the test session as an additional source of insight into both the patient's internalized object relationships and the transference-countertransference interactions that develop during psychotherapy. Thus, a male tester who finds himself unusually buoyant with an attractive female patient, perhaps flaunting his psychological testing brilliance in an exhibitionistic manner, should not be surprised if blatant oedipal imagery appears in her inkblot perceptions or in the thematic content of her TAT stories. The self-representation of a flirtatious, attractive little girl, genetically linked to an oedipal attachment to an eminently seducible father, may evoke both in tester and therapist a countertransference resistance in the form of either seductive or counterseductive behavior.

A modern approach to psychological testing involves a delicate, essentially measured use by the tester of his own personality reactions in order to gain a more therapeutically relevant understanding of the patient. The ability to note and jot down various personal reactions during the course of the testing session is an essential skill of the sophisticated tester. I ask my supervisees to cultivate the habit of jotting down personal feelings and interactional observations in addition to the more typical process recording during testing sessions. Personal recording of this sort may typically involve such statements as "I feel myself being subtly intimidated by the patient" or "I find myself becoming angered by something about this patient." Other personal observations may involve unusual degrees of assertiveness, exhibitionism, or passive withdrawal in response to some aspect of the interaction with the patient. Of course, the tester must be aware of his own personality and typical testing reactions in order to make reliable and valid phenomenological inferences of this sort.

It is important to emphasize that the observational process described in this chapter, although essentially a way of focusing on the countertransference, need not involve a transformation of the testing situation into a psychotherapy session. It is assumed that such a process of phenomenological inquiry occurs within the context of a tightly organized testing format in which standardized instructional procedures are closely followed. Thus, while recording verbatim the responses to standard test items, the examiner may additionally note such facts as that very little demand is being placed on him by the patient for eye contact or interpersonal engagement; or, with a different patient, that a tremendous amount of engagement is required and that the examiner feels emotionally drained by the end of the session. Such observations, when integrated with the more traditional inferences derived from the structural and content aspects of the test responses, allow for a richer and therapeutically more useful study of object relationships.

It is, of course, assumed that the examiner will be sensitive to his own affective and attitudinal state going into a test session and will carefully separate personal reactions that are independent of the tester-patient interaction from those directly stemming from it. For instance, being in a mildly dysphoric state prior to meeting a patient is obviously quite different from a fairly sudden shift to a sense of sadness (from a happier mood) during a testing session. Since the affective dimension is such an important and often neglected aspect of the tester-patient interaction, it is incumbent on the experienced tester to pay careful attention to his moods before, during, and after each session. Over time, a sophisticated tester will gain an increasing capacity to discriminate interpersonally generated affects, for the purpose of making reliable inferences with regard to the patient's self- and object representations, from intrapsychically motivated feeling states which relate largely to the self- and object representations of the tester himself.

Resistance-Counterresistance

In addition to the exploration of countertransference within the testing interaction, it is also possible—via a guided and systematic use of tester activity—to explore the dimension of resistance-counterresistance. Appelbaum (1959) has developed a rather creative addendum to the traditional Rorschach procedure that allows for the novel use of systematically arranged tester activity (in this case, a form of diminished activity) in order to assess in a deeper fashion important aspects of the patient's resistance. Appelbaum's Altered Atmosphere Procedure is a technique for loosening the associative processes of tightly guarded or severely inhibited patients who tend to produce constricted Rorschach protocols with a paucity of clinically useful imaginative responses. Appelbaum describes his novel procedure as follows:

> Directly following the usual test administration, I have come to discard some of the paraphernalia of the testing situation, implying by my behavior that the test is over. While putting down my pen, shuffling response sheets together, leaning back in the chair, adopting a more conversational tone, I hand all the cards back to the patient and suggest that he go through the cards again to see whether he might see something else, something he perhaps did not notice before. These directions might best be taken as conveying the gist of what occurs rather than as an inflexible prescription, for different patients elicit spontaneous alterations in the technique necessary to establish and maintain the desired atmosphere. [p. 179]

The creation of a more relaxed, informal setting after the traditional standardized Rorschach administration permits the spontaneous emergence of imaginative responses that may have been suppressed or repressed. The Appelbaum procedure can be considered a form of testing the severity of a given patient's resistance—important, since it will doubtless be played out in the course of psychotherapy. A patient who can produce revealing imaginative responses to the Altered Atmosphere Procedure can be assumed to be less resistant than one who cannot. My own impression, gleaned from extensive personal use and supervision of the Appelbaum procedure, is that it generates a sophisticated and therapeutically useful analysis of resistance tendencies.

The use of "paradigmatic" techniques (Strean, 1959; Nelson, 1962) also allows for the exploration of resistance tendencies during the testing session. The experienced examiner, once in touch with induced counterresistance feelings, can use such feelings to explore certain qualities of the patient's object relationships. The delicate use of ironic observations, which either nonverbally mirror or verbally confront a given patient's resistances, can be effectively used to test the limits of that patient's characterological rigidity and defensiveness.

Such techniques are particularly useful as a method of exploring the degree of flexibility in passive-aggressive defensive structures. Thus, children with histories of academic underachievement who manifest such tendencies on the intelligence test (via forms of constriction, avoidance, or a general holding back of specific cognitive capabilities) can be confronted with such tendencies at appropriate points in the testing. The examiner might register his awareness of a characterological quality of negativism or obtuseness by asking the patient why he is trying to convince the examiner of his stupidity. A more ironic confrontation might be the following: "I see that I am testing a retarded child." The examiner, by such statements, directly confronts the defensive structures underlying the pseudoretarded characterological posture and often engages the child as a "consultant" (Strean, 1959) in what one hopes will be a humorous mutual exploration of the degree of permeability or plasticity of these resistances.

Paradigmatic interventions can also be used to test the patient's capacity to introspectively explore masochistic defensive structures and resistances. Thus, an awareness by the examiner of angry or sadistic feelings toward the patient may be used to engage the patient's intropunitiveness or masochism. By making a statement about how ridiculous or inadequate the patient seems at a given point in the test session, the examiner actively engages both his own induced counterresistance feelings and the patient's masochistic defenses, which no doubt will be played out transferentially in the ensuing interaction with the therapist.

It should be emphasized that these paradigmatic techniques must be used very sensitively. They are not to be used merely as a cathartic outlet for feelings generated during the course of the tester-patient interaction. Used properly, however, they are a way of openly registering the mutual awareness that certain feelings have been induced and that it is permissible to explore, during the test session, the self- and object representations underlying them.

Perhaps the most effective device for exploring resistances during testing is the self-interview technique. At various points during the examination, the patient is asked to reflect upon the possible psychological meanings of his responses. This technique may be used selectively—particularly in connection with projective tests such as the TAT and the Word Association Test—or in a more comprehensive fashion on all tests, including the more structured intelligence test. The purpose is to engage the patient in more active exploration of the possible psychological meanings of his responses. The patient is in effect asked to use his own psychological-mindedness rather than resign himself to a passive testing experience.

This ability to introspect may be conceptualized either as an autonomous ego function or as a characterological composite of the defensive or resistive tendencies of the patient. At any rate it is an essential attribute that will certainly have great significance for the ensuing resistance-counterresistance interaction with the therapist. The so-called difficult patient may very well be the individual whose resistance tends largely to be played out in the sphere of psychological-mindedness. The patient who cannot introspectively explore the psychological meanings of his test responses will probably be severely resistant to the inquiry process during psychotherapy.

Conclusions

In a previous paper (1971), I explored some of the possible reasons for a diminished reliance on psychological tests in the formulation of treatment goals for various patients. Perhaps a major reason lies in the fact that no systematic art and science of testing has as yet been formulated. Numerous contributions toward this end have, however, been made (Schlesinger, 1969; Appelbaum, 1969, 1970, 1972; Kissen, 1973). While maintaining the proper boundaries between psychological testing and psychotherapy, one may still find it possible to sensitively explore important parameters of psychotherapy during the typical testing session. The practical therapeutic derivatives of such an expansion of the testing function will no doubt contribute to the attractiveness of psychological testing to young clinicians. In addition, the object relations patterns implicit in the tester-patient interaction can provide a solid phenomenological feel and action language orientation for the inferences generated in the course of testing.

References

Appelbaum, S. (1959), The effect of altered psychological atmosphere on Rorschach responses: A new supplementary procedure. *Bull. Menn. Clin.*, 23:179–189.

——— (1969), Psychological testing for the psychotherapist. *Dynam. Psychiat.*, 2:158–163.

——— (1970), Science and persuasion in the psychological test report. *J. Consult. Clin. Psychol.*, 35:349–355.

——— (1972), A method of reporting psychological test findings. *Bull. Menn. Clin.*, 36:535–545.

——— (1976) Rapaport revisited: Practice. *Bull. Menn. Clin.*, 40:229–237.

Balint, M. (1968), *The Basic Fault: Therapeutic Aspects of Regression.* London: Tavistock.

Fairbairn, W. (1954), *An Object-Relations Theory of the Personality.* New York: Basic Books.

Giovacchini, P. (1975), *Psychoanalysis of Character Disorders.* New York: Aronson.

Guntrip, H. (1969), *Schizoid Phenomena, Object Relations and the Self.* New York: International Universities Press.

Jacobson, E. (1964), *The Self and the Object World.* New York: International Universities Press.

Kernberg, O. (1975), *Borderline Conditions and Pathological Narcissism.* New York: Aronson.

Kissen, M. (1971), The status of psychological testing in current clinical practice. *J. Clin. Iss. Psychol.*, 2:20–22.

——— (1973), The importance of psychological testing for the psychotherapy process. *J. Clin. Iss. Psychol.*, 5:11–13.

——— (1980), Therapeutic use of self- and object representations in the treatment of character disorders. Unpublished manuscript.

Mayman, M. (1976), Psychoanalytic theory in retrospect and prospect. *Bull. Menn. Clin.*, 40:199–210.

Nelson, M. (1962), Effect of paradigmatic techniques on the psychic economy of borderline patients. *Psychiat.*, 25:119–134.

Schafer, R. (1954), *Psychoanalytic Interpretation in Rorschach Testing.* New York: Grune and Stratton.

——— (1976), *Language and Insight.* New Haven: Yale University Press.

Schlesinger, H. (1969), Diagnosis and prescription for psychotherapy. *Bull. Menn. Clin.*, 35:269–278.

Strean, H. (1959), The use of the patient as a consultant. *Psychoanalysis and the Psychoanalytic Review*, 46:36–44.

Winnicott, D. (1975), *The Maturational Processes and the Facilitating Environment.* New York: International Universities Press.

Wolstein, B. (1964), *Transference: Its Structure and Function in Psychoanalytic Therapy.* New York: Grune and Stratton.

Chapter 12

TREATMENT IMPLICATIONS OF OBJECT RELATIONSHIPS AS THEY UNFOLD DURING THE DIAGNOSTIC INTERACTION

FRED SHECTMAN and MICHAEL K. HARTY

A common criticism of psychological diagnosis has been that the diagnostic enterprise tends to be self-contained, even solipsistic; not only crude diagnostic labeling, but even the most sophisticated descriptions of personality structures and dynamics, often fail to have a significant impact on the disposition or management of cases (see Shectman, 1976, for an overview). At a general level, our own observations support this criticism, in that too often the diligence expended in a diagnostic examination seems to contribute more to the bulk of a file than to the betterment of the patient's condition. But should the diagnostic enterprise therefore be drastically limited or abandoned altogether? We think not. Diagnostic practice can be carried on in ways that make for much greater clinical relevance, especially if a broad object relations viewpoint is utilized. It is toward that aim that this chapter is directed.

What we propose is not so much a particular technique of diagnostic

This chapter is based on a workshop on psychological evaluation which the authors gave at the annual meeting of the Society for Personality Assessment, San Diego, March 1977. The authors gratefully acknowledge that many of the ideas in this paper derive from presentations made by Drs. Herbert Schlesinger and Howard Shevrin in various seminars and discussions with postdoctoral fellows in clinical psychology at the Menninger Foundation. We are indebted to Drs. Ann Appelbaum and Richard Maxfield for their editorial suggestions and encouragement in the preparation of the manuscript.

practice as a general orientation to the process of diagnosing. We will be referring both to diagnostic interviews and to psychological testing, but the "process approach" we advocate may be applied to other situations as well. Whatever the specific setting of the diagnostic assessment—individual interview, family interview, psychological testing, etc.—there are, in our view, regular features of the unfolding clinical process. We look to these regular features to provide an integrating frame of reference, relating the diagnostic understanding, however gained, to whatever additional interpersonal process is designated as "treatment."

Psychological diagnosis is never carried out in a vacuum, but always for a more or less specific purpose. Here we will concern ourselves with situations in which *the presumed purpose is to help someone, or some group of people, to obtain appropriate assistance for psychological difficulties*. This is not the only valid purpose for a psychological assessment; very often, for example, people are psychologically evaluated to determine suitability for employment or liability to prosecution, for research purposes, or, as is frequently true when the assessor is a student, to provide an opportunity for someone else to learn professional skills. The findings of the assessment may be greatly influenced by such considerations, and if only for that reason it is important to be clear about the kind of context we wish to assume.

For our purposes, it is also essential to be clear about this because distortions of the assessment's purpose often occur as it proceeds. Often the "real" or official purpose is pushed into the background as the personal concerns of the participants dominate the process. Probably all clinicians have experienced situations in which the patient acted as if his main purpose were to make a favorable impression on the diagnostician, or to antagonize him, make a fool of him, and so on, instead of to obtain his professional help. And diagnosticians may also recall occasions when they have acted as if they were primarily interested in placating the patient, teaching him a lesson, or selling him something, rather than helping him understand his difficulty and figure out what to do about it. These are the kinds of departures we are calling distortions of the purpose of the assessment, and in what follows we take the position that such distortions can be worked with, understood, and constructively used, rather than regarded only as nuisances to be avoided or circumvented whenever possible (see Shectman, 1977, 1979). This point of view would be difficult to apply without some clarity at the beginning about the "real" purpose that constitutes the background against which to view the distortions.

If we assume that the diagnostic assessment is aimed toward some kind of helping process, then we can also assume that it is aimed toward some kind of *interpersonal* process. That is, no matter whether the recommended intervention is called psychotherapy, counseling, psychoanalysis, vocational training, or whatever, it cannot rightly be thought of as an abstract manipulation which will impinge on the client outside an interpersonal context. This will strike no one as a great revelation, since most forms of psychological intervention are explicitly based on the importance of the interpersonal relationship as a vehicle for bringing about change. However, what has not been emphasized enough are the parallels and similarities between this eventual treatment process and the interpersonal process of psychological diagnosis which precedes it. The psychological assessment need not be thought of as simply a kind of ''snapshot'' procedure—one that yields a static, cross-sectional view of how the patient happened to be at a particular point in time. A better photographic analogy in our terms would be the screen test—a ''casting'' procedure which tries to make maximum use of the similarity between the test situation and the situation which is predicted to. In the screen test, unlike the snapshot, the subject's functioning is observed under a variety of conditions which approximate those of ''real'' interest; and changes which occur are available to observation, in addition to the constant features. This is something like what we mean by a ''process approach.''

Viewed in this way, the diagnostic and evaluation process can become a kind of testing ground for psychological treatment, and as such can become highly relevant to the planning and conduct of such treatment. From this point of view, the major aim of the diagnostic process is not simply to label or classify the problem; nor is it to formulate an understanding of the difficulties in psychodynamic terms, although this may be part of the task. Rather, we conceive of the most central diagnostic task as that of *assessing those difficulties and those capacities of the person which are most directly relevant to the way that person can use a helping relationship* (see Shevrin and Shectman, 1973). The diagnosing is carried out under conditions which inevitably bear important similarities to ''treatment'' conditions, and which can and should be exploited because of those similarities.

For us, then, ''diagnosing'' refers less to descriptive diagnosis and more to the process of understanding, assessing, and making explicit those factors which bear directly on the subsequent treatment situation. A broad object relations perspective—one that emphasizes the role of internalized relationship patterns in both adaptive and maladaptive psychological functioning—provides the frame of reference which links the two clinical situations with each other and with the life situations in which the patient's difficulties originally appeared. The further elaboration and application of this point of view is the subject of these pages—that is, how can the diagnostic process be used so that it contributes maximally to the treatment process toward which it is aimed?

The discussion is organized in a way consistent with the approach we advocate: not around particular techniques or diagnostic questions, but rather around phases or aspects of the clinical process that develop in the diagnostic situation.

On Beginnings

To consider ''beginning'' only as a point in time underestimates the complexity of such openings or startings. It is possible to think of beginning instead as an unfolding process—a process that can go on across time (Schlesinger, 1973). An example may clarify this point:

> A middle-aged man is referred for psychological testing after his neurologist finds no organic basis for the patient's headaches, but notes that there is some correlation between his headaches and periodic outbursts of anger. The psychologist introduces himself and asks if the patient has ever been tested before. The patient abruptly says that he has never seen a ''shrink,'' that he is not nuts, that it is not all in his head, and that something is really wrong with him! The psychologist responds that he is interested in assisting the neurologist by providing a comprehensive examination, and that includes psychological testing. Grudgingly, the patient goes through the testing in a matter-of-fact way, cautiously and tentatively producing few responses, and making his discomfort and irritation obvious. The psychologist administers the tests in a determinedly businesslike fashion, though inwardly angry at feeling that getting test responses from this patient is like pulling teeth. Looking ahead to his eventual test report, the psychologist is already formulating statements about how resistive the patient is, how poorly motivated for thinking psychologically about his problems, and hence how guarded the prognosis is for any successful therapeutic outcome.

What can we make of this way of beginning? Clearly something happened, and the participants began (and continued) in a particular way. One aspect of the interaction is that an angry patient managed to put the examiner on the defensive, made the psychologist feel as frustrated and irritated as the patient felt, and got the diagnostician to say some ''bad'' things about him—under the guise of technical jargon about resistance and motivation. We may also observe that instead of openly bickering, the two people went through the motions of collaboration; they called an unspoken truce after the patient's original outburst and kept one another at arm's length thereafter. But as a result there was very little of an unfolding process. Instead, things quickly came to a psychological standstill for patient and examiner alike. Neither was able to learn anything new—for example, under what conditions that patient might be less resistive and more motivated, and how a treater might use himself to create such conditions. Raising such "process" questions about this beginning could have been a way of exploiting the similarity between assessing and treating, to the betterment of the future treatment (see Shectman, 1977, 1979). Instead, by responding in a static fashion, the psychologist labeled and disposed of the patient. For example, the psychologist regarded the patient as "poorly motivated," as if one is either well motivated or not, independent of the particular conditions which influence one's motivation.

By avoiding the difficulties of beginning and fleeing into the tests, this examiner indicated that he was as unready as the patient to risk participating in an unknown journey of discovery. Each protected himself from taking a chance on a more unfolding (and therefore uncertain) process by keeping the quality of the interaction pretty much frozen right where they started. In that way their exchange exemplified "beginning" as a point in time, rather than as a process—a point at which both participants were stuck.

We will return to this vignette shortly. However, this example already illustrates that one's way of beginning holds many clues to the way one is predisposed to participate in and use what follows. Thus, our patient's way of starting a diagnostic process

> has much in common with other beginning processes, such as entering a new school, taking a new job, going on a blind date, or starting [a treatment undertaking]. . . . In each instance, at least one of the parties will wonder: Will they understand me? Do I dare let them know me? Will they reject me if I do? Is this person competent to do what I need to have done? And, conversely, am I worth his bothering with me? Can I meet and afford his requirements? [Holzman and Schlesinger, 1972, p. 397.]

Such concerns are heightened when one is in the especially vulnerable role of patient. But rarely is the patient alone in having such doubts and fears, for if the process is indeed mutual and the diagnostician is open to his own experience, then he too must grapple with such worries.

Indeed, the initial phases of the interaction are perhaps best thought of as a mutual diagnostic process, in that the patient is also evaluating the examiner, what will be required of him, and what will be the quality of the interaction. These concerns may take the form of seemingly innocuous questions ("Your accent isn't a Midwestern one, more like an Eastern one where I grew up. Is that so?"). Or there may be doubts over the appropriateness of the assessment procedure itself (as in our vignette), or exaggerated scheduling difficulties, questions about the details of the assessment task, etc. Once it is recognized that even such "realistic" issues may be the vehicle for concerns about beginning, it becomes possible to learn something from the particular form such expressions take. For example, the patient's feeling scared and worried that he may not be understood or helped may be expressed blatantly by his angrily asking the examiner if he is competent. A less troubled patient could express the same concern by inquiring how long the examiner has been a professional. Successively refined transmutations might lead to questions about the diagnostician's age, the school he attended, the painting on his office wall, and the patient's perhaps stating that he knows nothing about such art—all indicating progressively more subtle and reality-attuned ways of dealing with "beginning" anxieties.

Thus, the more anxiety-laden question of "What am I getting into?" may well underlie many of the patient's first questions or concerns as he enters into the assessment process—these questions and doubts being part and parcel of the way we all begin. If the examiner can be aware of the underlying questions being asked, he is better able to deal with them by staying within the metaphor that the patient is using to convey his underlying, probably preconscious, feelings.

Hence, the nature of the few minutes' interaction after the participants first meet, and before the "real" examination begins, can markedly alter the outcome (see Masling, 1966). Specifically, the examiner's behavior helps set the stage for the patient's relationship with him, and the nature of this relationship will have a systematic influence on the material that emerges. The examiner who strives to hold his behavior constant in order to "standardize" the situation thus risks deceiving himself; he may readily misinterpret patient behavior that represents the individual's response to the examiner's perceived rigidity (see Schafer, 1954). In particular, rigid procedures restrict the patient's behaving as freely as he is optimally able, neither struggling to conceal nor trying to reveal his difficulties.

We are *not* proposing that, in the case of psychological testing, one conduct an in-depth interview before starting testing, but rather that the examiner needs to recognize the legitimacy of the patient's uncertainty over beginning. For who of us is ever really ready to begin without such help?

This viewpoint makes more understandable a frequent assessment occurrence: the patient referred for testing is asked if his referring doctor talked to him about the testing, and the patient says no. It would be tempting for the psychologist to feel angry at how unprepared the doctor left the patient, thereby making the psychologist's task more difficult. Or, if the psychologist knows that the psychiatrist did talk about the testing to the patient, the psychologist may feel angry at the patient for distorting things; or perhaps he may wonder if the patient is a psychopathic manipulator! Some psychologists respond to the patient's stated ignorance about the imminent testing by providing a brief description of the diagnostic instruments and procedures—as if cognitive information alone were wanted and needed. From our standpoint, however, the patient is expressing his unpreparedness to begin. And his expressing it in terms of informational ignorance should not obscure that it is an understandable emotional insecurity that is being expressed. To respond with cognitive information alone is to mistake the *form* in which the need is expressed for the underlying *content* of the need. In short, when the patient says he doesn't know about the testing, he may actually be implying, "Sure I've been told about all this, but not what's really important—what you'll learn about me, and me about myself, and what we'll both think about me afterwards." Thus, one might respond to a patient who says he has been told nothing about the testing, "Then it's probably difficult for you, not knowing what to expect," or "You must feel uncertain about being here and proceeding. And you may have some questions of your own."

We are not suggesting that the tester seek to satisfy the needs of the patient, as these are expressed in his uncertainty about beginning. That is not the examiner's task. Needs ought to be recognized and responded to, to the extent necessary to facilitate the process developing in a more meaningful diagnostic fashion, that is, so that the patient can be freer to let himself be known and to collaborate in that endeavor as much as possible.

How then, applying these ideas about beginnings, might we want our earlier vignette to be different? Let us begin with the patient's response to being asked if he had ever been tested before. Recall that he said he'd never seen a "shrink," that he wasn't nuts, that it wasn't all in his head, and that something was really wrong with him. The dialogue might go as follows:

Psychologist: I know that you're not happy about seeing a shrink now.

Patient: Brilliant deduction, Doctor.

Psychologist: And I think that you're angry because you feel your doctor is saying you're crazy by sending you here for testing.

Patient: Well, wouldn't you be angry? This isn't in my mind and I'm not screwy. My head really hurts.

Psychologist: Are you maybe worried that your doctor isn't taking you seriously and maybe that I won't either?

Patient: (Visibly relaxing) Well, he said he couldn't find anything physically wrong. (Anxious now) Anybody would worry.

Psychologist: And be frightened as well.

Patient: (Visibly tensing) I don't know what to do. I get so frustrated sometimes.

Psychologist: I know that really upsets you or else you wouldn't have come now, because it's so hard for you to be here.

Patient: I just don't see what good more tests will do. I've had so many already.

Psychologist: It's hard to keep on with more tests after your doctor disappointed you—not finding anything physically wrong, and then sending you here.

Patient: (Shrugs as if to say "what the hell") I guess I've got nothing to lose since I'm here already.

Psychologist: Okay, but let me know how these angry or discouraged feelings are influencing you as you respond, or if there's anything else you especially notice about your responses as you take the tests.

With such a beginning, the chances are much better for a process to unfold, and for the patient to reveal himself more and for a collaborative alliance to be deepened. Moreover, not only has the examiner facilitated a more meaningful interaction, but he has added to the traditional data bases of formal test scores and test content a third source of data: diagnostic information based on the patient-diagnostician relationship. From the way the patient described above began, much diagnostic understanding has been gained: his fears of being labeled crazy (perhaps reflecting a secret belief that his anger and his mysterious headaches would justify such a label); his fears of not being taken seriously, of being disposed of, instead of helped; his tendency to mask how threatened and discouraged he feels by being angry and attacking instead; but also his potential for overcoming these fears and moving toward collaboration with the examiner. And the psychologist, having directly observed these manifestations in the diagnostic interaction, is in a better position to use his other data sources. Projective test material, for example, may help to clarify what "being crazy" connotes for this patient, and to what extent this felt danger corresponds to an actual likelihood of decompensation. Or the tests may provide added information about the patient's initial, defensively motivated experience of not being taken seriously: to what extent is this likely to characterize other relationships; what alternative modes of relatedness seem available; and what are the effects on various psychological functions when one or the other self-other relationship prevails?

Another important point about beginnings is implicit in this vignette. The patient actually "began" before he ever saw the psychologist, because he experienced his doctor's referring him for testing in a way which shaped his experience of the psychologist and the testing before he encountered either. "Thus the tester is not merely a detached observer of the patient but an active participant in the testing situation. He cannot avoid being a participant though he can avoid knowing about it"—as this psychologist did at first by fleeing into the testing. By inactively participating, he unwittingly helped the patient to harden his attitudes and intensify his fears about what the testing would reveal. Active or not, "the tester is necessarily a part of the context in which the test response is obtained. Moreover, the tester who is [aware of that] is an active and changing part of that context as the testing proceeds" (Schlesinger, 1973, p. 498).

Let us broaden the focus to consider further how beginnings always occur in the context of a relationship with at least one other person—even though that other person may not be physically present. Consider a psychological assessment interview.

> The psychodiagnostician often forgets that he is becoming acquainted with a person through a personal relationship no matter how transitory and tentative. If psychological functioning is to be elicited and observed, it can only be done in the context of one person responding to another with the psychological means at his disposal. When viewed in this way, it is clear that psychological assessment does not begin when the patient arrives. It has started before, or he would not even be coming for help. And how it has started is related to how the patient has perceived his future relationship with the clinician (e.g., his fantasies, wishes, fears, anxieties). The clinician, then, is entering into an ongoing process which plays a role in shaping the patient's response to the diagnostic process even before the patient is seen. And it is just this perceived relationship which can greatly color what follows. [Shevrin and Shectman, 1973, p. 468]

It is impossible, then, for a relationship not to exist as the context for beginning.

> The only choice is whether to recognize it and take it into account, because one cannot choose to have it be absent since the patient will clearly form one [in his mind and experience] anyway. [You may ask] but what if a teaching machine were used, so that a human treater would not have direct contact with the patient? Even under those conditions, the influence of a personal relationship would still need to be taken into consideration. This is so because the patient's performance would be a function of how he perceived the [diagnostic] context; that is, his psychological functioning is influenced by qualities of the perceived relationship, for example, its impersonality, scientific purity, etc. [Shectman, 1977, p. 200]

This point is equally applicable to a person filling out a paper and pencil test in a room all alone, without ever having seen the diagnostician or therapist. Although the patient himself may not be fully aware of it, he is not taking the test in a vacuum. Somewhere in his mind he is filling out the test and shaping his responses in anticipation of who will be reading it, what reactions that reader will have, what goals the patient has, etc.

Perhaps one further example can pull together these ideas on beginning.

A fifty-year-old clergyman applied for an outpatient evaluation after what he described as a "life crisis." Feeling overwhelmed in his work with his present congregation, as he had with two previous ones, he had become so fed up with their felt demands that he abruptly resigned. In his negotiations with the admissions officer, he balked at filling out a self-report questionnaire in advance because of its many "irrelevant and superfluous items." He similarly sought to shorten the proposed week-long diagnostic evaluation, because a week would "take too much out of me"—even though he was without a job and told of how little he had to occupy his time.

This patient, in our terms, was clearly engaged in beginning long before he ever met the diagnostician. That person, on undertaking the evaluation, would be entering into a relationship the patient had already begun to establish with the admissions officer. Moreover, a major process issue was already clearly evident in that beginning relationship, in the seemingly paradoxical observation that the patient was fighting against the very help he had sought—a noteworthy discontinuity. The diagnostician could hypothesize that the patient was already experiencing the "demands" of the admissions officer as he had those of his congregations—feeling unfairly burdened and responding with angry, ultimately self-defeating attempts to resist. Above and beyond other issues, then, this process issue based on an already unfolding relationship is a central one, because it is occurring between the two participants in a virtually palpable way and will likely color whatever else transpires between them—before they have even met. Recognizing and making explicit such discontinuities, then, as issues for the patient to consider, is an essential task of beginnings (see Shevrin and Shectman, 1973, especially pp. 468–471 and 477–482, for an elaboration of the concept of "discontinuity").

In short, then, the more one can be alert to and help the patient to see that he has started before ever seeing the clinician, the more clearly can the patient's own way of revealing himself and his problems stand out—so that his encounter with the clinician can become a microcosm of his way of relating to certain other people and of showing the nature of his problems in the very functioning which he displays in the way that he begins.

So, for our minister patient, attention to his way of starting helped us form questions about him even before the patient had arrived in person. He did eventually consent to stay for a week, but with obvious reluctance. While somewhat cooperative, he was not yet truly collaborative. Following his lead, the initial task the diagnostic team set itself was to see if the patient could examine his "beginning" behavior, acknowledging and perhaps shifting his oppositional stance.

So, though the patient was starting, he was not yet ready to really begin. Notice we are using "begin" in a third way here. The first way is to regard it as a static position in time. The second way is to view it as a process term, a point of view toward an interaction—a way of looking at a process, exemplified by how our patient with headaches was expressing his way of beginning with a psychologist around the testing. This third use of the term applies to the patient's state of readiness to do a certain kind of work, to look at himself with help. From this standpoint, a beginning could occur after a patient has been in treatment for months or even years! For example, a patient may agree to take psychological tests, begin an assessment interview, or start psychotherapy, but not really be ready to begin in this third sense of the term. It is just this viewpoint which Portnoy's analyst has in mind when, after 274 complaint-ridden pages, he says, "Now vee may perhaps to begin. Yes?"

The Middle Phase

In discussing a middle or data-gathering phase of the diagnostic process, we emphasize two major concepts. The first concerns the clinician's orientation to his task; it is the distinction between conceiving of the task as fact gathering and conceiving of it as *eliciting psychological functioning* (Shevrin and Shectman, 1973). The second concept is that of the *diagnostic alliance*.

Before taking up these topics, however, we note that the designation "middle phase" can be as misunderstood as "beginning." Like "beginning," it is not intended to refer concretely and exclusively to time, but rather to a point of view, a perspective. By "middle phase" we refer to an *aspect* of the process, that aspect which involves ongoing work and the development of understanding relevant to the questions that exist at the time. Middle phases are defined less by when they occur than by the kind of work they involve. The tasks of clarification, of testing out ideas, of sorting out the more from the less relevant—these can be regarded as specific to middle phases, in much the same way as the tasks of identifying discontinuities and formulating issues are specific to beginnings.

Now what do we have in mind when we distinguish between fact gathering and the eliciting of psychological functioning as alternative definitions of the evaluator's task? Could we not say that these are but different parts of one task, and that one does not preclude the other? True enough in principle, but rarely so in practice. One orientation very frequently seems to displace the other, to the detriment of the diagnostic process. And there is an asymmetry in the way this occurs. The role of fact gatherer is one which is in many ways protected. It implies a certain distance between the observer and the observed, and it clearly locates the problem "in" the latter. It is also a role which, because of its "objectivity," has considerable professional sanction. By contrast, the task of eliciting psychological functioning involves more ambiguity and requires more involvement and thus more risk from the one who takes it on—especially when the psychological functioning of central interest is that which occurs in a relationship context. Therefore, when one role is favored over the other in the assessment process, it is likely to be fact gathering that crowds out what we consider the more useful approach.

At the same time, in a significant sense the fact-gathering orientation does preclude the optimal elicitation of functioning, whereas the converse is not true. Observations of functioning can readily be preserved and treated as newly gained "facts," but if one starts with "the facts" considered as disembodied historical events, fixed character traits, or the like, one is on speculative ground in attempting to extrapolate the psychological functions which have produced these facts.

We emphasize that the fundamental distinction is not at the level of technique, but rather at the level of the clinician's conception of his task. What the clinician *does* is largely a consequence of what he *thinks he is doing*. If he thinks of himself as collecting items of information, historical or current, which are static—which have some existence of their own that is independent of who is reporting them, to whom, for what purpose, and under what conditions—then he is engaged in what we are calling a fact-gathering approach. If, on the other hand, the clinician considers that his task is to *develop* facts—if the "facts" are expected to emerge from observing the patient's psychological functioning and examining it in context—then he is engaging in the approach we advocate. Such a clinician still can, and should, attend to the importance of past events. However, beginning with a focus on discontinuities in current functioning should enable him more selectively to trace back and highlight that portion of the past which is "alive" in the present—really the only part of the past warranting diagnostic attention anyway!

The fact-gathering and function-eliciting approaches are not necessarily distinguished by the degree of "cooperation" present. The patient may cooperate in furnishing facts, or he may not. The difference is that in our approach, the cooperation or noncooperation is an object of interest in its own right, not simply a help or a hindrance in getting the job done. We may be interested in knowing, for example, what illicit drugs a patient has used, over how long a period, and so on. But for purposes of understanding the patient in a way which facilitates treatment planning, we are even more interested in *how* he tells us, or does not tell us, these presumably objective facts.

Perhaps the distinction between approaches can be made clearer by further examples. Suppose that in an initial interview a patient describes a troublesome symptom—say recurrent anxiety attacks. The way the clinician defines his task will have an obvious influence on the way he takes this up with the patient. If he approaches the situation primarily as fact gatherer, he will naturally try to find out certain things about the symptom. He will ask about when the symptom started, about the circumstances under which it occurs, about what seems to bring relief, and perhaps he will ask the patient to describe what the internal experience of this anxiety is like.

One can gather a great deal of important information in this way, and it is information which, depending on the patient's skill as a self-observer and reporter, may be highly meaningful. But we would raise the question, Meaningful to whom? In our view, the danger of this approach is that no matter how skillfully or ingeniously the patient is questioned, and no matter how complete the picture that is gained of how the difficulty manifests itself, it is likely to be a picture much more meaningful to the clinician than to the patient. With regard to his own understanding of the problem, and, more important, of what he might contribute to its resolution, the patient is likely to be left exactly where he was at the beginning of the interview. The "facts" of the problem, as he knows them, are already familiar to him; it is likely that he has been through the same explanation before.

Meanwhile, consider the model of the clinical process which has been encouraged, or at least reinforced, in the "fact-gathering" interview. The patient has presented himself as a passive partner, to be interrogated by the expert who will then presumably solve the problem, or at least give some kind of prescription or directive which promises to solve it. We know that important psychological difficulties are not solved in this way; every major therapeutic school, from psychoanalysis through Gestalt and client-centered therapy to behavior modification, recognizes the importance of the patient's assuming appropriate responsibility for change. But in the purely fact-gathering interview, little has been done to help the patient move in that direction—or, perhaps more realistically, to explore his ability to move in that direction. In fact, though, something may well have been done to discourage precisely such a shift!

Now how would we approach the same situation if we define our clinical task as the eliciting of psychological functioning? We would still want to know about the phenomenology of the symptom, its origin, the circumstances of its occurrence, and so on. But we would not regard such material as facts which have some existence of their own, independent of the context in which they are being reported. Thus, even though we might ask a similar question (e.g. "When did you first notice this symptom?"), we would do so with a different intent. Our ultimate aim would be to see what manifestations of the problem are observable within the present situation, and then to engage the patient, to whatever extent possible, in a collaborative attempt to understand those manifestations.

Thus, when the patient tells us something about the first occurrence of the symptom, our next question might be, "What sense can you make of that?" The response to such a question will guide our further inquiries. The patient may be able to provide further instances, to discover commonalities among them, and to begin in the context of the interview to make sense of things for himself. On the other hand, if the patient is unable to provide a response, and if this is repeated with other inquiries, we are presented with a discontinuity in psychological functioning which can usefully be made the focus of our attention: "You have told me about a problem which has interfered with your life in various ways, and which has caused you much distress. Yet as we talk about it, you seem to doubt that it makes any sense at all. How can we reconcile this?" Thus, as in any good clinical interview, the interviewer follows the patient's lead, but with a constant invitation to the patient to collaborate with him, and with a constant effort to assess how well the patient is able to do so.

The similarity to a psychotherapy process should be apparent, and we recognize the dangers of inappropriately falling into the role of therapist, rather than diagnostician, when employing such an approach. But the statement of this problem in a sense contains its solution as well. In applying this approach, it is incumbent on the clinician to be aware of the boundaries of his task. To us, it is not a contradiction to advocate exploring the patient's capacity to use help without trying to offer all the help the patient can use.

With this we come to the second topic of our "middle phase" discussion, that of the diagnostic alliance. We use this term to emphasize that there exists in the diagnostic process something analogous to what, in the context of the therapeutic relationship, is referred to as the "therapeutic alliance" or "working alliance." Greenson (1967), writing about psychoanalysis, defines the working alliance as "the relatively non-neurotic, rational relationship between patient and analyst which makes it possible for the patient to work purposefully in the analytic situation"; this alliance involves "a partial and temporary identification that the patient makes with the analyst's attitude and method of work" and enables the patient to continue to work in the analysis in spite of the discomfort it may involve (p. 46). This concept has strong similarities to what we want to call the diagnostic alliance, although there are differences as well.

In a real sense, a diagnostic experience that involves this kind of alliance can be a very effective preparation for therapeutic work. So we do want to encourage the patient or client to identify, in part, with the diagnostician's task and his way of working; at the same time, we regard it as a crucial part of our task to diagnose the patient's ability to do so: How readily can the patient engage in this kind of collaborative self-scrutiny? In what areas of his functioning is this more or less difficult? What interventions by the examiner seem to facilitate or hinder his involvement?

In this regard, we would not want to speak only of the presence or absence of a diagnostic alliance, any more than we would feel we were doing an adequate job by speaking only of the presence or absence of schizophrenia or obsessive-compulsive neurosis. These are matters of degree, and matters in which the qualities of the patient's functioning, and the conditions which facilitate or hinder it, are at least as important as the labels we may choose to attach.

Finally, we also have to bear in mind the limits of the diagnostic contract, which is the main issue that distinguishes it from the therapeutic. As diagnosticians we have undertaken to clarify the patient's difficulties, to point the patient toward some way of finding a solution, but not necessarily to provide the solution ourselves. This too is not an all-or-none distinction, but still the diagnostic task is a comparatively limited one, and the alliance with the patient around that task, if it is to be a realistic ("nonneurotic") alliance, must recognize those limits. In fact, there are situations in which the patient's failure to recognize these limits is itself an important diagnostic observation.

In considering how one recognizes elements of (and resistances to) the diagnostic alliance, we again refer to a diagnostic testing situation and hope the applications to other circumstances will be fairly evident.

First, what is the quality of the patient's *cooperation with the tasks* which are posed for him by the examiner? Does he avoid them, oppose them, submit to them, attempt to make light of them, distort or misunderstand them, aggressively disrupt them? And when, in his own way, the patient does engage in the task, what happens when he encounters difficulty? Does he give up and withdraw, ask directly or indirectly for help, deny that there is a problem, or plunge aggressively ahead?

Second, what is the patient's *attitude toward the material* he has produced? Does he rapidly disown it in some manner, perhaps even forgetting responses that were given a few moments before? Does he use every observed difficulty, or every bit of self-revelation, as ammunition in his attack upon himself? Or conversely, does he feel that he has to aggressively defend his responses, as if anything he says may and probably will be used against him? Or, to put it more positively, to what extent does he seem capable of accurately remembering, objectively evaluating, and reflectively considering his own behavior as elicited in the assessment situation?

Third, *what development occurs in the relationship* of the patient to the examiner? This is, of course, the area in which manifestations of the diagnostic alliance are most obviously to be sought, and perhaps for that reason the area where they are most easily misunderstood. When we look for favorable development in this relationship, we are not implying that the patient and examiner should get to be good friends as the assessment proceeds, or that conflict and difficulties should disappear from their relationship. We are talking about a process of unfolding, not of neat packaging. From this point of view, for the psychological testing, or the diagnostic interview, to proceed in a rosy glow of friendship and good feeling is probably as much an indication of a miscarriage of the diagnostic alliance as would be the situation in which the patient abruptly storms out of the office and refuses to complete the procedures.

This incidentally touches on another issue of importance in assessing the diagnostic alliance, and that is *the way the contact ends*. However, we will be discussing that more extensively when we take up the general topic of endings. For now, since this discussion of the diagnostic alliance may still be somewhat abstract, let us present two passages from reports of psychological testing as a way of illustrating our various observations and how they might be brought together. The first passage is from a report on a thirty-year-old woman who had experienced recurrent acute paranoid episodes and had broken off several previous treatments:

> Despite her proneness to projective thinking, she displays considerable capacity for self-observation and psychological-mindedness. Perhaps most important, there is sufficient flexibility in her defensive arrangements to allow for the establishment of a fruitful and cooperative alliance with a helping figure, even though such an alliance is certain to be severely tested. This flexibility was demonstrated in the course of the Rorschach test, to which she first responded in an angry, avoidant manner, maintaining that the test was "a cliche" and "not relevant," and restricting her responses to a minimum. When she was invited to discuss her feelings about the test, however, she was able to do so in a constructive way, making some acknowledgment of the difficulty it posed for her, and was able to shift her test-taking attitude to one of increased openness and productivity. It bears emphasizing that her responses as such were equally as disturbed following this shift as they had been before; what she seems capable of changing—given an opportunity to express and examine her angry feelings in a respectful and tolerant atmosphere—is not the degree of her disturbance, but her willingness to reveal it.

Later this same report took up a new difficulty which became apparent in the testing situation with her acceptance of help from the examiner, namely her tendency to overidealize the helping person and to experience strong wishes for, and fears of, a totally engulfing, symbiotic kind of relationship with such a person. Thus the report points up the relationship between observations within the testing situation and the important clinical issue in this case, which was the patient's inability to sustain a treatment long enough to get adequate benefit from it.

Consider another passage, this again referring to a patient who presented a picture of repeated treatment failure.

> His prevailing approach to the psychological testing (and, by extension, to psychological treatment and to relationships in general) is best summed

> up by one of his Rorschach responses: "a man lying on his back . . . watching himself masturbating." He treated the testing primarily as an opportunity for an exhibitionistic display of all varieties of perverse fantasies, toward which his attitude was one of passive admiration and absorption. He became offended and suspicious at the examiner's effort to confront him with this attitude, and did not show any increase in reflectiveness as a result of such interventions. Although referring frequently to his embarrassment at revealing sexual material, he usually followed such a statement with additional unnecessary elaborations on the "embarrassing" theme. His interpersonal behavior showed a striking obliviousness to what was appropriate under the circumstances; he treated the examiner by turns as if he were a long-lost friend, a powerful authority, an admiring audience, a potent rival, or a foolish child, depending on his own state at the moment, but never gave any indication of viewing the examiner as a collaborator in understanding his difficulties.

This is, of course, a somewhat extreme example, but it is chosen partly for its contrast to the first. Note especially that although obviously a lot *happened* in the patient-examiner relationship in this second case, there was no *development* of the relationship in the sense we are looking for. By contrast, considerable development took place in the first case, although we could not say by any means that the difficulties in the patient-examiner relationship were resolved.

To return now to the question of how one fosters a diagnostic alliance—or better, how one might test out the possibility of its development—perhaps the largest part of the answer is already apparent. These issues will remain obscure unless the diagnostician is attuned to them and interested in them, and unless he provides opportunities for them to develop. Knowing what one is looking for in this regard is the surest guide. In terms of specific techniques, we may do such things as the following: inviting the patient to discuss a particular difficulty he seems to be having in taking a test, or in responding to certain kinds of questions; providing a graded series of helps with a difficult problem, to determine whether adding degrees of structure to the task enables the patient to participate at a different level; offering for the patient's consideration our own observations of a similarity between some difficulty portrayed in response content and one which seems to be present in the testing situation; inviting the patient to freely and spontaneously comment on his own responses; sometimes readministering a test, or a portion of a test, to find out what alterations in test responses seem to follow from some apparent shift in the patient-examiner relationship (see Appelbaum, 1959); and so on. We would emphasize the importance of making such interventions in a controlled and intentional way. If we are able to bring about some shift in the alliance, but unable to understand how it happened, we have fallen short of a major goal of the middle phase.

Treatment Recommendations

In discussing the middle or data-gathering phase of the diagnostic process, we distinguished between eliciting psychological functioning for both patient and clinician to observe and deal with, and simply gathering historical "facts" from the patient "computer." The former viewpoint implies an active, developing, forward-looking process in which the two parties are mutually engaged. On the other hand, the latter way of working makes for a passive, static, backward-looking procedure in which the emphasis is on the presumably immutable information, rather than on the ongoing process out of which the significant data arise.

The same kind of distinction is applicable to the treatment recommendations. Traditionally the information-gathering approach has led to a recommendation being *given by* the clinician *to* the patient—with all the implications of an active party operating on a passive one. In this traditional conception, the process is analogous to what happens when one presents oneself to a physician for a physical problem: questions are asked, lab and other studies are done, the patient may be poked and probed, and then presumably the results are tallied and a prescription given. Of course, even in such relatively clear-cut circumstances, the prescription for treatment may not be followed. And even if the patient does follow the prescription, he may do so in a spirit of compliance, without conviction that he is acting on his own behalf—that is, without being really engaged as a person at all. As Erikson (1964) has noted, "Any good doctor knows . . . the patient's complaint is more extensive than his symptom, and the state of sickness more comprehensive than localized pain or dysfunction. As an old Jew put it . . . , 'Doctor, my bowels are sluggish, my feet hurt, my heart jumps—and you know, Doctor, I myself don't feel so well either' " (p. 51).

Now it may be possible, even if undesirable, for a patient to comply with a prescription for a physical disorder without having much conviction about either the doctor or the merit of the prescription. However, such a way of proceeding not only embodies a false analogy between how one deals with patients with physical maladies and those with psychological ones; it also misses the very essence of the process necessary for psychological work. In fact, this way of operating greatly jeopardizes the treatment recommended, because the patient is not helped at all to be in a frame of mind and spirit to internally experience, and act on, a felt necessity for implementing the treatment recommendation. Furthermore, presenting a treatment recommendation to a ''passive'' patient assumes that the patient is suddenly wholly rational, cooperative, and free of the very interfering conflicts and resistances which led him to seek help in the first place. In fact, one can expect the interferences to resurface as the recommendation is discussed. Indeed, part of that discussion typically needs to include a focus on the patient's reactions to the recommendation.

Apropos this point, issues raised in the beginning and middle phases of a psychological assessment process will surface again in the treatment recommendation phase, for these phases are all parts of an unfolding unity. Indeed, if one genuinely believes that these phases are all interconnected, ''then the treatment recommendation should flow naturally from the diagnostic process. The issues should lead to the formulation of a treatment program. Ideally, then, the patient should become gradually aware of what is needed as a result of what has already taken place'' (Shevrin and Shectman, 1973, p. 487). As we pointed out in discussing beginnings, the patient and clinician often start with different goals. If the patient has been helped to actively participate, share, observe, and reflect, he has taken part in a new experience, has learned something new about himself, and has developed a sense of what he needs in order to continue a process already set in motion. Of course he may not be able to make a technical recommendation, but he can have a better idea than when he started of what kind of issues need to be worked on and how he needs to involve himself in that. He may be aware that he has not received what he may have desired or feared. Instead, he has perhaps become aware of a plan of action, rather than a tangible solution. Consequently, ''The diagnostic process should bring about enough of a shift so that the patient can act on the recommendation. In fact, it is our belief that it is just this point which differentiates psychiatric diagnosis from other kinds of diagnosis. To our knowledge, in no other diagnosis is it necessary for the diagnostic process itself to prepare the way for accepting the recommendation'' (Shevrin and Shectman, 1973, p. 488).

And in order to facilitate such a preparation and shift, one needs to be aware of the frame of mind of the patient, the mood and spirit in which he comes for help, and how he has experienced the diagnostic process. In this way the current issues, often based on mutually observed psychological discontinuities, form a bridge between patient and diagnostician which makes for their concurrent involvement and active participation in developing treatment recommendations growing out of this mutually participatory process. Hence the importance of formulating the issues close to the level of clinical interaction, as a way of facilitating the patient's involvement in a diagnostic alliance that can develop with continuity into a later therapeutic alliance.

Some clinicians feel quite reluctant to accept an evaluation patient as a treatment patient. Having defined the diagnostic task as primarily doing an evaluation and "selling" treatment, they feel that their potential effectiveness as therapists is compromised. This may be true enough when the diagnostic process has in fact been conducted according to the model of an active clinician doing something for a passive patient (prescribing a treatment), or seeking to get a resistive patient to comply with a treatment recommendation. But the diagnostic and therapeutic tasks need not be so antagonistic. The diagnostician, in offering recommendations, may view himself "as one who works with resistances, which, when understood, will allow for the necessary shift in the patient to take place" (Shevrin and Shectman, 1973, p. 489).

A case example used in the section on beginnings demonstrates why we think the recommendation should be considered an intrinsic part of the diagnostic process. Recall that the patient was a clergyman who had abruptly resigned his position with a congregation because he felt burdened and angered by unfair demands. He also resisted accepting the format of the outpatient evaluation, perhaps again feeling unfairly burdened.

Before even seeing the patient, the diagnostic team wondered if this very tendency would surface as a major obstacle to working out a successful recommendation. Concomitantly, such behavior posed a significant diagnostic question: What leads the patient—who is obviously suffering, and without even a job to sustain him financially or psychologically—to apparently experience potential help as a demand, so that he winds up opposing (if not defeating) the very help he seeks? This discontinuity could well serve as the opening dialectic of the consultation. Raising this issue could (1) advance the diagnostic process by zeroing in immediately on the patient's feelings about coming in the first place—an experience which would undoubtedly color subsequent diagnostic interactions; and (2) help to increase the likelihood of subsequent recommendations being accepted, because the patient's resistance to accepting the very conditions for the evaluation is an issue from the start.

When this issue was brought up, the patient recalled a previous therapist, who seemed more interested in talking about himself than in listening to the patient. "I felt I was his counselor," he said, as if he had unfairly had to give more than he had received. The examiner related just that feeling to the current evaluation, and the patient agreed and added that he really had little hope of receiving help. Little by little, the examiner came to understand this way of experiencing help as the expression of an important object-relations paradigm. The patient needed to depreciate helpers as the needy ones, and to portray himself as the one who was demanded from and who had to give. In this way he protected himself against the envy and inadequacy he would deeply feel if he truly let himself receive—but in the process he insured that he would continue to feel unfairly burdened. With gentle but firm diplomacy, that viewpoint was presented to the patient. Most explicit was the examiner's anticipating from the very start the patient's need to reject any recommendation, to avoid feeling that the examiner could offer something the patient needed and could use.

Note that by focusing on the process unfolding between them before their eyes, the examiner made the issue of the recommendation part of the overall diagnostic process and included the patient in looking at how prone he was to reject the recommendation even before he came. Thus the issue of the recommendation itself could become a topic for gathering the psychological data as part of the middle phase. Specifically, in subsequent interviews the patient spelled out his distress but continued to hint at feeling put upon and doubting that anything valuable would be suggested. It was as if he were talking primarily to give the examiner enough rope to hang himself; the patient could then say that he had given much but received little in return.

Since this pattern had already been recognized and underscored as the very way in which the patient had begun, the examiner could point to its happening again and again as a theme pervading the diagnostic process—almost independent of the topic being discussed. From the beginning, and subsequently, the examiner was able to make the recommendation an integral part of the process; for instance, he could preface his discussion about the recommendation by saying that, whatever the recommendation, he anticipated the patient would be very likely to reject it as virtually worthless. Eventually, the patient tearfully confided that he feared never being able to end any treatment if he accepted any recommendation for it. In particular, he sensed his frightening wish to give in and rely totally on the therapist, becoming unacceptably dependent and as contemptuous of himself as he was of those whom he saw as being demanding because so internally resourceless.

Endings

In closing, it is appropriate that we consider in a more focused way ''ending phenomena'' in the diagnostic process (see also Appelbaum, 1961). Let us consider a fairly common clinical situation which is a good introduction to the topic of ending difficulties: the patient who suffers from incomplete mourning. What we see in such a case is someone who has been unable to deal with the end of a relationship in a healthy way; instead the person remains so preoccupied with the loss, yet at the same time so wrapped up in defending himself against its implications, that he is able to give little attention or energy to the business of everyday living, and his psychological growth may come to a standstill.

We would propose that difficulties comparable to this can arise around the ending of any interpersonal process, and specifically around the ending of a diagnostic process as we have been describing it. As with distortions of the process which arise in the beginning phase, in data gathering, and around treatment recommendations, these ending difficulties may be approached as resistances—that is, as maneuvers carried out for the purpose of protection against the painful implications of the new perspectives and plans for action which have been generated.

Often, of course, ending difficulties are simply continuations of characteristic resistances. For example, the externalizing patient may want to speak only of the environmental pressures which prevent him from implementing the treatment recommendation, or which "force" a premature end to the assessment; the counterphobic patient may show an exaggerated eagerness to plunge ahead with his treatment; the hostile, paranoid patient may try to pick a fight with the examiner and end the process on an angry note. This is a version of the familiar "recapitulation phenomenon" which often occurs at the end of psychotherapy; old complaints reappear and need to be worked through again in the context of the end of the treatment relationship. When this occurs—that is, when already familiar resistances appear, perhaps in an exaggerated form, in an ending phase—we are again presented with a diagnostic opportunity. Certainly we do not expect that the security operations the person has developed over a lifetime will change in a dramatic and lasting way in the course of a relatively brief diagnostic process. However, if the process has involved some collaborative work on understanding these maneuvers, then their reappearance in the ending phase is a chance to again bring that earlier work to bear, test out anew the patient's capacity for shifting his psychological perspective, and perhaps further encourage or solidify the patient's commitment to a more constructive course of action.

But there are other resistances which are more specific to endings; they have the purpose of ending a process and a relationship in such a way that its impact is reduced, denied, or distorted. We can illustrate these most vividly by portraying some common examples in the form of a statement which might summarize the patient's prevailing attitude.

1. "Wasn't this a marvelous experience!" Without rejecting or depreciating the patient's gratitude for our efforts and for any benefit he may have derived from them, we may still wonder why an exaggerated idea of this kind is displayed at the end of an assessment process. After all, if the process has gone well it is likely that the problems are in sharper focus, or are seen from a different perspective, but they are by no means resolved. Most often, an attitude of exaggerated appreciation is a disguised way of disposing of the process prematurely, of regarding it as more "over" than it really is or should be. Indeed, optimally a process has been set in motion which will continue after the actual diagnostic situation ends.

2. "You're such a brilliant doctor, and I don't know what I would have done without you." This is a variant of the first attitude mentioned, and one which is perhaps even more difficult to deal with. But again, we must wonder

what is being covered up when this kind of idealization prevails. After all, the assessment process was designed for the patient's benefit, not to enhance the assessor's self-esteem. If we too readily take the patient's idealization of us at face value, we may be diverted from one of the important tasks of ending, which is to clarify as much as possible where the patient will go from here.

3. "That wasn't so bad, was it?" In part, relief at finally being able to share troubling problems with another person, and finding that no catastrophe occurs, is a natural and appropriate reaction. But the fact is that when the difficulties are clarified and the necessary courses of action have been considered, new anxieties will also likely emerge, just because new options (and consequent risks) are available. In such a context, the statement quoted could represent a denying or minimizing of the seriousness of the problems which have been brought to light, and could indicate a wavering of the patient's painful recognition of what he needs to do. This is perhaps a good example of how the principle of being alert to discrepancies or discontinuities in functioning applies to endings as well as to other phases; if the patient's ending attitude seems mismatched with the kind of process which has occurred, it is a signal for some added investigation.

4. "Speak a little more slowly, Doctor; I want to get it all down on paper so I'll remember exactly what you told me to do." Certainly we want the patient to remember and preserve whatever understanding has been generated in the assessment process, in order that he can act on it. But an exaggerated attitude of attention and compliance at the end of the evaluation can amount to a disclaimer of the patient's own role in developing that understanding, and likely of his role in putting it to use. As we have mentioned repeatedly, it is not the doctor's understanding of the difficulties which is most crucial, for it is not the doctor who must take the next step.

5. "It's terrible that we have to stop, just when we're really getting underway!" This is a particularly seductive resistance, for we often share the same feeling. When an evaluation process has gone well, when some important shifts seem to have taken place and a process of growth is set in motion, it may be as difficult for the clinician as for the patient to see it end. But an attitude of this kind is, or can be, a resistance nonetheless. The end of a process need not nullify the benefit which has been gained from it, and to fall in with the patient's acting on such an assumption is to leave unexamined an important obstacle to continued change. Often in our experience, patients who end their evaluations in this way are in fact those whose life stories involve repeated cycles of raised hopes followed by disappointments, so that the experience of ending the evaluation can often be directly linked with the difficulties under examination. Incidentally, this kind of ending may also be a signal of a particular problem in the evaluation process, that of the evaluator's

falling too much into the role of the therapist, and seeming to offer more than is consistent with his relatively circumscribed role. This is a pitfall which is especially likely with "good" patients, unless the boundaries of the task are carefully kept in mind.

Let us now turn the issue around, however, and briefly consider what might be the characteristics of a "good ending." Such an ending, we think, would reflect the idea that *endings—like beginnings—are not just points in time but points of view toward an interaction.* How a diagnostic process ends, then, is a function of the way it has developed and unfolded, with both its mutual fulfillments and disappointments. Whatever difficulties are encountered during and at the end of the diagnostic process, we hope that the patient will end it in a state of increased *awareness:* awareness that he probably has not received what he originally desired, but that a plan of action, rather than a tangible solution, is possible; awareness that he has experienced a new relationship and thereby taken a step toward discovering what is achievable for him, what he can and cannot change, and when it would be better for him to compromise; awareness of what he is like and what his problems involve, including his own contributions to them; and awareness of the options available (or unavailable) to him.

We would add to this list what is implied above, i.e. an awareness of what the evaluation itself has meant to him, but in real rather than idealized terms—implying that not only the insights and the gratifications, but also the pain, frustrations, and disappointments are acknowledged. *Just as one can start without beginning, so one can stop without ending.* The latter implies, for us, an acceptance of that event, a true acceptance implying attitudes other than the kinds typified by the five discussed above. As a concomitant of this increased acceptance and awareness, we hope for the patient to end with an increased sense of control over his fate.

We would emphasize that such an increased sense of mastery can be present even when the outcome of the evaluation is a decision for such a radical course of action as long-term hospitalization. Even then, the patient may have been helped to feel that the decision is his, taken in his own best interests, rather than imposed by others and submitted to because there is no choice. (See Schafer, 1976, for an elaboration on the value of viewing the patient as an active agent who is forever doing and hence choosing—consciously and unconsciously.)

We want to mention one other characteristic of a good ending, or perhaps it should be called a characteristic of a good diagnostic process that is most apparent at the end. This is the convergence of goals between patient and clinician which we referred to earlier, when discussing the diagnostic alliance. To say that there is a convergence of goals does not mean that the patient comes to see things our way, any more than it means that we come to see things his way. In the kind of diagnostic process we have been advocating, it is in fact impossible for the clinician to have "the answer" from the beginning, since the best answer can only be one that is jointly arrived at. The kind of convergence we mean is necessarily a mutual process; it means that the two participants have found some way of understanding the situation that makes sense to both of them, even though each will retain his own additional ways of thinking outside this common ground. In our view, a diagnostic process which ends with this sense of moving toward collaborative understanding, and which has clarified what is required for such movement to continue, is a diagnostic job well done.

References

Appelbaum, S. (1959), The effect of altered psychological atmosphere on Rorschach responses: A new supplementary procedure. *Bull. Menn. Clin.*, 23:179–189.

——— (1961), The end of the test as a determinant of responses. *Bull. Menn. Clin.*, 25:120–128.

Erikson, E. (1964), The nature of clinical evidence. In: *Insight and Responsibility*. New York: Norton, pp. 47–80.

Greenson, R. (1967), *The Technique and Practice of Psychoanalysis,* Vol. 1. New York: International Universities Press.

Holzman, P., & Schlesinger, H. (1972), On becoming a hospitalized psychiatric patient. *Bull. Menn. Clin.*, 36:383–406.

Masling, J. (1966), Role-related behavior of the subject and psychologist and its effect on psychological data. In: *Nebraska Symposium on Motivation*, Vol. 14, ed. D. Levine. Lincoln: University of Nebraska Press, pp. 67–103.

Schafer, R. (1954), Interpersonal dynamics in the test situation. Chapter 2 of *Psychoanalytic Interpretation in Rorschach Testing: Theory and Application*. New York: Grune & Stratton, pp. 6–113.

——— (1976), *A New Language for Psychoanalysis*. New Haven: Yale University Press.

Schlesinger, H.J. (1973), Interaction of dynamic and reality factors in the diagnostic testing interview. *Bull. Menn. Clin.*, 37:495–517.

Shectman, F. (1976), Provocative issues in psychiatric diagnosis: A dialogue. *Bull. Menn. Clin.*, 40:435–458.

——— (1977), Conventional and contemporary approaches to psychotherapy: Freud meets Skinner, Janov and others. *Amer. Psychol.*, 32:197–204.

——— (1979), Problems in communicating psychological understanding: Why won't they listen to me? *Amer. Psychol.*, 34:781–790.

Shevrin, H., & Shectman, F. (1973), The diagnostic process in psychiatric evaluations. *Bull. Menn. Clin.*, 37:451–494.

Part IV
Psychosocial States

Chapter 13

ASSESSING CHILDREN'S MENTAL CONSTRUCTION OF THE OBJECT

BONNIE BATTER SLADE

In 1970 Piaget encouraged and predicted the synthesis of cognitive theory with psychoanalytic theory into a more adequate model of psychological functioning (Piaget, 1973). The groundwork for that synthesis had already been laid with Wolff's detailed analysis (1960) of the similarities and differences between Piaget's and Freud's ideas. A larger event contributing to combining the two systems may have been the emergence of object relations theory in the psychoanalytic literature. Both Piaget's theory and some aspects of object relations theory (e.g. Mahler, Pine, and Bergman, 1975) are rooted in careful observations of infant and child development, with the former focusing on intellectual development and the latter more on emotional development and clinical phenomena. Thus, it is perhaps not surprising that the two might, in Piaget's words, "fuse in a general theory which will improve both, through mutual correction" (1973, p. 250).

A major focus of object relations theory is on the child's development of internal or mental self- and object representations. Within a developmental framework, it studies the synthesis of these internal representations to create a constant and stable concept of self, and a differentiation of the self from objects. Object relations theory and Piaget's conceptually overlap in their mutual interest in the cognitive aspects of self-differentiation. Thus, object

Acknowledgment is due to Nancy Moss and Dianna Hartley for their comments on an earlier draft of this paper.

relations theory can benefit from an examination of Piaget's systematic observations and his network of conclusions about the development of the mental concept of the object and the growth of representational intelligence.

The past decade has seen the fruits of that examination, with the publication of papers comparing the two theories and attempting to synthesize them (Blatt and Wild, 1976; Greenspan, 1979). In addition to these theoretical endeavors, empirical reports have appeared, particularly in the area of attachment research, which further an interchange between the two models (see Bell, 1970; Gouin-Decarie, 1974). Finally, recent applications of Piaget's concepts to psychiatric problems (e.g. Suchtoliff, 1970; Blatt and Wild, 1976; Cowan, 1978) encourage the development of a model which can synthesize the two theories.

The present chapter joins the growing literature which applies Piagetian concepts to clinical phenomena. The utility of Piagetian concepts in assessing children's mental construction of the object will be demonstrated by the analysis of a Rorschach record. The first part of the chapter will briefly outline the basic concepts of Piaget's theory, while the second part will illustrate the clinical application of Piagetian and object relations concepts.

Theory

Piaget was a biologist and a genetic epistemologist. His interest in the development of knowledge led him to systematically observe the ontogeny of intelligence beginning at birth. From his laborious observations and experiments he was able to produce a tightly woven model of intellectual development which can be summarized as follows.

Piaget acknowledged three broad categories of intelligence—content, structure, and function—and focused primarily on the latter two. ''Function'' refers to the two basic tools with which the child organizes experience. These functions do not change. They further development of intellectual structures through interaction with the external environment and through ongoing internal reorganization. These functions are (1) *organization* and (2) *adaptation* or *equilibrium* (Piaget, 1952). The latter comprises *assimilation* and *accommodation*.

''Organization'' refers to an invariant characteristic of intelligence. Intelligence always consists of some internal coherent, interrelated, organized structure which progresses from simple, or undifferentiated, to complex, or highly differentiated. This organized internal structure is called a *schema* (Flavell, 1963).

''Assimilation'' is the mental process by which the organism ignores certain characteristics of the object in order to fit into the preexisting internal schema. ''Accommodation'' is the mental process by which the organism changes the internal schema in order to come to grips with the novel features of the object (Flavell, 1963). "Adaptation" or "equilibrium" refers to the balance between assimilation and accommodation. In an adaptive, equilibrated act, the organism makes an incremental change in the internal schema as well as a minor distortion of the object; it is, then, a balance between the person's unique internal representation and the external environment.

The child begins with basic inherited schemata (e.g. sucking) which, through experience with the world and adaptation, become increasingly complex and interrelated, furthering the mental construction of reality (Piaget, 1954). For Piaget, the motivating force behind intellectual development is the exercise of the schema for the sheer sake of exercising it (Flavell, 1963). As the organism develops, schemata become increasingly interrelated with each other, forming complex and mobile chains. For example, a first coordination of schemata occurs in early infancy, with the coordination of sucking and grasping.

Piaget wrote volumes about the structure of intelligence. The structure of intelligence refers to the clusters of mental properties which determine behavior. These continually change as the child develops. For example, the child's concept of object permanence is a structure. Because Piaget's theory is so well woven, it is difficult to discuss some of its structural aspects in isolation from the total theoretical context. However, at the risk of simplifying and somewhat injuring the elegance of the theory, this chapter will be limited to a few core concepts.

The child is born in an undifferentiated, egocentric psychological state where assimilation and accommodation are initially indissociable. The child proceeds to slowly construct a universe, which we call reality, in which the self is included as an element separate from but among other objects. In the initial egocentric state there is no self and no other. Rather, they are experienced as the same. The self, paradoxically, is least aware of itself at the height of egocentricity and most aware of itself as it develops away from egocentricity. Like the self, the object's existence comes to be apprehended as having permanence (Piaget, 1954).

In the beginning, the infant's thinking consists of a series of reflexive actions which quickly develop through assimilation and accommodation to increasingly deliberate concrete actions upon objects. The infant cannot think without simultaneously acting on an object. The neonate initially conceives of objects as fleeting sensations and pictures. In early infancy, with the development of schemata, the objects come to be seen as extensions of the child's own actions. In this sensorimotor period of development, all thinking *is* external action (Piaget, 1954).

With ongoing experience the child refines the concept of the object, progressing from a view of the object as a fleeting picture, a mere extension of the effort of looking, to one which allows the infant to anticipate a hidden object simply from seeing a part of it. Even then, however, the infant appears to conceive of objects as being formed as they are uncovered and eliminated as they are covered. In the second year, although the child develops a better sense that objects do not disappear and reappear as they leave or enter the visual field, there remains a sense that the object is still only part of its action context (Piaget, 1954). Thus, a child conceives of many replicas of the object, depending upon the context, rather than a single object in different contexts. Like the objects, then, representations of the self and others may be internally represented in separate and discontinuous images. Further development is needed to synthesize those images and thus create an experience of a more coherent self.

The child attains a mature concept of the object in the third year, as he or she mentally constructs the object as independent of his or her actions, can infer its existence when it is not perceptible, and can spontaneously evoke a mental image of it. This is the beginning of representational intelligence. The child not only can evoke a mental image of the object, but can also internally imagine a series of actions with that object without actual motoric action on it. According to Piaget, at that point action becomes interiorized. The child will then learn to construct the object on this representational or symbolic level, as earlier he or she learned to construct it on the sensorimotor level (Flavell, 1963).

The preoperational stage of development partly refers to the period of mental construction of the object during which the child gradually constructs the object on the symbolic level. The symbol now becomes the thing to mentally act upon, as earlier the concrete object was. For our purposes here, only a few concepts from this stage will be discussed. The logic of preoperational children appears shifting, contradictory, and literal. In part this is due to the egocentric notions held about their newly found ability to think internally. There is a lack of critical examination of their own logic and a belief that everyone is thinking just like the child. At this stage, children feel little need to justify their ideas.

Preoperational logic seems arbitrary for several reasons. First, the thinking is ''centered,'' meaning that there is a tendency to focus on one salient feature at a time to the exclusion of other characteristics. Second, thinking is ''static'' or binary. The child sees the static states and not the transformations between states. Logical explanation for state change at this stage of development relies on juxtaposition, or the inference of causality by reason of temporal or spatial contiguity. Third, thinking is irreversible. The child can progress along one chain of logic but cannot reverse it. The child is unable to hold a symbol constant while manipulating other symbols (Flavell, 1963).

For preoperational children, symbols take on a very real quality. Just as the object had been inseparable from action for sensorimotor children, so now is internal thinking fairly inseparable from external reality for preoperational children. Words and thoughts can be experienced as having a real-life quality sometimes synonymous with action. In this period of intelligence, the heavy cognitive demand of relating present events with past while internally manipulating symbols manifests in marked disequilibrium and swings in the assimilation-accommodation balance (Cowan, 1978). The sense of self and others, while more continuous and constant than in the earlier period of development, is experientially subject to a tenuousness of existence.

Through constant social interaction, the child's intelligence develops the capacity to conserve and manipulate symbols, reaching a state of much increased equilibrium. This begins the concrete operational period of development, the first stage of rational logic. This chapter, however, will not address intellectual development beyond the preoperational stage.

Clinical Application

An important contribution of Piaget's theory is the meticulous attention it gives to the process of the construction of reality in children. Piaget himself spoke of the necessity of a stable caretaking relationship as the context of this progress. For Piaget, affective and cognitive development are inextricably linked with each other, neither causing the other but rather developing hand-in-hand (Piaget, 1962). This relationship can be seen clearly in the projective material of young disturbed children. The Rorschach record provides an opportunity to integrate an understanding of the cognitive with the affective to arrive at a fuller view of the child's internal representation of reality. The following analysis of a Rorschach record illustrates such an application.

This record was produced by a nine-year-old boy with low average intelligence. The mother brought him to the clinic because he was setting small, controlled fires. He lives with his mother, two younger brothers, and an older sister. His history included sexual molestation by his father during his early preschool years and the subsequent divorce of his parents. His mother became depressed following the divorce. She allows the boy minimal autonomy and erratically displaces verbal and physical aggression upon him. An example of this problem in her caretaking behavior was a recent observation of her walking down the street, her son by her side with his head tucked under her arm in such a way that he walked rapidly and in a bent-over position to keep up with her. The boy has supervised visits with his father on weekends during the daytime. The mother accompanies the child during these visits and chats with the father. When alone with the boy, however, she continues to remind him about the molestation by the father. The father has been described by a mental health professional as very passive, not very intelligent, and interested in his son's welfare.

This child was assessed in four sessions. He was a sallow-complected, lanky boy with a floppy quality to his body. His speech was notable for its nasal quality and poor articulation. He spoke in a slow, whining manner. He was wriggly and handled the examination materials excessively. At times he draped his body over the table in a prone position. During the Rorschach administration he slid under the table several times. The examiner's office had a sparse but visible supply of toys. This child complained several times that the examiner's toys were far superior to those of his therapist, and he coaxed and pleaded to be allowed to use the toys. At one point he left his chair to examine a small mirror attached to a toy bureau. He was unsure about whether it was a mirror and asked whether the reflection was of himself.

The Rorschach was administered in the Gesell tradition (Ames, Learned, Metraux, and Walker, 1974) in the third session. The responses were not timed and the card remained with the child during inquiry. However, the inquiry and location were more precise than the Gesell method. The child's responses to each card and the inquiry are presented here and followed by an analysis. The location of the percepts are indicated on the accompanying location chart.

Response	*Inquiry*
Card I. A bat. I can't think of it. Who does it. Who did it. A hand. (Anything else?) Wings like this. (Flaps his arms.) (Anything else?) No, I can't see.	(What about the blot made it look like a bat?) Um, it had, it had wings and it had han- it had a face on it, a head—hands on it and had these things on it, and a line down the middle. (A line?) A line to keep it together. (Giggles.) Are some of these different colors? (Spins blot.) (What made the blot look like a hand?) A little hand like this. (Puts his hand into a pincer shape.) A claw. (What about the blot made it look like the wings were flapping?) It like it was flapping. (It was flapping-looking. What made it look that way?) I don't know.

In this first card, the boy initially attains a good assimilation-accommodation balance with the percept of "bat." His following question ("Who does it? Who did it?"), however, may indicate a beginning tendency to confuse the past with the present. The good equilibration he attained with the percept of "bat" may have taxed his ability to relate present perceptions to representations of the past. That is, his slippage on the verb tense may be a reflection of the amount of effort needed to maintain an equilibrated response. In the inquiry he shows a tendency to become momentarily captured by various features of the blot, and then arbitrarily combines the percepts into one percept. He creates an impossible bat with a face which would be much too large and displaced in relation to the wings. Perhaps his anxious comment that the line holds it together reflects a fleeting awareness that the logic of the percept has become poor. However, he is not able to correct it. Here one can begin to sense his experience of helplessness in ordering reality; that is, he is dimly aware of the disorder but relatively unable to develop stability. The preoperational qualities of this response are clear with the centering on a salient aspect of the blot and an arbitrary combining of two percepts (the face and wings). Through the inquiry the response begins to become less assimilative, in that the boy overaccommodates his mental image of a bat to fit this perception.

The child's motoric imitation of flapping wings and a pincer-shaped hand suggests an overaccommodation to the blot in terms of becoming his percept. There appears to be difficulty in boundary articulation between self and object. A problem with separation-individuation may also be inferred from his reference to the line in the blot. A line is more commonly used to demarcate boundaries and to keep things apart. This child's understanding of the line as something which keeps things together may reflect conflict about separateness.

Response	*Inquiry*
Card II. (Examiner is about to hand over the card: Is it the same color?) It has red marks. It looks like blood. (Giggles.) And it looks like a monster and a dinosaur.	(What made it look like blood?) That red stuff. (What made it look like a monster?) Big hunk in it. This black stuff. Who made these? That big black stuff and it had a head like a vulture head. (Can you see the vulture head?) Something what the vulture eats. (But what about the blot makes it look like a vulture head?) He eats people and a dinosaur does too if it's a meat-eater. (What made it look like a dinosaur?) This stuff. This. It got a neck like a dinosaur (rubs ink). (What else made it look like a dinosaur?) Because this thing, the tail and the lumps on there.

The second card seems to begin with what may be the child's hope that the examiner will not tax his equilibrium too badly by changing the color of the inkblot. Alternatively, it is possible that the blackness of the ink is disturbing to the child and he may hope for the comfort that colors can provide. The child is immediately captured by the salience of the red and black ink. The blackness becomes the most important determinant of the percept and the child cannot decenter and consider aspects of the blot which would modify the perception. The incorporative fantasy about this monster becomes enlivened. The child appears to be imbuing his symbols with reality. His language and percept appear to be infused with private attributes which make it difficult for him to logically respond to the examiner's questions. The rubbing of the inkblot seems to be the child's attempt to test out the reality of his internal thoughts. Like his question about who made the blots, it may also indicate an attempt to distance the internal images from the inkblot by reassuring himself that these are only inkblots.

The poor differentiation of the percepts may reflect a poorly differentiated sense of self. The fantasy about eating people may be the first indication on the protocol of some trouble distinguishing inside from outside. The vulture, dinosaur, and monster all seem curiously enmeshed with one another. This may reflect a confused internal feeling of "thick" enmeshment with the other that is a further indication of difficulty with separation.

Response	*Inquiry*
Card III. I can't think of anything. It looks like people sitting down. That's all I could think of.	(What made the blot look like people sitting down?) They sitting down like. Here's the feet, arms, sitting down again at a table and it's raining. (What about the blot made it look like it was raining?) This red stuff. (What about the red stuff makes it look like it's raining?) It's red. When we have storms. (When we have storms it rains. What about the blot reminded you of rain?) God. (Were the people boys or girls?) Girls. (What made them look like girls?) These lumps. "Stand up!" (He raises the card perpendicular to the desk.)

This response begins with a good, equilibrated percept. There is a hint of static thinking when he says, "sitting down *again,*" as though, as his responses are elaborated, it is constantly a new state of affairs rather than a gradual transformation. His thinking becomes difficult around the concept of raining. He seems to have centered on the redness of the ink and attempts to explain the percept on that basis. He gets further trapped and perhaps finally invokes God as an explanation, as if juxtaposing God with the problem is sufficient.

At the end of the inquiry, standing up the card was possibly a maneuver intended to counteract the passive percept of people seated. The sadistic voice and absence of playfulness in this behavior suggests that the child may think that these people are extensions of his own actions and that the percept actually has life. It is possible that the examiner's question about the gender of the people in the inkblot aroused fear about sexuality, causing some regression in thinking ability. The very active stance the boy takes in his command contrasts with prior observations of passivity. It is as though there is an unintegrated sadistic "introject" which represents past experiences with others but is now also experienced as being part of the self. This would appear to lend discontinuity to the experience of self and a confusion about the source of the sadism.

Response	*Inquiry*
Card IV. Looks like a monsters. Got two heads on it. Two feet and arms on it. How come these cards won't stand up? Do you share the office?	(What about the blot made it look like a monster?) It had big feet and it had, uh, heads on it and arms on it. (Hides eyes with arms.)

In this response there seems to be a concern about "twoness," manifestating the mistaken pluralization of monster, the presence of two heads, and the inquiry about whether the examiner shares the office. The monster seems to be a passive but potentially powerful figure. Perhaps it represents the boy's two representations of his father. It is as if there are two separate images of the father: the active father-who-molested-him and the passive father-who-now-lives-far-away. It may be a manifestation of a splitting of the object into good and bad as a way to preserve the good object. One can speculate that the child may have integrated his sexual experience with the father by attributing the bad to the father's genitals and seeing the genitals as some separate entity appended to the father, thus preserving his father's goodness

In Piagetian terms, it may be that the child sees the object as part of an action context such that there can be different versions of the object depending on the context. The concept of twoness may also represent conflict about separation-individuation, as suggested earlier. The concept of twoness may reflect the child's concern about the hard work involved in separating his internal world from the external reality. The inner world often seems to take on a reality which matches the outer world. Hiding his face during inquiry may be an attempt to demarcate inner object representations from external objects as well as to protect himself from the percept.

Response	*Inquiry*
Card V. Got big ears on it, and big feet on it and it got, and it's flying. (Does it look like anything you know about?) It got heads coming out-a-here and it got arms, here. (What could it be?) A monster.	(What made it look like it was flying?) It's making it fly. (What made it look like a monster?) It got what this stuff on it. Just a flying monster. (What made it look like a monster?) It's all black. (Hides face.)

This response shows a swing toward accommodation to the detriment of assimilation with the reluctant creation of a creature that encompasses all the separate parts. The avoidance of integrating the separate body parts may have allowed the initial ability to maintain equilibrium. There seems to be some continuation of experience from Card IV. It may be that the deterioration on Card IV and the blackness of Card V contributed to the boy's difficulty in imposing some internal organization on this inkblot. It is interesting that the inkblot which most readily lends itself to a whole response elicited perceptions of body parts. This may reflect an experience of the self as discontinuous and a series of unintegrated parts and introjects. As previously observed, the boy's construction of the object is at times reminiscent of the sensorimotor stage, when the object is conceived of as part of a context such that there are many objects in different, discontinuous contexts rather than one object in several continuous contexts.

Response	*Inquiry*
Card VI. A honey bee. Big one. Got a big nose on it. (Hides eyes.) I see feet going out like this. (Stretches legs.)	(What made it look like a honey bee?) It's got shape like a honey bee. This big part, where they get, keep the honey when they get home. (Puts hands up beside head.) My computer says it's right. (Long

	conversation ensues, at the examiner's initiation, about this computer and about how his computer talks to his mother's computer.)

Like some previous percepts, the honey bee is something with an appendage stuck on it. This may be a hint about concerns about sexuality. For a child, the initial percept seems well equilibrated. However, his logic fails in the inquiry when he reports that the wings and nest are the same part of the blot. He appears unable to monitor his thinking, moving from one thought to another, and unable to retrace his steps while holding an idea constant. This can be summarized as trouble with decentering and with reversible thinking.

The image of a honey bee suggests the theme of nurturance. The fusion of the percepts of the wings and the nest makes it unclear whether the honey is in the inside or the outside, and whether the bee is holding the honey or needs to get it. This is highly suggestive of a boundary confusion between inside and outside which may occur with the arousal of nurturance issues. The discussion about his computer talking with his mother's computer raises questions about the extent of fusion he experiences with the mother. It is interesting in the light of previous indications of difficulty with separation-individuation.

Response	*Inquiry*
Card VII. I don't know, a "N." (I didn't hear you. What did you say?) N. (Anything else?) I don't know. Lemme see if my computer. He knows. He saw it a N too.	(What made it look like an N?) Looks just like N.

This seems to be an overassimilative process where the child ignores many of the features of the blot so that it can be an "N." It may be an effort to distance his internal self from the external stimuli in order to preserve some sense of order and separateness. It may be that when affectively aroused the child attempts to prevent overaccommodation and loss of self by becoming overassimilative. It is interesting that this rigid attempt to maintain separateness occurs on the card which is thought to elicit feelings about the mother. The barren and impermeable quality to the response is also striking.

Response	*Inquiry*
Card VIII. It's a different kind of monster. Super monster. Superman monster. Are these chairs glass? (Covers eyes.) (Anything else?) The orange stuff. It looks like, I don't know, a hill with two lions crawling up it. Computer says it's right and it's V-I-I-I.	(What made it look like a monster?) It's a hill with two jaguars going up it. (A hill. What made it look like a hill?) These, hill, all this stuff. Crack isn't a hill.

The first part of this response seems to depict a struggle to better differentiate a global percept and to reach equilibrium. The creation of a superman monster seems to reflect an attempt to synthesize good and bad by placing them together rather than synthesizing them. The uneasiness of this response results in a slippage to a more familiar task of color naming. Contrary to past responses which deteriorated as time passed, the color naming seemed to help the child and he finally produced an adequate, equilibrated percept. The image of the lions crawling once again seems to be one of a powerful being in a helpless stance. In inquiry, the lions become jaguars. Although that may be a better adapted percept, it suggests static thinking and a difficulty in conserving identity.

The reference to the crack in the hill as not belonging to the hill speaks to the boy's difficulty with boundaries. A crack, in reality, is inseparable from the hill, as they define each other with their boundaries. This seems to be similar to the child's error about a line holding a percept together. Separateness may be viewed as a precipitous and dangerous act which results in an unwelcome disruption of unity and coherence. The child's idea that his chair is made of glass may be a reference to the potential separation from and shattering of important appended external objects.

Response	*Inquiry*
Card IX. I don't see nothing. It looks like a me. (Points to himself.)	(What made it look like you?) All this green stuff, red stuff, and blue stuff. (Misnames colors.) Green is hamburger. It's mustard, hot mustard. (I don't understand. How does it remind you of you?) It got the same things like me. Like meatballs, ketchup, and other stuff like relish.

Perhaps the inability to relate the blot to any internal schema was initially dealt with by rejecting the blot as unadaptable. This stance fades as the child's assimilation and accommodation become indissociable and the internal schema and percept are united as one entity. The child becomes disoriented such that he misnames the colors. That the percept becomes food may speak to a confusion of internal and external, and fusion of internal sensation with external visual perception as in early infancy. It represents a serious loss of boundaries.

Response	*Inquiry*
Card X. Ugh! Looks like crabs.	(What made it look like crabs?) The blue. It looks like crabs. (What about the blue looks like crabs?) Just crabs.

The initial revulsion to the card raises questions about whether the card produced a kinesthetic experience for the child. He quickly recovers and produces an adequate percept. He seems unwilling to think any further, possibly as a way to keep the outer world from impinging on the inner world and vice versa. There is a notable change from the amorphous fluid response on Card IX to the percept of a crab, a creature with a hard, impermeable exterior. This shift from permeable to impermeable seems to help him recover from and prevent further loss of self-boundaries. This highly differentiated inkblot may have helped him maintain a sense of self-differentiation. His ongoing overaccommodation of inner experience to the outer world leaves him vulnerable to undifferentiated self-experiences in the face of a low amount of external differentiation and, conversely, better able to self-differentiate when the external is more differentiated.

Summary and Conclusion

A summary of the card-by-card analysis of this child's Rorschach illustrates the complementary aspects of Piaget's theory and object relations theory in arriving at an understanding of the child's construction of reality and the implications of that construction for development, the experience of self, and for psychotherapy.

The Rorschach revealed not only the boy's delay in object construction, but also the vulnerability of the achieved construction. The delay was clear in the examples of the boy's difficulty in conserving the symbolic representations of the object. His thinking was characteristically static, centered, and irreversible. With decreased external structure, and emergence of issues related to both nurturance and his father, internal tension seemed to increase, and the construction of the object on a sensorimotor level became vulnerable. There seemed to be a regression in the mental grasp of the object as separate and permanent. The object seemed to become embedded in its action context. There were indications on the Rorschach that the symbol of an object was viewed as a continuation of the action-object context such that internal thoughts took on real, substantial property.

Such a delayed and vulnerable construct of the object would have implications for the child's experience of himself and his ability to maintain a relationship with another (Blatt and Wild, 1976). His highest level of functioning appeared to be preoperational, the qualities of his thought implying a changing, moment-to-moment experience. Disequilibrium due to struggles in manipulating symbols manifests itself in arbitrary assertions which are embraced one moment but discarded the next. Thus, even his highest level of functioning is characterized by a shifting and somewhat discontinuous sense of self. This kind of discontinuous self-experience might be less disruptive were it not for repeated shifts in his object concept. He radically regresses from a preoperational to an early sensorimotor level under some conditions of internal drive state. This seems to leave the boy feeling passive, helpless, and unstable. The intensity of that experience could be seen in his inability to correctly identify colors in Card IX. Thus, he may not be able to rely on his own basic skills when stressed. This instability could be seen in his fear that the very chair he was seated upon might be made of glass.

The boundaries between self and the other can quickly become fluid as the tension increases in his grasp of object constancy. There are instances on the Rorschach suggesting that he may attempt to prevent this deterioration by a suddenly assimilative stance whereby he would actively create an impermeable, rigid boundary around his self. It is as though he becomes another aspect of himself. He appears to call up a past accommodation or introject and to use that temporarily to prevent the passivity and loss of boundaries. This minimal ability to balance the assimilative and accommodative processes is similar to his difficulty in synthesizing the two aspects of self.

The shifting between overaccommodative and overassimilative stances in the Rorschach record was striking. This disequilibrium has been thought to be characteristic of disturbed children (Cowan, 1978). It is not necessarily unhealthy to have the capacity for such disequilibrium. However, the few equilibrated responses in this boy's Rorschach record and his apparent lack of control over disequilibrium (as indicated by an absence of humor and an inability to monitor his thinking process) are indicative of marked dysfunction.

The blending of the Piagetian and object relations approaches contains

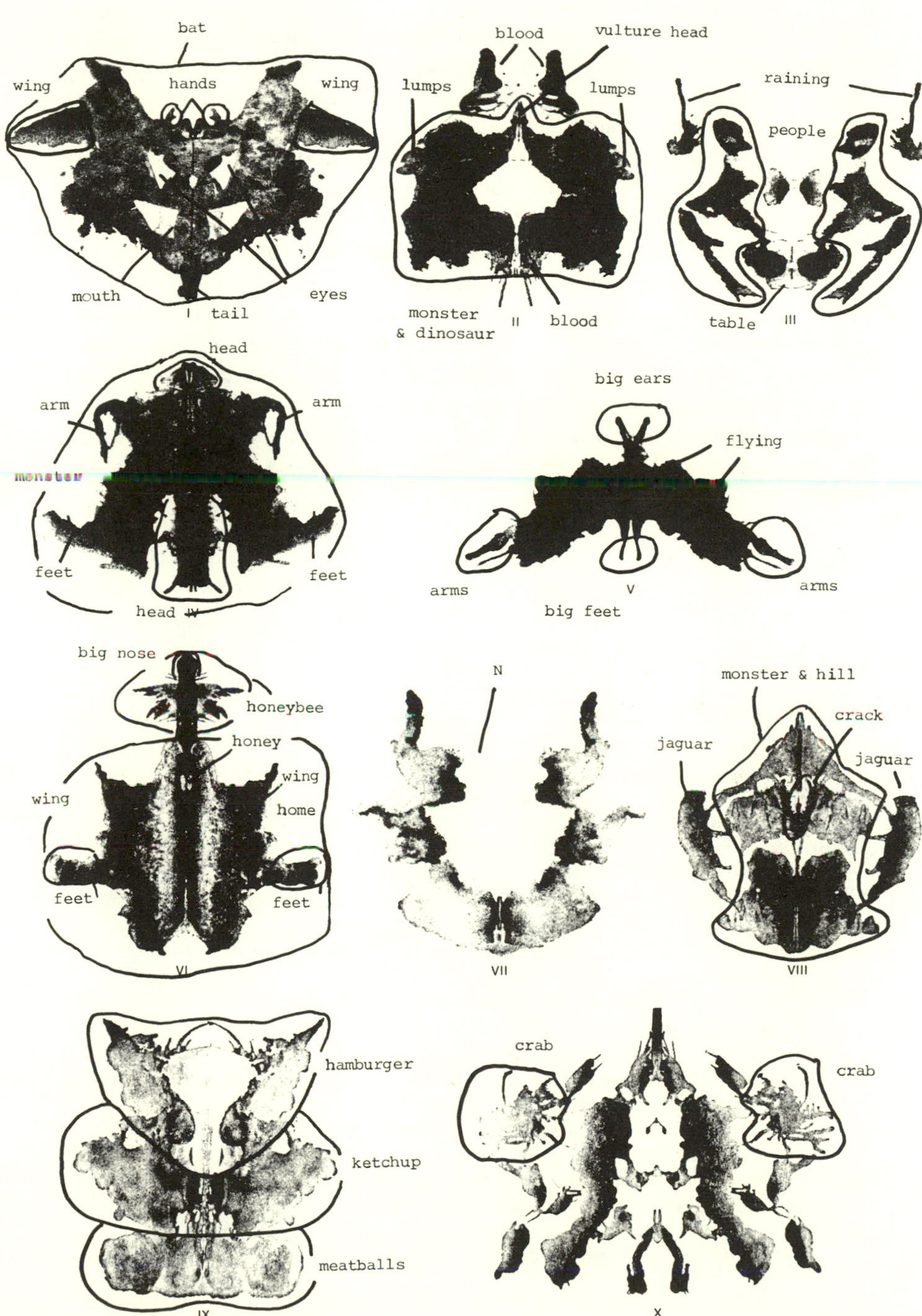
bat
wing
hands
wing
mouth
I
tail
eyes
blood
vulture head
lumps
lumps
monster
& dinosaur
II
blood
raining
people
table
III
head
arm
arm
monster
feet
feet
head
IV
big ears
flying
arms
V
arms
big feet
big nose
honeybee
honey
wing
wing
home
feet
feet
VI
N
VII
monster & hill
crack
jaguar
jaguar
VIII
hamburger
ketchup
meatballs
IX
crab
crab
X

an implicit treatment framework. For example, the child's regression in his construction of the object is likely a disorienting and fearful experience. Development cannot proceed well in an unstable and fearful internal or external environment. First, it would seem that an important treatment goal would be to lower the incidence of these regressive fluctuations by creating structure in the therapy hour as well as in other social spheres (e.g. family and school). Second, the therapist and the treatment milieu would need to be extremely constant and stable, both affectively and concretely, in order to sharpen the distinction between inside and outside fluctuations of state, as well as to increase the probability of creating a stable internal experience. Third, the child would need the therapist to actively serve as an interpreter of reality and a clarifier of the sources of tension. Because of the child's history of molestation, there might be a tendency to focus on that trauma in treatment. However, it would seem that a working through of the child's experience could not occur until he attained a more stable construction of the object.

References

Ames, L., Learned, M., Metraux, R., & Walker, R. (1974), *Child Rorschach Responses*. New York: Brunner/Mazel.

Bell, S. (1970), The development of a concept of object as related to infant-mother attachment. *Child Development*, 41:291–311.

Blatt, S., & Wild, C. (1976), *Schizophrenia: A Developmental Analysis*. New York: Academic Press.

Cowan, P. (1978), *Piaget: With Feeling*. New York: Holt, Rinehart, & Winston.

Flavell, J. (1963), *The Developmental Psychology of Jean Piaget*. New York: Van Nostrand Reinhold.

Gouin-Decarie, T. (1974), *The Infant's Reaction to Strangers*. New York: International Universities Press.

Greenspan, S. (1979), Intelligence and Adaptation. *Psychological Issues*, Monogr. 47/48. New York: International Universities Press.

Mahler, M., Pine, F., & Bergman, A. (1975), *The Psychological Birth of the Human Infant*. New York: Basic Books.

Piaget, J. (1952), *The Origins of Intelligence in Children*. New York: International Universities Press.

——— (1954), *The Construction of Reality in the Child*. New York: Basic Books.

——— (1962), The relation of affectivity to intelligence in the mental development of the child. *Bull. Menn. Clin.*, 26:129–137.

——— (1973), The affective unconscious and the cognitive unconscious. *J. Amer. Psychoanal. Assn.*, 21:249–261.

Suchotliff, L. (1970), Relation of formal thought disorder to the communication deficit in schizophrenia. *J. Abnorm. Psychol.*, 76:250–257.

Wolff, P. (1960), The Developmental Psychologies of Jean Piaget and Psychoanalysis. *Psychological Issues*, Monogr. 5. New York: International Universities Press.

Chapter 14

MESHING CHARACTER STRUCTURES IN MARRIAGE PARTNERS

MORTON KISSEN

Psychological test data offer us a rather unique opportunity to projectively explore the object relations implications of various complex psychosocial states. The self-representations, object representations, and more differentiated ego identity states implicit in the character structures of marriage partners can be illuminated through their test responses. An exploration of the meshing character structures in marriage partners can shed further light on the complex issue of object choice underlying the coupling process.

The issue of object choice in marriage has puzzled and fascinated psychoanalysts as well as the average individual over the years. What sort of personality types choose each other for an intimate dyadic relationship such as marriage? What are the personality factors involved in the ultimate compatibility or incompatibility of such a relationship? Although a commonsense argument can be made for the purely chance nature of marital object choices, the principle of psychological determinism implies the existence of subtle but nevertheless systematically observable motivational and personality factors underlying such choices.

A number of writers have attempted to meld ego psychoanalytic and object relations theory in their conceptualizations of the processes underlying the choice of a partner in marriage. Giovacchini (1958, 1967), an important

---

A preliminary version of this chapter was published in 1978 in the ASPP Newsletter, Adelphi University.

psychoanalytic theorist, has in particular developed the notion that marriage relationships typically involve an intimate meshing of characterological structures. The more intrinsic and well fitting the characterological mesh the more enduring (but not necessarily adaptive and free of emotional disturbance) the marriage relationship.

Recently, a number of psychoanalytic writers exploring issues around the treatment of patients suffering from character disorders (Grinberg, 1962; Wangh, 1962; Malin and Grotstein, 1966; Kernberg, 1969; Giovacchini, 1975; Langs, 1976) have begun to focus more and more on the central significance of the concept of ''projective identification'' for understanding the dynamics of character disorders and the development of more effective treatment techniques suitable for these more difficult patients. Langs (1976), in particular, has emphasized the largely ''interactive'' nature of the processes of projective identification and sharply differentiates them from the more ''intrapsychic'' processes of projection and identification. ''It is well to remember,'' he states,

> that the interactional processes of projective and incorporative identification have many important nuances that we have not as yet investigated. Here, I'm stressing something that I have not seen discussed in the literature—that the recipient of a projective identification is by no means totally passive. Instead, the object of a projective identification actually may invite such a process from the subject, or on the other hand, communicate reluctance to accept such processes into himself. [p. 149]

The interactive nature of the process of projective identification is further highlighted by Grinberg (1962) in his explication of the concept of ''projective counter-identification'':

> When this counter-identification takes place, the normal communication between the analysand's and the analyst's unconscious will obviously be interrupted. In this case, the unconscious content rejected by the analysand will be violently projected onto the analyst, who, as the recipient object of such projective identifications, will have to suffer its effects. And he will react as if he had acquired and assimilated the parts projected on to him in a *real and concrete* way. [p. 437]

Wangh's notion of the ''evocation of a proxy'' (1962) comes closest to elucidating the truly interactive nature of projective identification processes. Using numerous case examples, Wangh convincingly demonstrates the subtle yet clearly observable capacity of certain severely disturbed patients to incite thoughts, feelings, and impulses in a mate in order to cope with a difficult separation-individuation conflict with which they themselves are struggling. Thus, a woman who is unconsciously terrified and rageful over the impending rupture of a symbiotic bond to her son may subtly induce in her husband the feelings of rage and the acting-out impulses that she herself feels incapable of containing and mastering.

> Essentially, then, what happens is that anxiety is induced—or evoked—by one member of a couple in the other, and we learn from our analytic examples that the husbands consequently become not only agitated but also angry against a third person, their progeny. In contrast to the partner's agitation and rage, the older sister and the wives remain calm and assume a benevolent and protective attitude. [p. 457]

Wangh goes on to systematically elucidate the various dynamic, economic, and structural aspects of such complex forms of projective identification. He emphasizes the subtle interactive use of a marriage partner as a "container" for feelings and action-tendencies that are either consciously unavailable or deemed too ego-disruptive and threatening to the more severely disturbed mate.

It can be inferred from Wangh's exploration of proxy-evocation as a special form of projective identification that many bipersonal interactions facilitate the occurrence of such a process. Marriage relationships, in particular, offer a unique opportunity for an exploration of the use of partners as containers for ego-dystonic projective identifications. In object relations terms, the actual choice of a mate may involve an unconscious appreciation of the latent character structures of the mate and their suitability for proxy-evocation. Contrasting "character styles" (Shapiro, 1965) may well offer married couples an opportunity to projectively identify threatening or potentially ego-disruptive thoughts, feelings, and action-tendencies into each other. A paranoid mate may be a perfect container and an eventual proxy for the aggressive feelings and impulses of a seemingly docile and benign passive-dependent personality, while a psychopathic mate may act out primitive impulses for a more compulsively organized individual.

The character structures of mates may allow also for the projective identification of higher levels of behavioral and personality organization. For instance, a compulsively organized mate may offer fairly rigid superego (and ego ideal) boundaries for an individual whose character structures are organized in a more hysterical, infantile, or narcissistic direction. The more hysterical individual thus uses the compulsive partner as a proxy for latent, very tenuously integrated superego and ego ideal projections.

The basic hypothesis being proposed, then, is that marriage partners use their contrasting characterological styles for purposes of projective identification and proxy-evocation. To explore the tenability of such an hypothesis, the test data obtained from two married couples will be descriptively presented, with an emphasis on inferences with regard to characterological patterns. In addition, the actual object choice of marital partner may be inferred to stem, at least partially, from such projective identificatory interactions.

The Tested Couples

The couples are two of many who have been tested at an outpatient Community Mental Health clinic. In some cases, both marriage partners came in seeking couples therapy or marriage counseling. In others, only one partner seemed initially to be in difficulty, and the other was brought in for evaluation in order to better understand the marital interaction. In a few cases, the couple came in around difficulties with a child and subsequently were evaluated themselves, in order to better understand the nature of family dynamics and parent-child relationship patterns.

Couple A

Mr. and Mrs. A. were evaluated in connection with their application for marriage counseling. The husband, an apparently successful, self-made businessman, was involved in a love affair that threatened the stability of the marriage. They have two children, the younger a seventeen-year-old girl who is apparently overshadowed by a brilliant and intellectually gifted older brother.

The following inferences were drawn from Mrs. A.'s test report:

> She comes across, in a number of ways, as a rather headstrong and willful individual who can occasionally behave in an oppositional or negative manner. This was particularly evident in her approach to the figure drawings. Her interaction with the examiner during that test was a subtly stubborn and defiant one. She persistently raised the fact that she was blocked imaginatively and insisted that she could not elaborate upon or associate to the personality characteristics of the figures she had drawn. Her unconscious need to take the examiner on in a subtly defiant manner would appear to link, at least in part, to her current difficulties with her husband. It was interesting to note that, despite her defiance, a tendency to idealize the examiner was also evident. She thus, paradoxically, also manifested a wish to please the examiner—much as a little girl might wish to please her father.
>
> Phallic personality features were plentifully evident in her responses. She is essentially a quite assertive, strong-minded, and com-

> petitive woman who attempts to mask and camouflage her assertiveness beneath a docile, compliant, and hyperfeminine defensive facade. . . . In a sense, to be aggressive or assertive is to be essentially "crazy." Such a noxious self-representation stems from a very competitive oedipal relationship with her mother. By being brave, domineering, and assertive (like the father) she risked the alienation of her jealous mother, who could never be quite as adventurous or bold. The risk was thus that she might be abandoned by the mother and left in a depressive state. . . . She has, thus, internalized her quite tense and conflictual interaction with her mother in the form of a latent masochistic-depressive characterological orientation.

The diagnostic formulation for Mrs. A. was "Adjustment Reaction of Adult Life with Phallic and Masochistic-Depressive Features."

The report for Mr. A. follows:

> He is an intensely competitive man who seemed threatened by the testing situation—particularly the fact that the examiner was experienced as an authority figure. He was able to verbalize the fact that he is generally "in command" in most situations and that the testing hence posed a dilemma in that he was not able to exert very much power or control. He nevertheless attempted to intimidate and turn the tables on the examiner in a number of different ways. His sarcastic manner often had a provocative quality and seemed geared toward establishing a reversal of roles with the examiner. Phallic personality traits were plentifully evident in his test responses. He responds to most interpersonal situations in the exhibitionistically cocky manner of a little boy who has just discovered that he possesses a penis. There was a clearly counterphobic element to his cockiness, in that the underlying fear is that he will be seen as vulnerable and essentially castrated.

The diagnosis for Mr. A. was "Phallic Narcissistic Personality."

It can be hypothesized from these test findings that Mrs. A. projects into Mr. A. her own latent phallic drives and aspirations. He offers himself as a proxy for his wife's competitive strivings and assertive potential. She, on the other hand, plays out for him the role of dutiful and hyperfeminine wife and enhances his inflated sense of macho superiority and domination.

Couple B

Mrs. B. has a master's degree in fine arts and is an art teacher currently on child care leave from her teaching assignment. She recently experienced what seemed to be a postpartum depression following the birth of her child, who is now two years old. Mr. B. is a union organizer.

The following excerpts are from Mrs. B.'s test report:

> She is a very unusual person. Her idiosyncratic qualities were very much in evidence. A certain willful, distant, and basically ethereal quality could be observed. She relies quite heavily on defense mechanisms typical of borderline or severely narcissistically damaged character disorders. She frequently uses the defense mechanism of splitting, which tends to give a vague, distant, and ethereal quality to both her inner experiential world and her characterological, expressive exterior. . . . Her proneness to split off latent elements of her character structure (i.e. her competitiveness, achievement strivings, and phallic assertiveness) is dynamically linked to an unconscious association of such strivings with strongly repressed aggressive and sadistic impulses. The quality of her dissociation is that typically seen in anorexic individuals whose dissociative defenses allow for a chronic sort of denial of painful, depressive aspects of inner and outer reality. Having been an only child, she probably moved more and more into an inner world of fantasy ideation. She verbalized the fact that she had an imaginary childhood playmate. Although she had probably been overprotected, it is unlikely that she was a wanted child.

The diagnosis for Mrs. B. was "Schizoid Personality."

Mr. B., on the other hand, was described in the following manner:

> Although outwardly he seemed a rather assertive and aggressively self-confident individual, this expressive demeanor would appear to reflect a rather brittle characterological facade which only partially masks his latent sense of inferiority, self-doubt, and essentially damaged ego structure. He is thus not nearly as cocky and actively assertive as he would like others to believe. His phallic tendencies and seeming aggressivity and capableness—in light of his projective test responses—came through more as overcompensatory bluff and counterphobic bravado than true self-confidence. He thus manifests a rather damaged sense of self-esteem and ego identity camouflaged beneath a surface, highly willful "persona" that suggests the opposite. His aggressivity and seeming cocksureness may thus be viewed more as personified ego ideal aspirations than as truly synthesized personality traits and capabilities.
>
> He possesses an essentially very narcissistic personality structure and his rigid self-orientation may, under certain circumstances, allow for charismatic leadership interactions with others. His attractive physical

appearance, excellent intellectual capabilities—taken together with his narcissistic orientation—may on occasion also lead to a psychopathic-like manipulative posture toward others in his outer environment. There is a certain ''slippery'' quality of evasiveness to his expressive demeanor which suggests a latent paranoid characterological orientation of guardedness and hypervigilance that is covered over by a surface attitude of seeming authenticity, spontaneity, naturalness, and a caring attitude toward others.

As a youngster he would appear to have been forced to shoulder rather severe burdens and responsibilities. The latter may have stemmed from an intense oedipal entanglement with his mother and a consequent proneness by the two of them to disparage his father as a viable phallic identificatory figure. His need to subsequently play out the role of ''superman'' in his marriage (given the outward contrast of his own personality with that of his seemingly fragile, withdrawn, and vulnerable wife) stems from his early enmeshment in a similar interactive matrix in his childhood milieu. His latent misgivings, sense of uncertainty, and fearfulness, however, are covered up by his surface attitude of being the ''Rock of Gibraltar'' upon which his wife can lean. He may very well have been tempted to flee the marriage (perhaps in some form of extramarital relationship) at some earlier point in time.

The diagnosis for Mr. B. was ''Narcissistic Personality.''

Thus, Mr. and Mrs. B. come through as profoundly damaged and emotionally needy individuals who nevertheless manifest a projective identificatory interaction matrix somewhat similar to that described for Mr. and Mrs. A. There, too, the husband plays out the role of phallic and seemingly quite dominant leader while the wife remains in the background. Mr. B. may occasionally act out the aggressive feelings and impulses that are largely dissociated from Mrs. B.'s conscious awareness. He thus becomes a proxy for Mrs. B. by acting out her latent assertive strivings. She, on the other hand, probably offers him certain externalized superego controls and ego restraints.

Discussion and Conclusions

The test data of both couples are compatible with the hypothesis proposed. The particular idiosyncratic mesh of characterological structures in these two couples seems ideally suited for processes of projective identification and proxy-evocation. In both cases, the husbands offer themselves as aggressive surrogates for their wives and the wives offer themselves as seemingly hyperfeminine, docile adornments to their husband's narcissistic, self-aggrandizing mastery needs.

Of course, in many marriages the proxy pattern may go the other way, with the wife acting out the more passive husband's latent hostile and aggressive fantasy-wishes. It would appear, nevertheless, that the projective identification process is a very basic one cutting across all sorts of marriage relationships—happy and unhappy, mildly neurotic and more severely disturbed. By playing out the role of proxies for each other, marriage partners expand each other's personality differentiation, facilitate each other's ego functioning, and allow for vicarious experiences of a potentially pleasurable and useful nature. Problems arise, however, when these projections or proxy attitudes become unduly one-sided, noncomplementary, or stereotyped.

Personal growth in one marriage partner without a simultaneous personality differentiation in the other may lead to marital problems. Ideally, contrasting characterological structures mesh together in a potentially satisfying and harmonious marriage relationship. The idiosyncratic nature of each member's character style (e.g. paranoid, masochistic-depressive, psychopathic narcissistic-infantile, hysterical, passive-aggressive, obsessive-compulsive) allows for a useful containing or acting-out experience for their mates. Although the proxy process is often more visible in more active mates (i.e. those who offer themselves as id to their mates), it is also established in an equally viable manner in those who serve largely "containing" functions (i.e. those who offer themselves as ego, ego ideal, or superego to their mates).

Thus, the primary goal in treatment with couples may very well be an intensive exploration of the mutual projective processes occurring in the marriage interaction. As couples become more aware of their useful and ego-enhancing proxy functions for each other, they are less prone to unrealistic expectations and demands. A deepening respect and "postnarcissistic" attachment may very well be derived from a thorough exploration of these projective identificatory relationships. On the other hand, more pathological forms of proxy interaction can be diminished through this focus on the projective identifications implicit in the marriage relationship.

References

Giovacchini, P. (1958), Mutual adaptation in various object relationships. *Internat. J. Psycho-Anal.*, 39:1–8.

——— (1967), Characterological aspects of marital interaction. *Psychoanal. Forum*, 2:7–13.

——— (1975), *Psychoanalysis of Character Disorders*. New York: Aronson.

Grinberg, L. (1962), On a specific aspect of countertransference due to the patient's projective identification. *Internat. J. Psycho-Anal.*, 43:436–440.

Kernberg, O. (1969), The treatment of patients with borderline personality organization. *Internat. J. Psycho-Anal.*, 49:600–620.

Langs, R. (1976), *The Bipersonal Field*. New York: Aronson.

Malin, A., and Grotstein, J. (1966), Projective identification in the therapeutic process. *Internat. J. Psycho-Anal.*, 47:26–31.

Shapiro, D. (1963), *Neurotic Styles*. New York: Basic Books.
Wangh, M. (1962), The "evocation of a proxy": A psychological maneuver, its use as a defense, its purpose and genesis. *The Psychoanalytic Study of the Child*, 17:451–469. New York: International Universities Press.

Chapter 15

EXPERIENTIAL AND STRUCTURAL ASPECTS OF THE (C) RORSCHACH RESPONSE IN PATIENTS WITH NARCISSISTIC CHARACTER PATHOLOGY

PAUL M. LERNER

Consequent on recent advances in psychoanalytic theory and technique, increased interest is being shown in patients who present with severe character pathology—narcissistic disorders and borderline personality organization. This interest challenges the psychodiagnostician to use his armamentarium of psychological tools and concepts to contribute, in a meaningful way, to the assessment, understanding, and treatment of these patients. A determinant that has received comparatively little currency in the Rorschach literature, yet appears with insistent regularity and frequency in the Rorschach records of a selected subgroup of these patients, is the (c) response.

The score is applied to responses which are delineated and determined by variations in shading, whether it be variations within a heavily shaded area or those within a brightly colored one. As these variations in shading are subtle and not at all striking, to achieve a (c) response one must seek out, discover, and attune to finer nuances as well as feel one's way into something not readily apparent. To do this requires perceptual sensitivity in addition to

Shortened versions of this chapter were presented to meetings of the Society for Personality Assessment, Scottsdale, Arizona, March 1979, and Tampa, Florida, March 1980.

a searching, articulating, and penetrating type of activity. Schachtel (1966) has described this mode in terms of a perceptual attitude "of a stretching out of feelers in order to explore nuances" (p. 251). While such an attitude of heightened sensitivity and penetrating activity can reflect and underlie an adaptive capacity for achieving highly differentiated responses, attuning to subtleties of feeling, and empathizing with the nuances of another's experience, it can also go awry. We are all familiar with the person who has his antennae out, as it were, to feel out an anticipated hostile, cold, and unfriendly environment. In such individuals I have observed a constant state of hypervigilance, hypersensitivity, and excessive vulnerability.

In a testing report I have described one such patient in the following way:

> The patient presents as a passive, indefinite, seemingly dependent individual whose weak, wispy voice adds to her overall impression as a fragile, tragic, lonely child. To judge from her tentativeness and unwillingness to take a stance, she senses the environment as well as herself as lacking substance and solidarity. One may liken her to a thin, frail branch, barely attached to a tree, and vulnerable to the slightest breezes. She is hypervigilant, overly sensitive, and painfully open—open like an unprotected wound. This state of vulnerability is vividly captured in her Rorschach percept of a "snail without a shell."

In a group of fifteen patients presenting with severe character pathology, I have found this state of unremitting hypervigilance, heightened sensitivity, and extreme vulnerability related to an identifiable self-system, mode of object relatedness, defensive structure, manner of experiencing affects, line of cognitive regression, and way of being and behaving in treatment.

Self-System and Object Relatedness

Each of these patients presents a passive attitude toward the environment, either an unspoken willingness or an inability to prevent being influenced. Their vigilance and sensitivity, like radar, constantly scans the immediate outer milieu in search of potential dangers as well as cues to guide and direct their desires, values, and behaviors. Like chameleons they sensitively attune to the expectations and anticipations of others and mold themselves and their behavior accordingly; this sensitivity and accommodating, however, is defensive and in the service of warding off potential threats to a rather fragile self-esteem. In this regard, they differ from the "as if " character (Deutsch, 1942) whose compliance and imitative behavior is more related to a search for an identity—an identity which will do justice to their inflated sense of self.[1] Because the accommodating is without investment, the other is left with a sense that something is "wrong." In like manner, the patient, himself painfully and helplessly aware of his compliance, is left feeling ungenuine, false, and despairing. Intimately related to the compliance is a presentation of fragility and vulnerability. The fragility is disarming in that one quickly senses that the wrong word, the forgotten act, or the slightest hint of disapproval will strain an already strained relationship to a point beyond repair. Thus, their relationships are tenuous and transitory.

Based on a chronic frustration of legitimate childhood needs which interfered with the building up of necessary psychic structures, these patients manifest disturbances in the cohesion, continuity, strength, and harmony of their self (Tolpin and Kohut, 1978). Because the requisite self-object matrix out of which the self gradually crystallizes had been unreliable, the nuclear self lacks reliable firmness and their self-perception is one of being fragmented, discontinuous, and unreal.

In keeping with Kohut's formulations (1971), I have found that patients who offer the (c) Rorschach response, because of disturbances in their nuclear self, relate themselves to others as "self objects." That is, the other is perceived not as separate, distinct, and whole, but rather as an extension of the self, and is used to correct or make up for something that is felt as missing inside. Thus the object is needed to serve a basic function that is normally internalized and, hence, carried out intrapsychically. While the object may serve any one of a number of functions (for example, that of the judging, regulating and controlling superego), Kohut has drawn attention to specific interactions in which the object is used to enhance the sense of self and/or to provide idealizing direction.

Affects and Defensive Structure

Their parents' emotional unavailability or unresponsiveness to early psychological needs gives rise to lowered self-esteem, disintegration anxiety, and feelings of depletion. Annie Reich (1960) has suggested that because of the archaic nature of their ego ideal, they are doomed to vacillate between a hypercathexis of the self (grandiose self-image) and a phase of lowered self-esteem. Disintegration anxiety (Tolpin and Kohut, 1978) is the anxiety experienced by a precariously established self in anticipation of further deterioration. While it involves a threat to the cohesion of the self, specific fears include fear of fragmentation of the self and loss of vitality and aliveness. Associated with disintegration anxiety is a subjectively perceived tension state

[1]Unlike the "as if" character, who tends to be grandiose and treats his objects with contempt and disregard, these patients suffer from lowered self-esteem and fear involvement with their objects.

which, when felt as intolerable, initiates a series of ego maneuvers directed toward lowering this state (Easer, 1972). Their depressive affect corresponds to Tolpin and Kohut's depletion depression (1978) and involves unbearable feelings of deadness and nonexistence and a self-perception of emptiness, weakness, and hopelessness.[2]

The hypervigilance and hypersensitivity are used to ward off affects, especially those feelings which could lead to greater intimacy (Easer, 1972). With an increase in tension, various forms of acting out become prominent, and if these escape outlets are cut off, then projection and paranoid suspicion quickly ensue. In a previous study (Lerner and Lerner, 1980), the (c) determinant, when combined with the Dr location score and content involving distorted part or full human forms, was found to be a reliable measure of projective identification.

Appelbaum and his colleagues (Appelbaum and Holtzman, 1982; Appelbaum and Colson, 1968) found that an attunement to the nuances of shading when combined with and in a colored area was indicative of suicidal tendencies. In that the patients I have identified offer the (c) response indiscriminately to both achromatic and colored areas it is not surprising that one form of potential acting-out behavior is suicide. While Appelbaum and Holtzman sensitively detail the experiential state which might lead a person offering the color textural response to consider self-destruction as an available course of action, they are less clear as to precipitating motives or circumstances. Among this character disordered group of patients I have found several precipitates of suicidal behavior, all involving the nature of their self-experience and the quality of object relations. These include fear of impending fragmentation of the self, a dramatic or cumulative loss in self-esteem, and a yearned-for symbiotic attachment with a lost object.

Cognitive Regression

Beginning with Singer's pioneering work (1977), it has become axiomatic that patients with a borderline personality organization appear as more intact on more structured tests such as the WAIS than on the more unstructured material such as the Rorschach. This is thought to relate to the patient's ability to make use of the external structure to avoid or recover from regressive bouts (Sugarman, 1980). While I would agree that in such patients peculiarities of content and lapses in formal thought processes tend to be restricted to the

[2]Depletion depression is similar to Blatt's concept (1974) of anaclitic depression, which is also characterized by feelings of helplessness, weakness, and depletion; however, whereas Blatt's concept is rooted in classical psychoanalytic theory, Tolpin and Kohut's notion evolves from Kohut's efforts to systematically develop a psychology of the self.

less structured tests, I would not agree that their WAIS performance is as benign and unrevealing as commonly assumed. Rather, I have found that in general, and with character disordered patients in particular, one may observe both in the patterning of scores and in the content cognitive equivalents of significant self, developmental, and relational difficulties.

In this subgroup of hyperalert, overly sensitive thin-skinned patients, I have found a specific subtest pattern on the WAIS as well as an identifiable line of cognitive regression which appears on both the WAIS and the Rorschach. In keeping with their heightened attunement to the expectations and anticipations of others, these patients do comparatively well on the Comprehension and Picture Arrangement subtests. By contrast, their performance on tasks having to do with the capacity to abstract, such as Block Design and Similarities, is appreciably lower. This test finding is in agreement with Winnicott's observation (1960) that patients who present a marked discrepancy between the true self and the false self have difficulty using symbols. A closer inspection of their approach to the blocks and the quality of several of their Rorschach responses reveals a tendency to lapse into concretistic, stimulus-bound thinking in which there is a glaring loss of perspective. That is, they demonstrate a nearsighted clarity with an attendant loss of the backdrop. This heightened attunement, in a concrete way, to very specific properties with a loss or distortion of perspective, could well underlie the type of thinking involved in the primitive defense of splitting. Further, this thought style also corresponds to the level of object representation found in anaclitic depression. Blatt (1974) has noted that in anaclitic depression the object representation is at a sensorimotor level and there is a need to maintain direct, concrete, physical, sensory contact with the object.[3]

Treatment Considerations

I have discussed the treatment behavior of these patients, especially in the opening phases, elsewhere (Lerner, 1979), relying heavily on the thoughtful and sensitive descriptions and illustrations provided by Ruth Easer (1972, 1974). Treatment begins under a cloak of great vigilance, with a readiness to be distrustful. They are, as it were, there, but with one foot out the door. Upon beginning, a rapid and massive regression occurs involving feelings of terror and panic, outbursts of affect toward the therapist, and a rush of activity directed away from but laden with meaning regarding the treatment. Easer (1972) furnishes examples of such activity, including one patient who, upon agreeing to psychoanalysis, took out a large life insurance policy. Quickly,

[3]Basic to his position are the assumptions that the development of object representations is, in part, a cognitive process and that one can distinguish subtypes of depression on the basis of a developmental model of object representations.

all aspects of the therapist, including his attire, tone of voice, or shifting of body, comes under careful scrutiny. If the therapist recalls an incident or memory mentioned several sessions before or responds in a particularly empathic manner, then the patient feels together and whole and considers the therapist an ally; but let the therapist cancel a session or respond with a trace of irritation in his voice, then the patient reacts with hurt and pain and regards the therapist as hostile, distant, and uncaring. The therapist's experience is one of being viewed under a microscope. Not only is his every movement closely monitored, but his comments are carefully scrutinized and regarded as evidence to weigh before allowing the relationship to continue and possibly deepen. This stance evokes a marked countervigilance and hypercaution on the part of the therapist. Realizing that interpretations will be met with an overreaction and be taken as an attack on the person, the therapist finds himself less spontaneous, less relaxed, and more careful with his interventions.

The patient's heightened attunement to visual, gestural, and emotional aspects of the therapist may be likened to the young infant's early experience with his mother and, as such, permits a reconstruction of that experience. Genetically, the perception of emotional tones and of tension by the young child precedes the learning of language and the understanding of spoken content (Schachtel, 1966). It develops from the infant's perception of his own sense of comfort or discomfort with the mothering one, including her moods and tensions. As development progresses, and with "good enough" mothering (Winnicott, 1960), attention to the obvious and to verbal content overshadows the need for perceiving finer visual and emotional nuances of the environment. In the absence of such mothering this transition is tenuous and incomplete. While several authors (Deutsch, 1942; Winnicott, 1960) have pointed to a defect in empathy in these mothers, I have been more impressed with the extent and depth of their depressive affect and how this has interfered with their capacity to continuously attend to and minister to their infants as well as permit the offspring to fully and satisfactorily hatch from a state of symbiotic relatedness (Mahler, Pine, and Bergman, 1975).

The Holding Environment

I have found Modell's concept of the "holding environment" (1976, 1978), by which he means the full range of the mother's caretaking functions, particularly useful with respect to the treatment of these patients. Psychoanalysts are beginning to view the structure of the analytic setting itself as containing symbolic equivalents of the mother-child relation. Modell has identified several aspects of good analytic technique that are reminiscent of a psychologically idealized maternal holding relationship: the analyst is consistent and reliable, empathically responds to affects, is there for the patient's needs rather than his own, and has a better grasp of the patient's inner psychic reality than does the patient. In his capacity to thoughtfully set limits, accept what is provocative and alienating, and do what in his judgment is best for the patient, the analyst, like the caring parent, may be said to be symbolically holding the patient. Therapeutic interventions are effective only if there is an affective relatedness between patient and therapist; however, as Easer (1972) has observed, these patients use their hypersensitivity to ward off any affect that leads to a stronger affective bond. The sharing of feelings and more intimate thoughts is not only anxiety-arousing, but at the very core of their character. Continuously struggling to maintain a sense (often illusory) of autonomy and self-sufficiency, these patients fear the communication of feelings, as this raises the danger of humiliation and annihilation of their fragile sense of self (Modell, 1978). What is called for during the initial phase of treatment, therefore, is an empathic acceptance and awareness of the patient's pain, interpretations that are perceived as empathic, and quiet waiting. Although during this period the therapist might feel that little is happening, the treatment process has already been set in motion by the action of the holding environment. In this context, the holding environment serves as a protective container which permits and facilitates necessary consolidation of the self so that eventually a therapeutic alliance can be established and a more classical analysis of conflicts and defenses can be conducted.

Clinical Illustration

A unique opportunity to explore the various processes involved in the (c) Rorschach response was provided when a patient, who in the course of her diagnostic testing had offered four such responses, was referred to me for psychoanalysis. In presenting excerpts from this case I would like to draw particular attention to the importance of self-sufficiency and the role and vicissitudes of early object loss.

Background Information

The patient is a thirty-six-year-old interior designer, twice divorced, who sought treatment following a painful termination of a six-month relationship with a married man five years her junior. Realizing that becoming intimately involved with men who are married or otherwise unavailable had become a distinct pattern, she began wondering as to whether she was destined to spend the remainder of her life unmarried and essentially alone. This coincided with a palm reading in which the reader suggested that she had been fated by her father's death.

The youngest of three girls, she suffered the first of several losses at age six when her father died of a brain tumor. Three years later, when the patient was nine, her mother had a severe stroke resulting in a loss of speech and paralysis to one side of her body. Following her mother's stroke, an uninvited uncle intruded and split the family. The two older sisters were sent to boarding school while the patient and her mother were taken to the uncle's farm in rural northern Ontario. During the next several years a maternal grandmother died, her oldest and favorite sister married a professional football player and left Canada, and she and her mother were thoughtlessly shifted from relative to relative. When the patient was sixteen, her mother suffered another stroke and died. Thus by midadolescence the patient had lost both parents and a grandmother through death, a sister through marriage, and had essentially raised herself.

Excerpts from the Analysis

The patient began analysis by providing, in a highly controlled and rather affectless manner, a comprehensive, exhaustively detailed chronicle of her life, starting with her father's death and extending through other deaths and losses, her two marriages and subsequent divorces, the birth of her daughter, her cervical cancer (which was discovered and operated on soon after her daughter's birth), the various places she had lived, from Toronto to San Francisco, and her many and varied affairs. As she spent hour after hour meticulously recalling and describing each of these events in their entirety, I became aware of her inordinate need for control, defensive use of compliance, heightened investment in self-sufficiency, longing for but intense fear of belonging, long-standing search for the ideal man, and pervasive desire to feel genuine. Throughout this period I felt, paradoxically, an ignored bystander watching her conduct her own analysis, in her typically self-reliant manner, as well as a captive audience being constantly monitored to guarantee that I, or my attention, would not wander off. In addition, I periodically felt like a protective container into which she was pouring the hardships and burdens life had visited upon her. Aware of the uninvited, intrusive uncle of childhood, what few remarks I did make involved attempts to empathize and recognize with her the immense pain and sadness that had accompanied her much of her life. She responded to my comments with genuine but controlled gratitude—as if they were mildly intrusive, unexpected, and unasked for, but precious gifts nonetheless.

In the eleventh month of treatment we had our first extended break. During the three-week separation from analysis her efforts to be totally self-sufficient failed to quiet and control intense feelings of emptiness, loneliness, and isolation, as well as the unbearable but persistent thought that I might never return. An analysis of these thoughts and feelings, together with the accompanying defenses, led to her first direct, unashamed, and undefended grieving for her father, who had died more than thirty years earlier. With the activation and release of her grief, the patient began to recapture a flood of early memories—painful ones, as of a time, around the onset of his tumor, when he became lost while the two of them were out driving and she had had to navigate them home, but also fond and pleasurable ones of how, before his illness, he was able to infect her with his joyful, fun-loving, devil-may-care attitude toward life. As she filled her analytic hours with these forgotten experiences, her hours outside of treatment were devoted to what can best be described as a desperate but unwavering effort to "reclaim" her father. For the first time since his funeral she visited his gravesite—not once, but week after week. In her search for information about him, neglected relatives were contacted, hospital records secured, and long-ignored photo albums hungrily explored. In the midst of all this she reported the following dream: "I went to the hospital to visit my father. Two people were in the room and my father was furthest away. It was the first time in eighteen years I had seen him. I walked in the room and he recognized me. He had only one eye. Where his right eye once was, skin had grown over it. I felt that he felt self-conscious. I hugged and held him for a long time with my hand behind his head and kissed the right side of his face, the side with the missing eye. I sensed that he knew I was not repulsed by him. Later, I moved to the other side of the bed and from that perspective he looked the same as always. I then began having a conversation with the man in the other bed. I had vague sexual feelings toward him which I can't explain." Two associations to this dream, one involving her view of her father from the right side, and the other related to her view of him from the left, were particularly significant. Seeing him in the dream with the right side of his face covered over by a layer of skin provoked a highly painful, previously repressed memory. She recalled that during his illness he was sent to the Mayo Clinic for brain surgery. In meeting him upon his return at the local railroad station, she remembered being stunned, mortified, repulsed, and horrified by his appearance. He looked like a broken, damaged, deformed, and aged relic of the father she had once known. Clad in pajamas and a bathrobe, with a bandage covering one side of his head, he had lost considerable weight, his color was ashen, and he was helplessly confined to a wheelchair. His fly was open, exposing his genitals. This she found profoundly humiliating, both for him and for herself. Her other association, to the left-side view, involved feelings of elation over the fact that this was the first time since his death that she had been able to evoke a full and undistorted inner image of him.

Discussion

The metapsychology of self-sufficiency, particularly as it bolsters defenses aimed at blocking the expression and sharing of feelings, has been thoughtfully detailed by Modell (1975). He notes that severe environmental trauma can induce the formation of a false self-organization, including the illusion of self-sufficiency. Because the sharing and communication of affects is object-seeking, the illusion that nothing is needed from others and that one can provide the source of his own emotional sustenance, removes the individual from the fear of closeness to objects by denying any instinctual demand to be made upon the object. Winnicott (1960) put it this way: one can keep oneself hidden by failing to share genuine feelings. In my patient, for instance, profound fears of loss and abandonment were associated with closeness and defended against by the illusion of self-sufficiency. Further, during the opening phase of treatment this illusory self-sufficiency constituted the major resistance.

Death is not only traumatic for a child but, as Nagera (1970) has suggested, also represents a "developmental interference." Unlike the adult, the child is not a finished product but rather is in the middle of a multiplicity of developmental processes, processes that require for their normal unfolding the presence of the absent object. Thus, there is a need to bring the lost object back to life in order to satisfy the requirements of psychological development. Within this context, the patient's failure to establish any satisfactory long-term heterosexual relationship and her tendency to choose unavailable men were not simply manifestations of a classical, unresolved nuclear oedipal conflict; rather, they signified an oedipal conflict complicated and influenced by a defect in psychic structure—namely, an impairment in the process of internalization of her father. In other words, following a pattern noted by Teicholz (1978), she relied on external objects to serve a function that should have been carried out intrapsychically. Further, and in line with Blatt's observations (1974), the impairment in internalization and the resultant failure to establish a whole inner representation of her father left her vulnerable to depressive affect and handicapped in coping with loss. It is my belief that had these manifestations of faulty structure formation been mistaken as purely disguised derivatives of a repressed oedipal conflict, her sense of being ungenuine, her impairment in internal object representation, and her failure to achieve object constancy would have remained unchanged.

There is one additional finding I would like to report. My conclusions with regard to the structural aspects of my patient's personality have so far been based on the sheer presence of the (c) response. But I also had the opportunity to review, with the examiner, the patient's Rorschach protocol, and while examining the record we found that of the four (c) responses given, the *content* of two involved distorted and deformed human faces in which part of the face was hidden or covered over. Very striking, then, was the similarity in content among these two Rorschach responses, the right-sided view of her father as reported in the dream, and the recollection of her father as recaptured in her early memory.

Pertinent to this finding is the concept of object representation. Defined broadly, object representation refers to the conscious and unconscious mental schemata, including cognitive, affective, and experiential components, of objects encountered in reality. Beginning as vague, diffuse, and variable sensorimotor experiences of pleasure and unpleasure, they gradually expand and develop into differentiated, consistent, relatively realistic representations of the self and the object world. Earlier forms of representation are based more on action sequences associated with need gratification, intermediate forms are based on specific perceptual features, and higher forms are more symbolic and conceptual. Various authors (Blatt, 1974; Krohn and Mayman, 1974) point to the constant and reciprocal interaction between past and present interpersonal relations and the development of representations. Whereas these schemata evolve from and are intertwined with the developmental internalization of object relations and ego functions (Mahler, 1968), the developing representations provide a new organization for experiencing object relations.

Two comprehensive scoring systems, one developed by Krohn and Mayman (1974) and another by Blatt, Brenneis, Schimek, and Glick (1976) have been found to be reliable, valid, and useful in experimentally assessing this concept. Although both systems have sparked an increasing amount of research (for reviews, see Hatcher and Krohn, 1980; Spear, 1980), studies regarding the clinical application of these scales, or of the systematic appraisal of object representations in a single case, appear far more sparingly in the literature.

Lerner (1980) applied three object representation scales, including that of Blatt et al., to the Rorschach responses of an adolescent girl who was tested upon admission to a psychiatric hospital. He found that inferences based solely on an appraisal of her object representations as manifest on the Rorschach accurately reflected the nature of her hospital stay and her response to the course of treatment. More specifically, he noted that

> her tendency to evoke extreme (infantile or malevolent) drive-drenched, non-mutual interchangeable representations of objects in action sequences coupled with content of an orally devouring, destructive, or extreme infantile nature all point to a representational configuration consistent with an anaclitic personality structure characterized by an early history of deprivation, unfulfilled neediness, and a profound sense of longing associated with a fear of abandonment and the loss of gratification. In fact, her hospitalization was permeated with numerous AWOL's all associated with separations and loss. . . . These losses appear to have triggered intense feelings of abandonment, pain and disappointment which swiftly led to suspiciousness and rage which could then only be contained by denial, pseudo-autonomy, and ultimate flight. [pp. 8–9].

Graham (1978) reported a case in which he found that his patient's level of self- and object representations, particularly as reflected in manifest dreams, changed during the course of the patient's analysis. He observed that during the earlier stages of treatment self- and object representation were relatively undifferentiated and expressed through elements in the physical environment, whereas, as treatment progressed, the patient's representations became more differentiated and were expressed increasingly in more whole human forms. He also found that paralleling the change in form of expression was a concomitant maturation of cognitive functioning from concrete-animistic to abstract-depersonated forms.

The case reported here, like Lerner's and Graham's, clearly illustrates the centrality to personality organization of specific object representations and how they find expression through a variety of psychological pathways—manifest content of dreams, early memories, transference paradigms, Rorschach responses. Mayman (1977) put it this way: the structure and content of these inner imagos, both conscious and unconscious, provide a substrate for all subsequent relationships. With my patient, the recapturing, bringing into full conscious awareness, and reconstructing of an early paternal imago enabled us to better appreciate, understand, and explore how her choice of men was in part determined by a compelling desire to both find and restore to health and wholeness the damaged, deformed, sickly father of her childhood.

In agreement with others (Mayman, 1977; Graham, 1978; Lerner, 1980), I have found that the individual's representational world, including the structure and content of the self- and object representations which populate it, serves as a powerful and determining experiential influence upon his sense of himself and others, and also upon his behavior. As therapist and patient alike come to recognize, grasp, and meticulously study these organizing structures and their derivatives, the patient's seemingly inconsistent and often incomprehensible behavior begins to take on coherence and direction.

A middle-aged male patient who presented with depressive and somatic symptoms noted that for inexplicable reasons he would periodically not come home from work till the early morning hours. Despite knowing that his not informing his wife of his lateness would cause her undue concern and distress, and that his feelings of guilt would be followed the next morning by violent bouts of vomiting, his behavior persisted. The manager of several furniture stores, he reported a somewhat similar phenomenon that would sometimes occur at work. While generally reliable, helpful, affable, and personable with employees and customers, he at times would withdraw deeply into himself, leaving him feeling distant, removed, and aloof and appearing to others as "not being there." When I pointed out to him that in either case he seemed to become a "missing person," this quickly led to a highly meaningful interchange regarding his feelings, as a youngster, about his father's frequent and prolonged absences. In essence, the part of him that became a "missing person" represented an identification with the absent father as well as the turning of a passive experience (being left) into an active one (leaving).

Upon greeting a second patient in my waiting room, I commented upon his new and particularly flashy shoes. He replied that it was part of his plight of "being all dressed up and having nowhere to go." The ensuing theme of his analytic hour related exclusively to movement. Specifically, he offered numerous examples of how others around him, including his wife, children, and colleagues, were on the move, while he, both personally and professionally, was "standing still." In time, we came to appreciate how his sense of himself as motionless and of others as perpetually in motion, was rooted in early experiences with an unreliable, inconsistently responsive, often unavailable mother who, emotionally, moved in and out of his life while he stayed put.

Summary

Patients with severe narcissistic disturbances who offer the (c) Rorschach response appear hypervigilant, overly sensitive, and excessively vulnerable. They manifest disturbances in the cohesion of the self and relate to others as either split-off parts of the self or as there to serve in the maintenance and restoration of the self. They are especially vulnerable to feelings of lowered self-esteem, disintegration anxiety, and depletion depression. Under stress there is a tendency to lapse into concretistic, stimulus-bound thinking in which there is a marked loss of perspective. Their heightened attunement to the visual, gestural, and emotional aspects of others, including the psychological examiner or psychotherapist, is understood as a recapitulation of very early, preverbal experiences with a sporadically responsive and often depressed mother. Excerpts from the presentation of a case illustrated the importance of self-sufficiency as a defense as well as the impact on structural development of early object loss. In addition, the content involved in several of this patient's (c) Rorschach responses matched similar content in manifest dreams and early memories, thereby pointing to the centrality in personality organization of selected object representations.

References

Appelbaum, S., & Colson, D. (1968), A re-examination of the color-shading Rorschach test response and suicide attempts. *J. Proj. Tech. Personal. Assess.*, 32:160–164.

——— Holtzman, P. (1962), The color-shading response and suicide. *J. Proj. Tech.*, 26:155–161.

Blatt, S. (1974), Levels of object representation in anaclitic and introjective depression.

The Psychoanalytic Study of the Child, 29:107–157. New Haven: Yale University Press.

——— Brenneis, C., Schimek, J., & Glick, M. (1976), A developmental analysis of the concept of the object on the Rorschach. Unpublished manuscript.

Deutsch, H. (1942), Some forms of emotional disturbance and their relationship to schizophrenia. *Psychoanal. Quart.*, 11:301–321.

Easer, R. (1972), Some observations on the treatment of the narcissistic character. Paper presented to the Canadian Psychoanalytic Association, Toronto, Ontario.

——— (1974), Empathic inhibition and psychoanalytic technique. *Psychoanal. Quart.*, 43:557–580.

Graham, I. (1978), Representational and cognitive aspects of a depressive personality. Paper presented to the Toronto Psychoanalytic Society, Toronto, Ontario.

Hatcher, R., & Krohn, A. (1980), Level of object representation and capacity for intensive psychotherapy in neurotics and borderlines. In: *Borderline Phenomena and the Rorschach Test*, ed. J. Kwawer, H. Lerner, P. Lerner, & A. Sugarman. New York: International Universities Press, pp. 299–320.

Kohut, H. (1971), *The Analysis of the Self*. New York: International Universities Press.

Krohn, A., & Mayman, M. (1974), Level of object representations in dreams and projective tests. *Bull. Menn. Clin.*, 38:445–466.

Lerner, H. (1980), An object representation approach to psychological assessment. Paper presented to the Society for Personality Assessment, Tampa, Florida.

Lerner, P. (1979), Treatment implications of the (c) response in the Rorschach records of patients with severe character pathology. *Ontario Psychologist*, 11:20–22.

Lerner, P., & Lerner, H. (1980), Rorschach assessment of primitive defenses in borderline personality structure. In: *Borderline Phenomena and the Rorschach Test*, ed. J. Kwawer, H. Lerner, P. Lerner, & A. Sugarman. New York: International Universities Press, pp. 257–274.

Mahler, M. (1968), *On Human Symbiosis and the Vicissitudes of Individuation. Vol. I: Infantile Psychosis*. New York: International Universities Press.

——— Pine, F., & Bergman, A. (1975), *The Psychological Birth of the Human Infant*. New York: Basic Books.

Mayman, M. (1977), A multi-dimensional view of the Rorschach movement response. In: *Rorschach Psychology*, ed. M. Rickers-Ovsiankina. New York: Robert E. Krieger, pp. 229–250.

Modell, A. (1975), A narcissistic defense against affects and the illusion of self-sufficiency. *Internat. J. Psycho-Anal.*, 56:275–282.

——— (1976), The holding environment and the therapeutic action of psychoanalysis. *J. Amer. Psychoanal. Assn.*, 24:285–307.

——— (1978), The conceptualization of the therapeutic action of psychoanalysis: The action of the holding environment. *Bull. Menn. Clin.*, 42:493–504.

Nagera, H. (1970), Children's reactions to the death of important objects: A developmental approach. *The Psychoanalytic Study of the Child*, 25:360–400. New York: International Universities Press.

Reich, A. (1960), Pathologic forms of self-esteem regulation. *The Psychoanalytic Study of the Child*, 15:215–232. New York: International Universities Press.

Schachtel, E. (1966), *Experiential Foundations of Rorschach's Test*. New York: Basic Books.

Singer, M. (1977), The borderline diagnosis and psychological tests: Review and research. In: *Borderline Personality Disorders: The Concept, the Syndrome, the Patient*, ed. P. Hartocollis. New York: International Universities Press.

Spear, W. (1980), The psychological assessment of structural and thematic object representations in borderline and schizophrenic patients. In: *Borderline Phenomena and the Rorschach Test*, ed. J. Kwawer, H. Lerner, P. Lerner, & A. Sugarman. New York: International Universities Press.

Sugarman, A. (1980), The borderline personality organization as manifested on psychological tests. In: *Borderline Phenomena and the Rorschach Test*, ed. J. Kwawer, H. Lerner, P. Lerner, & A. Sugarman. New York: International Universities Press, pp. 39–57.

Teicholz, J. (1978), A selective review of the psychoanalytic literature on theoretical conceptualizations of narcissism. *J. Amer. Psychoanal. Assn.*, 26:831–862.

Tolpin, M., & Kohut, H. (1978), The disorders of the self: The psychopathology of the first years of life. In: *Psychoanalysis and the Life Cycle*, ed. G. Pollock & S. Greenspan, NIMH Publication, Government Printing Office.

Winnicott, D. (1960), Ego distortion in terms of true and false self. In: *The Maturational Processes and the Facilitating Environment*. London: Hogarth Press, 1965.

Chapter 16

SELF- AND OBJECT REPRESENTATION IN BORDERLINE DISORDERS

HENRY M. BACHRACH and FREDERIC J. LEVINE

In recent years the study of borderline and related narcissistic disorders has captured the imagination of an extraordinary number of clinicians. Some say it is because changes in family structure and societal attitudes have altered the nature of psychopathological formations and that the type of patient seen today is somewhat different from that of years past. Other explanations are offered, but it certainly seems that Kernberg's brilliant, immensely successful, and now classic paper, "Borderline Personality Organization" (1967), did much to spark this interest. That paper offered the first comprehensive psychoanalytic schema for conceptualizing the psychopathology of a group of frequently encountered patients who before had been refractory to understanding and effective therapeutic management.

Kernberg proposed that among the many difficult-to-diagnose patients, who were not clearly either neurotic or psychotic, there existed a group whose intrapsychic organization was set stably between the two ranges of ego weakness. These were neither decompensating neurotic patients nor psychotic patients in remission. Rather, they were representatives of a syndrome with definable characteristics and typical conflicts and defenses. Descriptively, such patients presented more instinctualized and pervasive symptomatology than is generally seen in neuroses, but in familiar circumstances their functioning remained relatively adaptive and revealed no evidence of primary thought disorder. The extent of their ego weaknesses became manifest only when core conflicts were stirred and especially in relatively unstructured circumstances. To conceptualize their characteristic ego pathology, Kernberg (1966, 1967) blended object relational and ego psychological concepts. Such patients were seen as struggling with primitive (primarily oral) aggression and need, and as making defensive use of archaic levels of mentation, e.g. splitting, in order to segregate internal representations of "good," nurturing maternal objects (and associated "good" self-representations and affects) from projectively conceived "bad," depriving object representations (along with associated "bad" self-representations and affects). The primitive defensive operations of splitting, projective identification, primitive idealization, and denial were considered the fundamental causes of the ego weakness manifested in disturbances in anxiety tolerance and impulse control, an overdependence of reality testing on stimulus nutriment (external structure), and other "non-specific" disturbances in the ego functions of judgment, thought organization, and reality testing. The diagnosis therefore "depends on characteristic ego pathology and not on the descriptive symptoms" (Kernberg, 1975, p. 9). Kernberg's formulation led him to recommend a specific form of expressive psychotherapy (not psychoanalysis) as the treatment of choice. In this method, the main focus was on the interpretation of the archaic defenses within the *here and now* of the therapeutic interaction, and judicious management and interpretation of the latent negative transference in order to protect the volatile object tie to the therapist from disruption.

Since that time Kernberg has produced a score of papers on this subject, Kohut has set down his thoughts on related matters from a different perspective, new names have appeared on the scene (e.g. Masterson, Rinsley, Stolorow), the work of the British object relations school (e.g. Klein, Fairbairn, Guntrip, Winnicott) has received fresh attention, and symposia on borderline disorders have become the order of the day. There certainly is a lot of activity, and though not all agree with these new formulations, only a few have questioned them. Those who have are not convinced that the patients of today are very different from those of past years, that object relational and ego psychological concepts can be readily blended, or that the currently popular views and prescriptions deliver as much as they promise (Pruyser, 1975; Appelbaum, 1979; Calef and Weinshel, 1979). They suggest that the apparent clarity and precision of these formulations does not always do justice to the actualities of clinical practice.

The aim of our inquiry is neither to join this debate nor to further herald the coming of a new emotional plague. We are not compelled by the evidence put forth regarding a decrease in the incidence of disorders that can be understood and treated psychoanalytically. However, we have in our own work found many of Kernberg's formulations helpful in understanding and treating a delimited group of patients whom we consider representative of a borderline syndrome. In what follows we shall address ourselves to the presentation of self- and object representation characteristic of this syndrome in diagnostic psychological testing.[1]

Our focus will be on those patients who most clearly exemplify and epitomize our understanding of borderline personality organization—namely, individuals who are able to maintain relatively adaptive attitudes in familiar, average expectable circumstances, and who have no history of extended or frequent psychosis but whose functioning is highly vulnerable to regression, at times to a psychotic-like degree due to the activation of significant intrapsychic conflicts, particularly in relatively unstructured circumstances. Such individuals have basically good reality testing and stable if primitive attachments to objects and the object world. Expressive psychotherapy is the treatment of choice, though external structure may sometimes be required as an adjunct. This is essentially Fenichel's characterization (1945) and corresponds also to Rapaport, Gill, and Schafer's perspective (1945). It is long-established clinical lore that such patients are able to maintain relatively productive problem solving attitudes on structured diagnostic tests (e.g. the Wechsler Scales) with only a minimum of transient lapses in critical attitude when salient conflicts are elicited, whereas their functioning on less structured tasks (e.g. the Rorschach) is dominated by varying degrees of primary process thinking. Singer (1977) made note of this observation in her presentation on the diagnosis of borderline disorders from psychological tests at the first International Conference on Borderline Disorders, and Carr, Goldstein, Hunt, and Kernberg (1979) have confirmed it empirically. Kernberg (1977) has made special note of this phenomenon in his paper on diagnostic interviewing.

[1]Because the specific nature of test stimuli and their manner of presentation can influence the data generated, we feel that we should specify our approach to psychological testing. Our approach follows in the manner and tradition of diagnostic testing developed by Rapaport, Schafer, and their colleagues (Rapaport, Gill, and Schafer, 1945; Schafer, 1954, 1967). An attempt is made to construct a model of the patient's intrapsychic functioning, particularly in its structural, dynamic, and adaptive aspects, based on the organization of thought processes expressed in test responses. The fundamental rationale is that thought organization is integral to the personality it reflects, and that the study of thought content together with its organization under various known conditions permits clinical formulation of the content and structure of conflicts. For this reason it is necessary to provide opportunities for studying a broad range of ego functions under varied conditions of structure. A test *battery* is therefore always employed, consisting, at a minimum, of a Wechsler Scale (for the assessment of a broad range of ego functions under average expectable conditions corresponding to the structure of everyday life), a Rorschach test (for the assessment of the resilience of ego function in the absence of structure-maintaining cues), and the TAT (for its ability to elicit information about the interaction of dynamic themes and structure, and especially for its ability to elicit representational themes). We also often employ additional tests for further confirmation of inferences derived from the core battery (e.g. Word Association Test, Early Memories Test). Our inferences from these data are guided by the psychoanalytic model of the mind, with particular emphasis on structural propositions.

Although theories such as Kernberg's may seem to provide the basis for a sign approach to differential diagnosis, we believe this to be neither possible nor desirable, and we will make no attempt to provide a differential diagnostic system or "cookbook." Kernberg's conceptual lexicon is set at a relatively high level of abstraction (the level of clinical theory, according to Waelder, 1962) and does not translate in a one-to-one fashion into observable acts or descriptive traits. For example, Kernberg (1967) holds that splitting "is an essential defensive operation of all borderline personality organization which underlies all others which follow"; he uses "the term 'splitting' in a restricted and limited sense, referring only to the active process of keeping apart introjections and identifications of opposing quality" (p. 667). While one may find *instances* of concrete test responses which appear to reflect this process, such as rapid or isolated oscillation between "all-good" idealized images and "all-bad" devalued ones on the Rorschach (Grala, 1980), such imagery is not frequent or dramatic, nor is it necessary or sufficient as an indicator of borderline personality organization. We believe it an oversimplification to seek direct observable referents of highly complex and abstract clinical propositions.[2] However, we do find that when the patterning and configuration of test performance is viewed as a whole, it is possible to detect subtle tendencies for representations to be cast in extreme and instinctualized terms, reflecting the coloring of ego functions by pervasive splitting.

The clinically derived formulations of borderline functioning, then, cannot be directly or literally translated into test signs, and are not manifest in the simple terms that might be anticipated from the contemporary literature on borderline personality. Nonetheless, these formulations are valuable in developing a comprehensive picture of a personality by using a test battery to systematically vary structure and other stimulus dimensions. They point

[2]It is not uncommon to find levels of abstraction confused in efforts to apply clinical and theoretical concepts derived from psychoanalytic observation to the task of interpreting test data. Sugarman (1980), for example, confuses levels of conceptualization in his efforts to identify Rorschach manifestations of borderline functioning. While correctly observing that borderline patients often relate to persons as part-objects, he incorrectly translates this clinical finding into the expectation that borderline patients will produce more part than whole human responses. The basic error here is that "part-object" ways of relating does not mean an interest in literally disembodied human parts, but rather that objects are related to mainly in terms of their isolated (partial) need-gratifying and punishing functions in the context of limited empathy. There is scant recognition of the needs and other qualities of the objects. Part-object functioning is discernible only in the overall pattern of representation in the entire test performance. An actual inability to perceive whole responses could reflect extreme impairment of the response process and often bespeaks a greater (or a different) type of ego weakness than is generally characteristic of borderline patients. For further discussion of the tendency to mingle and confuse levels of abstraction in clinical and theoretical work, see Slap and Levine (1978).

to ways of using the examination to delineate the nature and types of environmental influences to which a given patient may respond and to the relevance and possibilities of interpretive interventions in psychotherapy. Further, they provide a framework within which to identify specific salient core conflictual fantasies, the extent and kinds of regression that can occur, and potential transference and countertransference paradigms expressive of the individual's characteristic conflictual fantasy themes.

Self- and Object Representation

The Unconscious Fantasy Function

Our approach to understanding the representational world of borderline patients begins with our understanding of the nature of unconscious fantasy activity and its relationship to secondary process functioning. During childhood all people develop characteristic conceptions—organized, regnant, and persisting—of their bodies, themselves, and their archaic objects. Because such fantasies are the products of childish minds, they reflect, in symbolically condensed form, the conflict-laden passions and imagined dangers of childhood, along with the defenses against them. Since normally these are repressed, they do not accommodate to later experiences and persist unconsciously in their primeval form, shaping and guiding subsequent experience and forming the core of character structure and self- and object representations. There is a unity to such conflictual fantasies in any individual that is expressed both in cognitive contents and in ego structures, in feelings and actions as well as in thought. These fantasies are *structures*.[3] (This isomorphism of form and content can be seen with special clarity in the test battery, especially the Rorschach.) A life story can be understood as a playing out of the scenarios derived from these powerful, unconsciously organized structures.

Since unconscious fantasies are ubiquitous, then, their presence and persistence is in no way a reflection of mental aberration. In the hypothetically normal individual, one might postulate that they would remain so effectively repressed as to be, to all intents and purposes, innocuous and undetectable (although perhaps receiving direct expression in the brief and reversible regressions of creative activity, as well as exerting a continuous but "silent" influence on characteristic ego functioning). Psychopathology, in contrast, can be understood as a disturbance in the relationship between unconscious fan-

[3]For more extended discussions of unconscious fantasy and its relation to personality functioning, see Rapaport (1957), Beres (1962), Arlow (1963, 1969), Arlow and Brenner (1964, 1969), Jacobson (1964), and Klein (1976). Luborsky (1977) and Levine and Luborsky (1981) have provided an experimental paradigm for exploring the vicissitudes of unconscious fantasies in the content of treatment hours.

tasies and the adaptive behavioral surface. In neurosis, where there is a firm attachment to the object world, characterized by whole objects in which "good" and "bad" elements are combined, we see the return of the repressed in the form of ego-alien symptoms or character pathology with little loss of ego autonomy or distortion in relations to reality even under highly conflictual circumstances. At the other extreme, in psychosis, stable ties to the object world have not been attained, and the boundaries between self and object, fantasy and external reality, are substantially impaired. Here we see severe flaws in reality testing and in adaptive and critical functioning even under average expectable circumstances. Borderline patients fall between these extremes, and share characteristics with each, in various ways. There are three interacting factors that determine the way and the extent to which the unconscious fantasy function will influence any manifest act: the strength and structure of the ego, the presence and strength of salient conflict, and the amount of external structure present. The latter two factors are systematically varied in the diagnostic examination, and we expect the following results. The neurotic will show little primitivization of function, but will react with defensive failures (symptoms) when conflict is aroused. The psychotic's defensive efforts will be primarily narcissistic and not aimed at protecting ties to the object world. These patients will show primitivization in all conditions of structure, with gross disturbances in reality testing. The borderline patient will show primitivization of ego function specifically when dealing with unstructured situations and most intensely when conflict is aroused. Defenses will be oriented toward maintaining "good" images of important objects, and regressive distortions in self- and object representations and reality testing will occur to this end. They will be greatest and most frequent in the context of primitively conceived, blatant versions of superordinate organizing fantasies, especially those related to intense archaic rage. Because of his relatively stable object ties, the borderline patient will recover from these regressions quickly; we will therefore find dramatic contrasts and inconsistencies in the primitiveness of his functioning. Consistent with these archaic structural characteristics of borderline patients, certain archaic thematic contents will characterize their fantasies, their self- and object representations, and the unconsciously determined scenarios underlying their relationships with objects. Here will be found conflicts centering on oral aggression and rage; intense but usually terrifying dependent longings; fantasies of return to an imagined early state of union with "good" maternal representations; extreme wishes for power and possessiveness with objects, often coexisting or alternating with fantasies of submission; bodily sensation and deformation; and extremes of primitive sadomasochism.

Unconscious Fantasy and the Primitivization of Ego Function

From the structural point of view, what distinguishes the vicissitudes of unconscious fantasy formation in borderline disorders is the degree to which unconscious fantasy activity impinges upon the conflict-free ego sphere. While there is no person, however "normal," whose ego functions do not partly develop in accord with unconscious fantasy activity, the perception, thought, motility, memory, etc. of relatively normal or neurotic persons shows a greater autonomy from its influence than is the case in borderline conditions. In psychosis, the domination and distortion of the conflict-free ego sphere by unconscious fantasy is greater than in borderline conditions. What is therefore diagnostic is the degree of ego autonomy or, conversely, the primitivization of ego function. From the perspective of the test battery, persons functioning within neurotic ranges of ego weakness will be able to maintain critical and productive attitudes on both structured and unstructured tasks, though their responses may be colored by unconscious fantasy and defense. For example, when asked Why are laws necessary? one somewhat angry and compulsive neurotic patient answered, "To control what people do; without laws you would have chaos." Unconscious fantasy activity colors the response, but only at a reasonable level of critical thought. A patient with masochistic preoccupations cast his response in terms of victimization: "Without laws women and children would be exploited." By contrast, a patient functioning within the psychotic range of ego weakness is less likely to maintain critical attitudes on this sort of structured task. This is what psychosis is: the distortion of adaptive and critical functioning by unconscious wishful and defensive demands in average expectable circumstances. "Laws are necessary to keep people from experimenting on one another. You know how the Nazis tried to turn the Jews into homosexuals with their medical experiments . . ." On structured tasks the performance of borderline patients is not markedly different from patients functioning at a neurotic level.

On relatively unstructured tasks, however, such as the Rorschach, the performance of the borderline patient diverges from that of the neurotic. Where the neurotic patient is able to maintain relatively critical attitudes in the absence of external structure or reality-orienting cues, the borderline patient has difficulty. The regressive impingement of primary process becomes more the order of the day. However, unlike the psychotic individual, the borderline patient is more resiliently able to go on to restore the integrity of his test responses and object relations after a regression. This mode of functioning can be described from a number of interrelated points of view.

George Klein (1976) and Slap and Saykin (1980) have described unconscious fantasy activity (and other mental contents) using Piaget's concept of the schema. Normally, they point out, mental schemata are the basis upon which reality is understood. New experiences are assimilated to existing schemata, which may in turn be modified by accommodation to new data. Repressed schemata, however, do not accommodate to new experience, but instead tend to alter the perception of new stimuli by assimilation. We have found it useful to conceptualize the continuum of ego weakness in these terms. From this perspective, for example, borderline patients assimilate new experiences to a greater degree than do neurotics, thereby rendering unconscious fantasies more prominent and regressions more fantasy-specific.

From a developmental point of view, these observations have much in common with Winnicott's description (1951) of *transitional phenomena,* experiences in which there is a kernel of reality heavily infused with (assimilated to) wish-fulfilling fantasy. Here there is a merger of aspects of the self with the perception of the object. Transitional phenomena occupy an important place in the development of object constancy during the normal separation-individuation phase of development. They aid the toddler in developing a sense of separateness by containing the fear of object loss. They give him the fantasy of control over his important primal objects and mitigate his rage when he is frustrated by them. This is similar to the internal struggles that occupy borderline patients, and there are many descriptive and functional parallels between their highly distorted, egocentric (but stable) modes of relating and the toddler's transitional mode. Like the infant of rapprochement, the borderline adult is reassured by the clear-cut presence of external objects (as on structured tests) to which he is able to relate adaptively, but becomes frustrated and threatened when the object is not clearly evident in familiar and well-defined ways (as on unstructured tests). What results is that the borderline patient tends to seek stability by assimilating any new and unstructured stimulus to his unconscious schemata. Perceptions lose their differentiation from fantasies, meanings, and feelings, and become united in the animistic reifications of transitional phenomena (Modell, 1968, p. 33).

The borderline patient's difficulties in modulating regressive experiences provides another useful perspective on the nature of his dealings with objects. Controlled regression, after all, is required for optimal performance in the test battery. Adaptive regressions are required, for example, for imagining movement on the Rorschach test and for the construction of motives and feelings on the TAT. Adaptive regression is the metapsychological parallel of empathy. Temporary and controlled identifications with others are required to sense their motives and feelings, but as Reik (1948) put it, "What is heard with the third ear must be heard again and examined in the control room of reason" (p. 438). Without the latter step, "sensing" cannot be distinguished from perception, empathy from sympathy, and the recognition of the feelings and motives of another from unconsciously fantasized "oneness" bereft of critical judgment. Limited in this latter capacity, the borderline patient thinks *with* his objects instead of thinking *about* them in the sense of *einfülung* (Schafer, 1958; Bachrach, 1968; Beres and Arlow, 1974). The neurotic individual imagines, creates, and senses feelings, motives, and relations among the characters of a TAT story, for example, *but does not lose sight of the fact that these are imaginative products of which he himself is the author*. Similarly, the perception of inkblots may be imaginatively imbued with activity, but without a loss of perspective as to the origin of that perceived activity. By contrast, borderline patients think *with* test stimuli and believe the motives and feelings they "see" are *actually* depicted by the perceptual givens of the stimulus; they believe that what they "see" in the TAT figures is actually shown in facial expressions, or that perceived relationships in Rorschach inkblots are in fact *meant* to be there. This is thinking *with* an object in a manner in which regression is not transient or subject to reversal by critical judgment.

Rapaport, Gill, and Schafer (1945) have identified several manifestations of primitivized ego functioning on the Rorschach, i.e. the response categories of *fabulized combination, confabulation*, and *perceptual distortion*. Responses of these types are frequently found in borderline patients and can be understood as expressions of these patients' pervasive tendencies to assimilate the ambiguous test stimuli to their dominant unconscious schemata, without the corrective influence of critical judgment and perspective. For instance, illustrating a remark by Rapaport, Gill, and Schafer (1945), "What appears to lie at the core of the fabulized combination is that a spatial relationship in the inkblot is taken as an immutable, real relationship" (p. 433), one borderline patient took certain aspects of one inkblot too literally and produced an image of a man with *four* arms. Though the perceptual accuracy of the response was not in question, the disturbance here (of thought) was that people do not have four arms and the momentary valence of the stimulus (and its associated unconscious fantasy) dominated critical judgment. Another borderline patient, whose life was dominated by fantasies of bodily and intellectual imperfection, saw the whole of an inkblot as the body of a woman and a tiny speck at the top as the head (size distortion). A provocative borderline patient rendered Card IV of the Rorschach as "King Kong taking a great big shit." Here the portion of the inkblot referred to as King Kong was a popular enough response, and the portion referred to as feces could readily be seen as feces—but, when the two were combined, the feces were disproportionately large, nearly as large, in fact, as King Kong himself.

Rapaport, Gill, and Schafer (1945) define confabulation in the Rorschach as a lack of justification for the specificity and affective loading of a response (i.e. "two people lying down . . . somebody helping them, nature might be helping them . . . might be God"), or thinking in terms of "participation" (i.e. two conceptually separate areas of an inkblot connected for arbitrary, stimulus-specific reasons, e.g. color), or "transductive reasoning" (i.e. "two people too tired to get up, so the other *must* be helping them"). One borderline patient put it this way, referring to the two popularly seen animals on Card VIII: "They are holding on tight and struggling to see which one will overcome the other.'' Another believed ''they have to maintain their delicate balance so they won't be carried off into oblivion.''

Patients functioning within a neurotic range of ego weakness show no more than marginal amounts of the kind of reasoning expressed in fabulized combination or confabulation, and no more than marginal levels of perceptual distortion, at least insofar as they are attempting to maintain realistic attitudes. (This is why the attitude of a patient producing such responses must always be assessed. Narcissistic patients without ego weaknesses often attempt to be fanciful or provocative in these ways.) However, the presence of perceptual distortion, confabulation, and fabulized combination does not clearly distinguish the borderline patient from the psychotic. While it is true that some psychotic patients show greater primitivization in ego functioning or in the content of their fantasy expressions, what *clearly* distinguishes the psychotic patient from the borderline is that primary process reasoning is evident on structured tasks as well.[4] The psychotic's tendency to regress during times of internal stress is not readily subject to correction by critical judgment and reality testing, even when dealing with clear, structured situations, because ties to fantasy representations are far greater than to the world of external objects.

Frequent Fantasy Themes of Borderline Patients

Throughout our discussion, we have emphasized the close intertwining of response contents, formal thought characteristics, and orientation to the test task and the examiner. All of these modalities of functioning express the shifting, conflicted currents of unconscious fantasy systems, and all are intimately interrelated. We have also stressed that what primarily characterizes borderlines, at least for differential diagnostic purposes, is the nature and extent of assimilatory encroachment of unconscious fantasies on the conflict-free ego sphere (Kernberg's ''nonspecific'' and ''specific'' ego weaknesses). However, we also find a number of common themes characteristic of borderlines' fantasy lives, especially as compared to patients with less severe ego weaknesses. In schematic form, as we have indicated already, the major concerns of borderline patients can be described as clustering around primitive orality and oral aggression, regressive merging fantasies (often with the pur-

[4]This statement requires a certain qualification. Contaminated responses and severe disturbances of language (i.e. neologisms) are not present in the test performance of borderline or neurotic patients. A contaminated response confuses and integrates distinctly separate conceptual and perceptual realms. For example, one schizophrenic patient saw the two popularly seen people on Card III of the Rorschach as ''close friends'' because the red area of the inkblot between them looked like ''joined hearts.''

pose of protecting the love object from aggression),[5] fusions of oedipal and sexual wishes with orality, wishes for power and submission, and intense sadomasochism.

The passive, defensive attitudes of many borderline patients are an especially prominent area of expression of their often acutely masochistic object relationships. They may feel helplessly unable to use imagination to make up TAT stories, for example, because they feel empty, or feel constrained by the perceived realities of the test stimulus (''I can't tell what this character is thinking by looking at his facial expression—just can't do it. I'm sorry''). Such patients often attempt unconsciously to engage the examiner in sadomasochistic struggles. The examiner may feel tempted to ''pull teeth'' in an effort to encourage responsiveness, or conversely to become so gentle and inhibited as to fail to conduct sufficient inquiry. Borderline patients also often express their intensely painful, masochistic impulses in Rorschach imagery: torn leaves, raw wounds, animal skins which have been recently, freshly removed from the animal (''not a bear rug, but a jaggedly unfinished hide'').

For many borderline patients, primitive pain is a prominent feature of their infantile experiences with their mothers—dominating mothers who love through control, depressed mothers who ''model'' pain. ''The nature of the object tie during the earliest period of life is critical for the qualitative structuralization of affects. . . . If the affects, especially those primal and primitive affects associated with the early self and self-object experience, take a predominantly painful direction, then a set is established wherein pain . . . connotes the original self-object . . .'' (Valenstein, 1973, pp. 373–374). This is consistent with Kernberg's emphasis on the borderline's coloring of oedipal and sexual longings with oral rage.

Narcissistic and borderline patients find separation from love objects unbearable, and frequently attempt to prevent loss through total submission, including acceptance of humiliation and physical abuse. Such patterns of object relationship are commonly seen in the TAT stories. One woman patient told a story of a woman who caught her husband in marital infidelity, but as she went on the story metamorphosed strangely so that this situation was construed as the *wife's* fault, and a reason for her to be nicer and more submissive to him. Instead of an offense against the wife, the patient gradually, and with brazen unconcern for logic, transformed the husband's act into

[5]In their ''The Psychopathology of the Psychoses: A Proposed Revision,'' Arlow and Brenner (1969) suggested that conflicts over aggressive impulses are more frequent in psychosis than in neuroses and that consequently psychotic patients have special needs for protecting their objects from their projected aggression. This is seen as a fundamental cause of the serious disruptions in their relationship with the world of objects. This finding merits considerable attention in the understanding of borderline disorders.

something that hurt *him,* and a subtle signal intended to alert the wife to problems in their marriage: ''Some kind of a hint. 'Why do you think I . . . destroy something we had together that was so good?'' The wife goes on to try to help him, ''she shows him some warmth.'' Ultimately, despite her love and convoluted efforts to please, ''he turns away anyhow.''

Because of their intolerance of separation and loss, the object relationships of borderline patients are often marked by extreme possessiveness. Efforts are made to unite self and object as one in fantasy, so the needed object has little real independent existence, and serves mainly as a prop (Beres and Arlow, 1974). This provides yet another perspective on borderline patients' highly arbitrary ways of dealing with the diagnostic examination. The examiner and test stimuli may be seen as props without a fully independent existence. Thus, totally idiosyncratic Rorschach inkblot areas may be invested with special meanings, the fabric of TAT stories twisted and rationalized with empty intellectualization, or frequent digressions made from the tasks at hand in order to tell personal anecdotes. Borderline patients often talk *at* the examiner, as though he were a tireless, feelingless stenographer, or go on rapidly with lengthy responses, ignoring requests to pause so that the examiner may catch up with his note taking or request clarification.

A final important feature of the thematic content of borderline patients' productions is its relatively great responsiveness to major ongoing life events. These may be depicted with great frequency and clarity in manifest content. This is because current or recent conflict-evoking situations will lend strength to the patients' unconscious fantasies, *and these will then exert a very strong assimilative impact on test behavior and responses.* It is therefore often useful to obtain information about these patients' lives. Such data, when integrated with the examiner's inferences, often make it possible to better understand fantasies and precipitating situations, much more than in neurotic patients.

Case Illustration

The patient was a forty-one-year-old unmarried businessman highly successful in a specialty involving numbers and calculations. He lived with his aged parents and had few other social relationships. His only long-lasting relationship with a woman had ended around the time he sought treatment. His main interest, ''more important than work,'' was in a sporting activity around which he arranged his life. He had done well in school and in his military service.

The patient's mother suffered from crippling infirmities which she had developed while he was away on vacation several years earlier, and he had not taken a vacation since. He said that he suspected that her illness was partly psychogenic, a reaction to his vacation. He described his father as a man who had always "been afraid to express emotion and let people know about it," including positive feelings the father may have felt toward the patient. His only sibling was a sister seven years younger, a divorcee with two children, who had frequent difficulties with men. He said he did not "really know her."

The patient sought psychiatric consultation for severe anxiety and somatic symptoms occurring when he had to make public presentations, as well as for his distress over losing his girlfriend. He had no history of psychosis or other disabling disorders, and supportive-expressive psychotherapy was recommended. He was referred for diagnostic testing several years into this treatment because of a mutually perceived impasse in the progress of the work; he intellectualized endlessly and got nowhere.

Consistent with his clinical history of adaptive success in familiar, average-expectable circumstances, the patient maintained productive problem solving attitudes on relatively structured tasks, and he turned in IQ scores within the Very Superior range (Verbal IQ: 137, Performance IQ: 123). He approached such tasks in an organized, precise manner and his responses were very much "to the point." In this manner, for example, he achieved a perfect score on the Information subtest of the WAIS, made only one error on the Arithmetic subtest (he couldn't believe $60.00 could be a weekly salary), and performed almost flawlessly on the Block Design, Picture Arrangement, and Story Recall subtests. Here is an example. When asked *What should you do if you found an envelope in the street that was sealed, stamped, and addressed?* he directly answered, "Put it in the mailbox." But even on the well-structured tests, this controlled manner of responding did not always prevail. At times, when certain questions touched upon conflict-laden unconscious fantasies, transient primitivizations and regressive lapses in his usually realistic and critical attitudes occurred.

The first such clearly regressive lapse occurred on the Comprehension subtest when he was asked *Why should people keep away from bad company?* There was an immediate pressure toward regression (assimilation) which he was able to hold in check until the examiner inquired into the meaning of his response: "A simple answer is that bad company will *corrupt* in some way. (He goes on about the risks of being seen with bad company.) I've recently been thinking people can be corrupted to almost any degree with appropriate *prodding*. (He is asked what he means.) I've been talking to my doctor about possible *latent homosexuality* . . . and decided the issue doesn't come up if you avoid homosexual company, just as people who become *swingers* now wouldn't have twenty years ago . . . they are corrupted . . . Germans were corrupted into not seeing what they were doing to the Jewish people . . . I hadn't thought of all the ramifications . . . *cannibalism*. Now I'm more convinced than before." Thoughts such as *corruption* are instinctualized equivalents of their more autonomous counterparts, i.e. influence. Yet how far removed is *cannibalism* from the original question! The presence of specific conflictual fantasy themes of aggression, exploitation, control, self-doubt, identity, and passive feminine longing seem implied by his response. At this early point in the test battery, one might infer, although very tentatively, that primitive sadism and oral rage may be expressed within a passive masochistic fantasy involving projection and efforts to segregate self and object into good and bad. Is he struggling against succumbing to passive longing in his desire to avoid being "corrupted"? Perhaps we shall not be surprised if his thoughts of external influence later become elaborated into more direct expressions of nurturant longing, perhaps reflecting specific unconscious fantasies of union with idealized maternal part-introjects. Perhaps, too, we shall find further *formal* expression of such regressive wishes in confabulations and other primitive forms of thinking in which test stimuli are dealt with in a transitional object mode, showing incomplete distinction between fantasy and external reality. Yet, here, the regressive quality of this response is easily reversed as he goes on to deal with the next few questions in his more characteristically to-the-point style; all that it takes is a fresh, more neutral (for him) question, a small shift in the focus of his attention to the more familiar and comfortable.

But this man's need for control of instinctual pressures is intense. Several questions later, when asked *Why does the state require people to get a license in order to get married?* the regressive pull resurfaces and the conflictual fantasy themes of interpersonal dominance and submission reassert themselves with intensity and diminished judgment: "I'm tempted to say I just plain don't know. . . . (He ruminates.) Obviously the State wants control . . . a license is a way of ensuring that control. . . . It provides delays . . . it *forces* people to think for at least a day or two . . . and permits checking, theoretically, that people are who they say they are."

It is in this manner that the patient responds to relatively structured, familiar, average expectable tasks: well-organized, precise, and to the point when salient conflicts are not stirred up by test stimuli; more carefully, hesitatingly, and compulsively when he grows less sure of himself (e.g. his approach to the more difficult Block Design tasks); and occasionally, but infrequently, with transient reversible regression when test items touch upon salient conflict. The patterning of his subtest scores shows no marked elevations or drops, there is no systematic evidence of primary thought disorder, and while there are occasional instinctualized references in the contents of his ideas, none reach bizarre proportions. His usually controlled, efficient performance on structured tasks illustrates the borderline patient's ability to cling to clear-cut reality in nonconflictual situations, without primitivization of ego functions by the assimilative effects of unconscious fantasy. This is one indication of the relatively greater tie to the object world that distinguishes these individuals from psychotic patients.

When the reality-orienting structures of the examination are diminished, the picture begins to change, but in quantitative and not qualitative terms. Regressions are more pronounced, unconscious fantasies more intrusive, but they are still reversible and set within an overall context of organization and task orientation, especially when test stimuli are perceived less conflictually. Many of his TAT stories thus remain critically attuned, but some do not. For example, on Card 2 confusion and paralyzing indecision emerge in an object related fantasy. "The key character is the young woman . . . who is very pensive. Going to school . . . the man plowing . . . reminds her of her boyfriend who is far away . . . would like to be with him. . . . In order to, she would have to leave this country setting which she likes very much." So far, a rather typical story of conflict. But now, at first in the guise of intellectualization, self and object distinctions weaken and the "ordinary" story becomes transformed into a highly dramatic, personalized fantasy, as the unconscious conflicts exert greater assimilatory effect. "The man symbolizes the robustness of the country and the good part of hard work. The woman leaning against the tree symbolizes the hard work . . . the harshness of the country, the cross that the country woman has to bear. . . . She is with another baby . . . and the girl in the foreground . . . relates to the robustness of the place [but] . . . is aware of the harshness and sorrow that we clearly see in the face of the [older] woman. . . . The man's horse appears to be distracted by something . . . appears to be very little connection among the three people. . . . Looking at it more closely . . . doesn't seem to be any plow attached [to the horse], that's the problem with it. In fact . . . doesn't even seem to be an obvious connection of the horse and man. . . . The woman is obviously very beautiful. . . . Part of what she is thinking is how she would be less beautiful if she were pregnant like the woman leaning against the tree. (He goes on for several minutes about details of the horse and another farmer coming from the next field.) The man appears to be . . . in control of what goes on. . . . The woman against the tree . . . would probably be his wife. (He again comments on the man and horse and reveals his burgeoning anxiety by joking that the strong wind outside the examiner's office may blow the window out.) Neither woman appears to be wearing a wedding ring . . . possibly the [older] woman is pregnant and not married . . . in which case it really is a hard life in the country . . . makes her an outcast among the country folk." Here the progressive failure of the patient's strained defenses is reflected both in the content of his thinking and in its formal aspects (i.e. the fluid shifts in his relationship to the stimulus and the examiner as momentary parts of his object world). He shows, on the one hand, a blurred distinction between fantasy and the objective properties of the test stimulus in his reference to the figures as "symbols," and, on the other, an inability to tolerate regression sufficiently to make the slight imaginative step needed to infer obvious connections between the horse and plow or the man and wife. The optimal balance between fantasy and judgment is lacking. Instead the subjectivity of ''symbol'' is juxtaposed to the hyperobjectivity enacted in his inability to infer connections among many of the figures. Here the content (i.e. poor connections between objects) may be a manifestation of his unconscious struggle against regressive dependent longings—perhaps a basis for his isolated, lonely life. The increasing disorganization of his story also reflects his difficulties in dealing with the examiner as a separate, stable object to whom he must communicate clearly. The specific unconscious fantasy themes reflected in the story are about dependence, separation, overidentification of one person with another, projective identification of people with quasi-natural forces, lack of connection or relationship between people, and submission to harsh fate as the alternative to separation and loss. These are all issues having to do with needs for objects, the fear of losing them, and also the fear of imagined consequences of being too close to the object. The imagery of pain and suffering that is often found in connection with such unconscious, masochistic struggles appears in this story.

The man's superficial awareness of his own difficulties in separating from his family (and his therapist) is depicted in his story in response to Card 3, which he knows is autobiographical. Here again, as with Card 2, repetitive thematic concerns emerge regarding weakness and dependence on the one hand, and loneliness and emptiness on the other. His ready identification with the female figure in the story also raises a question about the conflictual elements in his feminine identification and their contribution to his passivity. ''Woman here is in terrible distress, she has broken down and is crying . . . feeling very alone . . . mother has died, she just doesn't know what to do. . . . Be in this condition for some time . . . feeling very hopeless. She'll start pulling herself together . . . maybe as long as a week before she stops withdrawing. . . . It's not just collapse but complete withdrawal . . . suggest she'll never be able to lead an open life even when she recovers . . . never did before . . . very dependent on parents, so she is someone I would feel sorry for, nothing one can do . . . will just have to lead this sheltered, secluded life forever, certainly never marry.'' He added, ''Maybe I fear that this is what will happen to me if I don't hold myself together.'' As we shall see later, one motive to struggle *against* passive dependence is his need to control intense hostility directed at maternal introjects. The strength of the encroachment of his inner fantasy world is shown with special clarity in this story, both by his identification with the story character and by his extensive investment of the character with motives, feelings, and, indeed, a whole life-plan that have little or no basis in the picture. His reification of the story figure in the transitional object mode is shown by the fact that he has real, and strong, feelings about her.

In the next several TAT stories he was able to characterize objects with understandable, familiar, and even complex thoughts, feelings, and motivations. His approach was compulsive and showed good judgment, and the emerging themes centered about passive longing and separation set within the context of obsessional defenses. Perhaps he was becoming better acclimated to the task and therefore less confused and prone to regression. But then on Card 11, yet another decrease in structure, and yet another transient regression: primitivization in the *formal* aspects of his thinking and *contents* more intensely depicting his dominant unconscious fantasy concern with struggles with passive longing. He experienced parts of the picture "surrealistically," and the story character reacts to them *as though he had the perspective of an outside observer*. At one point these surrealistic elements even seemed to be described as mental creations *of the character* (i.e. "explosions in his mind")—like dreams. This shifting between the storyteller's and the character's frames of reference, in which fantasy and reality are interchanged, is similar to his idea on Card 2, where the characters "symbolize" states or ideas. There seems an identification between storyteller and character; both are driven by the fantasy of infantile nurture, but for both the prospects are a nightmare, a dangerous state in which oral aggression is rampant and projectively feared. Both character and storyteller struggle to be vigilant and to avoid regressive retreat into a sleeplike passivity. Card 11: "Am I supposed to look at it in this position? (A reaction to the lack of clearly defined forms.) I don't see any people here. (He begins to carefully explore the visible details.) I do see rock formations . . . some sort of reptile . . . an arched bridge heading . . . I guess into a castle because nowhere else would have a bridge like that. (After an intellectualized effort he tries to distinguish less clear forms and to synthesize a story. Then he regresses.) The sensations in this are all . . . prehistoric . . . science-fiction. . . . On top of this wall . . . some sort of surrealistic caterpillar . . . on bridge . . . a person fleeing . . . from the surrealistic part of the picture into the more realistic. It seems to have exploded in his mind. (He is asked about that phrase.) Like a nightmare and he is fleeing these horrible things that are going to envelop him and attack. . . . I guess he was walking down a ledge or a road in his dream and these things started coming up—the things in his mind is what we see attacking him—eventually he is going to flee these scary things to a fortress." After telling the story he added that it reminded him of frightening dreams he had had as a child. He does not dream now and says it is a major frustration to his therapist, who is an analyst. Perhaps he doesn't dream because he fantasizes so much when awake. He knows that in theory people are believed to dream every night, and in fact he knows someone who just had a sleep-EEG. But he couldn't subject himself to such experiments "because they could never get me to sleep." He "discard[s] the hypothesis" that he actually does dream and represses the dreams upon awakening.

The content of his story again reflects his unconscious, highly conflictual longings for a childlike state of protection. Since he sees the "caterpillar" (a fetal form) in an area of the card more frequently perceived as a lizard or dragon, we can infer that the passive fantasy-wish serves a defensive function against the implied aggression. However, it succeeds only in disguising that impulse, and the "enveloping" things express the projected oral rage. "Surrealistic" may also be a reflection of states of mind or feeling that embody these primitive fantasies. Certainly, along with the reified dream images in the story, it suggests that the regression is again to a *transitional* mode in which objects have no "real" existence. The regressive aspects of his manner with the examiner (and the storytelling task) are reflected in his difficulties in constructing a clear-cut story. In the form and content of this single story, then, we can see indications of the effects on this man's thinking, object relations, self-experience, and everyday functioning, caused by assimilation to his unconscious conflictual fantasy themes of regressive, passive longings, and the warding-off and projection of oral rage. The extent of his discomfort with what was stirred by the picture stimulus was emphasized when he returned to this story on a subsequent day to reinforce his defensive splitting and primitive denial of the aggression by saying that only *part* of the picture was nightmarish. And his comments on his treatment impasse reflect the fact that the same conflictual themes which are visible in his test performance are enacted also in the therapeutic transference: he fears that his "dreams" might result in a regressive, dependent relationship with his therapist and therefore feels he has to keep himself "awake." He mocks and belittles the object in his fight against the wish to submit, but feels that the struggles cause him to lose his therapist's interest.[6]

[6]Lewin (1954) has pointed to similarities between sleep and states of narcissistic regression and has suggested that both may represent an imagined satiated state of the infant at the breast. This is another vantage point from which the test performance of borderline patients can be viewed. The relatively effective performance of borderline patients on structured tasks may be conceptualized as a use of structure for keeping "awake," realistically in touch with the object world, and in firm control of impulses and fantasies. However, when clearly identifiable external objects and structure are not immediately available, there is a regressive pull toward narcissistic fantasied gratification (as in sleep). This regression brings with it a new set of fantasied dangers attendant on primitive gratification, such as object loss, merger, smothering, being devoured, and the like (the specific fears depend on the individual's unconscious fantasy systems). The "sleep" turns into a nightmare, and patients typically struggle to contain the regression and "wake themselves up." In many borderline patients, therefore, we see not only the well-documented increase in primitivization accompanying the shift from structured to unstructured tasks, but also efforts to regain a more realistic mode of functioning. Often this is evident in frequent, rapid shifts in the level of primitiveness, with severe regressions alternating with sudden recovery of adaptive functioning when some external stimulus can be used to "wake up" (e.g. when a new task or test card is presented). The case illustration provides many

The patient was asked to recount his earliest memory (the Mayman Early Memories Test). He remembered "being in a crib, being very upset, crying and shaking the crib, and being sufficiently clever to move it across the room while shaking it." His early memory is aggressive, omnipotent, and totally self-absorbed—there are no other people in it. Again, the fantasy theme of conflict with passive submission; he was furious because he "didn't want to be kept there."

Of all the tasks in the test battery, the Rorschach offers least in the way of familiar, reality-orienting structure. It thus provides the most stringent test of the resilience of intrapsychic structure. The greater the ego weakness or lack of autonomy, the greater the potential for poorly controlled regression, and the less likelihood of a rapid recovery of judgment and reality testing. And so it was for our patient. On the other tasks, transient regressions were interspersed among otherwise well-organized, task-oriented responses. But on the Rorschach his well-organized, articulately perceived responses were less frequent, and primary process thinking (assimilation of the stimuli to unconscious schemata) dominated. In the face of this lack of structure he gave way to an anxious verbal flood (73 responses) and the perceptual accuracy of nearly half his responses was open to serious question.

After some initial hesitation to Card I, he was able to muster all his critical resources to begin with the popularly seen butterfly, and he hoped the examiner would not press him further: "I'm not sure how long one is supposed to go on with these. I suspect the longer the time, the more expansive." But the examiner did not grant his wish and the patient went on. Summoning his resources further, he produced a well-articulated, imaginative response: "a ballet dancer." And then, "improbable breasts," improbably supported by the perceptual givens of the inkblot. And soon thereafter, "two strange-looking people with very long noses on each side . . . smiling . . . they seem to be connected with a mixture of Alice in Wonderland and a caterpillar. . . . (Then, after lengthy indecision:) The two people are walking away from each other . . . as they do it, their figure is evolving." With inquiry this was elaborated: "The two figures are growing out of . . . obtaining form from . . . the central figure which is a combination of Alice in Wonderland and caterpillar[7] . . . as they emerge from this source of form they take shape, grow." Here the regression is once again to a point suggestive of an unconscious fantasy expressing longing for and defense against passive infantile dependence (the figures are larval, in the process of growth, separating and

---

examples of such shifts, as well as many direct thematic references to concerns about sleep, dreaming, and awakening to reality.

[7]The merged image of these two figures is a type of response frequently encountered in borderline patients: a half-human, half-animal figure.

in birth).[8] He also thinks of Alice, a character who is undergoing a growth process and is a famous dreamer. His attitude to his perceptions, the response process, and the test stimuli again seems to suggest a transitional object mode, i.e. the fantasy of self-object merger.

A new stimulus provides fresh opportunities both for redeployment of attention (and the assertion of ego autonomy) and for regression (in the service of direct expression of unconscious fantasy). Recovering from the regression on Card I, he begins Card II with another well-articulated, popular, perhaps reassuring response: "Two dogs with noses touching. Sort of Scotty-type dogs. Cute little pleasant dogs." But then he becomes too bound to his thought and briefly has difficulty in continuing: "I'm trying to erase the dogs now." The fantasy product momentarily became too real, impairing his ability to manipulate and control his own imaginative process. When he does get past it, a theme of sexual conflict emerges in a confused, unrealistic percept of female genitalia and urinary apparatus in the red and white area of the inkblot. The color stimulates a highly charged fantasy that unfolds as contradictory, poorly integrated masculine and feminine self-image components, i.e. the conflictual fantasies again appear in primitive *form* and *content*. Next he finds two caterpillars "trying to communicate," a mild confabulation reflective of the redundancy with which regressive struggles emerge in borderline patients.

[8]Some might construe such images as depicting the separation-individuation stage, but we would consider that an instance of the genetic fallacy. It is more parsimonious to see it as reflecting the current struggle with impulses. In addition to the very high frequency of images of larval and fetal organisms in the patient's test responses, there are several other bits of evidence that point to the likelihood that this man's longings to be passive and cared for by his mother are woven into intense and highly conflicted fantasies of returning to the maternal womb (or claustrum). On TAT Card 11, in addition to the image of a larval caterpillar form, he referred to the danger of being "enveloped," which is suggestive of the wish for and fear of being encased in the womb. In addition, the references to things being "surrealistic" that were found in this story, and among many other test responses, suggested that he may experience feelings of unreality or depersonalization. Slap (1974) has argued that these feelings are "components of fantasies of sleep and return to the womb" (p. 853).

Although psychological testing can give us extensive information about the primitivization of ego functioning, it permits us only the *hypothesis* that this man is driven by the unconscious fantasy of returning to the womb. The presence of this fantasy can be definitely confirmed only by the associative method of exploratory psychotherapy or psychoanalysis, with its access to historical data. We can speculate, based on our knowledge of similar cases, that the historical source of this fantasy may have been in the child's observation of his mother's pregnancy with the younger sister, or in some similar circumstance which led him to feel enraged as well as hurt, and also to long for the ultimate closeness and comfort that his mother could offer. He would then express his rage, rivalry, and longing in condensed form, like Freud's Wolf Man, as "life makes me so unhappy, I must get back into the womb!" (Freud, 1918, p. 100). This wish may also be the origin of the fantasy theme of merger of self and objects which we have observed a number of times in this man's protocol.

Card III also begins with an autonomously conceived percept: ''Two men dressed in full dinner clothing.'' But soon we find the men ''holding on to black kidneys for some reason.'' Here the *spatial contiguity* between the men and the kidneys is interpreted as a *conceptual connection*. But he does express his recognition of the uncritical quality of this fabulized combination as he remarks ''for some reason.'' It is simply that he cannot limit the regression to a ''signal'' level. Next his mind turns again to a redundant theme: ''fetuses.''

Card IV yields a more rapid regression. His first association graphically depicts bisexuality and his masochistically crippling struggle with himself. ''First impression is a picture of a man with his head up his ass . . . funny creature . . . unreal beast with large feet that has arched itself over [backward].'' The ''unreal'' quality is again similar to the dreamlike state in which self- and object representation are arbitrarily assimilated to unconscious fantasy. The relatively more clear-cut structure of Card V provides sufficient cues to halt the regression. Even under the pressure of the conflicts aroused by the Rorschach situation, his regressions are still transient, conflict-specific, and readily reversible by the redeployment of attention and the imposition of added, reality-orienting structure.

Card VI begins again with well-conceived, popular responses (e.g. animal skin) which again give way to a primitive fantasy theme reminiscent of the sexually confused self-images suggested on Card II (i.e. vagina and urethra): ''Suggestion of a phallus (entire center), suggestion of a vaginal opening. . . . (On inquiry he adds that the vagina ''could be a cross-section of a male urethra.'') . . . major part of it (the area of the inkblot in which he sees the vagina) is elegant . . . almost like Indian or Eskimo design . . . topped off by strangely ugly head (the area in which he sees a phallus).'' Here we find more evidences regarding his conflicts about sexual identity, i.e. the phallic area is ''ugly,'' the vaginal area is ''elegant.'' One might even begin to speculate that the feminine aspects of his identifications may be related to early, maternally tinged fixations, and in conjunction with his previously expressed oral aggression, his concerns about putting himself in a passive, needful, and vulnerable position. This is the thematic fusion of sexual and oral-aggressive impulses discussed by Kernberg (1975). Its emergence in a confabulation response is another in our large store of instances of the conflict-specific primitivization in this man's ego functioning. Card VII yields more passive imagery (e.g. ''sofa cushions'') and other instances of the now more clearly developing homoerotic, feminine identity theme, i.e. ''somebody's rear end.''

The color of Card VIII takes us ''back in the land of surrealistic organisms . . . very basic sea bodies or something.'' This is by now familiar to us as a representation of primitive ego functioning, and perhaps also a mode of self-experience, that is clearly reflective of his fantasy of regression to fetuslike dependency on his mother, and his struggle against this wish. A popular response interrupts, again demonstrating the reversibility of the regressions, even if at times only momentarily, and we are soon again to become submerged in a world of unconscious fantasy longing: ''Jelly fish . . . exotic . . . from warm seas . . . crab . . . pink iceberg (arbitrary combination of form, content, and color) . . . *enough strange things*.'' He still can, and does, ''awaken'' himself.

Card IX ''seems like a close relation to what I was just looking at . . . except the colors have turned around. . . . The creature we saw before obviously undergoes changes . . . staring at me . . . two eyes . . . in the middle . . . not being nasty . . . just like a fish in an aquarium.'' In this response we see his ego functioning close to its most primitive. Cards VIII and IX are not separate and his percepts are reified. *It is the creature, rather than his ideas, that is seen as changing*. He also sees the creature ''staring at'' him, a projection that, even if later undone and denied, attains near-delusional intensity. But it is an ''as-if'' staring; judgment is retained at a transitional level. The enactment of the enveloping, submerging, and merging fantasies resembles projective identification with the creature, as a defense against the implied oral aggression. The creature, he specifies, is ''not nasty,'' a fetuslike being in a protective, nurturing tank of water. And here is also a major theme associated with splitting: passive, helpless babies can't be nasty.

Card X: ''Underwater seascape with all sorts of different creatures . . . crablike . . . jellylike . . . tiniest bit of pelvic *sensation* in the symmetry . . . brassiere (oral deprivation) . . . vaginal opening (female, claustrum) . . . sperm (male, tiny) . . . frogs (the adult products of a metamorphosis) in the same areas as sperm . . . cocoon.'' The last response on the Rorschach often communicates a great deal (Appelbaum, 1961). And this is the same man who was able to deal with most of the WAIS with efficiency and dispatch and who easily achieved near-perfect scores on the Information and Arithmetic subtests.

In this somewhat truncated and brief case illustration, we have attempted to *illustrate* how the ego functioning, modes of relating to objects and external reality, self- and object representation, and response contents of borderline patients, all reflect the powerful regressive influence of regnant, primitive unconscious fantasies in an interrelated fashion. As we indicated earlier, all people retain unconscious residues of childhood wishes, defenses, and experiences, in the form of individually characteristic, persistent unconscious fantasy systems that influence and guide their lives continuously. Borderline patients like this one are characterized by the manner and degree in which those fantasies influence everyday life and conscious functioning: They have a sufficient tie to the object world to enable them to function realistically when clear external structure is present, and when conflict is not intensely aroused. However, when either of these two conditions is not present, borderline patients are prone to experience relatively transient, conflict-specific regressions. These are reversed when the pressure of the unconscious wishes is diminished and/or when greater external structure is available. These regressions can be understood as caused by extensive assimilation of perception and other ego functions to the unconscious fantasy system, without the corrective effects of critical judgment. Objects and other external stimuli are imbued with characteristics derived from these primitive wishful fantasies, much as occurs in the transitional objects of infancy.

The primitivization of ego functioning by unconscious fantasy is more visible in the test battery than with other modes of observation, because the battery systematically varies stimulus structure and potentially conflict-arousing contents. We are thus enabled to observe, as we did with this patient, that there is a general increase in regressed, assimilatory functioning as structure diminishes; and we see that the same themes intrude repeatedly and with increasing clarity during periods of regression. The test battery also documents the borderline patient's characteristic struggle against his own passive and oral-aggressive impulses, which causes him to swing widely between primitive and realistic functioning under all conditions of structure; and it shows how this is manifest in response *contents, formal* aspects of thinking, and in the *relationship* to the examiner and the tests as objects. As we saw in this case, it is then often possible to draw highly specific inferences from the test protocols of borderline patients about the ways in which their conflictual unconscious fantasies are likely to be reflected in day-to-day functioning, object relations, and self-experience, as well as in treatment.

In the patient discussed here, the most prominent specific fantasy themes centered around intensely conflictual passive longing, the desire for protective nurture associated with a sense of "oneness," and wishes to retain ties with maternal introjects through identification as a defense against oral aggression. These are not only illustrative of the fabric of unconscious fantasies typical for many borderline patients, but they are also the major unconsciously conflictual themes that brought this borderline patient to treatment and which now impede the treatment effort. The passive longings inherent in the fantasies are also the fabric of powerful defenses: warding off, staying alert and awake, and denial and containment of primitive rage (e.g. the "not nasty" creature; the "ugly" phallic area; the "harsh" country of his TAT; the cannibalism of the WAIS Comprehension subtest). We have also seen the plasticity of these defenses in his vulnerability to regression when conflict-specific fantasies are stirred up, and especially on relatively unstructured, unfamiliar tasks. As he regresses he becomes even more frightened, as his unconscious fantasies take greater hold of his conflict-free ego functions and he struggles to "wake himself up." He is trapped between his passive nurturant longings and fury over feelings of being deprived, and is terrified of the primeval prospects of object loss and of permitting himself to become too close to objects for fear of destroying (and thereby losing) them. All this and more is played out intrapsychically in the web of unconscious fantasies and is reenacted in the world of external objects. This man can permit himself to become attached to no person as intensely as he would wish to, and therefore his objects can be neither loved well nor mourned well and then relinquished. He keeps his distance from people and yet lives at home with his aged parents. He wants to be both a male and a female and cannot really permit himself to be either. Just such a dilemma has immobilized his therapy and can be seen in his remarks about dreams. He wants to please his therapist and retain him as a nurturing, protecting object, but fears the submission and loss of control that his unconscious fantasies compel him to believe are required. His story—the particular unconscious fantasies and their relationship to his ego functioning and their consequent coloring of his self- and object representations—is not the story of all borderline patients, but it is the story of many, and is *not* the story of most neurotic or psychotic patients.

References

Appelbaum, S. (1961), The end of the test as a determinant of responses. *Bull. Menn. Clin.*, 25:120–128.

——— (1979), To define and decipher the borderline syndrome. *Psychotherapy*, 16:364–370.

Arlow, J. (1963), Conflict, regression and symptom formation. *Internat. J. Psycho-Anal.*, 44:12–22.

——— (1969), Unconscious fantasy and disturbances of conscious experience. *Psychoanal. Quart.*, 38:1–27.

——— & Brenner, C. (1964), *Psychoanalytic Concepts and the Structural Theory*. New York: International Universities Press.

——— ——— (1969), The psychopathology of the psychoses: A proposed revision. *Internat. J. Psycho-Anal.*, 50:5–14.

Bachrach, H. (1968), Adaptive regression, empathy and psychotherapy. *Psychotherapy*, 5:203–209.

Beres, D. (1962), The unconscious fantasy. *Psychoanal. Quart.*, 31:309–328.

——— Arlow, J. (1974), Fantasy and identification in empathy. *Psychoanal. Quart.*, 43:26–50.

Calef, V., & Weinshel, E. (1979), The new psychoanalysis and psychoanalytic revisionism: Book review essay on *Borderline Conditions and Pathological Narcissism*. *Psychoanal. Quart.*, 48:470–491.

Carr, A., Goldstein, E., Hunt, H., & Kernberg, O. (1979), Psychological tests and borderline patients. *J. Personal. Assess.*, 43:582–590.

Fenichel, O. (1945), *The Psychoanalytic Theory of Neurosis*. New York: Norton.

Freud, S. (1918), From the history of an infantile neurosis. *Standard Edition*, 17:7–122. London: Hogarth Press, 1955.

Grala, C. (1980), The concept of splitting and its manifestations in the Rorschach Test. *Bull. Menn. Clin.*, 44:253–271.

Jacobson, E. (1964), *The Self and the Object World*. New York: International Universities Press.

Kernberg, O. (1966), Structural derivatives of object relationships. *Internat. J. Psycho-Anal.*, 47:236–253.

——— (1967), Borderline personality organization. *J. Amer. Psychoanal. Assn.*, 15:641–685.

——— (1975), *Borderline Conditions and Pathological Narcissism*. New York: Aronson.

——— (1977), The structural diagnosis of borderline personality organization. In: *Borderline Personality Disorders: The Concept, the Syndrome, the Patient*, ed. P. Hartocollis. New York: International Universities Press, pp. 87–121.

Klein, G. (1976), *Psychoanalytic Theory: An Exploration of Essentials*. New York: International Universities Press.

Levine, F., & Luborsky, L. (1981), The core conflictual relationship theme: A demonstration of reliable clinical inference by the method of mismatched cases. In: *Object and Self: A Developmental Approach*, ed. S. Tuttman, C. Kaye, & M. Zimmerman. New York: International Universities Press, pp. 501–526.

Lewin, B. (1954), Sleep, narcissistic neurosis and the analytic situation. *Psychoanal. Quart.*, 23:487–510.

Luborsky, L. (1977), Measuring a pervasive psychic structure in psychotherapy. In: *Communicative Structures and Psychic Structures*, ed. N. Freedman & S. Grand. New York: Plenum, pp. 367–395.

Modell, A. (1968), *Object Love and Reality*. New York: International Universities Press.

Pruyser, P. (1975), What splits in ''splitting''?: A scrutiny of the concept of splitting in psychoanalysis and psychiatry. *Bull. Menn. Clin.*, 39:1–46.

Rapaport, D. (1957), Cognitive structures. In: *Collected Papers*. ed. M. Gill. New York: Basic Books, 1967, pp. 631–664.

——— Gill, M., & Schafer, R. (1945), *Diagnostic Psychological Testing*. New York: International Universities Press, 1968.

Reik, T. (1948), *Listening With the Third Ear*. New York: Farrar, Strauss & Young.

Schafer, R. (1954), *Psychoanalytic Interpretation in Rorschach Testing*. New York: Grune & Stratton.

——— (1958), Regression in the service of the ego. In: *Assessment of Human Motives*. ed. G. Lindsey. New York: Rinehart, pp. 119–148.

——— (1967), *Projective Testing and Psychoanalysis*. New York: International Universities Press.

Singer, M. (1977), The borderline diagnosis and psychological tests: Review and research. In: *Borderline Personality Disorders: The Concept, the Syndrome, the Patient*, ed. P. Hartocollis. New York: International Universities Press, pp. 193–212.

Slap, J. (1974), On waking screens. *J. Amer. Psychoanal. Assn.*, 22:844–853.

——— Levine, F. (1978), On hybrid concepts in psychoanalysis. *Psychoanal. Quart.*, 47:499–523.

——— & Saykin, A. (1980), The schema: Basic concept in a nonmetapsychological model of the mind. Presented at the Midwinter Meeting of the American Psychoanalytic Association, New York.

Sugarman, A. (1980), The borderline personality organization as manifested on psychological tests. In: *Borderline Phenomena and the Rorschach Test,* ed. J. Kwawer, H. Lerner, P. Lerner, & A. Sugarman. New York: International Universities Press, pp. 39–57.

Valenstein, A. (1973), On attachment to painful feelings and the negative therapeutic reaction. *The Psychoanalytic Study of the Child*, 28:365–394. New Haven: Yale University Press.

Waelder, R. (1962), Psychoanalysis, scientific method, and philosophy. *J. Amer. Psychoanal. Assn.*, 10:617–637.

Winnicott, D. (1951), Transitional objects and transitional phenomena. In: *Collected Papers*. New York: Basic Books, pp. 229–242.

NAME INDEX

Abraham, K., 9
Adler, G., 122
Allen, J., 5, 175
Allison, S., 225
Ames, L., 312
Appelbaum, S., 52, 189, 274, 295, 299, 336, 350, 370
Arlow, J., 353, 356, 359, 360
Athey, G., 5, 20, 22, 25, 32, 89, 175, 194
Atwood, G., 127
Averill, J., 207

Bachrach, A., 90
Bachrach, H., 349, 356, 372
Balint, M., 3, 7, 52, 271
Becker, W., 25
Bell, S., 308
Bellak, L., 53, 58, 59
Beres, D., 128, 353, 356, 359, 360
Bergman, A., 52, 128, 307, 338
Bertalanffy, L., 209
Billow, R., 243, 245, 248, 250, 256
Bion, W., 153, 225, 226-230, 231, 232-233, 235, 236, 240, 243-244, 248, 254, 255, 256, 257, 258, 264
Blanck, G., 6, 89
Blanck, R., 6, 89
Blatt, S., 20, 26, 52, 56, 58, 79, 81, 82, 98, 128, 129, 130, 132, 135, 136, 137, 145, 194, 225, 308, 320, 336, 337, 342, 343
Bleuler, E., 245
Bloom-Feshbach, S., 54, 81
Bloom-Feshbach, J., 54, 81
Blos, P., 84
Bremner, J., 231
Brenneis, C., 26, 52, 98, 128, 343
Brenner, C., 207, 353
Brentano, F., 207
Breuer, J., 229
Bursten, B., 56

Calef, V., 350
Campbell, D., 218
Carr, A., 77, 79, 351
Chethik, M., 80
Chevron, E., 52
Christopher, P., 90
Cleveland, S., 98
Colson, D., 336
Conklin, J., 248
Cowan, P., 210, 308, 311, 320
Coyne, L., 25

Deutsch, H., 334, 338
Dorpat, T., 146, 148

Easer, R., 336, 337, 339
Eigen, M., 241
Elkind, D., 85
Endicott, J., 132
Erikson, E., 9, 11, 296
Exner, J., 145

Fagen, R., 209
Fairbairn, W., 3, 52, 53, 175, 271, 350
Faris, M., 52, 189, 195
Fast, I., 80
Fenichel, O., 351

Ferguson, G., 218
Fine, R., 148
Fisher, S., 98
Fiske, D., 145, 218
Flavell, J., 210, 211, 308, 309, 310
Fleischer, J., 25
Freedman, N., 144, 147, 149, 151
Freud, A., 208
Freud, S., 5-6, 9, 11, 57-58, 93, 176, 225, 226, 227, 228, 229, 230, 231, 233, 240, 241, 247, 248, 251, 255, 256, 257, 307, 368
Frieswyk, S., 89

Gaughram, J., 132
Gediman, H., 53
Gedo, J., 143
Gill, M., 22, 24, 57, 77, 127, 158, 193, 225, 351, 357
Giovacchini, P., 3, 6-7, 8, 175, 186, 271, 323-324, 3
Glick, M., 26, 52, 98, 128, 343
Goldberg, A., 143
Goldman, D., 250
Goldstein, E., 77, 351
Gouin-Decarie, T., 210, 308
Graham, I., 344
Grala, C., 149, 150, 352
Greenson, R., 292
Greenspan, S., 82, 308
Grinberg, L., 324
Grinker, R., 84
Groff, H. 90
Grotstein, J., 154, 229, 237, 238, 248, 256, 324
Gunderson, J., 84, 85
Guntrip, H., 3, 53, 271, 350

Hall, A., 209
Hartley, D., 90
Hartmann, H., 6, 52, 91, 143, 175
Hatcher, R., 52, 343
Havel, J., 22, 56, 256
Heimann, P., 153, 226
Holt, R., 22-23, 24, 51, 56, 145, 158, 256
Holtzman, P., 22, 23-24, 283, 336
Horner, A., 10-11, 55, 176
Horwitz, L., 35, 89
Hoxter, S., 231
Hunt, H., 77, 351
Hurvich, M., 53

Inhelder, B., 209, 211
Issachs, S., 226

Jacobson, E., 3, 11, 175, 176, 271, 353
Johnston, M., 22, 23-24
Joseph, E., 128

Kant, I., 232, 241
Kaplan, B., 26
Kaye, C., 4
Kelly, E., 145
Kenny, A., 207
Kernberg, O., 3, 4-5, 6, 7, 9-10, 11, 20, 21, 28, 34, 59, 77, 78, 81, 84, 89, 91, 128, 130, 131, 136, 140, 143, 145, 146, 147, 148, 149-150, 153, 154, 155, 156, 157, 159, 160, 161, 162, 176, 186, 195-196, 209, 271, 324, 349-350, 351, 352, 358, 359, 369
Kissen, M., 7, 187, 188, 189, 203, 271, 276
Klein, G., 51, 53, 55, 353, 355
Klein, M., 3, 52, 145, 153, 155, 156, 225, 226, 227, 229, 231, 232, 233, 248, 252, 254, 350
Knight, R., 77, 78, 84
Kohut, H., 9, 89, 130, 229, 335, 336, 350
Krohn, A., 52, 98, 129, 144, 175, 213, 343
Krystal, H., 60, 71, 82, 208, 209, 212
Kuhn, T., 52
Kumin, I., 60
Kurash, C., 53, 80, 82, 83, 85
Kwawer, J., 10, 52, 194

Lachmann, F., 144, 147, 149, 160
Langs, R., 248, 324
Larson, D., 151
Learned, M., 312
Leichtman, M., 80
Lerner, H., 5, 52, 84, 131, 132, 136, 144, 150, 152, 155, 158, 159, 160, 162, 165, 336, 343, 344
Lerner, P., 5, 52, 131, 136, 144, 150, 152, 155, 158, 159, 160, 162, 165, 336, 337
Levine, F., 352, 353
Lewin, B., 366
Lewis, N., 250
Lichtenberg, J., 58, 59, 144, 147, 148, 149, 152
Loevinger, J., 213, 218
Loewald, H., 55, 91, 129
Loewenstein, R., 91
Lovett, C., 242
Lovett, J., 245, 248, 250, 256
Luborsky, L., 90, 145, 353

Machover, K., 180, 182, 189, 196
Mahler, M., 10, 51-52, 55, 128, 147, 148, 230, 307, 338, 343
Malin, A., 154, 324
Martindale, C., 212

Masling, J., 284
Masterson, 81, 350
Matarazzo, J., 225
Matson, F., 51
Mayman, M., 5, 8, 11, 52, 53-54, 55, 98, 128, 129, 144-145, 175, 176, 177-178, 189, 194, 195, 196, 197, 225, 271, 343, 344
Meissner, W., 89, 91
Meltzer, D., 231
Metcalf, D., 53, 81, 82
Metraux, R., 312
Modell, A., 80, 132, 159, 161, 162, 338, 339, 341-342, 356
Murstein, B., 217

Nagera, H., 342
Nelson, M., 275

Ogden, T., 154, 155

Palermo, D., 250
Piaget, J., 209, 211, 307-308, 309, 310, 311, 319, 355
Pine, F., 52, 128, 307, 338
Pitcher, G., 207, 212
Pruitt, W., 98, 145
Pruyser, P., 4, 146, 147, 149, 350
Pulver, S., 90

Quinlan, D., 52

Rabin, A., 225
Racker, H., 237
Rapaport, D., 5, 6, 22, 23, 24, 25, 26, 33, 52, 54, 55, 56, 57, 58, 77, 78-79, 127, 141, 158, 175, 193, 225, 262, 351, 353, 357
Redmore, C., 213
Reich, A., 335
Reich, W., 9
Reik, T., 356
Rinsley, D., 81, 132, 350
Ritzler, B., 20, 56, 79, 82, 98, 129, 145
Roback, H., 179, 189, 196
Robbins, F., 58
Robins, S., 132
Rosenblatt, B., 95, 128
Rosenfeld, H., 153
Rosenfeld, S., 80
Ross, N., 207
Ross, P., 250
Rossman, J., 250
Ryan, E., 52

Sadow, L., 58
Sandler, J., 95, 128
Sargent, H., 52
Satre, J., 222
Saykin, A., 355
Schachtel, E., 33, 70-71, 334, 338
Schafer, R., 6, 11, 22, 24, 27, 51, 57, 58, 77, 90-91, 92, 127, 143, 145, 146, 155-156, 158, 162, 163, 175, 176, 193-194, 225, 238, 253, 257, 272, 284, 302, 351, 356, 357
Schictman, S., 137
Schimek, J., 26, 52, 98, 128, 343
Schlesinger, H., 276, 282, 283, 286
Schmale, A., 208, 209
Schur, M., 207
Searles, H., 153, 203, 245
Segal, H., 82, 137, 247, 260
Shapiro, D., 71, 325
Shapiro, S., 80
Shectman, F., 20-21, 22, 279, 280, 281, 283, 287, 288, 289, 297, 298
Sherman, M., 179
Shevrin, H., 20-21, 22, 56, 59, 78, 281, 287, 288, 289, 297, 298
Singer, M., 21, 77, 78, 151, 336, 351
Slap, J., 144, 147, 148, 149, 152, 352, 355, 368
Smith, K., 20, 144, 150
Spear, W., 28, 49, 52, 129, 144, 343
Spilka, B., 98, 145
Spitz, R., 51, 53, 81, 82
Spitzer, R., 132
Sprince, M., 80
Sroufe, L., 207, 208, 209
Stoeri, J., 235, 248
Stolorow, R., 127, 144, 147, 149, 160, 350
Strean, H., 179, 189, 275
Suchotliff, L., 308
Sugarman, A., 5, 51, 52, 53, 54, 55, 79, 80, 81, 82, 83, 84, 85, 132, 154, 155, 158, 175, 193, 336, 352
Sundberg, N., 179
Sutherland, J., 4, 8
Swensen, C., 179, 189, 196

Teicholz, J., 342
Thompson, A., 207, 209, 211, 213, 217
Tolpin, M., 335, 336
Toussieng, P., 59
Tustin, F., 231
Tuttman, S., 4

Urist, J., 23, 24, 26, 52, 129, 130, 131, 136, 147

Valenstein, .,359
Volkan, V., 145

Waelder, ., 352
Waite, R., 225
Waldman, K., 213
Walker, R., 312
Wangh, M., 187, 202, 324-325
Wechsler, D., 241, 259
Weddell, D., 231
Wein, S., 52
Weiner, I., 239, 243, 244, 245, 256, 257, 258, 262
Weinshel, E., 350
Wender, P., 84
Werner, H., 26, 130, 209, 212
Wessler, R., 213
White, R., 6
Wiener, I., 23
Wild, C., 20, 56, 58, 79, 82, 129, 145, 308, 320
Winnicott, O., 3, 6, 7, 8, 53, 80, 92-93, 122, 161, 175, 271, 337, 338, 342, 350, 356
Wiseberg, S., 208
Whittenberg, I., 231
Wolf, J., 242
Wolff, P., 307
Wolstein, B., 272
Woo-Sam, J., 225, 239
Wyatt, G., 55

Yorke, C., 208

Zimmerman, I., 225, 239
Zimmerman, M., 4

SUBJECT INDEX

Action language, 175-176, 194, 272
Adolescence, borderline symptomatology in, 83-84
Affect
  affect-events, 209-211
  in borderline adolescents, 83-84
  cognitive aspects of, 207-211
  development, sensioromotor stage of, 210-211
  development of, concrete operational stage in, 211
  differentiation process of, 209-211
  intensional aspect of, 207
  in narcissistic personality organization, *see* Narcissistic personaltiy organization
  reversibility of 210, 212, 216-217
  and Rorschach, 127-132, 140-141
  tolerance of, 222
  TAT and, 207-224
  see also Emotion
Affect maturity, 211-213
Affect maturity scale, 217-219
  empirical validation of, 217-219
Aggression, 107, 110, 146-149
  in borderline personality organization, 146-152, 350, 354, 358, 371
Alpha functioning, 232
Autonomous ego functions, *see* Ego functions
Anxiety, 95-96, 153-154
  disintegration, 335-336
Altered atmosphere procedure, 274-275
As if personality, 334-335

Borderline personality organization, 186, 349-372
  borderline symptomatology in adolescence, *see* Adolescence
  boundary disturbances in, *see* Boundary
  clinical examples, 99-124, 132-140, 164-168, 360-372
  cognitive disturbances in, 81-85, 336-337
  and confabulations, *see* Rorschach test, fifth category scoring
  defenses, *see* Defenses in
  differential diagnosis of schizophrenia on the Rorschach, 77-80, 84-86
  discrepancy in functioning on psychodiagnostic testing, 77-78, 336-337, 351, 369-372
  ego functioning in, *see* Ego functions
  and ego-identity, *see* Ego functions and Borderline personality organization
  fantasy in, 83-84, 354-360, 370-372
  impulse control in, 82-83, 350
  and masochism, 359-360
  object relations vs ego psychological approach to, 78-81
  and object relations understanding of the Rorschach, 77-86
  object representation in *see* Object representation
  and paranoid ideation, 84-85
  primary and secondary process thinking in *see* Thought processes
  psychotic function in, 84-85

regression in, *see* Regression
responsiveness to ongoing events, 360
and Rorschach test, 77-86, 131-132, 143-169, 354-356, 369-372
self-representation in, *see* Self-Representation
separation and loss, 81-83, 359-360, 369-370
and separation-individuation, 149, 353-360
transitional phenomena in, 82, 161, 356, 365-366

Boundary
development, 58-60, 79, 92-94
disturbances in borderline personality organization, 79-83, 85-87
Inner vs outer, 53, 58-60, 90-93
internalization of, 91-92
projective-introjective cycle and, 95-96, 153-155
psychopathology of, 56-57, 80-84, 95-96
and Rorschach test, 56-60, 78-80, 96-97
self other, 53-60, 79, 85, 91-96
stages of self-boundary, formation, 94
Boundary deficit hypothesis, 20-21

Character disorders treatment, 6, 8, 132, 271
Children
clinical example, 311-319
infant development, 92-94, 307
and object loss, 342
object relations assessment using the Rorschach test, 307-322
object representations, 307, 311
reality testing, 311
thought processes, 307-308
Clinical Examples, 35-48, 60-70, 99-123, 132-140, 177-178, 182-189, 219-221, 237-264, 282-285, 288, 294-295, 298, 326-329, 360-372
Cognition, *see* Thought processes
Condensation, 56, 78
Confabulation, *see* Rorschach test, scoring
Conflict-free ego functioning, *see* Ego Functions
Containment, 7, 97, 119-120
Container-contained relationship 231, 234-235 *see* Rorschach test scoring

Defenses
in borderline personality organization, 148-169
denial, 4, 7, 143, 147-149, 350, 371
devaluation, 136-137 143, 147, 159, 162-164
externalization, 109-110
idealization, 4, 7, 143, 147, 159-160, 350
omnipotence, 145, 147 159-162
projection, 7, 53, 95, 123-124, 147, 154, 336, 362
projection vs projective identification, 154-155
projective identification, 4, 7, 143, 153-159, 324, 336, 350
reaction formation, 160
Rorschach assessment of, 143-169
self-depreciation, 4, 159, 163
splitting, 4, 7, 10, 53, 80, 136-137, 143, 145-153, 159, 337, 350, 352
splitting and object representation, 146-149
in Wechsler scales, 237-264
Denial, *see* Defenses
Depression,
depletion depression, 335-337
Depressive position, 232-233, 235
Displacement, 56, 78-79

Early memories test, 177
object relations aspects of, 195
affect states 195, 201
Ego,
body ego, 93
Ego functions, 52-56, 127-128, 367
autonomous, 52
in borderline personality organization, 77-80, 81, 85-86, 143-144, 146-153, 350-357, 369-372
conflict-free, 52, 354-355, 358
ego identity, 4, 53-54, 81, 85, 135-136
hierarchial view of, 54-57
Ego Psychology,
object relations and the Rorschach, 51-72, 77-79, 143-169
Ego functions
object representation, *see* Object representation
reality testing, 55-60, 79-80, 85-86, 210-211, 221-222, 354
reality testing and affect maturity, 210-213, 221-222
reality testing in borderline personality organization, 80-83
reality testing and self representation on the Rorschach, 51-72, 80-81
relationship to development of self/object representations, 55-57
synthesis, 52-55, 83, 127
and unconscious fantasy, 354-358
Ego psychology, 5-8
Ego states, 11-12, 176-177, 195-196
Emotion, cognitive aspect of, 207-211
development of, 207-224

and developmental lines, 208-211,
see also Affect
reality testing of, 210-211 221-222
reversibility of, 210-212, 216-217
and T.A.T., 207-224
Externalization, *see* Defenses
Fabulized combination, *see* Rorschach scores and ratios
False-self, 60, 83, 337, 341-342
Fantasy, in borderline personality organization,
see Borderline personality organization
unconscious function of, 353-358

Good-enough mothering, 6-7, 53, 59-60, 338

Holding environment, 92-93, 122, 338-339
Human figure drawings,
test administration, 180-182
assessment of object relations in, 179-180
object relations aspects of, 175-189

Idealization, *see* Defenses
Infantile character, 121-123
Internalization, 81-82, 90-96, 120
bodily experience of, 93-94, 120
development of, 81-83, 90-96, 147
introjection and projection as preconditions for, 89-124
and object relations theory, 128-130
psychopathology of, 94-96, 147, 342
and Rorschach test, 89-124, 129
and therapeutic alliance, 89
Introjection, 6, 12, 53, 95, 143, 147, 153, 177, 186
and the Rorschach, 89, 97-98, 161-162

Limiting Membrane, 92

Marital object choice,
contrasting character structures in 325-326
meshing character structures in, 323-331
Merger themes, 84-85, 336, 358, 368
Mirroring, 9-10, 356

Narcissism, 4, 81
Narcissistic personality organization, 334-339, 358
affects, 336
defenses, 144, 335-336
object relations, *see* Object relations
and Rorschach test, 333-345
treatment, *see* Psychotherapy

Object constancy, 9, 11, 53, 58, 81-82, 210, 356
Object loss
in borderline personality organization, 339, 359-360
and borderline phenomena on the Rorschach, 77-86, 143-169
Object relations
and borderline phenomena on the Rorschach, 77-86, 143-169
conceptual difficulties in, 52-57
and ego development, 52-57, 127-130
and ego psychology in assessment using the Rorschach, 51-72, 144-146
human figure drawing and early memories assessment of, 193-204
human figure drawing assessment of, 196
and internalization, 92
in narcissistic personality organization, 334-336
part objects, 4, 10, 345
part objects, in borderline functioning, 80-82, 136-137, 145-146, 352
patterns seen during testing, 271-277, 279-303
phenomenological focus, 4-8
and psychosocial development, 8-11
and Rorschach, 5, 51-72, 143-169
and structural principles of ego psychology, 4-8, 52-53, 127-130.
and T.A.T., 207-224
and thought organization, 20, 53, 230
and treatment implications, 280, 296-299
Object representation, 4-5, 10-12, 53-55, 176-177, 343
by borderlines on the Rorschach, 150-153, 354
in borderline personality organization, 77-78, 80-83, 143-147, 149-150, 337, 349-373
in children, *see* Children
development of, 55-56, 94-95, 128-130, 307-308, 343
in early memories test, 195, 201
in human figure drawings, 182
impairment in, 128-130, 147-154
primary vs secondary representation, 146
projective-introjective process in, 19, 123-124, 153-155
reality testing of, 56-60, 94
and Rorschach assessment, 127-141, 144-146
on the T.A.T., 359
and transference, 129-130, 137
Paranoid-schizoid position, 232-236
Part object, *see* Object relations
Patient examiner alliance *see* Rorschach test or Psychodiagnostic testing

Primary process thinking, *see* Thought processes
Process approach, 279-303
  application to testing, 280
Projection, *see* Defenses
Projective-introjective cycle, 95-96, 121-122
Projective identification, *see* Defenses
Proxy-evocation, 187, 202, 203, 324-325
Psychosis, 354-355, 358
  and borderline personality organization, *see* Borderline personality organization
Psychodiagnostic testing
  clinical examples, 35-48, 60-70, 99-123, 132-140, 177-178, 182-189, 196-204, 219-221, 237-264, 282-285, 294-295, 326-329, 360-372
  countertransference, 272-274, 286, 290
  data gathering phase of, 289-296
  and diagnostic alliance, 289, 292-296
  discrepancy in functioning by borderlines, 77-78, 336-37, 351, 369-372
  distortions of, 280, 301-302
  fantasies about (patient), 284-287
  goals of, 280-281, 289-291, 293, 302-303
  initial stages of, 284-289
  and object relations, 5, 52, 127-141, 279-281
  object relations vs ego psychological approach to, 52-57, 127-130, 140-141
  paradigmatic techniques, 275-276
  pathological test phenomena, 237-264, attacks on links, 240-253, bizarreness, 253-257 hallucination, 257-261, pathological elaboration, 261-264, pervasive aggressivity, 237-240
  process approach in, 280-281
  resistance, 274-276, 300-302
  Rorschach, *see* Rorschack test
  termination of, 299-303
  tester-patient interaction, 19-49, 160, 163, 236-237, 272, 276, 279-303, 360
  Thematic Apperception Test (TAT), treatment recommendations, 140-141, 296-299, *see also* TAT
Psychotherapy
  and affect maturity, 212-213, 219, 221
  choice of treatment, 5-8
  couples, 330
  expressive, 5-7, 9-10
  and holding environment, 338-339
  of infantile personality disorder with depression, 121-123
  narcissistic personality organization, 337-338
  therapeutic change, 89-90, 123-124
  therapeutic and diagnostic alliance, 295-296
  transference, 9-10, 153-154 221-222
  treatment recommendations, 296-299

Reality Testing, *see* Ego functions
Regression
  in borderline personality in organization, 336-337, 351, 354-356, 366, 367, 371-372
  in service of the ego, 27, 356
Representational functioning, 95-96, 123-124, 129-130, 143, 344-345
  and boundaries, 59-60, 81-84, 97
Rorschach test, 51-72, 97-124, 143-169, 177
  acting out, assessment, 336
  alternative administration, 274-275
  borderline personality organization, *see* Borderline personality organization
Representational functioning, 95-96, 123-124, 129-130, 143, 344-345
  and boundaries, 81-84, 59-60, 97
Rorschach test, 97-124, 177, 51-72, 143-169
  acting out, assessment, 336
  alternative administration, 274-275; *see also* Borderline personality organization
  boundaries on, 10, 78-80, 85, 96-97, 101-110, 118-119, 145, 157
  content analysis, 57, 85, 97, 101-110, 118-119, 144-146, 158, 163
  fifth scoring category
    confabulations, 56, 78-80, 357-368, contaminations, 56, 78, 85, fabulized combinations, 56, 79, 150-151, 357-358, perceptual distoration, 357, primary process, 158-159
  mutality of Autonomy Scales, 130-131, 136
  narcissistic personality organization, *see* Narcissistic personality organization
  and narcissistic character pathology assessed using the (c) Rorschach score, 333-345
  object relations aspects of, 77-86, 127-141, 143-169, 194
  object relations and borderline defenses, 143-169
  and object representations, 127-141, 143-169
  patient-examiner relationship, 19, 33-35, 160, 163
  responses,
    denial, 131; devaluation, 131, 136-137, 159, 162-164; externalization, 110; fearful empathy, 156-158; hyperalertness, 158; idealization, 131, 159-160; inner vs outer, 79, 97-98, 101-102, 105-106; mirroring, 10, 63, 66,

106-107; omnipotence, 159, 161-162; projection and introjection, 89, 98-99, 110-111; projective identification, 131, 155-159; self-representation, 109-110; splitting, 131, 136-137, 150-153, 352, 369; symbolic castration, 163
scores and ratios,
achromatic color (FC'), 57, 65; color (C) 57, 71, 158, 333-345; color texture, 336; detail rare (Dr) 158, 336; form ratios and response (F% F+%) 57-60, 70-71; human responses, 128, 130, 132, 140-141, 144-146, 150, 159-160; movement (M) 140; shading (Fch) 57, 157, 333-345
self-representations on, *see* Self-representations
thought organization assessment of *see* Thought Processes
transference manifestations, 137, 140-141

Schema, *see* Thought Processes
Schizoid, 11, 180
Schizophrenia
differential diagnosis, 77-80, 84-86, 132, 355-356
Self-boundary, *see* Boundary
Self-depreciation, *see* Defenses
Self-interview technique, 276
Self-object, 335
Self-representation, 4-5, 7, 10-12, 55-57, 123-124, 147, 176-177
in borderline adolescents, *see* Adolescence
borderline personality organization and, 77-78, 80-83, 147, 349-373
development of, 55-60, 80-83, 92-95
in early memories test, 195, 201
in human figure drawings, 182
and Rorschach responses, 56-72
Sentence completion, 177
Separation-individuation, 10-11 81-83, 356, 359-360, 369-370
differentation, 80-83
practicing subphase, 81
rapproachment subphase, 10, 81-83, 149, 162, 356
and Rorschach test, 131, 162
symbiotic phase, 10-11, 79, 338, 354
Splitting, *see* Defenses
Spouse, as container, 325
Structural model, 5-8, 353-355
Symbiosis, 10-11, 79, 336, 354
Symthesis, *see* Ego Functions
Thematic Apperception Test (TAT), 177, 207-224
affect maturity scale, 213-217
and object relations, 207-224
Termination
diagnostic assessment of, 299-303
Thought organization, 20-33, 57-58
Thought processes, 53-56, 81-83
adaption, 308-309
and affect, 207-211, 336-337
assimilation, 308-309
in borderline adolescents, 83-84
in borderline personality organization, 78-85, 336-337, 354-357
capacity to symbolize, 53, 59-60, 80-83, 128, 310, 337
of children, *see* Children
concrete operational stage of, 211, 310-311
disorder, 20, 22, 56
equilibrium, *see* Thought processes adaptation
fantasy, 226
formal operational thinking, 84
object permanence, 309-310
object relations theory of, 53-57, 80-81, 128-130, 145, 230
organization, 308-309
organization in Rorschach, 22, 24-25, 54-57, 78-85, 144-146, 336-337, 351
primary process thinking, 23, 56, 78-79, 351, 358
reversibility, 84, 210, 310-311
schema, 53, 55-56, 308-309, 355-356
sensimotor stage of, 81-82 210-211, 309-310
thinking in Bion's theory, 226-227
Transference, *see* Psychotherapy
Transference enactment, 19
Transitional phenomena, 6, 53, 59-60, 89, 161, 356
and cognitive development, 53
and practicing subphase, 80-83
Treatment, *see* Psychotherapy

Wechsler Scales
Bionian interpretation, 225-267
and borderline personality
disorder, 77, 336-337